Wisdom With Understanding is Better Than Rubies

Lurine Karon Greenberg
Fine Arts Collection

Valery Gergiev and the Kirov

Valery Gergiev, photo inscribed to John Ardoin: "To Johnchik—My friend, a real musician, with sincere respect, Valery Gergiev, July 10, 1992, New York, Kirov at the Met." PHOTO: HARRY HELEOTIS

VALERY GERGIEV
AND
THE KIROV

A Story of Survival

by John Ardoin

with a foreword by
Sir Peter Ustinov

Amadeus Press
Portland, Oregon

Research funds for this book were provided by the O'Donnell Foundation and the Eugene
McDermott Foundation of Dallas and the Ann and Gordon Getty Foundation of California.
Production was supported by a generous grant from Yoron Cohen and the White Nights
Foundation of America, Inc.

The author gratefully acknowledges permission to include work created by others, all
identified in the text and bibliography, including material
    From the Foundation for Russian Ballet and from the collection of Nina Alovert
    From *Choura* by Alexandra Danilova, Copyright © 1986 by Alexandra Danilova Reprinted
        by permission of Alfred A. Knopf, a Division of Random House, Inc.
    From *Dancing in Petersburg* by Princess Romanovsky-Krassinsky, translated by Arnold
        Haskell, Copyright © 1960 by Victor Gollancz Ltd. Used by permission of Doubleday,
        a division of Random House, Inc.
    From "Lost and Found" and "The Soloist" by Joan Acocella, originally published in
        The New Yorker.
    From "The Kirov" by Elizabeth Kendall, originally published in *The New Yorker.*

Printed in Hong Kong

Published in 2001 by
AMADEUS PRESS (an imprint of Timber Press, Inc.)
The Haseltine Building
133 s.w. Second Avenue, Suite 450
Portland, Oregon 97204 u.s.a.

Library of Congress Cataloging-in-Publication Data

    Ardoin, John.
    Valery Gergiev and the Kirov : a story of survival / by John Ardoin ; with a foreword by Peter
Ustinov.
       p. cm.
    Includes bibliographical references and index.
    ISBN 1-57467-064-6
    1. Gergiev, Valery, 1953– 2. Conductors (Music)—Russia (Federation)—Biography. 3. Leningrad-
skiæ gosudarstvennyæ akademicheskiæ teatr opery i baleta imeni S.M. Kirova. 4. Mariinskiæ teatr
(1991–) I. Title.

    ML422.G46 A73 2001
    784.2'092—dc21
    [B]   00-052583

For Lexo,
who began it all

Contents

Photographs

Foreword

by Sir Peter Ustinov

BEFORE THE APPEARANCE of this remarkable book, I had only learned about the Mariinsky opera house by hearsay, a haze of rumors and opinions unleashed by elderly Russian relatives of whom there was no shortage at the time. My celebrated great uncle Alexander Benois, the stage designer of *Petrushka*, among other ballets for Diaghilev, and one-time curator of the Hermitage Museum, lived in exile in Paris at the moment of my emergence as an actor in the London theater. He wrote me a charming letter to celebrate this fact, which stated that for two centuries and more our family had prowled around theaters. We have, at different times, administered them, built them, designed for them, composed for them, and conducted in them, but at last one of us has had the gall to leap onto the boards himself. It is a wonderful document of encouragement from a venerable artist to a young fledgling on his first solo flight from the nest.

I only found out later that Alexander Benois's uncle was none other than Alberto Cavos, the architect of the Mariinsky Theater, which I admired on my first visit to Russia in 1963. It is a lovely building of exquisite proportions which created a scandal at its inception for reasons difficult to comprehend today. It was apparently de rigueur in those days for opera houses to be finished in red, cream, and gold. The Mariinsky broke into a fastidious world in a mantle of blue, cream, and gold, which give it a pleasant aura of lightness. Thus it was as incongruous as a barefoot man in a tuxedo.

Alberto Cavos went on to rebuild and restructure the larger opera house in Moscow, the Bolshoi, after its destruction by fire in the 1850s. Quite recently, in 1998, I had occasion to direct an opera there and experience the greatest success I have ever enjoyed as a director of opera. In those august surroundings I am quite sure that a considerable amount of the prevailing state of grace was due to the heartwarming knowledge that the bricks and mortar were the work of a great great uncle. The opera in question was *The Love for Three Oranges* by Prokofiev, which had never had the frank success on its home ground enjoyed on this occasion thanks to a remarkable company, a brilliant choreographer, Misha Kislerov, and superb designs by Oleg Sheintsis. The production also played the Mariinsky under an exchange scheme. I was particularly pleased, since Prokofiev, a great composer by any standards, had had the wretched luck of dying on the same day as Stalin and not a flower was available in Moscow for his tomb. They were all reserved for the dictator's fragrant passage to Elysium.

Perhaps for a moment I may add a little research of my own on the background of the architect Alberto Cavos, whose sister Camilla was married to my great grandfather Nicolas Benois, also a distinguished architect. Alberto's father, Catterino Cavos (were they expecting a girl?), was the last Italian director of the Russian Imperial Opera. After him they were all Russian. I located his grave in the romantic Lavza cemetery in St. Petersburg, Russia's equivalent to England's Poets' Corner where practically all the nation's immortals are gathered. The Mighty Five of music are all in a tidy row, beside which a gigantic stone angel with a raised hand seeks to protect Tchaikovsky from the barbaric contagion. Down the pathway is the solitary figure of Dostoevsky, usually with a dead flower disintegrating on his shoulder. It was in a modest alley of this peaceful place that I found the black marble slab which marked the final resting place of Catterino Cavos. The inscription was in our alphabet, not in Cyrillic, and expressed the sense of values of the period: it remarked that he was a composer but insisted on the fact that he was a holder of the Order of St. Vladimir of the 4th Class. His emigration from Venice to St. Petersburg was a consequence of his magnanimity. As a young man, he had won the competition for the post of organist in the cathedral of San Marco. The second laureate was an elderly musician with a large family to support who urgently needed the job. The younger man voluntarily surrendered the post and accepted an offer to conduct in Russia where he was subsequently named principal conductor of the Imperial Opera. His generous nature caused him at a later date to withdraw an opera of his own based on the story of Ivan Susanin from the repertory when Glinka's opera on the same subject landed on his desk. He recognized at once that Glinka's work was superior. The only condition he laid down in exchange for his gesture was that he would have the honor of conducting the first performance of the earliest Russian opera to be part of the repertory to this day.

To pursue the research a little further back, we find the parents of Catterino Cavos in Venice. His father, Alberto, was the primo ballerino assigned to the Fenice opera house, then newly built. Where his choreographic genes disappeared to, I do not know. All I am sure of is that they reached not one living member of my family. His people had allegedly emigrated from Majorca at some earlier date. Alberto's wife, Camilla Baglioni, was one of four sisters, all coloratura sopranos famous at the turn of the eighteenth century. These sisters had a couple of brothers, both tenors. One of them, Antonio, created the part of Don Ottavio in *Don Giovanni* under Mozart's baton in Prague. He also sang the leading role in Mozart's *Clemenza di Tito* at its first performance. I may be forgiven if every time I hear *Don Giovanni* today I enjoy the warm sensation of listening to a kind of family heirloom. It is extraordinary, relatively late in life, to find out that a member of your family received musical instruction, or even enjoyed a bad joke, with Mozart himself.

But enough of the archives, the moribund wreaths of yesteryear, the dampness, and the dust. The Mariinsky is a living opera house, and it has never been so alive as it is today. Thanks to CDs and films, its artists and musicians are known the world over, especially in conjunction with a revelation of the wealth and diversity of the Russian operatic repertory. All this is due to the unique gifts of a single man, Valery Gergiev. His phenomenal ability in the field of public relations could, under normal circumstances, lead one to doubt his intrinsic quality as an artist. He allows no room for doubt. He is, quite simply, a great musician, an inspired administrator, and incidentally, a perfect spokesman for his passion, the Mariinsky, its reputation, and its future. This mission would be difficult under normal circumstances. Against a background of the collapse of the Soviet Union, the often desperate poverty of the people, and the huge ration of daily uncertainties, it is nothing short of a miracle. In short, the Mariinsky deserves Gergiev, Gergiev deserves the Mariinsky, and both deserve John Ardoin and this luminous book. My heartfelt gratitude to all of them.

Preface

THIS BOOK is an outgrowth of a year (1995–96) spent at the Mariinsky Theater in St. Petersburg. Actually, it is four books in one: a portrait of the company's present-day head, the conductor Valery Gergiev; a history of the building and those who have occupied it since the theater opened in 1860; a personal journal I kept in which the Mariinsky's composers, repertory, and personalities were seen through the sensibilities and interests of someone from the West; and, perhaps most important of all, the story of a major Russian theatrical entity attempting to survive in the turmoil and corruption of the post-communist period.

Anyone who takes on the formidable task of writing about any aspect of Russia faces two dilemmas. One is easily solved: the question of dating. In the nineteenth century the Russian calendar (commonly referred to as old style) lagged behind the Western calendar by twelve days, and in the twentieth century, up through January 1918, by thirteen. As mixing these two styles would create unnecessary chaos, I have used only Western (new style) dates, except in the case of Diaghilev's petition to Nicholas II.

The other problem—a curse, actually—is not so easily dispatched. It involves the transliteration of names. Russian spelling is phonetic, and the trend today among many scholars is to render names in English strictly according to the Cyrillic originals. But this leads to great difficulties and even greater confusion for the average reader. While someone might recognize and even accept "Nizhinsky" for "Nijinsky," there would be problems with other figures famous in the West if "Benois" were rendered as "Benua," "Chaliapin" as "Shalyapin," or "Diaghilev" as "Dyagilev." While such an authority as *The New Grove Dictionary of Music and Musicians* is for the most part doggedly faithful in its transliterations and spells Rachmaninov as "Rakhmaninov" (although he signed his name "Rachmaninoff"), it eschews "Chaikovsky." But it adds "Pyotr Il'yich" instead of the more familiar "Peter Ilyich."

The point is that absolute consistency is neither readily attainable nor, to my mind, desirable. The Russians themselves have long realized this and outside of Russia have adapted their names to Western spellings (which vary, of course, from country to country—"Moussorgsky" in France, for instance, and "Strawinsky" in Germany). To muddy the waters further, in the Kirov's recordings and the company's publicity and programs in America and England, the spelling of names is inconsistent, causing further complications. To cite one example, Philips Classics—and the Kirov and I follow suit—uses "Vladimir Galuzin" for the tenor's recordings, but he himself chooses to transliterate his name as "Galouzine." Furthermore, whereas it is logical to speak of Russia's penultimate czar as Alexander III, a problem arises with the last czar, Nicholas II. There are many important figures in this book whose first name, like his, is "Nikolai"—the Kirov's leading baritone, Nikolai Putilin, the composer Nikolai Rimsky-Korsakov—but again I felt inconsistency was the best policy, and I decided to use both forms of the name because Nicholas II is how this czar is best known in the West. The same is true of his great-grandfather, Nicholas I.

But whatever decision one makes, there is no way to win; it is impossible to be entirely consistent and not displease someone. Thus, arbitrary choices have to be made and lived with, whatever flak may result. My decisions included standard Western spellings for familiar names (including the use of "y" for the final "ii," and "yu" and "ya" for the Russian letters "ю" and "я," respectively) and the omission of marks for soft and hard sounds. This meant anglicizing places ("Dnieper," not "Dnepr"), institutions ("Bolshoi," not "Bolshoy"), and titles of works (*The Queen of Spades*, rather than its familiar French title *Pique dame*, and *Eugene Onegin* instead of *Evgeny Onegin*). Yet I have retained "Evgeny" as a first name when writing of musicians (such as Kissin and Mravinsky).

I have also used such American spellings as "theater" rather than "theatre." Finally, as "czar" rather than "tsar" is the style of Amadeus Press, Glinka's opera appears here as *A Life for the Czar,* while Rimsky-Korsakov's *Tsar Saltan* and *The Tsar's Bride* become *Czar Saltan* and *The Czar's Bride.* As to the question of Kirov versus Mariinsky, the theater uses both interchangeably (for the record, Gergiev speaks of "the Kirov Opera and the Kirov Ballet of the Mariinsky Theater"). I have employed them in a manner appropriate to the times I am writing about. The same is true with the use of "St. Petersburg," "Petrograd," and "Leningrad."

One last caveat: the books from which major quotations were taken can be found in the bibliography. Many of the short quotes, particularly those dealing with the dance, were drawn from such reference works as Oxford University Press's *International Encyclopedia of Dance* and the *International Dictionary of Ballet* from St. James Press.

As with any project as complex as this one proved to be, there are numerous people who must be thanked. The chief one is my research assistant, Myron Gamboa, whose perfect Russian and perfect understanding of the Russians opened doors and made possible a year's work that would have been inconceivable otherwise. Beyond translating the documents we unearthed and interpreting for me, he frequently shouldered the disagreeable task of doing verbal battle with Russian officialdom. The creatively devious ways he found to circumvent the political machinery and the stubborn personalities we encountered daily never ceased to amaze me.

At the Mariinsky itself, I was fortunate to have the close cooperation and goodwill of Gergiev's assistant, Katia Sirakanian, of the dancer Andris Liepa, and of the composer Alexander Tchaikovsky and his wife Ludmila, the assistant concertmaster of the Kirov Orchestra. A good friend of the Kirov's proved to be a good friend to me as well: Costa Pilavachi, of Philips Records, who supplied recordings and crucial video materials, as did the filmmaker Rainer Moritz. I am very grateful as well to Jeremy Noble, the director of the Foundation for Russian Ballet, for supplying a number of the dance photographs from the foundation's archives.

I must also thank those who generously allowed themselves to be interviewed for this book between 1995 and 1999. First of all is Gergiev himself. I tracked him from New York to Los Angeles, from St. Petersburg to Tokyo, and from Paris to Tel Aviv. In Russia I spoke with Olga Borodina, Lubov Kazarnovskaya, Andris Liepa, Victor Fedotov, Anatoly Malkov, Yuri Temirkanov, Alexander Tchaikovsky, Oleg Vinogradov, Inna Zubkovskaya and her family, Igor Belsky, Yuri Schwarzkopf, Brian Large, and Costa Pilavachi. I spent time in New York with Joseph Volpe and Sarah Billinghurst of the Metropolitan Opera; in Tel Aviv with Alexander Toradze; in Dallas with Igor Zelensky and Elena Prokina; and by phone with Ernest Fleischmann.

This book would not have happened without the tangible support of my former employer, the *Dallas Morning News*, and that of three sympathetic and compassionate foundations: the O'Donnell Foundation and the Eugene McDermott Foundation of Dallas, and the Ann and Gordon Getty Foundation of California. I owe a great debt of thanks as well to my old friend Clovis Morrison, who wisely suggested that I seek financial support locally when all other avenues had dried up, and to Yoron Cohen, whose immediate interest in this book and generous support of it made possible its two color photo sections. Finally, I am very grateful to two exceptional friends who watched over me from afar while I was in Russia— Marian Lever and Meg Starr—in a way I can only describe as "angelic."

It has been said that if you manage to have a Russian as a friend, you have a friend for life. That has been the case for me with Alexander Toradze, to whom this book is dedicated. I would never have reached Russia as soon as I did without a push from him, nor would I have had the good fortune to know Gergiev and other Russians intimately. But Lexo did more than open doors. He was there in Russia and later in the United States, where he now lives, to encourage and console me when the going got rough, and he always seemed blissfully certain that all would turn out well and the book would get done, something about which I had recurrent doubts. He is an extraordinary pianist, but more important, he is an extraordinary friend.

JOHN ARDOIN
San Ramón, Costa Rica

PROLOGUE

Valery the Great

I N THE FINAL DECADE of the twentieth century the Mariinsky Theater regained its original name and won back its status as Russia's premier opera theater. It reestablished a prominent position in the world of opera thanks to the impatience and daring of Valery Abissalovich Gergiev, a conductor of enormous charisma and talent, who was named its artistic director in 1988 and became its absolute master in 1996.

Gergiev had been a member of the theater's conducting staff since 1978, so he is no metaphorical Prince Charming who simply appeared on the scene and by his embrace brought the Kirov back to life. Instead, he structured the theater's rebirth on the foundation of discipline and professionalism laid down by his mentor and predecessor at the theater, the conductor Yuri Temirkanov. But it was Gergiev's energy and foresight and the breadth of his phenomenal gifts (as well as Russia's new political climate) that turned the tide.

It is not necessary to search unduly for apt parallels between Gergiev and Russia's mythic czar, Peter the Great. They all but leap out at one, and it is hardly hyperbole to dub Gergiev "Valery the Great." Like Peter, a visionary who demanded that a capital arise out of a marsh, Gergiev rules by dint of his power and personality. Both men decried the established norm and forced changes that often went against the grain of the old ways of life.

Again like Peter, Gergiev grabbed all within his reach by the scruff of their necks and pulled them, often protesting, into a new era, one founded upon his will and his vision of a riveting amalgam combining the theater's past with modern Western ways. A further quality Gergiev shares with Peter the Great is a tendency to head west, sometimes at the most inopportune moments and for long periods of time, leaving his kingdom in the hands of others less capable. All too often the fortunes of Mariinsky are put on hold while Gergiev conducts, tours, or attempts to raise funds elsewhere. But his odysseys and his background enable him, like Peter, to think in both Eastern and Western terms, something denied most Russians.

In true imperial fashion, Gergiev achieves his ends with single-mindedness, ruthlessness, and an ego that ignores everything and everyone that does not fit into his grand design. At times he appears to be oblivious to the broader needs of the theater, and without question he understands Louis xiv's maxim *"L'état, c'est moi,"* which, in Gergiev's case, could be slangily paraphrased as "The Kirov, that's him."

Gergiev's standing at the theater depends on whom you ask, for he is admired and feared, loved and disliked. In fact, in a land that has historically distrusted outside ways and ideas per se and in which paranoia is still rampant, there are those who are against him solely because he is from the south—Ossetia—and not truly Russian. His word, however, is final, and his wishes are law. The reasons are simple: he engenders greatness, generates desperately needed revenue, and, at his most inspired, produces results that are dramatic in every sense of the word and reduce all other complaints to insignificance.

Gergiev was born in Moscow on 2 May 1953 of Ossetian parents. His remarkable creative talents appear to have been a fortuitous confluence of fate, for his mother and father were not musical (although his older sister, Larissa, became an excellent pianist, coach, and accompanist). His father was an army regular who rose to become an officer during World War ii and who died from a stroke at the age of forty-nine, when Gergiev was fourteen.

The family moved back to Vladikavkaz, the major city in Ossetia, when Gergiev was five. "My father had become disenchanted with the army," Gergiev told me, "and the communist system—I learned this from my mother—and he wanted to distance himself and his children from Soviet life. It was in Ossetia that I met for the first time many of our relatives, as well as people my parents had grown up with, and learned what it meant to be Ossetian. My people are from the south, the mountains, the Caucasus. Theirs is a very communal society, and when you share a table with a family there it is a ritualistic thing. Families there are very tightly knit, and you feel very close, for example, to your extended family—uncles, aunts, and cousins. You may live independently of each other, but there is always a great feeling of warmth, and with all Ossetians there is a great commitment to traditional values.

"Ossetians were originally Scythians—my great-great-grandfather was Scythian—and this was a great state, a big people, a power. The Scythians were practically destroyed by the Mongolians, and their descendants, the Ossetians, were eventually absorbed by Russia. We are Indo-Europeans, and our language is within the European family of languages. This means we are equally Eastern and Western, which probably best explains where I stand emotionally and philosophically.

"My father was a highly respected man who had a gift of leadership, of obtaining people's respect and trust without becoming arrogant. I believe he passed this quality on to me, and, after all, isn't this what conducting is all about—the ability to lead, to make people listen to you and accept what you say? My mother's influence, of course, continues today. When she is unhappy about something, I immediately know that not everything is all right.

"This has been particularly true since I took over the Kirov, which to me is like a family. My decisions there affect the lives of hundreds of people. When I say 'Do this,' it is done. This makes my responsibilities very heavy, but they are made lighter because my mother keeps me Ossetian—I remain her son and the son of her husband. I might have easily become a less responsible person without her guidance. In her quiet way, she has been a more effective administrator of the Kirov than anyone who has held this post."

Gergiev's mother helped him start his musical education when he was seven, although neither could have known it would turn out to be a bad experience. She took him to the best music school in the town, where a committee of teachers was auditioning about a hundred children. From these they would choose fifteen to be admitted to the school. When it was Gergiev's turn to be interviewed, a woman on the committee beat a simple rhythm, but she beat it so weakly and in so inexact a way that he couldn't figure out what she was doing.

"When she said to me, 'Can you repeat this rhythm?'" Gergiev recalls, "I beat out a rhythm very strongly, as if to say, 'Well, this is my rhythm, whether it is yours or not.' Then they asked me to sing a melody and repeat a series of notes that was played on the piano, and this I did well. But after the examination, they told my mother, 'Your boy is a nice kid, but he is absolutely ungifted. He has no memory, no sense of rhythm, no gift for music. You had better just send him to a normal school.' My mother was surprised, for our neighbor was a musician, and he had told her over and over again, 'Your boy is very talented. You must let him study music.'

"My parents were very gentle people, and it was not in their makeup to go to the music school, make a fuss, and demand that I be admitted. But one of my father's friends, who was a composer, heard that I had been given this examination and had been turned away as hopeless. He asked my father if this was true, and my father answered that it was. 'Well,' said the friend, 'I'd like to see the boy for myself.' So he came by one evening and played on our piano a chord of three or four notes—and it wasn't such a simple chord—and asked me if I could sing all the notes, which I did immediately. He got very upset and said, 'But his ear is better than those teachers'!' "

Eventually Gergiev was admitted to the school, but only in a preparatory class —the "zero" class, it was called. "The other kids there were very slow," he remembers. "If you asked them to sing [the interval] 'si-do' or beat a simple quarter-note pattern, they couldn't do it. I was so bored, I stopped going and instead went off to play soccer [this is the one sport about which Gergiev remains passionate both as a spectator and as a player—when he is given the chance].

"Things became better when I began piano lessons at the school. My first teacher, Zarema Lolaeva, who also taught my sisters, believed in me. She told my father, 'The future of this boy is in music,' and he accepted this because he realized she was a serious person. She was the one who told me when I was ten years old, 'Someday you will be a conductor.' Now this was as realistic to me as it would be if I had been told I was going to fly to the moon and had better start preparing for it now.

"But she was totally committed to this idea of my becoming a conductor—the first real conductor from Ossetia. Yet I had no idea what a conductor was or what he did. I didn't even know how many symphonies Beethoven wrote! Where I lived there was no way of hearing symphonies or operas. I had once seen a local conductor, but he looked like a clown to me with the exaggerated way he beat time. My only real touch with music was to have a piano teacher of quality.

"I became a good pianist, but I did not enjoy spending time on purely technical things. I would choose my favorite eight bars and repeat them over and over again, each time with more pleasure and more quality. I remember loving certain harmonies and colors in a piece even more than the piece itself. And even today, when I rehearse, I tend to take one important section of a work and spend a lot of time on it to set the mood and atmosphere that I want."

Only after his father's death did Gergiev realize with certainty that music had to be his life. The turning point came when he met Anatoly Briskin, a conductor who had been a student of Ilya Musin, with whom Gergiev would later study at the Leningrad Conservatory, and Kurt Sanderling. Briskin was a member of the faculty at Gergiev's school and attended one of Valery's recitals. He immediately recognized Gergiev's potential and agreed to train him as a conductor.

"The role Briskin played in my life was very big," Gergiev told me. "When I started working with him, my sister Larissa accompanied me at my lessons; she would play piano reductions of symphonic scores which I conducted. He was the one who gave me the first symphonic score I ever held in my hands, and as part of my training, he would assign me a piece of music, like the Mozart G Minor Symphony, to study and then would ask me to play any instrumental part from it—the viola line, for example—from memory. In a year with Briskin I was playing the first eight Beethoven symphonies in four-hand arrangements and all the Beethoven sonatas. And with him conducting, I eventually performed the Beethoven Triple Concerto.

"He gave me only one compliment, if you can call it that, during my studies with him; actually, it was the most negative moment in our relationship. He screamed at me, one day when I was late to a lesson, 'You idiot, if it weren't for your piano playing I wouldn't have dreamed of working with you. You have a responsibility to yourself which you do not understand, and you waste your talent fooling around with your friends. You don't prepare your work properly because it is more important for you to see a soccer match.'

"It didn't occur to him that I was only a boy and wanted to enjoy the things I loved and understood. He was completely focused on music and wanted me to be the same. He told me that if I did not want to work seriously he would have nothing more to do with me. He wasn't going to spend six hours a week working with me just to see me become a football player. Now you might think it strange that I called this a compliment, but it was the first and only time that he ever referred to my talent. Never a word before. He would just say, 'Learn this, do this.' Naturally I was very shocked at his outburst, but it made me think really seriously about where I was heading.

"At the time I didn't know why he reacted so strongly. Later I found out. Music was all he had. To understand this you must understand the terrible tragedy of his family. His father, who was a Jew, and his younger sister were captured by the Germans in Ukraine during the war. They had been betrayed by someone who knew them. When the Germans arrested Briskin's father, they said, 'You two'—the father and the daughter—'this side. You'—to the mother, who was not Jewish—'that side.'

"But she refused to leave her husband and daughter and went with them to be executed. Briskin was then away in the army and only learned about their deaths later. Can you imagine anything so terrible? Musin, of course, knew about this, and he loved Briskin like a son. So when Briskin wrote a letter to Musin asking him to meet this eighteen-year-old boy, who was his student, he received me my first time in Leningrad like a grandson."

Briskin sent Gergiev to Leningrad to study at its renowned conservatory, which was founded in the nineteenth century by Anton Rubinstein. The school became a cradle that nursed composers from Tchaikovsky to Shostakovich and produced such renowned conductors as Evgeny Mravinsky, the longtime music director of the Leningrad Philharmonic. Musin accepted Gergiev as his student and became the major figure in the molding of Gergiev as a conductor, building on everything that Briskin had begun.

Gergiev believes that it was the presence of Musin, who was born in 1903, that had made the Leningrad Conservatory so very important. Gergiev is convinced that Musin "was one of the greatest teachers of the century. All his obituaries in the biggest papers said this when he died in 1999. He made the Leningrad Conservatory one of the world's centers of music. Although Shostakovich taught there and it had many important piano and string teachers, none of them so consistently produced fine students as did Musin, from the late 1920s until his death.

"He had great wisdom. He was living history, a brilliant narrator of important events in Russian music and in the musical life of Leningrad. He described for us, for example, the premiere of *The Love for Three Oranges* at the Kirov, and he told us why Prokofiev made changes in the orchestration of *Romeo and Juliet* when it was first played at the Kirov. Musin could speak of these things with authority because he was there. I never saw Otto Klemperer or Bruno Walter conduct, but Musin did. He attended their rehearsals with the Leningrad Philharmonic and heard Walter do *Queen of Spades* at the Kirov and Klemperer [do] *Carmen*. And he talked to them about tempos, rehearsal techniques, the German tradition of conducting, and he passed all of this along to us. He made me feel as if I had heard and talked with them as well.

"Musin's career as a conductor was never a big one like Mravinsky's because he had no interest in communist politics and wouldn't play that game. He also openly criticized the way Mravinsky made music. They didn't like each other, and Mravinsky kept him from conducting the Leningrad Philharmonic. But then Mravinsky did not like many other conductors. He was a great musician, but he was a dictator, a man of implacable will. It was the same with all strong men in the Stalin era."

While still a pupil of Musin's, Gergiev was heard by Temirkanov, who had studied with Musin and was about to take over the artistic direction of the Kirov Opera. In 1977 Temirkanov asked Gergiev to be his assistant at the theater. Eleven years later the Kirov would be Gergiev's—although not quite all his; supreme power such as no one at the Mariinsky had enjoyed before him would come only another eight years later.

Gergiev came to the artistic directorship of the Kirov during the final decade of the twentieth century, when Russia was in a rush to divest itself of everything that reflected its turbulent generations of communism. Statues of Soviet heroes were toppled from their pedestals, and hammer-and-sickle emblems suffered the same fate that had befallen Russia's double-headed eagle seventy-five years earlier.

Names, in particular, in this huge, mysterious, and still exotic land became a significant issue, for they often told a story all their own about the use and abuse of power and the rise and fall of political and historical fortunes. They are an especially poignant issue in Russia's former imperial city of the north, St. Petersburg, known simply as "Peter" by its natives. Even today it is not that unusual to meet someone who was born in Peter, grew up in Petrograd, married in Leningrad, and now has retired in St. Petersburg.

Although much loved by those who live there, this pastel-tinted town was always a thorn in the side of the communists. Even though it gave birth to their movement and they consistently paid lip service to its role in the history of their party, it was distrusted by Lenin, and even more by Stalin. St. Petersburg was too intellectual, too independent in spirit, too European. But its creator, Peter the Great, meant it to be this and more. It was not only his oft-described "window on the West," but a symbol of the new Russia he wished to create. It stood as an answer to the land's pagan past and became a seat of contrasts, where the old and new, the alien and the native rubbed shoulders and coexisted in a sometimes shaky, sometimes surprisingly comfortable alliance. The progressiveness and artistic license that came to be associated with St. Petersburg, however, were anathema to the Soviets. As soon as it was feasible, they moved their capital back to Moscow, which, during the imperial era, had played a secondary role in Russian life.

Moscow was recast to represent the new strength in the land, as well as the hub of new ideas and new politics. St. Petersburg (Petrograd at the time of the Revolution) was renamed Leningrad in an effort to make it a part of this new order. Little by little the dark, monolithic skyscrapers erected in Stalin's Moscow became a reflection of communist Russia, just as St. Petersburg's eighteenth-century fantasy palaces (designed by Italy's Francesco Rastrelli and others) had mirrored imperial Russia. This shift in power was endemic in all phases of Soviet life, and nowhere more than in the arts. Moscow's bloated red-and-gold Bolshoi Theater became the symbol and showcase of the new culture, while the smaller, more graceful Mariinsky Theater in St. Petersburg (named for Marie of Hesse-Darmstadt, the German wife of Czar Alexander II, who ordered it built) was relegated to a cultural backseat.

With the coming of communism, the Mariinsky underwent an identity crisis. Stripped of its imperial trappings, it was nationalized in 1917 as the State Academic Theater of Opera and Ballet. Then, in 1935, it became the Kirov Theater, in memory of the city's slain (supposedly on the orders of Stalin) communist party chief, Sergei Mironovich Kirov.

Whereas every element at the Bolshoi—scenery, dance, voices, staging—was amplified in an exaggerated, pseudoheroic manner to blare out the message of Soviet supremacy, the Kirov (after a valiant attempt to retain an identity of its own while becoming a part of the new spirit in the land) had, by the 1930s, become in general little more than a glorified regional company. It lost much of its sense of adventure and purpose and was finally reduced to being a feeder of talent to the Bolshoi (from the ballerina Galina Ulanova to the choreographer Yuri Grigorovich and the tenor Vladimir Atlantov). It remained, however, a bastion of bygone restraint, its traditions kept alive after two world wars primarily by its extraordinary dance company. Though change was inevitable—for ballet is a living as well as a lively art—the Kirov's distinctive style somehow managed to stay more or less intact, often impervious to what was going on outside and even within the borders of the Soviet Union despite decades of Bolshoi dominance and Russian insularity.

The Kirov reclaimed its original name with the fall of communism in 1991, when Leningrad once again became St. Petersburg. Ironically, since the name "Mariinsky" means little in the West, the theater's opera and ballet troupes continued to tour and to be merchandised as the Kirov Opera and the Kirov Ballet of the Mariinsky Theater. It is an odd hybrid, for while the name "Kirov" has solely Soviet resonances, "Mariinsky" rings with the glories of the czarist era and the memory of such artistic giants as Feodor Chaliapin, Anna Pavlova, and Vaslav Nijinsky. But perhaps this hybrid is not as inappropriate as it seems at first, for conflict and contradiction have long played roles in the theater's history.

It has been said that an opera house is the living room of a city, and from the beginning the Mariinsky fulfilled this function brilliantly. Located on a central square in St. Petersburg that also contains the city's Conservatory of Music, the imposing sea-green building with its white-icing trim became and has remained the core of the city's cultural life. The theater, which seats 1,621, opened in 1860 on the site of a burned-out building that had been constructed for the circus and then rebuilt for operetta and Russian opera performances. It is significant that this grand building came into being in a metropolis that has long had an exceptional empathy for the arts and whose parks, promenades, and architectural splendors combined to create an atmosphere of harmony that encourages beauty and symmetry as a natural part of life. In fact, the city's many parks and squares can still be seen as a series of immense stages, with their peripheral buildings positioned like scenic units. On them are enacted hundreds of human dramas each day.

Gergiev was only thirty-five when he took up the reins of the theater's artistic life in 1988. By the time he turned forty, he had, through extensive tours and recordings, made the Mariinsky the symbol of Russia's performing arts in the post-communist era. While the Bolshoi languishes from a lack of funds and dynamic leadership, the Kirov under Gergiev has gone from one foreign success to another, although, in the process, it has been paying a tremendous price for its newly acquired acclaim.

Gergiev is not interested primarily in glory or money, although both cling to him like pins to a magnet. Rather, he is possessed by a sense of mission, and that mission is, in large measure, to protect and preserve the traditions and the repertory born and nurtured at the Mariinsky. At the same time, he is attempting to bring the house into line with the finest of the theaters in the West—no casual juggling act. These aims are not entirely altruistic on Gergiev's part, for his staunch allegiance to the Mariinsky (a nonunion house, needless to say) is tied in with his freedom to work there on the music he fervently loves in the possessed, round-the-clock way he thrives on. No other major conductor in the world has quite the power and presence enjoyed by Gergiev at home.

One of Gergiev's attention-grabbing acts after taking over the artistic directorship of the Kirov company was to launch a series of festivals that concentrated on specific composers and showcased the theater's history. This was, after all, the house where the premieres of such Russian masterpieces as *Boris Godunov, Prince Igor,* and the *Nutcracker* took place. Gergiev's first festival in 1989 was devoted to Mussorgsky and featured both operatic and symphonic music, for he has made the concert life of the Kirov's splendid orchestra, both at home and abroad, as important as its life in the pit. In fact, it has been elevated to a position rivaled only by the orchestras of the Metropolitan and the Vienna State Operas.

Next in line for an in-depth reappraisal at the Kirov were Prokofiev and Rimsky-Korsakov; later, on a less exhaustive level, the spotlight was turned on Tchaikovsky and Stravinsky. In an effort to broaden the theater's horizons and conserve his limited funds, Gergiev began a series of coproductions with other leading opera houses, and he imported productions such as *Boris Godunov* from Covent Garden, in the admired Andrei Tarkovsky staging; *Tosca* from San Francisco; *Aida* from La Scala; and the Metropolitan Opera's old but still effective sets and costumes for *Madame Butterfly.* For the theater's new productions, he invited outside designers and directors to work at the Mariinsky and arranged for expatriate singers to return to the fold, at least on a temporary basis, for performances and recording projects.

Gergiev's Mariinsky became an inviting and ongoing adventure that has brought many to St. Petersburg for the first time. My initial journey to Russia in 1986 was not for opera, however, but for the much-heralded return of the pianist Vladimir Horowitz to his homeland after an absence of more than sixty years. I went there through the intervention of the Georgian pianist Alexander Toradze ("Lexo" to all who know him), who had defected to the West three years earlier and become my friend. It was he who had first spoken to me of growing up in Russia and of his friendship with Gergiev. He insisted that I must know both the land and the man, and he stage-managed my first visit.

Lexo and Gergiev had first met in 1979 in St. Petersburg. "After one of my concerts," Gergiev told me, "I went to a restaurant at the Union of Composers with six or seven other musicians. Suddenly I heard someone playing jazz on a terrible, out-of-tune upright piano. But it was incredible playing, and I jumped up and went to see who the pianist was. 'Who are you?' I asked, interrupting his playing.

" 'I'm Lexo,' he said.

" 'Oh, Toradze,' I said, because I knew his name and had heard of him as a marvelous pianist.

" 'And who are you?' he asked.

" 'Valery,' I answered.

" 'Oh, Gergiev,' he replied, for he had heard of me as well.

"Unfortunately, he was about to leave to catch the midnight train back to Moscow, but we exchanged phone numbers, and the next time I was in Moscow I called him from the station at 8:30 in the morning—not a good time to phone either one of us! 'I just arrived,' I told him.

" 'Ah, Valera'—he recognized my voice. 'Where are you?'

" 'At the Leningrad station,' I told him.

" 'Wait there,' he shouted and hung up. Fifteen minutes, he arrived in a car, waving at me. We spent the day with his friends and mine, and instantly we were like brothers. We still are."

The two first made music together in 1980—a Mozart concerto with the Kirov Orchestra. Soon afterward they performed the Prokofiev Piano Concerto No. 3 with the Leningrad Conservatory Orchestra. "There was a great personal warmth between us," Lexo told me one evening while we were both in Israel, "and we hit it off right away, for we thought about and felt music alike. But to be honest I didn't realize at first that I was playing with a conductor of a unique magnitude. That came later. We were just friends making music together.

"I remember he was always coming to Moscow when there were interesting concerts or operas. And there were always dozens of friends and relatives with him. This was confusing for me, and I couldn't imagine how he could manage to function under these conditions. I told him, 'Slow down. I know you love all these people, but you have to concentrate more and conserve your energy.' How could I have known then that this was the very thing that gave him his energy? He is the same way now, only more so. Not only is he still on the go all the time, but he is still surrounded by people whom he feeds with his talent and inspiration.

"There was a six-year gap in our friendship after I defected, but during that time he went to Georgia to see my mother and my father [the esteemed Georgian composer David Toradze]. Through them he tracked me down in the United States, where I was living in Arizona. One day the phone rang, and it was Valery calling from Japan. After that we would talk for hours whenever he was outside of Russia and could call. This was so important to me, because he was the only close Russian friend I spoke with during those years.

"I kept trying to get him to join me. He would listen carefully and then say, 'But first I have to make it here.' Even after he became artistic director at the Kirov, I didn't stop urging him to come to the West. But finally I realized what he was doing and how important the theater was to him, so I shut up. We at last met again in Holland in 1989 and began making music together again and haven't stopped since."

I asked Lexo, who has made music with many different conductors, what set Gergiev apart. "So many things," he replied. "It's hard even to try listing them. But I am always amazed how he can change any orchestra to conform to the sound he wants. Also, most conductors hate doing concertos, but not Valery. He sees the whole piece, not just the piano part or the orchestral part, and he is consumed with the whole. He is never just an accompanist. He works on the orchestra part with the same intensity he does when rehearsing a symphony.

"My father, being a composer, always used to tell me why he was giving a particular line to a particular instrument in one of his works and how much weight this instrument should carry in the overall sound. Valery thinks the same way. In addition, unlike many conductors, he listens to what I have to say about a piece—not only about the piano part but the orchestral part. Not that we always agree. But there is always an exchange of ideas. Beyond this, his imagination and inspiration are always working and can create something extremely spontaneous and unexpected during an actual performance. I love that. I like to do it myself. This can be very dangerous, however, especially in ensemble playing. But I understand what's happening when he does it, and he picks up on it when I do it. Often this enables us to go even further with a piece of music than what we had rehearsed. Even with works we have played together dozens of times and recorded, he still finds convincing new things. He never just settles for one interpretation. I love his Wagner, his Mahler, his Prokofiev, his Tchaikovsky, his Berlioz, Stravinsky, and Debussy. But although these are perhaps the composers dearest to him, I feel his musical and mental capacities are as boundless as his talent. Of course, when you have such a talent there is a temptation to get lazy. Not Valery. He never stops challenging himself."

Unfortunately, despite Lexo's efforts, I did not meet Gergiev on my first trip to Russia; he was away giving a concert in another city. But on my second trip, in 1988, the spring before he assumed the artistic leadership of the Kirov, we finally got together. It was during a festival of contemporary music in Leningrad, for which he was one of several conductors. Lexo had arranged an invitation for me through the composer Alexander Tchaikovsky, and Gergiev and I spent hours walking together through the parks and streets of St. Petersburg, talking about his impending directorship and about what could and should be done at the theater (at his suggestion, I played hooky from the festival several evenings to see Temirkanov conduct *Boris Godunov* and his staging of *The Queen of Spades* at the Kirov).

By the time I returned in 1993 for the inaugural Stars of the White Nights Festival, Gergiev was already making prodigious waves in Russia and the West through his recordings, videos, and tours. Late one night, after a dazzling all-Rachmaninov concert that had included *The Bells* and Lexo's blazing performance of the Piano Concerto No. 3, there was a late-night bout of drinking, eating, smoking, and talking (four passionate Russian pastimes) with a roomful of Gergiev's cronies and friends that included Mstislav Rostropovich.

About 3:00 A.M., as the party began to disband, Gergiev announced that he needed some air, and five of us piled into his car and drove to the nearby Neva embankment. As is common during that magical time of year in Russia known as White Nights, when the daylight elbows out most of the darkness and the city seems to be in a trance, there were many others out walking the river as well, creating an odd, off-hours feeling of festivity.

Leaving his friends sitting on the embankment, Gergiev struck out at a brisk pace along the river, motioning to me to follow. I discovered two further things about him that morning. He often waits until the last minute to discuss something that is pressing on his mind (I was due to leave the next day), and he frequently does it outdoors while on the move. "Johnchik," he began, using the affectionate nickname Lexo had given me, "why don't you write a book on the Kirov? It needs to be done. I have had several publishers approach me, but I don't believe they want to do something serious."

It is a good thing we were mobile or my legs might have buckled under me. I could immediately think of at least a dozen reasons why the idea was impractical. For one thing, I don't speak or read Russian. For another, it would take at least a year of research in St. Petersburg, for which outside funding would have to be found, before any writing could begin. Neither the theater nor I had the money to underwrite the project, and it was impractical to presume that a publisher would be willing to do so.

Gergiev, however, rarely concedes that something is impossible, and he is accustomed to getting his way in most things. Being intuitive and a born gambler (in life, not casinos), he seems to draw strength from living on the edge and to thrive on situations that are riddled with question marks. But when his mind is at last made up, he usually acts resolutely, whether right or wrong, and at that moment he was adamant that a Kirov book should be done, and that it must be done by a non-Russian with a nonparochial point of view.

Not by chance, but by his disposition and talent, Gergiev's god among musicians is Wilhelm Furtwängler, as is mine. I had just published a book on this influential conductor (Amadeus Press, 1994), which Lexo had given Gergiev to read while it was still in manuscript. The book convinced him I should tackle the story of the Kirov. We discussed the matter for a while longer as he countered my objections, and then said good-bye. To my amazement, I realized I had promised him to look into the problems involved and see if there were practical solutions.

Leaping the first hurdle was easy. Russian was the second language of a close friend of mine, Myron Gamboa, who had gone to school in Leningrad and graduated from its university. He knew the town, he understood the people, and he, too, loved the Mariinsky. He said he would be willing to go back and spend a year there as my translator and assistant. The next problem—the question of money—was not solved so simply.

Over the next year I tried a succession of national foundations that had Anglo-Russian interests and was turned down by them all. Then an old friend, who was a fund-raiser for a large university in Texas, suggested I try local foundations. In short order—and to my utter disbelief—I was promised half the funding in the form of a matching grant. With something concrete in hand, I was able to go to my employer and ask for a year's sabbatical, which was approved. The matching funds were soon found, and the pieces began falling into place with unexpected ease. Gergiev's crazy idea seemed less crazy; in fact, it seemed destined to work.

In mid-June of 1995, Myron and I boarded a plane with six bags of clothes for every possible temperature, a mini-drugstore, a typewriter, cameras, a tape recorder, and a portable photocopy machine, and we headed for St. Petersburg and Gergiev's third Stars of the White Nights Festival. What happened between that and the fourth festival the following June forms the core of this book.

It was unseasonably hot when we arrived, yet dazzlingly green. St. Petersburg has been described as both a white and a green city, and friends of mine frequently debated whether it was more beautiful in the snow and ice or in the lushness of spring and summer. Though I now see both sides of the issue, I tend to agree with those who love it best when its trees and parks are decked out like shimmering emeralds, for this is the time of year that includes the bewitching White Nights.

About two months each year, beginning in late spring, night in northern Russia all but disappears. Even when it gives way to something approximating darkness, the sky retains a rosy purple glow that lasts but a few hours before sunrise begins to light up the land. One can read about the fabulous White Nights and hear descriptions of them, but pictures and words are poor substitutes for the phenomenon itself. This is a time when the light is so pure during the day and so phosphorescent at night that the city's parks, its classic skyline, and its noble buildings take on an almost living quality.

The all-pervasive mood of White Nights is heightened for me by the sort of feverish music making that occurs at the festival when Gergiev and his artists are operating at maximum strength. In the space of two weeks, one is served an overflowing plate of opera, dance, orchestral concerts, and recitals at the Mariin-

sky and Hermitage Theaters and downtown in both the large and small Philharmonic Halls (now renamed for Shostakovich and Glinka, respectively). The festival is Gergiev's way of showcasing the best of what is happening at the Mariinsky.
Sometimes there is a theme, or at least an attempt at one, but usually the festival
is a grab-bag-in-excelsis, a mix of Mariinsky classics and the best of the season just
completed, be it repertory, artists, or a new production. Or, better said, it consists
of what has caught and held Gergiev's attention over the past twelve months, or
what fits in with his upcoming tour plans or recording projects. It is hard to fault
what often seems self-indulgence on Gergiev's part, for his gifts are of so fine a
quality and his use of them so unstinting and revealing that they often alter one's
perception and ideas about a composer or a work in a way that only the finest musicians can.

No one foisted the role of crusader or paterfamilias on Gergiev; he could have
easily settled into a posh, well-paying berth in the West as other Russian musicians
have done and not given the Kirov or its future a second thought. There was no
lack of offers; he is probably the most sought-after conductor today under the age
of fifty and has appeared as a guest on the major podiums of Europe and North
America. Nor is Gergiev indifferent to money; no one carrying the burdens of a
theater like the Mariinsky on their shoulders could afford to be. He is keenly aware
of what a dollar, a peseta, or a mark will buy for the Kirov in terms of helping the
company survive.

The search for funds is an ever-pressing one that Gergiev has described as necessary "to enable the best Russian singers to continue working and developing in
the Russian national opera tradition." To this end he established the Friends of the
Kirov in Great Britain and the United States, as well as a string of mini–Kirov Festivals outside of St. Petersburg that generate much of the theater's annual income.
A strong beginning was made first in the Netherlands, Finland, Great Britain, and
Japan, and seeds for mini-Kirovs are taking root in Germany, France, Spain, Israel,
and the United States. In a very real way, these satellite festivals are dependent on
what happens at the Mariinsky during the course of a season, but often they are
most dependent on what is chosen for White Nights, a time when Gergiev tests
his ideas and resources to the fullest.

My excitement at being back in St. Petersburg was matched by the excitement
of being back within the cradling, plush interior of the Mariinsky. I first heard
opera here in 1986, a performance of Yuri Shaporin's *The Decembrists*. On that and
subsequent trips, it became and remains for me the most personal of opera houses,
one with a rich past, a sympathetic present, and a bright future. I can do no better than to echo the words of Igor Stravinsky, who grew up literally in the shadow
of the Mariinsky. In his book *Expositions and Developments*, he wrote that the the-

ater "was a delight to me, no matter how often I saw it, and to walk from our house through the Offitserskaya to the Ulitza Glinka, where I could see its dome, was to be consumed with Petersburger pride. To enter the blue and gold interior of that heavily perfumed hall was, for me, like entering the most sacred of temples."

The Mariinsky is an ideal of what an opera house should be—luxurious yet functional, a setting that enhances the theatricality of what takes place on its stage. Although it lacks imposing public areas, the interior of the house exudes an air of sovereignty, from its blue velvet–covered armchairs in the parterre to the shining tiers of chandeliers, the imposing central imperial box, and its ornate trademark blue-and-gold curtain. It is a necessary stop, whatever the bill of fare, during the progress of a pilgrim who has come to St. Petersburg in search of the city's imperial past. As much as any of the palaces in and around the city, the Mariinsky is a contemporary reminder of a splendor that once was.

When I arrived, the 1995 Stars of the White Nights Festival was off to a riveting start with a new production of *Katerina Ismailova*, which had premiered at the theater in late spring. It was the first opera by Shostakovich to be staged by the company. As Gergiev is more often than not drawn to a composer's original ideas, it was surprising that he would choose to mount the revised and somewhat sanitized version of this controversial opera (a year later, at the next White Nights Festival, he would unexpectedly shift gears and present both *Katerina Ismailova* and *Lady Macbeth of Mtsensk* during the same twenty-four-hour period).

But Shostakovich himself was somewhat ambivalent about the two versions. Not many realize that he had begun a revision of the opera less than a year after its premiere in 1934, even before the work disgraced him with Stalin and the Soviet power structure. Furthermore, the other changes he made after being censored by the establishment were more because of his continued dissatisfaction with aspects of the libretto and the score itself than because of outside pressures. Shostakovich, who died in 1975, wrote that he disliked most productions of the opera during his lifetime (as well as the Soviet film of the opera) because the emphasis was never sufficiently centered on the music. Would that he could have heard how Gergiev endowed his score with overriding prominence and vividness! The Kirov performances for the eye and the ear amounted virtually to a new lease on life for *Katerina*, although Gergiev's decision to combine acts 1 and 2 as a single unit perhaps asked too much of both the performers and the audience.

Of almost equal importance in this gripping realization were the conductor's artistic partners: Georgy Tsypin, a visionary Russian designer now living in the United States, and the director Irina Molostova, a close friend of the composer. Tsypin is best known in the West for his operatic collaborations with the director Peter Sellars, and his *Katerina* designs did what scenery at its best should do:

reflect the music and draw a listener deep into the score. He used primarily mobile planks of polished wood—splitting, dividing, and swinging inward and outward. Separately and together they assumed various shapes and created abstracts of the Ismailova farm and house.

Molostova's staging took full advantage of the sparseness of the sets and the ample stage space they provided. She was particularly adroit at dealing with the conflicts that arise between the opera's leading characters. Her staging imbued the work with humor and parody as well as claustrophobia and terror, and she created a particularly mighty moment with the overwhelming passacaglia in act 2. The extra brass required for this interlude were paraded onstage in uniforms and lined up at the footlights, while the orchestra rose almost to stage level via the pit elevator. At the same time, the house lights were brought up, creating a startling coup de théâtre that doubled the impact of the music.

Gergiev's conducting was a prodigious feat of concentration, drive, and a savvy balancing of the peaks in the score with those moments when the music tamps down or tapers off. On the whole the cast was a strong one, although the Katerina, soprano Irina Lostkutova, was cautious on the first night (becoming steadier and more commanding in later performances, however). Yuri Marusin was a strong presence as Katerina's lover, and it is difficult to imagine a more compelling realization of Boris Ismailova than that delivered by the bass Sergei Alexashkin.

Aida, which followed on the heels of *Katerina*, was intended as the centerpiece of the festival, and vocally it was for the most part a formidable evening. There had been a grand plan to bring the original director, Franco Zeffirelli, to restage this 1963 La Scala production by Lila de Nobili, but after a cat-and-mouse game initiated by Zeffirelli the plan foundered, supposedly because of the Kirov's inability to come up with the sort of fee to which Zeffirelli was accustomed. At the last moment a staff member of the Kirov, Yuri Alexandrov, put the opera together in a generally creditable manner, complete with a pair of horses galloping onstage at full tilt during the Triumphal Scene. It was pure circus, but then so is this section of the score.

Although obviously much used and tired, there was still a faded grandeur to de Nobili's sets and costumes, which had been so acclaimed when they were new. Zeffirelli's idea had been to recreate *Aida* as it might have been done during Verdi's lifetime. This romantic concept could still be savored at the Mariinsky more than thirty years later. Yet the performance could not really be called Italianate. Gergiev is not as conversant or comfortable with this score as he is with *Otello*, an opera he has conducted more often and with more flair. The sort of swiftness and tautness that dominate Gergiev's approach to *Otello* worked only intermittently in *Aida*, which requires greater sweep.

The Bolshoi Kamenny Opera House and Theater Square in the late eighteenth century
where the Circus Theater and then the Mariinsky Theater would be built.
PHOTO: VILI ONIKUL

Old Circus Theater, 1858.
COURTESY MARIINSKY THEATER

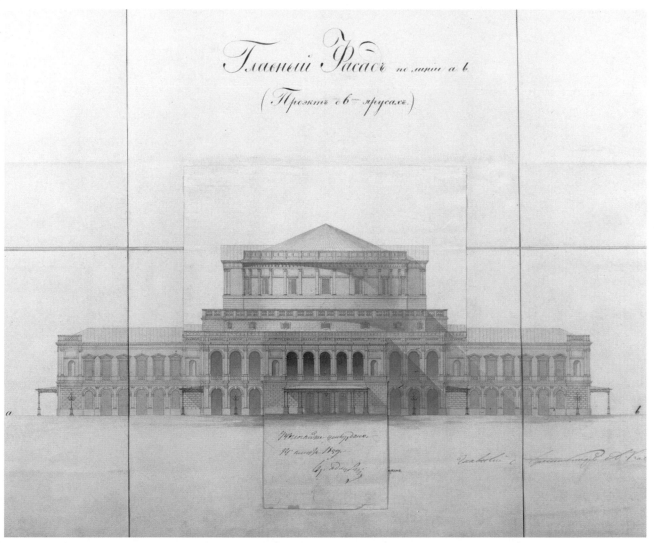

Alberto Cavos's design for the Mariinsky's exterior, 1860.
PHOTO: VILI ONIKUL

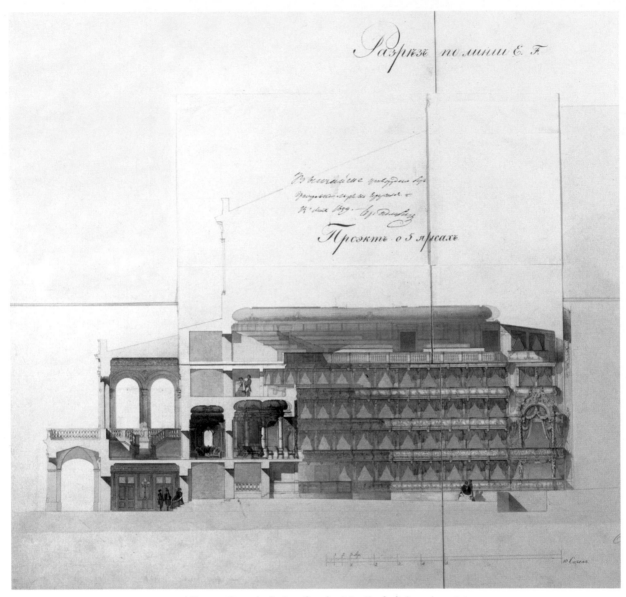

Alberto Cavos's design for the Mariinsky's interior, 1860.

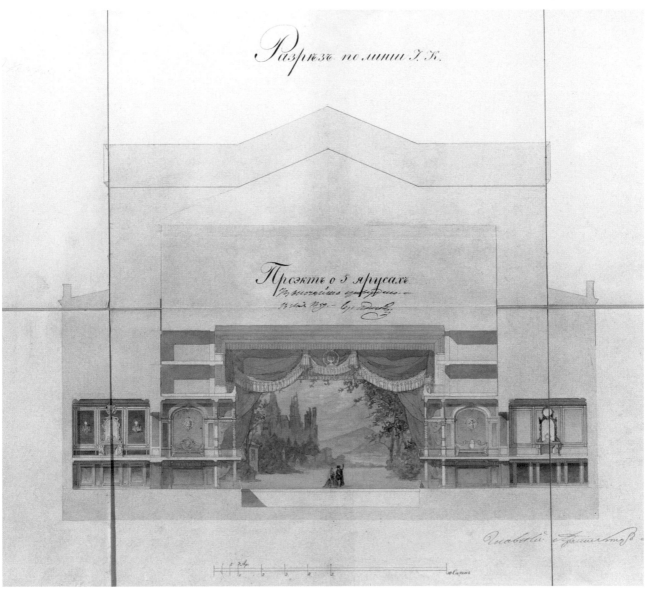

Alberto Cavos's design for the Mariinsky's stage, 1860.
PHOTO: VILI ONIKUL

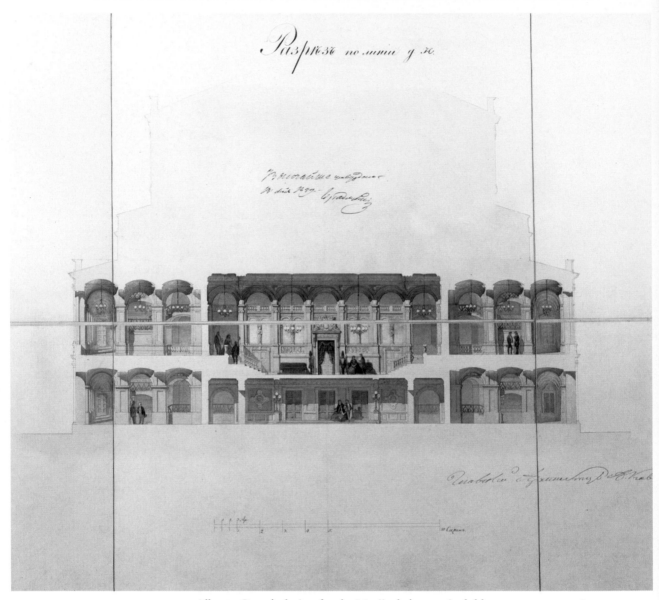

Alberto Cavos's design for the Mariinsky's upstairs lobby
with the entrance to the imperial box, 1860.

Alberto Cavos's design for the Mariinsky's boxes, 1860.
PHOTO: VILI ONIKUL

Mariinsky Theater, present-day exterior.
PHOTO: VALENTIN BARANOVSKY

Mariinsky Theater, present-day interior.
PHOTO: VALENTIN BARANOVSKY

Mariinsky curtain.

Mariinsky upstairs lobby.
PHOTO: VILI ONIKUL

Mariinsky poster advertising *Katerina Ismailova*,
a concert, *Carmen*, and a royal gala.
PHOTO: VILI ONIKUL

While the singing was at times uneven, the evening was nonetheless filled with vocalism to be reckoned with. The finest performance came from the mezzo-soprano Olga Borodina, who was an imperious, silky-voiced Amneris. The Amonasro, equally impressive, was Nikolai Putilin, whom I had earlier heard only in smaller roles. In *Aida* he rose to stellar dimensions. His voice is an exciting, at times dry sound; yet during my year at the Kirov he proved to be one of the stalwart wonders of the company.

As for Galina Gorchakova's Aida, there was no denying that her voice was dark and mighty. But it had also suffered a great deal of wear and tear in the three years since she burst upon the international scene as Renata in the Kirov's stunning production of Prokofiev's *The Fiery Angel*. By 1995 Gorchakova was often capable of only rudimentary vocal subtlety, for she was relying entirely upon muscle to sustain notes high above the staff. In *Aida* she was able to bat out B-flats and Cs in steely fashion, but her pitch sense was unreliable. This has become a great voice in great trouble. Yet, compared to other performances I heard from her in the months ahead—Tosca in London and Leonora in *La forza del destino* in Paris— her Aida was not that problematic.

Matching her in terms of vocal strength (though his overall performance was infinitely more secure) was Vladimir Galuzin as Radames. His trumpetlike voice easily stayed the course in *Aida*, and I would be hard pressed to name a current tenor in the West capable of making as much of the role. Finally, adding a further layer of importance to the performance was the Ramfis, Vladimir Ognovenko, Russia's finest bass these days.

Two nights later, Gergiev and the Kirov Orchestra moved downtown to the cradling warmth of Philharmonic Hall for the first of four concerts. The program included a spectacular, primitive performance of Stravinsky's *Le sacre du printemps* that was filled with crushing power and snaky primordial sounds. It surpassed even the violent colors and textures I remembered from Leonard Bernstein's fiery *Sacre*s.

Gergiev also offered the Russian premiere of an important new score by Alexander Tchaikovsky, his Concerto for Viola No. 2. The soloist was the incomparable Yuri Bashmet, and the composer was on hand to play the score's exacting piano part. In addition to being one of Russia's chief musical voices these days and a composer of variety, invention, and individuality, Tchaikovsky (no relation to Peter Ilyich) serves the Mariinsky as an artistic advisor and one of Gergiev's talent scouts.

Another example of Gergiev's turning a disappointment to advantage (as he had with Zeffirelli's defection) was the gala evening he created on the spur of the moment when Placido Domingo withdrew from a scheduled White Nights concert. As a replacement Gergiev put together staged performances of the third act of *Eugene Onegin* and the first Polovtsian scene from *Prince Igor*. Gorchakova, in better form than in *Aida*, was the Tatiana, while Borodina sang Konchakovna. The evening, in fact, belonged to Borodina, and her sensual performance was superbly backed by Putilin's regal Igor. Another Borodina-Gergiev collaboration came a few nights later with a mesmerizing performance of *Khovanshchina* in the marvelously old-fashioned sets by Feodor Fedorovsky. Borodina, Russia's major singer in the 1990s, performed her penetrating Marfa in the company of Ognovenko as Khovansky and the Kirov's admirable character tenor Konstantin Pluzhnikov in the dual roles of the Scribe and Prince Golitsin.

Back at Philharmonic Hall, Gergiev undertook his first performance of Beethoven's Ninth Symphony after the cancellation of yet another guest, the conductor James Conlon. Rehearsal time was at a premium, a less than ideal condition under which to prepare one's first performance of this difficult work, and Gergiev concentrated what few rehearsals he had mainly on the first movement. But watching him in numerous rehearsals over the next dozen months, I realized that he prefers taking a single movement or a specific section of a work out of context and spending what seems a disproportionate amount of time honing it to a fine point to set the sound he wants and the stylistic parameters of the piece. He then trusts his orchestra to take the lessons learned and apply them throughout the entire composition.

To a surprising degree, this highly personal approach appears to work more often than it fails. Beethoven's Ninth was an instance where it failed. The opening movement was the best part of the performance—in fact, it was extraordinary. But from the scherzo onward, the performance careened downhill. If any good could be said to have come out this roller-coaster ride, it was the opportunity to glimpse briefly the silvery voice of the soprano Marina Shaguch, one of the Kirov's current assets.

The next evening Gergiev was back in his element with a galvanizing performance of Tchaikovsky's Fifth Symphony. There was also a mystic, memorable account of the prelude to *Parsifal*. Its serenity and spaciousness left me convinced that Gergiev is one of the world's major Wagnerian conductors. An all-Stravinsky evening followed, and once more Gergiev took us to the heights, with a complete *Firebird* followed by Lexo's riveting first performance of the Piano Concerto. I thought the concerto was a bristling success, but it seems neither the conductor nor the pianist was happy with the first movement, so they made the unprecedented decision to repeat it on the spot as an encore. The second time around brought them the precision and excitement they were after.

Just as the music making at White Nights appeared to be verging on the utopian, I was brought down to earth with a performance of Stravinsky's two one-act operas *Mavra* and *Le rossignol*, staged in the elegant confines of Catherine the

Great's theater in the Hermitage. The cast for the double bill was weak, and the productions were commonplace (Gergiev conducted only *Rossignol*). It is best, as well, to draw a curtain over the contributions of the Kirov Ballet to White Nights (*Don Quixote* and *La sylphide*), for the main company and its stars were away in London; the dancers left were decidedly second class. No one, including Gergiev, seemed to think this mattered, however—as though the ballets were not to be taken seriously, merely filling time and space between the opera evenings and the concerts.

The festival ended with a new production of *Salome*, a work not seen at the Kirov for more than seventy years. It had been premiered in the late spring of 1995 at Germany's Oberammergau Theater and televised. But as it received only a single performance at the Mariinsky before the season ended and was not absorbed into the company's repertory until September, I will leave more about this *Salome* for another chapter.

The day after the Strauss premiere, the theater in effect shut down for two and a half months (although its stage was leased for a few weeks to the former Kirov dancer Askold Makarov, whose small dance troupe offered a program of popular ballets in modest productions aimed at the summer tourist trade and shamelessly hawked by scalpers as "The Kirov Ballet"). Meanwhile, Gergiev and his artists decamped to the festival he had founded a few years earlier in Mikkeli, Finland.

Myron and I stayed behind to move from the depressing former Soviet hotel in which we had been lodged to a pleasant, airy apartment only five blocks from the theater. It was in a small residence hotel, Matisov Domik, that had been created from a former office building and that the Kirov frequently used to house visiting artists. A new wing had just opened, and we were among its first occupants. Our apartment looked out onto a large courtyard with a garden and included two bedrooms, a bath, and a much-needed kitchen, for food in St. Petersburg is either very expensive, very bad, or both.

The balance of July was filled with unpacking, exploring the city, and establishing credentials and contacts at the superb Saltykov-Shchedrin Library on Nevsky Prospect, the nearby Library and the Museum of the Performing Arts behind the Alexandrinsky Theater, and the State Archives, where prerevolutionary papers are housed. The work—and the adventure—had begun.

CHAPTER ONE

Setting the Stage

Although St. Petersburg is younger than New York, it is older in spirit. Founded in 1703, the city was modeled along the lines of the great European capitals. Few cities have inspired so many words, ideas, and myths. Writers, including Russia's literary god Alexander Pushkin and his friend Nikolai Gogol, searched feverishly for phrases to capture its beauty and explain the hold it exerts on those who succumb to its beauty. St. Petersburg has been dubbed the "Babylon of the Snows," the "Venice of the North," and the "Northern Palmyra." However it is labeled, there is no mistaking the power of "this city of gold, on a horizon of silver," as the French poet Théophile Gautier described it.

"The grandiose buildings of the city," the author Suzanne Massie has written, "which surprised the eye with their colors of yellow, turquoise, green, orange and red; the wide avenues and squares, which seemed made for parades and revues; the swift-moving river, the misty canals, the rippling green islands and parks all gave to the city a unique mystery and charm. But like every great city, St. Petersburg is more than a collection of buildings; it is also a state of mind. . . . Its way of life, which poetically adapted the tastes of both east and west to the northern latitudes, evoked for Europeans a special romance. The city was born from the collision of two cultures, and the tension arising from this collision became the persistent theme of a remarkable succession of artists. In this city, suspended between water and sky, illuminated by iridescent white nights in the summer and sunk in gloomy darkness in the winter, human relationships attained a strange intensity. It was a city of power, of fortune seekers, of officials, of the court. It was also a city of dreamers, of poets, and of artists."

Like Venice and Amsterdam, St. Petersburg, with its network of canals, has always been dependent upon water, its life and history bound up with triumphs over this primal element of nature. The city has struggled since its creation to stay alive, for there was no reason for it to be, other than the whim of one of the mightiest men the world has known. Where others saw only marshlands, Peter the Great saw a potential for both a fortress—a city that would be a protected gateway facing hostile lands to the north—and a portal for bringing into Russia the scientific advances being made in the West. In his heart, Peter was first a sailor, and he must have fallen in love at once with the great expanse of the Neva River, three-quarters of a mile wide and three miles long. Its noble vista was surely as satisfying to him as the purity of its water was at one time thirst quenching. Peter built his palace on its banks to be close to his shipyards, and the Neva became not only a symbol of the city, but the focus of daily life.

Before long, the Neva was matched by another remarkable expanse, the city's main thoroughfare, Nevsky Prospect. This great boulevard extends from the golden spire of the yellow-and-white admiralty building adjacent to the Winter Palace eastward to the blue-and-white buildings of Nevsky Monastery. Today, only one of Nevsky Prospect's buildings does not date from the late eighteenth or early nineteenth century. The street is still lined with palaces and shops, and it remains a magnet of town life.

A stroll along Nevsky Prospect is one of the first things a tourist does after arriving in St. Petersburg. Here one encounters a remarkable variety of faces and races in an endless stream of humanity. The sidewalks are packed with flower stalls, newsstands, ticket kiosks, ice cream vendors, sellers of lottery tickets, beggars, and shoppers, and the varied parade of people never ceases to fascinate no matter how often one becomes part of it.

At some point during a visit to St. Petersburg, a tourist will no doubt discover the open-air market opposite the Church on the Spilt Blood, a monumental, old-style Russian edifice erected on the spot where Czar Alexander II was assassinated (its bulbous, multicolored turrets are wonderfully incongruous amid the classical splendors of the surrounding city). The lure of the market is not just its bargains in amber, balalaikas, and the ubiquitous *matryoshky* (nesting dolls), but its military souvenirs from the Soviet era, particularly army and navy caps, overcoats, and medals.

Soviet Russia, however, is not what most tourists are seeking. The majority are in search of imperial Russia—remnants of its czars, their treasures, and their former residences. An important stop in this quest is the Winter Palace, or the Hermitage; this complex of imperial buildings along the Neva is best known by the name given the wing Catherine the Great added to display her paintings. But few visitors to this breathtaking treasure house realize that here, along with its countless rooms of paintings, sculpture, and artifacts, can be found the cradle of Russian opera and ballet.

The Hermitage Theater was begun on Catherine's orders in 1783, the same year that the Bolshoi Kamenny ("Big Stone Theater") opened its doors across town. The architect for the Hermitage was the Italian builder Giacomo Quarenghi. His work in St. Petersburg emphasized the debt he owed his countryman, Andrea Palladio: the inspiration Quarenghi drew upon for the Hermitage Theater was Palladio's imposing Teatro Olimpico in Vicenza, which dates from 1579. Quarenghi took not only the elegant proportions and the fan shape of this Italian marvel; he was influenced as well by its decorations. He lined the walls of the Hermitage Theater with columns interspersed with niches housing statues of Apollo and the nine Muses. They, in turn, were surmounted by medallions of celebrated playwrights and composers. The theater has neither a large seating capacity nor an adequate orchestra pit. But its stage can comfortably accommodate the dramatic needs of most eighteenth-century operas and ballets. The Mariinsky's opera and ballet occasionally perform here, and in addition to a Stravinsky double bill I saw, several Kirov concerts were given at the Hermitage during my time in the city.

It is a harmonious space and has, of course, great historic importance as the only eighteenth-century Russian theater to survive intact. In the preface to a book about the theater, Quarenghi writes that it "was designed for the private use of Her Majesty and her Court. There is enough space to put on the most magnificent spectacles, and it does not in this respect fall behind the most famous theaters. All the seats are equally well placed, and anyone can sit wherever he pleases."

In her book *The Palaces of Leningrad*, Audrey Kennett, in addition to quoting Quarenghi, cites an anonymous English writer who visited Russia in 1790 and witnessed a gala evening in Catherine's theater. In his book *Letters from the Continent*, he reports that "on Saturday next there is to be a grand play. It was written by the Empress and is called *Olga*. It is a tragedy with choruses, like the ancients, with a kind of Greek music. There are no less than thirty personages in the play . . . the suite consists of six hundred people who are all . . . on the stage at once . . . a marvelous sight. When the play is over the wittiest thing would be to call for the author as they do in Paris, 'L'auteur, l'auteur!'"

Catherine II brought to St. Petersburg a succession of leading Italians to fill the post of court composer, including Giovanni Paisiello (whose best-known work, *Il barbiere di Siviglia*, was premiered in St. Petersburg), Domenico Cimarosa, and Giuseppe Sarti. She treated them lavishly, but the Italian opera company she attempted to establish did not flourish and was disbanded in 1807. The empress's love of dance and singing, however, is the root of Russia's performing arts.

Peter the Great's niece, Anna Ioannovna, who reigned before Catherine, is correctly credited with taking the first real step toward a Russian school of ballet. In 1738 the Frenchman Jean-Baptiste Landé, who had come to Russia to teach dancing, asked the empress for "twelve children—six males and six females—to create ballets and theater dances. . . . These pupils by the end of the first year will dance with cadets; in two years they will execute different dances; in three years they will not be less than the best of foreign dancers." He received not only a dozen children, but also two rooms in the Winter Palace in which to train them. This was the beginning of what was to be a steady flow of ballet masters and dancers from throughout Europe.

The first visiting troupe of Italian singers, headed by the composer Giovanni Ristori, also arrived in St. Petersburg during Anna's reign. Ristori's opera *Calandro*, given in Moscow in 1731, was the first ever seen in Russia. In 1735 Anna had an Italian opera troupe of her own recruited in Venice, with the twenty-six-year-old composer Francesco Araia as *maestro di cappella*. The company performed for the first time on the occasion of the empress's birthday in 1736. The setting was the Winter Palace, and the work was Araia's *La forza dell' amore e dell' odio*. Araia continued to produce operas during the reign of Peter the Great's daughter Elizabeth, who followed Anna to the throne in 1741; he eventually created eleven works for the Russian court, including one to a Russian text.

Dance continued to develop alongside opera. Elizabeth brought to St. Petersburg the Austrian dance master Frantz Hilferding, who was among the first to realize the possibilities of ballet as an artistic expression that could combine music, dance, mime, scenery, and costumes into an expressive whole. Some idea of what these expressive aims were can be grasped from the titles of the ballets being created in Russia at the time: *The Victory of Flora over Boreas, Apollo and Daphne, Cupid and Psyche*, and *Pygmalion*. However, along with these mythological and allegorical works, comic ballets were also being developed and applauded. The folk dances incorporated into them gave these entertainments a decidedly Russian flavor from the start.

But it was left to Catherine, in her solid German way, to tie up the loose theatrical ends of the time by setting up the Imperial System of Theaters, whose director was made responsible not only for opera, drama, ballet, and Russian and French theater, but also for the schools attached to these arts. Naturally, the main purpose of these various musical and dramatic units was to supply entertainment for the court. But many of them also gave performances in city theaters to which tickets were sold, a practice that increased in the decades ahead until the public performances far outstripped those at court.

Catherine raised dance to a professional level by hiring the Italian dancer, composer, and choreographer Gasparo Angiolini, a student of Hilferding. In 1772 he created the first serious Russian dance work, *Semira*, based on a tragedy by the Russian poet Alexander Sumarokov. With its strong political themes, it brought to Russian ballet what has been aptly described as a "patriotic style," however embryonic. It was during his tenure at court that the first Russian dancer of importance, Timofei Bublikov, rose to prominence.

Angiolini left Russia in 1786. He was succeeded at the theater by Charles Le Picq, a pupil of the influential French ballet master Jean Georges Noverre, who had reformed dance in France by creating works that went beyond a simple series of divertissements—they had a plot. Noverre advocated a flow of action with appropriate gestures and facial expressions to help carry a story forward (which led to, among other things, the elimination of masks, until then an integral part of dance). Noverre also made the corps de ballet part of the drama instead of merely a stylized background for the principals. Although Noverre never visited Russia, through Le Picq's advocacy he became nearly as influential a figure there as he was in France.

The stage was now set for the man who has been called the father of Russian ballet, Charles-Louis Didelot. Czar Paul I made him ballet master and director of the Imperial School of Dancing, a post Didelot held from 1801 to 1811 in tandem with Russia's first native choreographer of importance, Ivan Valbergh. On Didelot's arrival from his native France, he found a company of 114 dancers and three excellent state-subsidized theaters, each with its own workshop for producing scenery and costumes.

During these years Didelot opened ballet up beyond courtly conventionalities by doing away with heavily powdered wigs and buckled shoes, which were worn by every character from kings to shepherds. He introduced light gauze tunics that freed dancers to move more gracefully and soft slippers that enabled women to dance on three-quarter point and even full point for a fraction of a second. At first Didelot confined himself mainly to familiar mythological subjects, as did Valbergh, although the latter's ballets seem to have been of a more moralizing nature and heavier on pantomime. With Valbergh, dances usually occurred in the form of divertissements at celebrations and weddings onstage. Didelot, a firm disciple of Noverre, sought to create a more integral picture, and there seems to have been no mistaking that he possessed the greater talent for choreography.

A writer of the time remarked that "Valbergh's ballets had great dramatic interest and were arranged with great mastery, but they lacked [Didelot's] beautiful groupings and charming dances." Another observer commented that Didelot "replaced all false opulence by the richness of his own fantasy. One could always do without velvet, brocade, and gilt in his subject matter: life, interest, and grace stood in their stead. Picturesque arrangement of characters and groupings was always at his hand to conceal any external defects."

Didelot left Russia and returned to France in 1811, supposedly because of recurrent disputes with Valbergh, although other circumstances probably contributed to his departure as well—the burning around that time of the Bolshoi Kamenny, which left the ballet homeless for seven years, and a reduction in his salary, which came about when the court began being paying him in paper money instead of silver. Whatever Didelot's reason for leaving, in 1816 Alexander I persuaded him to return and gave him absolute power over the Imperial Ballet. Didelot demanded and received a contract for himself and his wife for six years instead of the usual three in order to have sufficient time to mold his dancers and carry out his plans for new ballets, as well as a salary of 16,000 rubles and a yearly benefit performance.

He remained head of the ballet troupe until his retirement in 1831, by which time the company had grown to 186 dancers. By imposing a rigid performing discipline and an austere training regime, Didelot created an ensemble that rivaled the best dance troupes in Europe. He insisted that dance be "poetry in action," and it is hardly surprising that by adding expression to what had previously been largely convention, Didelot began to attract enthusiastic audiences, and ballet began to flourish. Another element of Didelot's ballets was spectacular technical feats, such as dancers being carried aloft on wires. These innovations also helped to capture and hold the imagination of the city's ballet-going public.

In her engaging book *The Land of the Firebird*, Massie provides a vivid idea of the sort of trappings one experienced during Didelot's reign: "Mountains fell, ships sank, and cupids flew. In one glorious scene the chariot of Venus was propelled into the air by fifty live doves attached to specially constructed little harnesses. His ballets were full of exotics [such as] caliphs, feudal lords, nymphs, and gods; his productions were sometimes so moving that spectators would burst into tears. So enchanting were Didelot's ballets that Pushkin found no way to better describe the epitome of [Eugene] Onegin's world-weariness than by saying that even Didelot could no longer amuse him."

Although it developed distinctively Russian traits, ballet remained essentially a foreign art—an amalgam of French and Italian styles—and would continue to be so for much of the rest of the century. Many foreign dancers visited Russia during this period, the most triumphant of them being Marie Taglioni. Although she was not the first ballerina to dance *en pointe*, she popularized what shortly became an integral part of dance technique. She first appeared at the Bolshoi Kamenny in 1837 in *La sylphide*, a ballet she had created in Paris five years earlier. This lovely work, which is still danced at the Mariinsky, established the romantic style of ballet and introduced to Russia the costume that would come to exemplify the art form: a tight-fitting bodice that left the neck and shoulders bare, with a bell-shaped skirt of white net that fell midway between the dancer's knees and her ankles. With this were worn pink tights and satin slippers. (Taglioni's slippers, it seems, were not blocked; that would come later. Her support for point dancing came from the heavy stitching on the tip of the shoe.)

What made Taglioni so cherished as a performer, and eventually so influential in Russian dancing, was what could only be described as an ethereal or spiritual quality, supported by her fluid technique and her prodigious elevation. She even melted Russia's sardonic playwright Nikolai Gogol, who pronounced her "the synonym of Air! Nothing more ethereal had existed heretofore on the stage." From the outset she was idolized by the city—and by Nicholas I, who showered her with gifts and even had a statue of her placed in the imperial box. Ballet became a profitable and popular part of the Bolshoi Kamenny's seasons, and for a long while Tuesdays, Thursdays, and Sundays were set aside for the ballet. (When it eventually moved to the Mariinsky, Wednesday and Sundays became the ballet nights.) The balance of the week was devoted to Italian opera.

In 1803 the new czar, Alexander I, reorganized the public theaters in Russia and created a crown monopoly that remained in place until 1883. His reorganization extended to the ballet school Anna had founded, still the fountainhead of Russian dance. Under Alexander's plan, the students were taught academic subjects in addition to dance and music; performances by the school were scheduled every six months. The czar put his various theaters under a single administrative head, Prince Alexander Shakhovskoi, who, as a librettist, formed a creative partnership with the composer Catterino Cavos, the director and chief conductor of Italian opera at the Bolshoi Kamenny. Born in Venice in 1775 to a father who was the ballet master of the Fenice Theater, Cavos had come to Russia in 1799 as the conductor of a touring Italian opera troupe. He found extra work composing music for French vaudevilles and decided to make St. Petersburg his home when the Italian troupe collapsed after one season. Ironically, Cavos made his mark not with an Italian work but with a popular operetta in Russian, *The Dnieper Mermaid*, with a score by Ferdinand Kauer for which Cavos supplied extra music.

On the strength of the *Dnieper Mermaid*'s success, Cavos was named the new head of the Russian opera, housed in the Bolshoi Kamenny, a post he held until his death in 1840. By all accounts a vivid personality, Cavos was valued not only as a musician of energy and talent, but also as an exceptional teacher who trained many of Russia's early outstanding singers and conductors. He held the titles of inspector of court orchestras and musical director of the Imperial Theaters, and he wrote more than fifty operas and ballets in different styles, making him the most important figure in Russian music prior to Mikhail Glinka.

Massie has graphically described what it was like to spend an evening in the Bolshoi Kamenny: "In the square before the theater, in six large specially constructed stone pavilions, bonfires burned continually to warm the crowd of waiting coachmen. In the lobby, dignified bearded retired military men in uniform took coats and furs. The theater was all crimson velvet and gold, with a profusion of rococo ornamentation, garlands, and curlicues. On the huge curtain were scenes of Peterhof, with its green painted roofs, its fountains, its arcades, and statues.

"Boxes were lined with crimson velvet and decorated with white medallions framed in gold on a rose background. Dominating everything, facing the stage, two stories high, was the immense imperial box framed by heavy velvet and gold-fringed curtains and surmounted by an enormous gilded double eagle. The first row of boxes around the imperial loge bore the name of 'beautiful floor' [*bel étage*] and . . . these boxes were by custom reserved for the highest aristocrats and dignitaries of the court.

"As a mark of respect for the performers, by custom everyone always dressed for the theater, adding great brilliance to the scene—men in white gloves, dinner clothes, and glittering uniforms; women beautifully coiffed and jeweled. Dandies wandered up and down the aisles carefully scrutinizing the *beau monde*, making sure they were seen. Pushkin often joined the groups of young officers and state servants who were a permanent fixture at the ballet, always seating themselves in the first rows of the left side of the theater. Styling themselves 'the left flank,' these young men passionately applauded their favorite ballerinas, covered them with flowers, and clamored for curtain calls."

It was during Cavos's tenure with the Imperial Theaters that the first true beginnings of a native operatic genre were made. Although nothing from these initial efforts has lasted, a significant step was taken in Moscow during the same period by the composer Alexei Verstovsky. He developed a form of Russian romantic opera that attracted attention and audiences. His most popular work was *Askold's Grave*, which premiered in 1835.

Verstovsky's operas became popular in St. Petersburg as well, but progress toward a truly viable Russian school of opera was slow. For one thing, there was no way for an aspiring composer to obtain formal training. For another, payments made to composers—under a schedule set up during the reign of Nicholas I—discriminated against those who were Russian born, and those Russian operas and operettas that did manage to reach the stage were usually slavish imitations of successful French or Italian scores.

A crucial turning point in the development of Russian opera came in 1836 with the premiere of Glinka's first opera, *A Life for the Czar*. Cavos, who had set the same story to music earlier, conducted the first performance. Here was native opera on a grand scale, one of impressive technical finish. Although it owed a debt to Italian opera, it nevertheless had a vivid profile all its own. This individuality was even more apparent in Glinka's other opera, *Ruslan and Ludmila*. This setting of a Pushkin tale demonstrated to a critic of the time that "Russian melody . . . may be raised to the level of tragedy."

Peter Ilyich Tchaikovsky has provided the best summing up of Glinka and his operatic achievements. To him, Glinka was "a dilettante who played now on the violin, now on the piano, who composed colorless quadrilles and fantasies on stylish themes, who tried his hand at serious forms and songs but composed nothing but banalities in the taste of the 1830s, who suddenly . . . produced an opera which by its genius, breadth, originality and flawless technique stands on a level with the greatest and most profound music!" This opera stood alone as the first stage work of importance by a Russian on a Russian theme, one that concerned itself with the people instead of the nobility and that quoted Russian folksong.

Glinka's blossoming as a composer is not so mystifying when one remembers that he had traveled for a number of years in Europe. He met Vincenzo Bellini and Gaetano Donizetti in Milan and spent a year in Berlin studying theory and composition. When he returned to Russia, he decided to set to music the life of a national hero, Ivan Susanin, who sacrificed his life to save that of the first Romanov czar. The subject fired his imagination. "As if by magic," Glinka wrote, "both the plan of the whole opera and the idea of the antithesis of Russian and Polish music, as well as many of the themes and even details of the working-out . . . flashed into my head at one stroke."

Although Glinka produced only two works for the stage, they had enormous influence, not only on opera but also on ballet. Through the ballet sequences in his operas, especially *Ruslan*, Glinka furthered the cause of narrative dance. With him, dance scenes were not tacked-on divertissements but were woven into the action of the story, becoming an integral part of the whole. His sensitivity to dance in opera was more than just an attempt to fuse a single expressive entity. He loved ballet and had even taken dance lessons in his youth. He was also passionately interested in Russian folk dances, frequently using their rhythms and patterns in his music. Glinka took the first steps toward creating what would become the genre of symphonic dance works of Peter Ilyich Tchaikovsky, Alexander Glazunov, and Reinhold Glière.

Ironically, the inroads made by Glinka with his first opera were offset the same year by Cavos's introduction to Russia in 1836 of Gioacchino Rossini's *opera seria Semiramide*. Rossini's *Il barbiere di Siviglia* and *La gazza ladra* had been a part of the repertoire of the Bolshoi Kamenny a decade earlier, but it was *Semiramide* that created the great sensation. It was given in part as a vehicle for one of the most important Russian singers of the time, the bass Osip Petrov, who sang the role of Assur (he had made an impressive debut as Sarastro in Wolfgang Amadeus Mozart's *The Magic Flute* in 1830). Petrov went on to create the roles of the Miller in Alexander Dargomizhsky's *Rusalka*, Ivan the Terrible in Nikolai Rimsky-Korsakov's *The Maid of Pskov*, Varlaam in Modest Mussorgsky's *Boris Godunov*, and Prince Gudal in Anton Rubinstein's *The Demon*.

Joining Petrov in *Semiramide* was his future wife, the contralto Anna Vorobio-va. Cavos's protégée and a voice student of Glinka's, she created the roles of Vanya in *A Life for the Czar* and Ratmir in *Ruslan and Ludmila*. Although *Semiramide* was sung in Russian, it did what all the visiting Italian opera companies up until then had been unable to do—create a rage for Italian opera. Rossini became a near de-ity, followed in short order by Vincenzo Bellini and Gaetano Donizetti. Interest-ingly, a year after the premiere of *Semiramide* at the Bolshoi, a Russian journalist saw the opera staged in London, and among his fascinating comments is this query: "How can one compare *Semiramide* in Petersburg with the London Pro-duction? Ours is lush, full, animated; here it is poor, thin, weak. We do everything that is possible; here they do not do even half of what is necessary."

Nicholas I himself, having succumbed to the opera fever that infected the city, ordered the establishment of a permanent Italian opera troupe. With a stroke of his pen, the czar put Russian opera in the shadow of foreign opera for more than two decades, and soon the Italian seasons in St. Petersburg reached a splendor that rivaled what could be heard in Paris, London, or Vienna. After the success of *Semi-ramide*, the next logical step was to import the greatest singers from Europe, a trend that started in 1841 with the debut in St. Petersburg of one of the most fa-bled sopranos of the nineteenth century, Giuditta Pasta, the creator of Bellini's Norma and Amina (in *La sonnambula*) and Donizetti's Anna Bolena.

Although her voice was nearly in shreds by the time of her Russian debut, the last significant event in her career, she did give St. Petersburg what Richard Tarus-kin in *The New Grove Dictionary of Opera* has termed "a fatal taste of international stardom." For her performances with the Russian company at the Bolshoi Kamen-ny, the native singers supporting Pasta learned their parts in Italian. She was fol-lowed two years later to Russia by the equally famous tenor Giovanni Rubini (the first Arturo in Bellini's *I puritani* and Elvino in *La sonnambula*), whose success was so pronounced that Nicholas I appointed him "Director of Singing for the Empire."

Rubini's task was to lure the best singers of Europe to Russia, and he began in 1843 by bringing to St. Petersburg the young Pauline Viardot and the stellar baritone Antonio Tamburini. This influx of foreign singers continued with such glittering artists as Giulia Grisi (the cousin of the ballerina Carlotta, who also visited Russia and triumphed) and Giovanni Mario. It climaxed with the stellar appearances by Adelina Patti in the early 1870s, although by this time Rubini had long since retired.

Viardot, the daughter of the remarkable tenor Manuel Garcia and the sister of Maria Malibran, decided to accept Rubini's invitation to come to St. Petersburg following reports by her friend Franz Liszt of the warmth and generosity of the city's audiences. She arrived in Russia the year after Glinka (who became her "fervent admirer") premiered *Ruslan*. Although hardly an attractive woman, her voice and presence had enormous allure, and they enslaved the Russian poet and playwright Ivan Turgenev, who volunteered to teach the soprano Russian and in 1845, when her second season of engagements in St. Petersburg was over, followed her back to France.

With her gift for languages, Viardot became the first foreign artist to sing Russian music in Russian; during a performance of *The Barber of Seville*, she even interpolated a Russian song into the Lesson Scene, and later she programmed songs by Glinka and Dargomizhsky on a recital program. The czar attended her performance of the *Barber* and applauded "like a madman," according to Viardot's biographer, April Fitzlyon. Two weeks later, during a repeat of the same work, Viardot, Rubini, and Tamburini appeared with a Russian choir between acts of the opera to sing "God Save the Czar" in Russian. The gesture was so frantically cheered that it had to be repeated.

The Italians were soon so entrenched that Russian opera was banished from the Bolshoi Kamenny to the Alexandrinsky Theater (the home of Russian drama in the capital), and by 1846 performances of Russian repertory even there had dwindled to a handful. The Italian seasons owed their success not only to the appealing nature of the music and the star quality of the singers, but also to the wide range of operatic works at the company's disposal.

Because the works were sung in a foreign tongue, they were not subjected to censorship as were operas sung in Russian. Italian opera thus became a rallying point for the city's idealistic, anti-imperial young people, who were inspired by Italian librettos with their frequent cries for "liberty." When, for example, the tenor Enrico Tamberlik, as Arnold in *William Tell*, trumpeted "Cercar la libertà" (Let us search for liberty), he was invariably and loudly cheered and forced to repeat the phrase.

Meanwhile, ballet at the Bolshoi Kamenny continued to be a popular form of entertainment, running side by side with the Italian opera seasons. Five years after Didelot's death in 1837, a man appeared who was destined to be a major figure in the history of Russian ballet: the Danish premier danseur Christian Johansson. He would remain in St. Petersburg the rest of his life and exerted enormous influence through his teaching after he retired as a dancer.

A pupil of August Bournonville, the founder of an exquisite and individual dancing style still practiced in Denmark, Johansson, who had at one time been a partner of Taglioni, began his career in St. Petersburg in 1841. Before it was over, he had established standards and a style that helped form the basis of the Russian school of dancing. As an elderly man, he taught a number of the giants of Russian ballet, including Pavel Gerdt, Mathilde Kshessinskaya, Anna Pavlova, Nikolai Legat, Olga Preobrazhenskaya, Tamara Karsavina, and Agrippina Vaganova. Bournonville, incidentally, visited St. Petersburg in 1874 during the reign of the foremost choreographer at the Mariinsky, Marius Petipa, and was not pleased with what he saw. He complained to Petipa about the excesses of Russian dancing at the time and the lack of choreographic structure in its ballets, criticisms Petipa took to heart.

Seven years after Johansson's arrival, the French dancer and choreographer Jules Perrot joined the Bolshoi Kamenny as the theater's ballet master. He remained for eleven years, creating more than a dozen works for St. Petersburg; of them, however, only *Giselle*, in various forms, has lasted. It is still a staple of the Kirov's repertory. Perrot created the dances for the first Giselle, Carlotta Grisi, who was his student and lover, at the ballet's premiere in Paris in 1841, while Jean Coralli, then ballet master at the Opéra, set the rest of the ballet and to Perrot's dismay was credited with the whole.

Upon arriving in St. Petersburg in 1848, Perrot mounted a production of *Giselle* in which he not only restaged the entire ballet, but also rechoreographed several of the dances he had made for Grisi, in particular deepening the protagonist's mad scene. His new version greatly strengthened the work's overall drama and filled out many of the supporting figures. In effect, these Russian performances of *Giselle* were of an entirely new ballet rather than simply re-creations of a French one, and they became the basis for future *Giselle*s.

The title role in Perrot's staging was danced by Fanny Elssler, the next foreign ballerina of importance after Taglioni to visit St. Petersburg. In 1850, Perrot remounted *Giselle* for the role's creator when Grisi came to Russia for the first time (often partnered on her tour by the young Petipa), but she left balletomanes unfulfilled; they felt she was too affected and unable to reflect Giselle's "inner state." In general, Elssler's technical and dramatic gifts were preferred.

Giselle, incidentally, had reached Russia even before Perrot did. It was first seen in St. Petersburg the year after its Paris premiere in a staging by Antoine Titus that featured Russia's first major native-born romantic ballerina, Elena Andreyanova, who later went on to triumph in Paris and London. In St. Petersburg, she also appeared with Petipa in the premiere of his new version of the ballet *Paquita* in 1847, and the next year she had an enormous success with another Petipa creation, *Satanilla*. She retired to France in 1855, where she died two years later.

Perrot was followed as the imperial ballet master by Arthur Saint-Léon, best remembered today for his creation of *Coppélia*, with music by Léo Delibes, in Paris. A dancer, choreographer, and composer, Saint-Léon was also a man who knew how to please, and his ballets were in effect, protracted divertissements. A critic of the time summed him up as "a past master at inventing separate dances and in particular variations devised to suit the talents of particular dancers.... On the other hand, he did not know how to manage crowds. His ensembles were lifeless and devoid of color."

It was said that Perrot worked only when inspired, and he was known to cancel rehearsals when inspiration didn't come. Saint-Léon, it seems, could work anytime, for, not being dependent on the creation of purely poetic images, he had no problems vis-à-vis inspiration. He seems to have been a man in a hurry not only to finish a job, but to please. His chief legacy apart from *Coppélia* was the creation of the full-length ballet on a Russian theme that is still danced and loved today—*The Little Humpbacked Horse.* This vivid dance piece, with its extensive use of folk idioms and a lively pastiche score by Cesare Pugni, was an immediate success at its premiere in 1864 and proved to be an exciting vehicle for Russia's next great ballerina, Marfa Muravyeva. Saint-Léon exploited her brilliant technique in many of his ballets, and she held her own against more glamorous visiting foreign ballerinas of the day. She did not have a long career, retiring after her marriage at twenty-seven, but like Andreyanova, Muravyeva had successes abroad, beginning with her debut in Paris in 1863 as Giselle.

In his book *Voyage en Russie*, published in 1858, a half-dozen years before the premiere of *The Little Humpbacked Horse*, Théophile Gautier conceded that the art of dance was much more highly developed in Russia than in France, and that full-length ballets cast in several acts with intricate plots made Russian ballet "a self-sufficient art, in no way dependent on opera or any other sort of spectacle. In St. Petersburg," he continued, "it is not easy to win applause for a *pas*. The Russians are great connoisseurs of ballets, and the dancer who has withstood the marksmanship of their opera-glasses must be very confident of herself. Their Conservatory of Dance supplies excellent soloists and a corps de ballet knowing no equal for perfection and speed.... It is in truth the world of pantomime, where words are absent and action never transcends its boundaries." By the time these words were written, the tree Catherine had planted had grown strong and tall. Eventually its branches would spread out beyond Russia's borders to give shade to both England and the United States.

The home Catherine established in St. Petersburg for dance and opera was situated in a part of the city that had long been the heart of the city's performing arts —Karuselnaya, or Carousel Square. Today it is Teatralnaya—Theater Place. This open area, bounded on the west by the Krukov Canal, was from the earliest times a popular part of the town, in part because it was close to Colomna, the district where many of the city's working class and poor lived. They flocked to Carousel Square and its open-air markets and carnivals. In 1723 the city's first public theater was erected there. Built of wood, it lasted only a decade before it was demolished. In 1775 it was replaced by a larger structure, also of wood, and in 1783 Catherine ordered a permanent theater to be built out of stone. Inaugurated with Paisiello's comic opera *La luna abitata*, this grandiose new building, the Bolshoi Kamenny, became famous in the West as the Imperial Theater. It was enlarged in 1802, severely damaged by fire in 1811, rebuilt in 1818, and remodeled in 1836, and with each renovation new structural elements were added—among them a higher stage ceiling to accommodate the machinery for more complicated theatrical tricks and an imposing Greek-temple façade for the entrance of the building. The theater's repertory was initially a mixture of drama, pantomime, dance, and opera, and the building served the city as an important venue for opera and dance until 1886, when it was abandoned as unsafe.

The Bolshoi Kamenny was razed a decade later to make room for the city's Conservatory of Music. This building honored the conservatory's founder, the celebrated pianist and composer Anton Rubinstein, on the occasion of his fiftieth jubilee as a performer. To the many concerned with an indigenous musical culture, this gesture was long overdue, for it acknowledged not only Rubinstein's world fame, but also the cultural importance of Russian musicians. Back in 1862, the year Rubinstein began the school, he had noted that "Russia has almost no artist-musicians in the exact sense of this term. This is so because our government has not given the same privileges to the art of music that are enjoyed by the other arts." In other words, a Russian musician in the mid-nineteenth century was still a second-class citizen.

In the 1840s a new theatrical element came into play in Carousel Square when the first touring circuses from Europe invaded Russia and captured the fancy of St. Petersburg. So immediate and great was the success of the circus that the city officials permitted an Italian troupe to construct a wooden structure opposite the Bolshoi Kamenny in 1845. Two years later the city took the building over, providing funds for its upkeep and gradually expanding its bill of fare to include other forms of entertainment. The original wooden Circus Theater was outgrown in a few years, and the city council hired the architect Alberto Cavos, the son of Catterino, to design a new structure. Catterino had sent Alberto to be trained at the University of Padua, and upon his return to Russia he found work assisting Rossi in the building of the Alexandrinsky Theater, which, although destined to become the Imperial Theater of Drama, frequently staged operas and ballets, and still does on occasion. Cavos was next engaged to renovate the Bolshoi Kamenny in 1836 and then the Mikhailovsky (now the Mussorgsky or Maly) Theater, and he was commissioned to rebuild the Bolshoi Theater in Moscow, which burned in 1853. He created the massive structure behind Red Square that we know today.

But prior to his work in Moscow, Cavos was asked to undertake the building of a new Circus Theater in St. Petersburg. Work began in the summer of 1847 and was completed in only four and a half months by a crew of 140 masons, 41 stone-cutters, and 55 other workmen. According to the custom of the day, the structure was left for more than a year to settle, having been constructed on top of a series of huge granite boulders that had been sunk into the ground to support its weight (they are still the support of the Mariinsky Theater).

Cavos's design, which cast the building in the shape of a cross, combined the needs of the circus, opera, and vaudeville. The theater was crowned by a dome directly above the circular riding ring in the center of the house; the stage itself was behind the ring at the rear of the hall. The public sat in a semicircle around the ring, with an amphitheater below and two tiers of boxes and a balcony above. Cavos decorated the Circus Theater in gold and dark-red velvet set off by white walls, and it was the first theater in Russia to be lit by gas.

As the public's fascination with the circus began to wane, the theater's management began staging Russian comedies, starting in the autumn of 1850. Before long the circus programs were gone, replaced with Russian and German drama troupes and a Russian opera company. These new uses for the building meant that the auditorium had to be reworked. The circular riding track was removed, seats were installed in its place, a pit was added, and a new ceiling was constructed to improve the acoustics. Finally, an imposing chandelier was installed, and the chairs and the trim on the boxes were redone in turquoise velvet.

In 1856, the year after the theater reopened, the next important step in Russian opera was taken with the premiere of Alexander Dargomizhsky's *Rusalka*, the second of his three operas and the one that has persisted through time. The composer perceptively summed up his achievement in a letter: "The more I study the components of our national music, the more varied the aspects I discern in them. Glinka, who alone up to now has given Russian music a grand scale, in my opinion, has as yet touched only one of its sides—the lyrical side. His dramaturgy is too plaintive, the comic aspect loses its national character. . . . To the extent that I am able, I am working in my *Rusalka* to develop our dramatic components."

Both *Rusalka* and *Ruslan* were in repertory at the Circus Theater when, late in January 1859, it was engulfed in flames. A year later there arose from its ashes and charred walls what was destined to be regarded as one of the world's most beautiful and admired opera houses: the Mariinsky. The stage was set for Russian opera to come fully into its own. Although Italian opera would make a last stand within the walls of the conservatory at the turn of the century, the race was in effect run, and Russian opera was the victor.

CHAPTER TWO

September: The 213th Season

ALTHOUGH the Mariinsky Theater was 135 years old when I took up residence in St. Petersburg in June 1995, the season I attended was designated the 213th. The Russians began their tabulations with the opening of the Bolshoi Kamenny. Thus, by the official count, it was the 213th season that was inaugurated on 24 September 1995, after the Kirov completed a preseason six-day visit to Korea without Gergiev. But he was back in St. Petersburg from performances with the San Francisco Opera in time for opening night, a repeat of Dmitri Shostakovich's *Katerina Ismailova*.

The season ran for just over nine months, through the fourth Stars of the White Nights Festival, and ended on 30 June 1996, with a performance of the ballet *La sylphide*. In between these extremes came new productions of *Salome*, Tchaikovsky's *Mazeppa* (which was recorded and videotaped), Sergei Prokofiev's *The Gambler*, and *Carmen*, plus an *Otello* from the Bonn Opera, the Kirov Ballet's first staging of George Balanchine's *Symphony in C*, and the premiere of *Resurrection*, a dance piece by Oleg Vinogradov set to the Prelude and "Liebestod" from Richard Wagner's *Tristan und Isolde*.

The repertory was made up of twenty-six operas (*Tosca* and *La forza del destino* were given in only concert form, with *Forza* performed only on tour) and twenty-eight ballets (full-length and one-act pieces, combined in different ways and sometimes paired with one-act operas). Not surprisingly, the repertory was predominantly Russian (fifteen works). During the course of the season it was possible to see five stage works by Prokofiev, six by Tchaikovsky, and three by Rimsky-Korsakov. Of the non-Russian operatic works, five were by Giuseppe Verdi; non-Russian ballets were even more in the minority, consisting chiefly of works by George Balanchine and Jerome Robbins.

There were also at least a half dozen concerts (including one by the visiting Berlin Philharmonic under Claudio Abbado) and a number of mixed evenings with the opera and ballet companies featured in arias, ensembles, and pas de deux.

In all, 246 performances were given. They took place either at 7:00 P.M. or, in the case of the Sunday matinees, at 11:30 A.M. Although Mondays were normally dark nights, the theater was flexible in this regard, depending on its rehearsal, tours, and recording schedules. A week's programs were generally split more or less evenly between opera and ballet, although one wing of the house might get the lion's share of the performances while the other was away.

Since it opened on a Sunday instead of a Tuesday and was dark Friday instead of Monday, the first week of the 213th season could not be called a normal one. But the fare was more or less typical for the Mariinsky: Sunday, 24 September, *Katerina Ismailova*; Monday, 25 September, *Salome*; Tuesday, 26 September, *Aida*; Wednesday, 27 September, *Swan Lake*; Thursday, 28 September, *Mazeppa*; Friday, 29 September, no performance; Saturday, 30 September, *Giselle*; Sunday matinee, 1 October, *La traviata*; and Sunday evening, 1 October, *La bayadère*.

During the year the opera company made four swings throughout Europe (the last one five weeks in length and featuring staged and concert performances of four operas) and traveled for the first time to Israel. On its own, the Kirov Orchestra made its first tour of Japan, crossing paths there with the Kirov Ballet's annual holiday performances of the *Nutcracker*. In general, 1995–96 was a slack touring year for the ballet after a projected return to the United States was canceled; apart from the Japanese dates, the dance company's biggest trip abroad was to Denmark in late spring.

It was a momentous season for Gergiev, however. He made his debut at Italy's La Scala theater with a new production of *The Gambler*, which he took on the Kirov's late-winter tour of Europe and which was recorded by Philips Classics in the Netherlands. The recording was an act of faith at a time when record companies were severely tightening their belts. Philips continues to back Gergiev to the hilt, for it sees him not only as one of the towering figures in today's music world, but also as a breadwinner, far down the road, for the family of labels now owned by Universal Music. Gergiev also accompanied the Mariinsky's new production of *Ruslan and Ludmila* to San Francisco in early September (it had been staged in St. Petersburg the season before by the San Francisco Opera's general manager, Lotfi Mansouri), returned to the Metropolitan Opera for a new production of *The Queen of Spades*, and gave concerts with the New York Philharmonic, the Rotterdam Philharmonic (which he has taken on as music director), the Concertgebouw Orchestra, and Italy's Santa Cecilia Orchestra.

In addition to extending and reinforcing his own career during the season, Gergiev often acted as a sort of talent broker, supplying Kirov artists to non-Kirov organizations and using them to stock his satellite festivals in Finland and Holland. The backbone of the cast for the San Francisco *Ruslan* was from the Mariinsky, and the theater provided the principals for concert performances of *Aida* in the Netherlands and *The Gambler* at La Scala. In addition, the Kirov regulars Nikolai Putilin and Ludmila Filatova made their Met debuts with Gergiev in *The Queen of Spades*, while the Kirov provided the entire package (soloists, chorus, dancers, and orchestra) for the performances of *Khovanshchina* presented in Tel Aviv.

It is often against Gergiev's best interests to tour with his finest artists, for some of them establish firm footholds outside of Russia and eventually move to the West, rarely, if ever, returning home. It is, of course, not so hard to hold on to dancers. Although some from the Kirov have taken up residence in the West, particularly in Germany and the United States, as performers and teachers, on the whole leading dancers tend to stay wedded to specific companies. While they frequently make guest appearances, they nearly always return to the nest; a star dancer who works mainly free-lance in today's world is an unusual dancer indeed.

Singers are another matter. The opera world is totally dependent on peripatetic artists for its stars and its box office, and singers go wherever they are best paid. That means singing at the Mariinsky—where a top fee can amount to a few hundred dollars at best—is an act of charity. Gergiev is, of course, well aware of the dangers inherent in promoting his singers, but again the gambler in him takes precedence over the pragmatist. He wants to put the best face possible on his and the company's performances abroad, even if this means risking the eventual loss of artists essential to the Mariinsky's well-being back home.

These losses amount to a new form of defection. They are a far cry from those of Rudolf Nureyev, Mikhail Baryshnikov, and Natalia Makarova, which once made headlines around the world. Their leaps to freedom were for artistic and quasi-political reasons. More recently, those of Vladimir Chernov, Sergei Leiferkus, Maria Guleghina, and Elena Prokina were economically motivated. Many of the Kirov's current defectors have been part of the audio and video projects for Philips Records, and a few of them still return to the theater solely for recordings. This has created what I term "the Kirov mirage": the company's splendid records and videos (like their carefully orchestrated tours) cannot always be taken as an accurate barometer of what goes on in the theater night after night. Not that the company on home ground is incapable of scaling the heights; it is simply that its starry nights are far and few between. The ballet's videos, on the other hand, are a far more accurate measure of that company's daily standard.

Life within the Mariinsky goes on at a vigorous pace. On a day-in, night-out basis, it is, in effect, a small factory with a budget (in 1995) of about $10 million a year, which employs about 1,300 people who are geared to produce an average of seven public performances of opera and ballet a week amid a demanding schedule of rehearsals and coaching sessions. In actuality, it is a small town, contained within a generous city block, with its own stores, offices, restaurants, library, dispensary, visa department, and travel agency. In short, it provides virtually everything its constituents require except a place to sleep.

The stores operate out of small rooms in the theater, sometimes the size of a large closet, and it is pure serendipity as to what you will find there. One day it was canned goods that had been bought in quantity at a bargain price; another day it was shoes. The theater's two canteens, one off the auditorium itself and the other in the ballet wing, provide meals and snacks for the Mariinsky's employees as well as the pastries, caviar, and dry cheese or ham sandwiches sold to the public at intermission. Although some effort has been made to dress up the dancers' canteen as a modish clubhouse, the main canteen is fairly utilitarian, as is the food it prepares and sells for surprisingly little.

Throughout all levels of the five-story building, amid offices and storage rooms linked by dingy, narrow passageways with peeling paint and faltering elevators, is a network of rehearsal spaces. The largest of these, naturally enough, are set aside for the ballet. In addition to its four main rehearsal rooms, it shares with the opera a rehearsal theater complete with a stage, a pit, and a few rows of seats. I quickly discovered, however, that no room in the theater contained what I needed most and had expected to find—an archive. The Mariinsky's historical papers and the designs of past productions have been scattered about town in at least a half dozen buildings, and some had even wound up in archives in Moscow.

In general, dossiers of artists and other papers relating to the theater's activities stretching back to the eighteenth century are housed in the Imperial Archives in the old senate building, across from the mighty equestrian bronze raised by Catherine in honor of Peter the Great and immortalized by Pushkin. On the opposite side of the city is a repository for the papers from the Soviet years. Fortunately, in 1982 the Imperial Archives compiled an index of the material it possesses that pertains to the Imperial Theaters, and these four volumes were a great help in narrowing down my research parameters. It was also a source of disappointment, for the files for many of the theater's most famous artists—such as Chaliapin, Pavlova, and Nijinsky—were either missing or sequestered elsewhere.

If the Mariinsky can be said to have anything approaching an archive, it is to be found in the building off Nevsky Prospect that formerly housed the administrative offices of the Imperial Theaters and that is still home to the Kirov's incomparable ballet school, named for the woman who did more to codify ballet Russian style than any other—Agrippina Vaganova. The Vaganova Choreographic Academy on Rossi Street is part of a block-long miracle of design, whose proportions are as famous as they are ideal.

The height of the buildings and the width of the street are exactly equal (66 feet), while the length of the street is ten times greater, or 660 feet. At its foot is a shaded oval park, and at its head is the rear of the regal Alexandrinsky Theater. It was laid out by the architect Carlo Rossi between 1828 and 1834 and was long known as Theater Street. I could never set foot on it without remembering a comment the dancer Andris Liepa made after I remarked one evening on the breathtaking quality of the Kirov's corps de ballet. "How could it not be," he replied, "when you remember that its dancers are trained in the midst of perfection? Every time they walked out the door of the Vaganova onto Rossi Street they were walking into perfection."

During the czarist era the building on the east side of Theater Street housed, in addition to offices and the ballet school and its dormitories, a performing arts library and the Mariinsky's music library, with its incomparable collection of scores and parts reaching back to the eighteenth century. Today these artistic resources still repose in the same rooms, which are virtually unchanged since the turn of the century. What is different is the addition of the St. Petersburg State Museum of Theater and Music in the former offices for the head of the czar's five official theaters (three in St. Petersburg, two in Moscow) and his staff. With the coming of the Soviet years, the documents and designs that had been stored in the theater and in the administrative offices on Rossi Street were divided between the Imperial and the State Archives, the Theater and Music Museum, and the Library of the Performing Arts, although some material wound up in the Mariinsky's music library and some crossed the Neva to the Academy of Arts.

Before arriving in St. Petersburg I had decided that the best place to begin my work was with the invaluable set of theater annuals published from 1890 to 1915, the *Yearbook of the Imperial Theaters.* These chronicled the activities of the czar's theaters, their artists, and their employees and included an indispensable day-by-day table of performances. I had read of these rare volumes in America, for they are closely associated with the brief, year-long career at the Mariinsky of the impresario-to-be Sergei Pavlovich Diaghilev. One of his assignments on joining the staff of the theater was to overhaul the annual in terms of style, content, and typography to make it more attractive and readable.

I first spotted a set of these chronicles in the press office at the Mariinsky behind glass doors in a padlocked cabinet. I was told by the press director that I could not touch them, but after a month or so I was actually allowed to hold one volume and look at it. Borrowing or photocopying it, though, was "absolutely out of the question." After a few more weeks had passed I was told that I might be able to work with one volume at a time, but only within the theater. I might even be able to have part of it copied by the press office.

Finally, the week before the season opened, I was forced to find some means of resolving this impasse. Since Gergiev was away in San Francisco, I asked for help from his assistant, Katia Sirakanian. She, in turn, set up an appointment for Myron and me with the theater's administrative director at the time, Anatoly Malkov, a small-framed fifty-eight-year-old man who looked like the classic Soviet politico. He had been the director of the Baltiysky Dom Theater in St. Petersburg and served on the Lensoviet Cultural Committee. This springboard propelled him to the head spot at the Kirov in 1990. His was purely a political appointment, and one that was not appealing to Gergiev, but at the time the conductor had held his post as the opera's artistic director for only two years and lacked the clout he has today.

Malkov greeted us graciously but guardedly. When I asked if I might make use of the theater's set of the imperial annuals, he told me I had to write a formal letter to him requesting permission to use any material in the theater for my work. I then took advantage of the meeting to bring up another pressing problem. The ticket situation for visiting press at the time was chaotic at the Mariinsky, and invited guests often found themselves with either poor seats or none at all. As Myron and I were going to be in the theater for a year, I asked Malkov for two permanent places so I would not have to make a nuisance of myself with repeated ticket requests. I added that it was essential that I be in the same place at each performance so that I could hear and see from a consistent vantage point.

He looked at me oddly for a moment and then said, "There are seats, and there are seats." I asked him what he meant by that. "Well, there are the seats you can buy," he explained, "which would be good ones, or the seats I can give you, which will be where I choose." I replied that as I had been invited by Gergiev to write this book, I presumed the theater would supply seats for me, and that my budget did not extend to the purchasing of several hundred pairs of tickets. He shrugged his shoulders in reply, and after we left his office, Myron, well accustomed to Soviet double-talk after his years in Russia, told me that Malkov was fishing for money. If I agreed to buy the tickets, the dollars would probably go into his pocket. This comment would come back to register forcefully a month later.

A few days after I wrote the letter of request, Katia telephoned to say that Malkov had given his permission for me to borrow one volume of the imperial annuals at a time, and that Myron and I had been assigned places in one of the theater's boxes. I asked her if I could come down and have a look at the seats. She took me up to the extreme left of the *bel étage* level. The spot Malkov had picked out for us was in box C, a space reserved for the company; it is directly above the orchestra with only a partial view of the stage. As no specific seat assignments were made for us, I realized that we would spend the season jockeying for position with members of the company.

I pointed out the box's shortcomings to Katia, and she suggested I take a look at the media box, also on the *bel étage*, to which no tickets were sold since it was reserved for television use. It turned out to be ideal, just left and down from the imperial box, and she said she would try to get Malkov to agree to give us space there. Whatever she did worked, and box 14 became virtually my home away from home for the next ten months (at the time I had no way of knowing how much trouble this switch in seats was going to cost me). The same afternoon, I took the first volume of the imperial annuals home, where I had set up my photocopy machine and a small office.

Two days later *Katerina* inaugurated the new season, and as anxious as I was for this reprise, I was even more impatient to see again the Kirov's unique new *Salome*, which had been given only once, on the last evening of the White Nights Festival. Gergiev had engaged the American director Julie Taymor (of *Lion King* fame) and *Katerina*'s designer, Georgy Tsypin, to create the production. This was the first time a Strauss opera had been given at the Mariinsky since *Der Rosenkavalier* in 1928, and the only time one had been sung in German. Although not every aspect of production rang true, it was an uncommon achievement that would have provoked interest and controversy anywhere in the world of opera.

Taymor and Tsypin emphasized both the decadence of the story and Oscar Wilde's many moon metaphors. The latter Taymor took literally by actually bringing onstage the Man in the Moon, except that he was only part man. Because Taymor saw him as an androgynous creature, he wore a long white ballet skirt and nothing more. He entered before the first notes of music and crossed the stage carrying a large paper moon; it would be silhouetted at important moments such as Salome's kissing of the head of John the Baptist.

Taymor introduced other fascinating additions. Herod made a dazzling entrance accompanied by two ballet dancers rigged in masks as greyhounds. They crouched, scampered about on all fours, and were continually at Herod's heels; he alternately petted, kicked, and fed them. A strong scent of impending doom kept the dogs in motion, sniffing the air for any hint of danger. Taymor also introduced a barely pubescent boy in a body stocking that made him appear nude. He was Eros, and at one point he brought Salome a basket of blood-red roses to strew over the cistern after her encounter with John.

Tsypin, too, made capital of the moon motive. In the sky to the rear of the stage he positioned a huge moon that traveled up and down behind the singers, and Herod's palace was tiered, crescent-shaped, and black-and-white; it resembled old prints of the Tower of Babel. With a stunning array of costumes that added what color there was to the production, it was all intoxicating for the eye.

Indeed, sometimes the effect was too much. Taymor employed a battery of complex lighting effects (including one that shone directly into the eyes of the audience, blinding it for a moment) and had John the Baptist brought from the cistern, tied to an immense cross that rose high above the stage. In theater, as in most aspects of the arts, the greatest freedom exists within the greatest limitations, and the problems Taymor created for herself and for the audience were a result of her attempt to extend her parameters unduly. Her biggest mistake in this regard was to begin and end the opera in silence. In opera, music defines boundaries, and you go against them, as Taymor did, at your peril.

To sing the role of Salome, Gergiev brought back to the company a prodigal daughter, the soprano Lubov Kazarnovskaya. After three years with Moscow's Bolshoi Theater, she had been engaged in 1986 by the Kirov as a young artist of twenty-three (she stepped into the role of Leonora for a new production of *La forza del destino* when the scheduled soprano became ill). Three years later she broke with the theater in order to live abroad and fulfill an increasing number of dates outside Russia. Eventually she was engaged by the Metropolitan Opera, where she debuted as Tatiana in *Eugene Onegin* in 1992. Not until Gergiev made his Met debut in the spring of 1994 conducting a new production of *Otello*, in which Kazarnovskaya was the cover for Desdemona, did the two see each other again. Their reunion in New York quickly paid off. Gergiev invited Kazarnovskaya to join the company in Paris that fall to alternate with Gorchakova in the leading role of Fevronia for tour performances of Rimsky-Korsakov's *The Invisible City of Kitezh*. Kazarnovskaya repeated the part with the company the next spring when the Kirov performed *Kitezh* at the Brooklyn Academy of Music. Gergiev then invited her to return to St. Petersburg for *Salome*.

At first Kazarnovskaya was reluctant to undertake the Strauss part, but eventually she agreed when Gergiev promised to keep the orchestra down. "I am not Birgit Nilsson or Leonie Rysanek," she told him. "I will do Salome my way. It's not music for screaming. It's *raffiné*. You have to sing beautifully, sexily." Her portrayal of Oscar Wilde's Judea princess turned out just that—sexy, as well as mesmerizing, in her lithe, catlike, sensual movements. Her singing of the role, however, was as slim vocally as she herself is physically, and she did not consistently rise to the challenge.

The most adroit member of the cast was Konstantin Pluzhnikov. As Herod, he was licentious, evil, overbearing, and thoroughly wonderful. *Salome*, however, turned out to be a score that Gergiev could not conquer through instinct and will, as he often does with music new to him. He had trouble making transitions work, and he seemed unwilling to take the lid off of his orchestra, something he is normally not at all shy about. Perhaps he was too consciously aware that he was walking a delicate line where Kazarnovskaya's voice was concerned.

Kazarnovskaya's personal history was a strong undertow at these performances, for it brought together and neatly tied up some of the many strands endemic to Soviet-Russian artistic life, past and present. In 1989, just after Gergiev had taken over the Kirov, the soprano had been forced out of the theater following her marriage to the Viennese agent Robert Roszyk. Gosconcerts, the state artist agency, refused to give her a visa that would allow her to take up residency in Austria unless she formally severed her ties with the Kirov. This she did; her new life with Roszyk and the Western engagements he negotiated for her were, at the time, of greater importance, for she had come to feel increasingly stymied by the sense of isolation that persisted among Soviet artists with respect to the West.

"Most Russians didn't really have a chance to know the true Italian school," Kazarnovskaya believes. "They were singing in the Soviet tradition, like all the Russian sopranos in the 1950s and 1960s. . . . But it was awful. They didn't know how to produce the right sound. But with glasnost, perestroika, and the breaking of the Iron Curtain, we started to hear what was going on in the West and to relearn style and languages. . . . The new generation of Russian singers now has the opportunity to perform in the West, so even if they've started a nice career in Russia, they want immediately to go to the West because it's very important to be known there. It's a big plus but maybe also a minus, because sometimes they're not fully prepared and don't grow. And if they go too early, there's the danger they will lose the Russian style."

Kazarnovskaya had been trained at the Moscow Conservatory by Elena Shumilova, a former Bolshoi prima donna who had studied with Italian teachers, and she instilled in Kazarnovskaya a love for this style of singing. After graduation, Kazarnovskaya began her career in the city's second opera house, the Stanislavsky. She considers this a lucky break. "It was a theater that had very small, intimate productions," she told me, "not like the grand ones at the Bolshoi, and for me this was very good at the time. It taught me the importance of details in creating a character."

After a year at the Stanislavsky, Kazarnovskaya arrived at the Bolshoi in the twilight of that company's glory. The company had boasted a golden era of singing from the 1930s to the 1950s, with artists of the magnificent dimensions of the mezzo-soprano Nadezhda Obukhova, the tenors Ivan Kozlovsky and Sergei Lemeshev, the baritone Pavel Lisitsian, and the basses Mark Reizen and Alexander Pirogov. A second peak was reached in the 1960s and 1970s with the sopranos Galina Vishnevskaya and Tamara Milashkina, the mezzo-sopranos Irina Arkiphova and Elena Obraztsova, the tenor Vladimir Atlantov, the baritone Yuri Mazurok, and the basses Evgeny Nesterenko and Alexander Ognivtsev. But by the 1980s, the character and quality of singing at the Bolshoi had begun to decay.

Kazarnovskaya traces the decline to the first foreign tours of the Bolshoi, especially the company's initial American visit in 1975. That engagement at New York's

Metropolitan Opera House made many Soviet artists overnight sensations—notably Atlantov and Obraztsova—and they wanted, as Kazarnovskaya would a decade later, to reap both the artistic and the financial rewards possible outside the Soviet Union. Still, it was not that easy for them at the time, because of the tight hold Gosconcerts had on all Soviet artists. But soon ways were found around the impasse.

"They would say to the Bolshoi's management, 'Let's give the younger generation a chance,'" Kazarnovskaya recalled. "And so younger singers went into important roles; this freed the older singers to sing less at home and more abroad. This was good in one way but very sad in another, because the level of singing in the theater came down immediately; the younger singers had little experience or personality. Fortunately the level of orchestral playing and conducting remained quite high, with men like [Evgeny] Svetlanov, who conducted *Onegin* for me. But gradually, our greatest singers were singing only once or twice every three months or so; they were saving themselves for their foreign engagements.

"Then, too, those who also taught at the Moscow Conservatory used the Bolshoi to promote their favorite students. So the theater was soon a shadow of what it had been. How different this was from the great era before World War ii, when all artists stayed at home, worked on their roles every day, and rarely, if ever, left Russia. I think Obukhova went once to France, but she was an exception."

After Kazarnovskaya's debut as Leonora, Yuri Temirkanov asked her to consider becoming a permanent member of the Kirov, adding, "We have very good conductors now, a very good orchestra, and good soloists." He sweetened the offer by telling Kazarnovskaya there would be more performances of Leonora, as well as Tatiana in *Onegin*, Donna Anna in *Don Giovanni*, Marguerite in *Faust*, and Violetta in *La traviata*. She accepted.

"I felt instinctively I had to do it. 'Never mind,' I said to myself, 'that Moscow is the capital. Here I can do serious work in an atmosphere that is more healthy.' I felt at home largely because of Temirkanov and Gergiev. They were never involved in intrigues, politics, and unmusical matters. They always attempted to cast very good and interesting artists, and the level of the Kirov performances was in general high.

"During my first season I remember in particular being impressed with a *Lohengrin* which Valery conducted and which was sung by Tatiana Novikova, Evgenia Tselovalnik, and Konstantin Pluzhnikov. It was overwhelming. Everyone was on the same level, a true ensemble, something that no longer existed at the Bolshoi. Of course, I had not known the Kirov before this, but I am told that Temirkanov had brought the company to this level by building up the orchestra and chorus and through artists like those in *Lohengrin* as well as Larissa Shevchenko and Alexei Steblianko," who now are regulars at the Bonn Opera in Germany.

Because of a shortage of first-rank sopranos at the Kirov during the 213th season (Maria Guleghina and Elena Prokina had left for the West a few years earlier, and Gorchakova returned only to record *La forza del destino* and to join the company for tour performances of *Prince Igor* and *Forza*), Kazarnovskaya stayed on after *Salome* to crown her homecoming with Elisabetta in *Don Carlo* and concert performances of *Tosca*. Then, in early 1996, she made her debut at La Scala in Prokofiev's *Gambler* with Gergiev, and later she toured the opera with the Kirov and recorded it. Her return to the Mariinsky was not without a few surprises, even jolts, for her. She admitted that it was a different theater in 1995 than the one she had known a decade earlier, and that performances were slack and at times "awful" when Gergiev was not around. "I said to him, 'Why are you doing *Aida* when you don't have the singers for this opera? You have only an Amneris. That's all.' The same is true with *Turandot*, which [Alexander] Tchaikovsky is pushing him to do. 'Better do a *Bohème*,' I told him, 'which can be cast today.' The company has no production of it—imagine! And now Valery talks about Wagner all the time—*Parsifal, Tannhäuser*. Where are the singers for these giant operas? Maybe *Walküre* might be possible. But to do it he will have to make a greater effort to find some new talent."

Kazarnovskaya believes the Mariinsky at the time of her return did too little to discover and promote new talent, relying instead on its regular roster or on guests who come and go. "It can't go on like this. There is too great a difference between the best in the company and the rest. There are a lot of natural, good voices in Russia. What they need is the right sort of training. Bring them into the theater and teach them not just how to use their voices, but how to move, what to do with their hands, how to walk.

"I told Valery that he must have gifted veterans like Tselovalnik and Pluzhnikov work with young singers and pass on what they know and do so well. They are not going to get this in the conservatory. The teaching in most schools is very poor these days. Those who can sing, sing. Those who can't, have careers as teachers. It's not like the ballet, where great dancers, after they retired, spent their time molding the new generation and guarding our great traditions. That's why the level in the Kirov Ballet is so high. Most singers, however, are more interested in money than in helping younger singers."

Certainly no one could accuse Kazarnovskaya of returning to the Kirov for the sake of money. The very idea made her burst into a gale of laughter. "Do you know what I am being paid for a performance of *Salome*?" she asked. "Four hundred dollars. But I know that even this amount is hard for them to afford. It is two million rubles. But for me, being back at the Kirov is like breathing fresh air. Money is not a question. I have to be here. I can't just live all the time in the West and take all the benefits possible there. I must give something back. My blood, my soul is inside Russia, inside its culture. There is a love and need for music here that is greater than [in] any other place I know. The energy that exists between me and this land and this people is something that cannot be explained. It comes from God, or the cosmos—I don't know which. I just know that what I am doing is essential for me. I always try to do my best in a performance wherever it is, but here I feel more is required of me. I can see this in the faces in my audiences. I can see they are waiting for something more."

After the first three performances of the opening week, Gergiev took the company on its first outing of the season. His staff nicknamed it the "Crazy Tour." In seven days the Kirov gave seven performances in six cities of four operas in concert form plus the Verdi Requiem. The tour opened in Bremen, Germany, with Tchaikovsky's *Mazeppa*; the Requiem followed in Amsterdam. Brussels, too, heard *Mazeppa*, as well as Rimsky-Korsakov's one-act opera *Kashchei the Immortal*, while Utrecht got *Tosca*. A concert followed in Rouen, France, and this frenzied week ended with a fund-raising gala concert performance of *Prince Igor* in London's Albert Hall for the Friends of the Kirov.

The next day Gergiev left for New York to prepare the Metropolitan Opera's new production of *The Queen of Spades*; he would not reappear in St. Petersburg until he joined his orchestra for its first concert tour of Japan. In the meanwhile, conducting chores for the opera were split between his assistants—Alexander Titov, Alexander Polyanichko, and Sergei Kalagin—and, from time to time, guests and others whose duties centered more on ballet than opera.

As its contribution to the first week of the season, the ballet led from strength with its pair of reigning ballerinas. Julia Makhalina, the younger of the two, was featured in *Swan Lake*, and the ethereal Altynai Asylmuratova followed three days later as *Giselle*. It was a feast. Both artists were trained at the Vaganova Academy. Asylmuratova was a student of the former ballerina Inna Zubkovskaya, one of the original dancers in Grigorovich's gripping 1961 ballet *Legend of Love*, while Makhalina was taught by Irena Bazhenova and Marina Vasilieva.

Although both Asylmuratova and Makhalina are easily recognizable as products of the same institution, they are quite unalike in personality and in the use of the materials provided them by nature and their schooling, Asylmuratova glows; Makhalina flashes. Asylmuratova takes your breath away; Makhalina stops your breath. The differences in their dancing say a great deal about the training they received. Although it is a bastion of classical dance, the Vaganova is not a school that straitjackets a dancer, nor is it bent on turning out cookie-cutter ballerinas. What is stressed is the development of an individual approach within a formalized, set framework.

Mariinsky Theater, 1860. COURTESY MARIINSKY THEATER

Mariinsky Theater, c. 1894, with new façade. COURTESY MARIINSKY THEATER

Feodor Stravinsky as Grandfather Frost in Rimsky-Korsakov's *May Night.*
PHOTO: VILI ONIKUL

Medea Mei and Nikolai Figner as Lisa and Herman in Tchaikovsky's *Queen of Spades.*
PHOTO: VILI ONIKUL

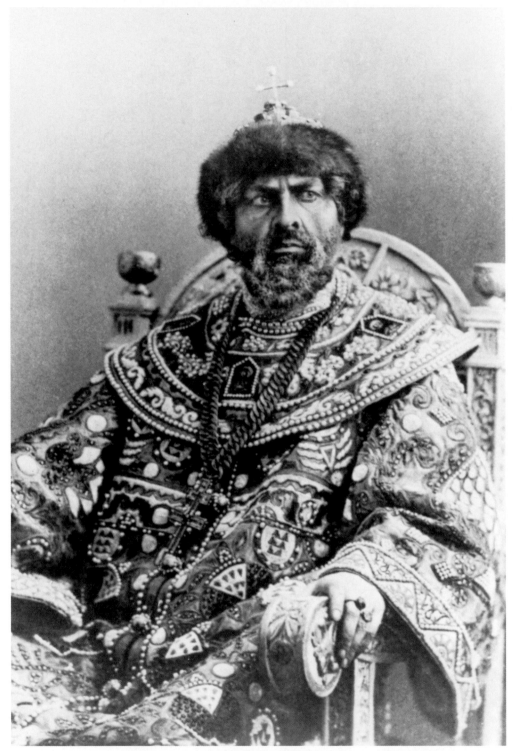

Feodor Chaliapin as Mussorgsky's Boris Godunov.
PHOTO: VILI ONIKUL

Leonid Sobinov as Lensky in Tchaikovsky's *Eugene Onegin*.
PHOTO: VILI ONIKUL

Ivan Ershov as Wagner's Siegfried.
PHOTO: VILI ONIKUL

Peter Ilyich Tchaikovsky.
PHOTO: VILI ONIKUL

Conductor Eduard Nápravník.
PHOTO: VILI ONIKUL

Tamara Karsavina in Fokine's *Le pavillon d'Armide.*
PHOTO: VILI ONIKUL

Vaslav Nijinsky in Fokine's *Le pavillon d'Armide*.
PHOTO: VILI ONIKUL

Anna Pavlova as Fokine's Dying Swan.
PHOTO: VILI ONIKUL

Ballerina Mathilde Kshessinskaya at home. PHOTO: VILI ONIKUL

Impresario Sergei Diaghilev.
© THE FOUNDATION FOR RUSSIAN BALLET

Choreographer Marius Petipa.
COURTESY ST. PETERSBURG STATE MUSEUM
OF THEATER AND MUSIC

Choreographer Mikhail Fokine as Siegfried in *Swan Lake*.
© THE FOUNDATION FOR RUSSIAN BALLET

In her *Dance Biography*, the former Kirov ballerina and academy graduate Natalia Makarova summed up Vaganova's way of training a dancer: "The natural possibilities of a human body were the cornerstone of Vaganova's system. She worked out a logical sequence of combinations that helped the body to find a way to the correct execution of prescribed movements, to develop its own coordination. . . . [Our] class was conceived in such a way as to make all parts of the body—hands, legs, feet, toes, back, and head—combine their movements into what became a classical harmony."

According to Makarova, this harmony was made up of a "delicate sketching of the plastic representation, airiness, and lightness in transmission of emotions . . . the pure aristocratic quality of pose and *port-de-bras*, the purity of classic positions, all the geometry of beauty and beauty of geometry that was sown in Russian soil by Marius Petipa. It reverberates with the architectonics of the city itself, where French classicism and a certain spirit of the Italian baroque merged so harmoniously. The Kirov style is determined by strict traditions of a culture that always stood behind St. Petersburg."

The salient phrase here is Makarova's characterization of the Kirov's port de bras as "aristocratic," always an appropriate Petersburgian word. This element, perhaps more than any other, sets the company's ballerinas apart from those with a different schooling. At the Kirov, one's legs and how they are deployed can be and often are more of an individual matter than the use of the arms. The fluid flow and line of the arms is the soul of Kirov dancing. This is just as apparent in a soloist as it is in the breathtaking work of the corps de ballet, which often dominates the stage and can satisfy and excite one as much as the dancing of a stellar ballerina.

Put another way, what happens with a Kirov dancer from the waist up is more characteristic of the company than what happens from the waist down. In *développé*, for example, Makhalina's leg will shoot up brilliantly and rest solidly in place to create a line that recalls the inevitability and wonder of a perfect line drawing. In contrast, Asylmuratova's leg will float into the same extended position. Yet both women are more closely matched in the sculpted, arcing use they make of their hands and arms.

If Asylmuratova's dancing is the purest and most affecting of poetry, this does not imply that Makhalina's is only prose; her movement is poetry couched in a more contemporary meter. In *Giselle*, for example, Asylmuratova's performance was a lyrical, effortless stream of motion. When Makhalina danced the role later in the season, the steps were more sharply etched, creating a sense of almost verismatic drama. Yet both performances took place within a similar technical context.

Although these prima ballerinas were nurtured by Oleg Vinogradov, who spotted their special gifts while they were in the corps de ballet and eased them into leading roles, one felt that Makhalina's manner as a dancer is more to the former ballet master's personal tastes. She is an overt giver and a technician whose body sends sparks flying. The performing arts do have those exceptional, splendid dancers, pianists, and violinists whose prowess is so total and so blinding that technique becomes a dazzling entity, one well worth serious consideration on its own.

For *Giselle*, Asylmuratova's partner was her husband, the marvelous *danseur noble* Konstantin Zaklinsky, who was nearing the end of a distinguished career, and in the first *Swan Lake* of the season, Makhalina was joined by Victor Baranov. Later, Makhalina would return as Odette-Odile with her husband, Evgeny Ivanchenko, as Siegfried, and in subsequent *Giselle*s Asylmuratova would be partnered by Andrei Yakovlev. The Kirov, incidentally, currently dances *Swan Lake* in at least two different stagings and uses at least two different sets of scenery, depending on whether or not it is touring.

While I was in St. Petersburg the company was dancing the more familiar 1950 variant of the original Petipa-Ivanov choreography staged by Konstantin Sergeiev. In it, Siegfried kills Rotbart and claims Odette as his bride, just as at the 1877 Moscow premiere. (Sergeiev also introduced the lively figure of the court jester in act 1 and built on the expanded dances for Siegfried and Rotbart fashioned in 1945 by Feodor Lopukhov, the theater's first major Soviet choreographer.)

Vinogradov has his version as well, which the company danced in London during the summer of 1995, and which included a reordering and regrouping of some of the dances in act 1. His chief choreographic imprint is found in act 3, where Siegfried duels to the death with Rotbart and loses. In this, Vinogradov echoes Modest Tchaikovsky's revised scenario for Petipa. In Modest's tragic ending, Odette throws herself into the lake and drowns, followed by Siegfried. Their deaths lead to a radiant apotheosis in which Siegfried, having proved his love, is reunited with Odette, and the pair sails away to a happier life together. Vinogradov, however, replaced this final tableau with the white swans avenging Siegfried's death by forcing Rotbart into the lake, where he drowns.

Throughout the season, a shining additive to ballet nights was the playing of the Kirov's orchestra under the direction of the veteran conductor Victor Fedotov. He is to dance at the Mariinsky what Gergiev has become to the opera—total authority combined with total control and expressiveness. Those of us from the West who cut our dance teeth on such touring ensembles as the American Ballet Theater or the old Ballets Russes de Monte Carlo long ago became inured to undermanned pickup touring orchestras whose playing was indifferent, poorly rehearsed, and often downright sloppy. Even a major dance company such as the New York City Ballet on home ground at New York's Lincoln Center (I am thinking of its full-length *Sleeping Beauty* in 1991) can be a sad mismatch of fine dancing and indifferent orchestral playing. The only way to reflect the full resonance of any ballet is with a superb orchestra in the pit, and this was a glorious fact of life night after night in the Mariinsky. To hear a Minkus score played by fine musicians is to appreciate fully the disarming period delights of *La bayadère* and *Don Quixote*. Admittedly, these pieces are part circus music, but the Kirov makes you realize as well their charm.

With the ice broken in the first week, the company was now geared up for the months and repertory ahead. Many ups and downs would follow, as they had during the first week, which included a substandard performance in Russian of *La traviata* whose singing was a match for its mediocre sets and staging. It was obvious that one of the chores and fascinations ahead would be balancing the scales between the various pros and cons of the season, which at times read like a fever chart.

CHAPTER THREE

Building the House

ABOUT 5:00 A.M. on 26 January 1859, the Circus Theater across the square from the Bolshoi Kamenny caught fire. According to eyewitnesses, the flames were first apparent in the upper stories of the building and spread so rapidly that the theater was soon engulfed in smoke, making it impossible to save anything in the offices or the dressing rooms. Later, a guard would testify that he saw the blaze begin in the buffet facing the Bolshoi. After questioning all of those employed by the theater, the police eventually ruled out the question of arson.

A fascinating document in the Imperial Archives details the scores and parts on hand in the Circus Theater at the time of the fire and gives a concise picture of the theater's repertory and activity at the time. The Russian operas included Dargomizhsky's *Rusalka*, Glinka's *Ruslan and Ludmila* and *A Life for the Czar*, and Verstovsky's *Askold's Grave*, while non-Russian works sung in Russian ranged from three Donizetti operas (*Lucia di Lammermoor*, *Marina Faliero*, and *Linda di Chamounix*) to Friedrich Flotow's *Martha*, Ferdinand Hérold's *Zampa*, Daniel Auber's *Le cheval de bronze*, and Carl Maria von Weber's *Der Freischütz*. There were a few other, now-forgotten works as well, plus music for overtures, intermezzi, *vaudevilles*, and ballets (the list of the nonoperatic works was destroyed along with the music). In less than a month, Alexander II ordered that a new theater be built for Russian opera.

One of the ironic and tragic figures in Russian history, Alexander came to the throne in 1855 after three decades of rule by his father, Nicholas I, which had brought Russia to the edge of a catastrophe. The country had been humiliated and devastated by war in the Crimea, and drastic reforms were being called for. Alexander took a significant step toward redressing the country's problems with his freeing of the serfs, whose centuries of servitude were holding back Russia's industrial development. Although he was widely disliked and distrusted at home, he was admired abroad, largely for ending serfdom and for making Finland and Bulgaria autonomous. He seems also to have been a man who cared, perhaps not passionately but at least honestly, for the arts. He died unexpectedly and violently at the hands of an assassin.

For a brief while there was some discussion with Alexander as to whether or not to rebuild the Circus Theater as a house for drama as well, but the plan was abandoned as being financially impractical: a theater that included drama would have cost more, since drama required a smaller auditorium, and the surviving walls of the old Circus Theater would have had to be demolished to create the proper space. A smaller house would have also meant less revenue at the box office. A report to the Ministry of the Imperial Court from an official in the Building Office, the branch of the czar's government in charge of construction work, survives, and it shows the chary concern of the czar when it came to money:

"Your Excellency knows that due to the fire in the Circus Theater the projected reconstruction of the Mikhailovsky and Alexandrinsky Theaters were ordered by the Czar to be postponed. At the same time His Majesty has ordered architect [Alberto] Cavos to undertake immediately the reconstruction of the burned-out theater with all the improvements that had been needed to be made when the circus building was turned into a theater. The Czar further orders that the architect preserve the interior decoration as it used to be.

"According to the plan of architect Cavos, which he has submitted . . . , with the surviving walls, staircases, and corridors being used, one can build a very comfortable opera theater. . . . In width the new theater will be equal to the Bolshoi Theater in Moscow, and in depth it will be [only a little bit] shorter. It is planned to add another tier of boxes, and the floor above the existing wings will be enlarged and the façade of the building changed. This will improve the exterior of the building and give additional space for dressing rooms and for storing sets.

"The stage will also be extended to provide further space for the proscenium [and] the enlarged hall will mean more box office returns for Russian Opera . . . up to 300 rubles more a performance. . . . Together with the decision to preserve the interior shape of the hall, His Majesty wants a big center box to be built. . . . As to the exterior, His Majesty wishes the roofed entrance with arcades to be preserved on the façade facing the Bolshoi Theater. His Majesty thinks it would be a waste of money to destroy the existing entrance. . . .

"The sum of money required for the reconstruction of the theater is estimated to be 900,000 rubles [a ruble at the time was worth a little more than today's dollar]. The Emperor [plans] to raise a loan of 590,000 rubles from the assets of the Imperial Ministry for a thirty-three-year term. The administration of the Imperial Theaters will make an annual payment plus interest with funds from its income toward the repayment of this loan. The remaining 310,000 rubles will be raised without interest from the operating budget of the Building Office."

The drawings Cavos made for Alexander's opera house have fortunately been preserved along with the overlays used for the changes requested by the czar. They show that the Mariinsky was a different, smaller, and less elaborate building than the one we know today. Cavos's reworking of the remaining parts of the Circus Theater resulted in a five-story building with wings of two stories on either side of the main building for offices and rehearsal rooms. The wings were constructed over what had formerly been stables that housed the horses and other animals used in the circus. Cavos also built several separate buildings for storage purposes, which were demolished a decade later when the first alterations were made in the building to meet the increased activities and needs of the company.

The theater's first façade was a simple one, described at the time as Romanesque in its lines and proportions. The vast differences between the old and the new building were most apparent inside. The new theater was more richly gilded, and its formerly round interior was reshaped to create the classic horseshoe design typical of the traditional European opera house. The fifth tier of seats increased the seating capacity to more than 1,500, making it smaller than La Scala but larger than Venice's La Fenice. The stage and its proscenium arch were also enlarged, and to heighten the room's acoustical properties the walls were ribbed with thin wooden planks, while the ceiling was made up of wooden panels decorated with pairs of dancing girls ringing a massive three-tiered chandelier.

Staircases on either side of the entrance led up to a narrow foyer on the *bel étage*, where the imperial box with its large anteroom, used for state occasions, was positioned in the center rear of the theater like a triumphal arch. Each of the smaller surrounding boxes had its own anteroom as well, equipped with a mirror, a table, and a couch. The gold of the hall was accented by blue rather than the traditional red, with the seats in the parterre covered in blue velvet and the boxes draped in blue silk with gold-and-blue velvet chairs. Throughout, the blue-and-gold of the auditorium was set off by chalk-white masks, statues, and ornaments.

When the Mariinsky first opened its doors on 2 October 1860 with Glinka's great nationalistic epic *A Life for the Czar*, conducted by Konstantin Liadov, it was described as "the most splendid theater of Europe." Yet, from at least one standpoint, it was a controversial building. Ironically, its stage was not considered good for ballet: it was thought to be too wide for dancing and not deep enough for the trappings and machinery needed to create the spectacular effects so popular at the time. The Imperial Ballet, with a few exceptions, remained ensconced in the Bolshoi Kamenny until 1886, where it flourished as one of the favorite diversions of the time.

According to the designer Alexander Benois, many people at that time considered ballet more of an entertainment than a serious art. He recalled that when he was a child, "grownups talked about it in the same vein as when they spoke of circus or operetta. Nevertheless, it was the custom to take children to the ballet, especially to the Christmas, Carnival, and Easter matinees." Even so, his visits to the ballet were less frequent than those to the opera, for, according to Benois, "Society in those days was still full of moral prejudices, and ballet was considered just a shade questionable. . . . This was an epoch of dresses to the ground and even long trains, whereas in the ballet very scantily-dressed young ladies appeared in skirts not reaching to their knees."

For its first few decades, the Mariinsky remained under the shadow of the Bolshoi Kamenny, not only because the Bolshoi was the home of the ballet, but also because the demand for Italian opera persisted. In its early years, the Mariinsky's music director was Konstantin Liadov. He was the father of Anatol Liadov, a leading composer and teacher at the turn of the century and Diaghilev's first choice to write the score for the ballet *Firebird.* The elder Liadov, a composer of ballets as well, would preside over the musical life of the Mariinsky until replaced by his assistant, Eduard Nápravník, in 1868. Nápravník would bring the theater to a zenith during the course of his tenure as chief conductor, which lasted nearly until his death in 1916. During this time, he became the most powerful musical figure in the life of the city.

While Konstantin Liadov and the Russian opera worked to gain a strong foothold in St. Petersburg's musical life, Italian opera at the Bolshoi Kamenny continued to be an influential force throughout the fabled appearances in Russia of the soprano Adelina Patti. She sang at the Bolshoi every season from the winter of 1869 through the winter of 1877. Russia's love affair with Italian opera, however, might be said to have peaked in 1862 with the czar's commissioning of Verdi's *La forza del destino.* No doubt Alexander II had wanted *Forza* to put a seal on St. Petersburg as a cosmopolitan opera center (the year of the opera's premiere, the city numbered a little more than a half million residents; by the time of the first major census in 1869, the figure had risen to 667,000).

Forza's history at the Bolshoi Kamenny began under a cloud, however. Originally its premiere was planned for 1861, and in November of that year Verdi, his wife, Giuseppina, and two servants set out by rail for St. Petersburg, where the composer planned to finish his orchestration of the score during the rehearsal period. Along with winter clothes lined in fur, Giuseppina brought along an ample supply of rice, pasta, cheese, salami, and wine. Unfortunately, the soprano Emma La Grua, who was to create the role of Leonora with the tenor Enrico Tamberlik as Don Alvaro, fell ill during what was a particularly severe Russian winter, and after a wait of two months it was decided to postpone the premiere until the next year.

In a letter from Russia to a friend, Giuseppina wrote, "The voices of singers are as fragile as—I leave you to finish this phrase—and the voice of La Grua is, to her and Verdi's misfortune, an upsetting example of this fragility." Interestingly, she goes on to note that "this terrible cold has not bothered us in the least, thanks to our apartments. One sees the cold but doesn't feel it. But . . . this curious contradiction is a benefit only of the rich who are able to shout 'Hurray for the cold, the ice, the sleighs and other joys of this world.' But the poor people in general, and the coachmen in particular, are the most miserable creatures on earth. Just think . . . many of the coachmen stay sometimes all day and some of the night sitting on their boxes, exposed to freezing cold, waiting for their masters who [are] guzzling in beautifully warm apartments while some of these unhappy beings are freezing to death. Such horrible things happen all the time. I shall never get used to the sight of such suffering."

When the Verdis returned to Russia a year later, *Forza* went ahead as scheduled, with a different Leonora, but this time the czar was ill and unable to attend the premiere; he and the czarina, however, appeared at the fourth performance and warmly applauded the work. Afterward he bestowed on Verdi the Royal Order of St. Stanislaus. Verdi was pleased with the cast and described the production as "extremely opulent." Although *Forza*, on the whole, was cordially received by the press, the opera rankled a group of Russian nationalists who were opposed to commissioning music from an Italian and who protested the performances. There were those, too, who were upset that an enormous amount of money had been spent on the production at a time when Russia was recovering from the financial and human losses of the Crimean War. In addition, the opera's length—four hours in the original version—annoyed many. Verdi later cut and rewrote many of its pages, but Russia would not hear the revised version of *Forza* until 1901, when it was presented by a touring Italian opera company; the first staged performance of the revision at the Kirov was in 1963.

A year after *Forza*'s premiere, Verdi's nemesis, Richard Wagner, came to St. Petersburg and conducted a concert of his music in the Bolshoi on 6 March 1863 (he had made his Russian debut in February 1863 in the Hall of the Nobility, now Philharmonic or Shostakovich Hall). These Russian concerts were among the first occasions on which the composer led extracts from *Die Walküre*, *Siegfried*, and *Die Meistersinger*, operas he was in process of completing. In St. Petersburg he also combined for the first time anywhere the Prelude to act 1 of *Tristan und Isolde* with the opera's "Liebestod."

Wagner was given an orchestra of 130 (which he described as "fiery" and "devoted") that had been drawn, according to his biographer, Ernest Newman, from "all the Imperial Theaters," meaning the Bolshoi Kamenny and the Mariinsky. Among those present for one of these concerts was the twenty-two-year-old Tchaikovsky, who years later wrote to his patroness Nadezhda von Meck, "I have only ever seen one . . . conductor command the authority and power that transforms the orchestra until all the players become as if one soul, one great instrument, and that was Wagner."

Wagner broke new ground in Russia with more than his music. St. Petersburg had never before seen a conductor stand in front of his musicians on a podium. Through the turn of the century, the conductor in a Russian opera house was positioned on a stool directly in front of the stage, facing the singers, with his musicians behind him, who in turn had their backs to the audience. Nor, it seems, had St. Petersburg seen a conductor who dispensed with a score and conducted from memory.

These Wagnerian innovations would not become standard practice in Russia until 1905, when Sergei Rachmaninov initiated them after joining the conducting staff of the Bolshoi in Moscow. Wagner's single concession to the concert decorum of the day was to wear white gloves while conducting, a convention he did away with in the West. In his landmark book on Alexander Scriabin, Faubion Bowers notes that Alexander II once ordered a conductor who appeared without his gloves to stop and put them on, "as if he were a butler serving plates of food."

Neither Verdi nor Wagner, however, was the first illustrious Western composer to journey to St. Petersburg. Robert Schumann and his wife, Clara, traveled there in 1844. But of greater importance, because of his profound influence on Russian music, was a visit in 1847 by Berlioz. In what is now Shostakovich Hall, he conducted excerpts from his *Damnation of Faust, Roméo et Juliette,* and the *Symphonie funèbre,* as well as the *Carnaval romain,* the *Symphonie fantastique,* and *Harold en Italie.* In his *Memoirs* he states, "I had a large and well-rehearsed orchestra and chorus, and a military band to boot. . . . Even the two kapellmeisters of St. Petersburg, [Henry] Romberg and [Ludwig] Maurer, had been recruited to play the antique cymbals in [the] 'Queen Mab' [scherzo]."

In between the concerts in St. Petersburg, Berlioz appeared in Moscow with what he describes as "third-rate musicians." This comment and Berlioz's reaction to a performance of *A Life for the Czar* at Moscow's Bolshoi provide strong evidence that performances in that theater at the time were on a less accomplished level than those in the capital. While he found the Glinka opera had "some graceful and original melodies . . . I had virtually to divine them—the performance was so poor." Berlioz returned to St. Petersburg for a second visit in 1867, a sick man of sixty-four who had barely a year to live (Rimsky-Korsakov remembers him as "bowed down by illness and therefore . . . utterly indifferent to Russian music and Russian musicians").

This second set of concerts—which were given with the orchestra of the Mariinsky Theater and were his last as a conductor—made a strong impression on Mussorgsky and Rimsky-Korsakov, however. He repeated the *Symphonie fantastique* and parts of *Damnation of Faust* and *Roméo et Juliette*, adding to these the overture to *Benvenuto Cellini*, as well as the second act of Gluck's *Orphée et Euridice* and Beethoven's Third through Sixth Symphonies.

Finally, before the trauma of revolution cut Russia off from the West, there were visits to St. Petersburg by Gustav Mahler, accompanied by his bride, Alma (Schindler) Mahler, in 1902, and alone in 1907 (he had earlier appeared in Moscow in 1897). At the first series of concerts in the capital, he conducted music of Haydn, Beethoven, Schubert, and Wagner with Mariinsky musicians. In her book *Gustav Mahler: Memories and Letters*, Alma recalls that they also attended a performance of *Eugene Onegin* at the Mariinsky, which "was on a very high artistic level."

When Mahler returned to St. Petersburg in 1907, he introduced to Russia his Fifth Symphony, a work that was only three years old. In a letter to Alma from Russia, Mahler, always an exacting orchestral taskmaster, remarks that "the orchestra behaves splendidly. Their enthusiasm never flags." The young Igor Stravinsky attended the performance and reported in later life that he was greatly impressed.

A decade after Wagner's trip to Russia, the Bolshoi Kamenny, along with Italian opera, began to lose its hold on the public. The coup de grâce came in 1877 during Patti's last Russian season at the theater. The soprano was suffering social ostracism à la Tolstoy's Anna Karenina: a scandal in her private life became public knowledge while she was in St. Petersburg, and her previous acceptance by the nobility came to a sudden halt. The parallel with Anna Karenina is not only apt but ironic, for in his novel, Tolstoy has Anna attending the opera on a Patti night after she, Anna, had broken with her husband over her younger lover. Patti had just done the same, casting off her spouse, the Marquis de Caux, for the tenor Ernest Nicolini.

"On the stage Adelina Patti, her diamonds and bare shoulders glittering, bowing low and smiling, with the help of the tenor who was holding her by the hand was collecting the bouquets that came clumsily flying across the footlights," writes Tolstoy. He goes on to relate how those in the most fashionable seats talked not of Patti or the opera but of Anna and her disgrace; one aristocrat in an adjoining box declares that she cannot remain in the presence of an adulteress and leaves the theater. This behavior was not far removed from that of the morally outraged women at performances by Patti and Nicolini who turned their backs on the stage whenever the diva appeared.

Although Patti never sang opera again in the city, she returned one last time to St. Petersburg in 1904 to appear in concert before an audience that included Nicholas II and his czarina. Princess Bariatinsky, a member of the court, was also present and recalled Patti as "a little woman, with refined and delicate features, but with very dark eyes that shone with great brilliancy out of her thin face . . . and she resembled nothing so much as a dainty piece of Dresden china." Igor Stravinsky, too, was at the concert, but his memory was less generous: "At that time, this tiny woman with the bright orange wig sounded like a bicycle pump."

As the Bolshoi Kamenny's fortunes declined, the Mariinsky's rose. In the beginning it had filled virtually the same niche in the life of the city that the Circus Theater had occupied before it; but its all-Russian seasons gradually grew in prominence and influence. The time was ripe for advancing the cause of Russian opera after the lead taken by Glinka, Dargomizhsky, and Alexander Serov (whose operas, although once enormously popular, are today not often produced in Russia or anywhere else). Suddenly significant new works from composers of the ilk of Tchaikovsky and Russia's Mighty Five (the name given to Rimsky-Korsakov and his friends Mussorgsky, César Cui, Alexander Borodin, and Mily Balakirev) flooded the stage, operas that took and held the spotlight in a string of successes that helped create the first fully formed Russian school of opera.

Italian opera would make one last stand, however, at the turn of the century, in the Great Hall of the conservatory (although its interior was eventually recast in a drab Soviet style, its splendid original lobby can still be seen today). The seasons at the conservatory brought to the city such renowned singers as Angelo Masini, Francesco Tamagno, Hariclea Darclée, Celestina Boninsegna, Marcella Sembrich, Titta Ruffo, Luisa Tetrazzini, Mattia Battistini, and Enrico Caruso. Foreign singers were still arriving in St. Petersburg as late as 1913—the Spanish soprano Elvira de Hidalgo, who later taught Maria Callas, and the Italian tenor Giuseppe Anselmi. World War 1 and the Revolution, however, would cut off the visits of Western singers for about four decades.

Of the illustrious foreign singers who journeyed to St. Petersburg at the turn of the century for performances at the conservatory, only Caruso and a few of his colleagues sang at the Mariinsky. During the 1899 season the Italian opera troupe moved across the square to give a single performance of *Aida* at the Mariinsky in December with Caruso and the Polish soprano Salomea Kruszelnicka. In February 1900 Caruso sang a solitary *La traviata* there with the soprano Sigrid Arnoldson.

Between the closing of the Bolshoi Kamenny and the opening of the Conservatory Theater there were stellar visits to the Mariinsky by Nellie Melba and the de Reszke brothers, Jean and Edouard, in February 1891, and by the American prima donna Sibyl Sanderson in January 1892. Sanderson, a great beauty with a phenomenal vocal range, had created the title role in Jules Massenet's *Esclarmonde* in 1889 at her Paris debut. She repeated the part eight times in St. Petersburg as well as appearing in *Faust*.

Another prominent foreign soprano, the Italian Olimpia Boronat, was also popular at the same time as Sanderson. She debuted as a guest with the Mariinsky in 1891, but following a bitter disagreement with Nápravník, she confined her appearances in the city to the Italian seasons given in other, less important theaters in St. Petersburg.

Melba and the de Reszkes came to Russia at the personal invitation of Alexander III. The trio appeared first in *Roméo et Juliette*, and then Melba and Jean, the matinee idol of his time, sang together in *Lohengrin*. Edouard joined Melba in *Faust*. The Australian soprano was followed to Russia by Philippe, Duc d'Orléans, the son of the pretender to the French throne, with whom she had begun an illfated affair. At the first night of *Roméo*, this smitten young aristocrat burst into applause after Melba's aria, which was a glaring breach of court etiquette: no one applauded any artist until the czar did. Alexander was not pleased and had a member of his staff inform the duke that he was no longer welcome in the capital. Although Philippe had no desire to leave Melba's side, he was given little choice in the matter after the czar made it clear that he intended to have the duke forcibly evicted from the city if need be. During this visit the czar, rather than thanking the de Reszke brothers with the usual imperial gift of gold or jewelry, confirmed their patent of nobility (they were Polish).

Although Melba did not return to St. Petersburg, the de Reszkes did. In 1898 they took part in a visit by the Breslau Opera, which gave thirty-one performances of eleven operas in February and March that included St. Petersburg's first hearing of *Die Meistersinger von Nuremberg*, *The Flying Dutchman*, and *Tristan und Isolde* (the latter with Jean as Tristan). One of the conductors for the Breslau performances was Hans Richter, who had led the premiere of the *Der Ring des Nibelungen* at Bayreuth in 1876; other prominent singers on the tour were Ernest van Dyck, Theodor Reichmann, and the Mariinsky's own Félia Litvinne. These performances, plus *Die Walküre* and *Siegfried*, further whetted the city's appetite for Wagner.

At the time Melba and the de Reszkes appeared at the Mariinsky, only *Lohengrin* and *Tannhäuser* were part of the theater's repertory. However, there had been a complete *Ring* in 1889, when a touring group formed by a tenor turned impresario, Angelo Neumann, with Karl Muck as conductor journeyed to St. Petersburg to present four cycles. Although this Russian premiere of the *Ring* made use of the Mariinsky's orchestra, it in effect lies outside the nominal history of the theater, as the singers, chorus, conductor, and sets were imported (the company also brought with it a set of Wagner tubas; the Mariinsky's brass players requested additional pay for performing on these "unusual" instruments).

Yet, these performances paved the way for the Mariinsky's own *Ring*, which was launched in the 1901–2 season with *Die Walküre* and *Siegfried*. But as Sergei

Levik points out in his extraordinary memoirs, which include a lively picture of opera during the imperial era, "The producers of Wagner [at the Mariinsky] were always faced with difficult problems, of which the first was the scale of the works themselves and the translation to be used, let alone the unprecedented length and range of the roles. . . . The length of the performances could be disastrous. The average member of the audience was not used to sitting out performances of six-hour length and wouldn't come back a second time, something the Mariinsky had to take into account. Therefore cuts had to be made . . . especially by Nápravník. . . . When the scores were handed over to others, the number of cuts increased in proportion to practical demands. Cuts were made in passages that were weak musically, although sometimes damage was done to the drama as well as to the poetry itself. As a result the complications of the dramas became even more difficult to follow and even the [most] alert member of the audience who had lost the thread of the stage action was reduced to enjoying the music for its own sake."

Neumann found during his 1889 visit that the Mariinsky orchestra compared favorably to that of Bayreuth, and the chorus for *Götterdämmerung* (amplified with twenty Mariinsky singers) was, in his view, the best he had ever heard. Muck, however, was not as happy with the orchestra and protested the poor quality of the horn playing to Neumann. He demanded that a player be brought from Germany specifically for the horn calls in *Siegfried*. In his autobiography, Rimsky-Korsakov provides a different take on the orchestra: "Imagine how astonished conductor Muck was when, having produced . . . *Der Ring des Nibelungen* with only six orchestral rehearsals for each of the four lyric dramas (abroad they have from twenty to thirty of them), he saw that in the first cycle of Wagner's work everything went perfectly, in the second cycle worse, in the third downright slovenly, and so on, instead of improving as the composition became more familiar. The cause of this lay in the fact that in the early days the orchestra had striven to show off before a conductor from abroad and really had shown off; while during the subsequent cycles self-confidence, routine, and weariness got the upper hand even of the spell of Wagner's name."

Whatever the problems with the orchestra, a great personal success was had by the soprano Therese Malten, who had been one of the three singers chosen by Wagner to sing Kundry at the premiere of *Parsifal* in 1882. Malten had been booked by Neumann for only the first cycle, but he was forced to persuade her to remain for more performances after an audience demonstration protesting her absence from the second cycle necessitated intervention by the police. The casts also included the celebrated husband-and-wife team Heinrich and Therese Vogl. Heinrich had created Loge at Bayreuth and shared the role of Tristan in the first Bayreuth production, and the couple had appeared as Siegmund and Sieglinde in

Die Walküre at its premiere in Munich in 1870, six years before the complete Bayreuth cycle.

Alexander III and the czarina attended the St. Petersburg *Ring*, as did many other members of the court, and the czar asked Neumann to repeat the operas in Moscow. This must have pleased the impresario, for Moscow had been part of his original proposal, but officials of the Imperial Theaters there had vetoed the idea. There were plans to bring his company back in the 1890s, but these had to be abandoned when politics entered the picture with the signing of the Franco-Russian Alliance.

The Mariinsky had been able to present Neumann's company because a few years earlier its pit had been enlarged to hold 102 players. This was one of a number of physical changes in the building that had begun to be made less than a decade after the theater opened. When Cavos died in 1863, the post of chief architect of the Imperial Theaters had gone to his brother-in-law Nikolai Benois, Alexander's father. Under his supervision a large storage area was built on the roof of the Mariinsky in 1869 for sets, and the acoustics in the auditorium were enhanced when he opened up space under the stage that had been filled with debris left from the Circus Theater.

More interior alterations followed in 1883 when Benois's successor, Viktor Shroeter, converted the upper balcony of the theater into an amphitheater. Then, between 1884 and 1886, with the closing of the decaying Bolshoi Kamenny imminent, Shroeter began a new series of major changes based on a plan drawn up by Benois. He extended and added a third floor to the left wing, which greatly altered the symmetry of Cavos's design but was urgently needed to house a boiler room, electric generators, shops, design studios, and storerooms. He also created a new private entrance for the imperial family and was responsible for enlarging the pit.

Even more drastic changes followed in 1894, when a third floor was added to the right wing and the front of the theater was entirely rebuilt, destroying its former classical simplicity in the process. The new façade, the one we know today, was set off by the addition of two tall stone towers on either side of the main entrance. The expansion of the façade, however, doubled the space of the promenade room outside the imperial box and made possible a second foyer above that of the *bel étage*. The reconstituted Mariinsky reopened its doors on in mid-October 1896, and the public that evening had to find its way through a new and unfamiliar network of stairways, foyers, and passages. In compensation, the interior was now even more brilliant, thanks to a ring of miniature chandeliers added to each level of boxes and a ceiling repainted to include dancing figures interspersed with angels.

Incidentally, the great blue-and-gold curtain, which is so closely associated with the Mariinsky, was not added until 1914. It was the work of the painter Alexander Golovin and was supposedly patterned after the design for a gown worn by Catherine the Great. It was originally red and gold (this version is still used from time to time for concerts); the more famous blue curtain was first seen in 1952. During the terrible 900-day siege of Leningrad there was damage to the roof and ceiling, and a direct hit on the right side of the Kirov in 1944 necessitated extensive rebuilding. The restoration of the ceiling was put into the hands of an eminent painter, Valentin Shcherbakov. According to Suzanne Massie, "Half the theatrical paintings and virtually all of the ornamentation of the silver, gold, and blue theater . . . had to be restored. . . . Bombs and artillery shelling had heavily damaged the colorful dome. The ceiling, made of many wooden squares, had broken through the canvas. In the blue sky of the huge painted ceilings, muses and cupids hung in shreds. Dampness and cold were finishing the job of destruction . . . Shcherbakov gently and patiently guided [the laborers] through their work, and under his direction the young students were able successfully to re-plaster the wooden foundation, glue the canvas back onto it, and repaint the damaged section of the painting." Later the ballet wing of the theater was extended, and in 1966–67 the last substantial modifications in the interior enlarged the pit (at a cost of several rows of seats) and added an elevator. More recently, Gergiev has redone the lighting equipment and feels it is "among the best in Europe." But he is unhappy with the current pit and feels it is too "near the public. I want to make it deeper and closer to the singers like the pit at La Scala. At present our sound is quite good there, but it can be a bit too dominant."

Out of these changes fostered by necessity, politics, and war emerged the building we know today. Although it is altered in shape and design from the original structure of 1860, it nevertheless remains decidedly imperial. When the theater reverted to its original name, the hammer-and-sickles throughout the house were replaced with an intertwining gold A and M for Alexander II and his czarina, Marie, and the secondary stage curtain, with its field of hammer-and-sickles, was laid to rest. After seventy years of Soviet rule, the theater was once more the Mariinsky, and it bore the name more comfortably and with a more commanding air than ever it had the name Kirov.

Feodor Chaliapin and Leonid Sobinov as Mefistofele and Faust
in Chaliapin's staging of Boïto's *Mefistofele*.

Feodor Lopukhov, first major Soviet choreographer.
© THE FOUNDATION FOR RUSSIAN BALLET

Vakhtung Chabukiani as Jerome
in Vainonen's *Flames of Paris*.
COURTESY ST. PETERSBURG STATE MUSEUM
OF THEATRE AND MUSIC

Agrippina Vaganova, Russia's premier dance teacher.
© THE FOUNDATION FOR RUSSIAN BALLET

Galina Ulanova as Adam's Giselle.
PHOTO: VILI ONIKUL

Konstanin Sergeiev as Frondoso in *Laurencia.*
© THE FOUNDATION FOR RUSSIAN BALLET

Natalia Dudinskaya as Glazunov's Raymonda.
PHOTO: VILI ONIKUL

Mariinsky Theater, 1945, with damage from World War II.
COURTESY MARIINSKY THEATER

Inna Zubkovskaya and Sviatoslav Kuznetsov in Goleizovsky's *Romance*.
COLLECTION OF NINA ALOVERT

Rudolf Nureyev as Albrecht in Adam's *Giselle*.
PHOTO: VILI ONIKUL

Yuri Soloviev in Belsky's *Icarus.*
© THE FOUNDATION FOR RUSSIAN BALLET

Natalia Makarova in Fokine's *Les sylphides.*

Mikhail Baryshnikov as Basilio in *Don Quixote*.

Valery Gergiev, c. 1958, with his parents and sisters, Svetlana (left) and Larissa.

Yuri Temirkanov, Gergiev's predecessor at the Kirov.
PHOTO: RICHARD HAUGHTON. COURTESY THE PHILADELPHIA ORCHESTRA

Oleg Vinogradov, choreographer and former artistic director of the Kirov Ballet.
© THE FOUNDATION FOR RUSSIAN BALLET

Oleg Vinogradov and Mikhail Baryshnikov in rehearsal.
© THE FOUNDATION FOR RUSSIAN BALLET

CHAPTER FOUR

October: House Revolt

A N OPERA HOUSE is like a beehive. When all is going well and functioning smoothly, both emit a contented hum. But when trouble threatens or something is amiss, a disruptive buzzing takes over that can be heard from a great distance.

It was a very loud buzz indeed that emanated from the Mariinsky during the first week of October 1995, signaling a scandal that shook the theater and St. Petersburg to their foundations. The house's administrative head, Anatoly Malkov, and its ballet master, Oleg Vinogradov, were arrested by the St. Petersburg police and accused of taking bribes from Western impresarios who wanted an inside track in booking the Kirov Ballet. Vinogradov was dramatically taken into custody only moments before a weekend performance by the ballet, and both men were held for several days before being released.

"It is one thing for such things to happen in the coal or oil business," the noted dance critic Igor Stupnikov was quoted as saying, "but ballet is supposed to be above this." The scandal came on the heels of the cancellation of a four-city tour to the United States by the Kirov Ballet because—as rumor had it—promoters had become "jittery over reports of unrest, chaos and corruption in the company."

The buzzing at the Mariinsky linked the scandal to a surprise move Vinogradov had made the preceding spring when he handed over part of his artistic and administrative responsibilities to two of his leading dancers, Farukh Ruzimatov and Makhar Vaziev. Such a development was entirely out of character for this iron-willed, dictatorial man, who had brooked little outside pressure, political or otherwise, since taking over the company in 1977. The feeling was that someone knew something Vinogradov did not want known and that he was forced to yield to their demands. His only comment was, "I am away so much that I must rely on them [Vaziev and Ruzimatov] to supervise the company and maintain discipline. I make decisions about repertoire and casting, they carry them out."

But the ballerina Altynai Asylmuratova commented to the *Times* of London that "the company was shocked" by these appointments. "At first nobody understood what had happened. A lot of strange things are going on here. . . . Nobody knows when and who will be dancing. It is abnormal. It's impossible to understand who runs the company." Ruzimatov countered by saying, "My main business is to keep an eye on the dancing. The company was not lazy, but you could feel some relaxation." This struck a sour note with Asylmuratova. Although she and Ruzimatov had once been a stellar team at the Kirov, they had parted ways and no longer danced together. As she put it, "It is very difficult working with a man who has no respect for anybody, who is fond of himself only."

The scandal broke when the *St. Petersburg Press* reported that Malkov had been "caught red-handed while receiving a $10,000 bribe from a Western impresario" and alleged that Vinogradov had been extorting bribes from promoters for years. Supposedly the $10,000 bribe was to ensure that Malkov, whose signature was necessary on all foreign contracts, would reduce the costs of future ballet bookings. Ironically, the key figure in the sordid disclosures, the Canadian impresario John Cripton, was at first quoted as saying, "The impresarios I know out there are not the type to do that. I'm almost sure that this has to do with internal decisions within the Kirov on how to distribute the money [earned on tour]." Yet it was Cripton who apparently contacted the local police and who was videotaped giving marked bills to Malkov in what was obviously a sting. It appears that the Canadian promoter had flown into St. Petersburg for only a day and left immediately after Malkov's arrest. A member of the Mariinsky's staff would later report having seen Cripton at the St. Petersburg airport in the company of Ruzimatov and Vaziev. This gave rise to the theory that the scandal was a setup, and Malkov and Cripton were the pawns.

In the meanwhile, although Malkov admitted receiving the $10,000, which he characterized as "a mistake," he maintained that it was not a bribe but "a bonus for the excellent organization of previous foreign tours." It was also reported that the police had turned up an additional $142,000 in cash belonging to Vinogradov and that the ballet master admitted to having an additional $1.2 million, earned from the company's tours, in a Swiss bank account. (Eventually $850,000 was returned to the Mariinsky. "We have never been able to determine where the rest of it went," Gergiev told me). Vinogradov maintained that this money was in his care for the needs of the company. Asked for a comment, Ruzimatov replied, "Someone wants to destroy this theater." No one disagreed. The question was why, and who that person or persons might be.

By the end of October, Malkov had resigned his post in the theater, and it was taken over on an interim basis by his deputy, Valery Shepovalov. Vinogradov, however, who was never formally charged with a crime, went on about his duties as usual, weathering the storm swirling around him and treating the accusations against him with contempt. What was not being reported in the press, but was being whispered about the house, was that this was no venal, penny-ante scandal. It was instead a full-scale palace revolt, an attempt to gain control of the theater itself, and it was carefully orchestrated to take place while Gergiev was away in New York, deep in rehearsals for a new production of *The Queen of Spades* at the Metropolitan Opera.

Supposedly, certain highly placed and ambitious individuals in the ballet wing wanted to rid themselves of Vinogradov and Malkov in order to gain control of the Mariinsky, and Cripton was their means of accomplishing this. The first step allegedly was to replace the theater's administrative and ballet heads with two puppet figures (who went along with the scheme, it was said, because they believed they would be truly in control). The next step was to eliminate them once Gergiev, the one incorruptible figure in authority, was out of the way. The conspirators reasoned that if life could then be made difficult enough for Gergiev, he would vacate his post for an untroubled berth in the West. They had not, however, fully taken the measure of the man they were intriguing against. Too much of his energy and too many dreams had gone into the remaking of the Mariinsky for him to be easily frightened off. Even from New York, Gergiev showed what power he could command when it was needed.

Because he could not personally go to St. Petersburg to deal with the crisis, the city came to him in the form of its democratic, crusading mayor (and close Gergiev friend) Anatoly Sobchok. Together they made a direct appeal to Russian president Boris Yeltsin and his minister of culture, Victor Chernomyrdin, for help. By early December there was a new, pro-Gergiev administrative head: Yuri Schwarzkopf, the former director of St. Petersburg's Komissarzhevskaya Theater. The revolt had successfully been put down; the crisis had been stemmed.

In December, during the Kirov's Japanese tour, Gergiev told me that "there are those who want do with the theater as they wish—sell it, like armaments or any other commodity that is going for quick dollars today in Russia. That would have been the end of the Mariinsky." It was his belief that the October revolt had been engineered by Vaziev and the administrative head of the Vaganova Academy, Leonid Nadirov. Their first aim, he believed, was to oust Vinogradov. Involving Malkov was just a means to an end; he was a man in the wrong place at the wrong time. Had they succeeded, Gergiev felt, they would have installed others as the theater's titular heads until the coast was clear, and then they would have moved in and taken over. Their hope was that Gergiev would give up in disgust and resign. He showed that he was made of tougher stuff.

As the scandal kept the hive buzzing, my work went steadily ahead. I realized that I could make only minor inroads with the Russian language in a year; indeed,

I never got past basic everyday pleasantries. But I knew that it was imperative to master the Cyrillic alphabet. This I did in a relatively short time so that I could read the posters outside the Mariinsky and their cast lists. Soon I developed a routine I went through before each performance.

The usher on our floor, Tatiana Sergeievna, who became both friend and ally, would let me into box 14 while the house was still empty and the stage was being prepared for the evening's performance. The curtain would be up, and there were always a few dancers on stage warming up, or some last-minute conference. During this quiet, magical time, the sets, lighting, and props for the evening were checked out before the audience was admitted. When all was in readiness, the house was plunged into darkness for a few moments, and then gradually the house lights came up, the prelude to another night of opera or dance. In these moments alone, I would translate the evening's cast list and other credits.

The programs include the statistics of the production, those responsible for it or for its revival, and how many times the company had presented the work. In 1995 they went for two thousand rubles (what was then twenty cents) for what was called the "Russian program" and five thousand rubles (a dollar) for the "English program." The only difference between the two was an insert in the latter that gave a synopsis of the evening's opera or ballet in a sometimes stilted or comical (or both) translation. Oddly enough, the English program never included cast or production credits in English.

A prime seat downstairs at the Mariinsky for a local was $5 (25,000 rubles), an expensive sum. But the same ticket went for ten times that amount to a foreigner and could cost even more (up to $75) if purchased at one of the city's luxury hotels. Although admittedly expensive, on a good night this was still a bargain compared to the cost of an opera ticket in New York, London, or Vienna. For some odd reason, the theater did not mark up its box or balcony seats, and those on the *bel étage*, in particular, were among the best in the house. It was, of course, possible for a non-Russian to go to the box office at the Mariinsky and buy a ticket, if he or she were possessed of a modicum of Russian or a gift for sign language. But here, too, there were two price scales designed to keep inexpensive ruble tickets out of the hands of tourists.

I had been told of people who had to make sacrifices to buy a ticket for an important ballet or opera night, and Tatiana Sergeievna frequently would introduce us to a friend or the friend of a friend who could not find or afford a ticket and ask if they might share our box. I always readily agreed, for I had come to know that an evening at the Mariinsky provides natives, as Elizabeth Kendall put it in a state-of-the-art report on the Kirov in 1992 for the *New Yorker*, with "a way to forget, however briefly, the overwhelming woes of the Russian economy. You sit in a delicate plush chair in the blue-and-gilt house; you hear the orchestra strike up the chords of one of those old tales of enchantment, sorrow, or revenge; you see the curtain rise on a panorama of a court or a peasant village, in which, with a graceful gesture, young dancers sketch their place in an ancient hierarchy; and you have an eerie sensation of somehow losing a century and finding yourself back in the twilight of the Romanovs."

We were transported to this twilight world in October 1995 with the return to the repertory of an exhilarating tripartite evening of dance whose elegant show curtain proclaimed it "Les Saisons Russes." It was the brainchild of the dancer Andris Liepa (the son of the electrifying Bolshoi dancer Marius Liepa) to commemorate the fiftieth anniversary of Mikhail Fokine's death. In a studio in Moscow, Liepa had directed the filming of three dance pieces—*Petrushka*, *Schéhérazade*, and *Firebird*, in their original choreography, sets, and costumes—by the Mariinsky's one-time ballet master and danced in two of them. All three had been created for Diaghilev's Ballets Russes and had never before been seen at the Mariinsky in the Fokine versions, although it had always been Diaghilev's dream to bring his best ballets back to where he and his company had begun. It took seventy-three years, but in giving these productions to the Mariinsky, Liepa righted more than one wrong, for Diaghilev had worked at the theater for a year (1899–1900) and been fired for insubordination.

To Liepa, it was important that St. Petersburg see these works and know that they, too, are part of the city's heritage. "After all," he told me, "they had never seen anything like these ballets, for what they got after the revolution was Soviet realism, nothing of such fantasy and beauty." In accepting this substantial gift, however, Vinogradov made one condition. As the company had his own, very different production of *Petrushka* (which Liepa had danced), he wished to substitute Fokine's *Chopiniana* as the gambit in the set. This landmark piece was in its final form the one work of the three to have been premiered at the Mariinsky, and it is credited as being the first abstract or non-storytelling ballet. While ultimately not as powerful an evening as Liepa had originally conceived, the switch did lighten the bill. It also linked the Fokine of St. Petersburg and the Fokine of Paris and proved to be an effective foil for the darker passions of the other two ballets. The Fokine triptych, which premiered in January 1993, has since toured to New York, London, and Tokyo. These performances amounted to a rebirth of the complete *Firebird*, which has been largely replaced in the public's consciousness by George Balanchine's choreography of the orchestral suite, and although Fokine's *Schéhérazade*, the first true creation of the Ballets Russes, had been staged by other companies, its reappearance in the repertory of so major a company as the Kirov amounted to a resurrection.

Repeated viewing of this uncommon evening made it easy to understand why *Chopiniana* (later taken over by Diaghilev and christened *Les sylphides*, forever muddying ballet's waters by causing confusion between it and Bournonville's *La sylphide*) has held its own through the years, but one wonders why *Schéhérazade* and the complete *Firebird* have not. Both were pace-setting works in their day, and *Schéhérazade* had dealt Paris a body blow at its premiere in 1910 with Léon Bakst's wild juxtaposition of colors (orange and pink, clashing with each other and set against emerald and turquoise). And it was *Firebird* the same season that put the name of a young, unknown St. Petersburg composer, Igor Stravinsky, on the world's lips.

Liepa feels part of the reason for the neglect of Fokine in the West was that he remained first of all a Russian choreographer and never tried to adapt himself to American dancing as Balanchine later did. "In Russia," Liepa believes, "he had worked with a special kind of dancer who instinctively understood him. This sort of dancer didn't exist in the West. That is why he returned to Russia after the Revolution, but he was unable to remain because of the difficulties of life there and the politics he had to cope with at the theater."

Coming up with a plausible replica of the original production of *Schéhérazade* could not have been easy for Liepa, who worked on the project with Fokine's granddaughter Isabel. Even for a well-informed spectator, it was sometimes difficult to chart accurately where authenticity began and ended in terms of the sets and the choreography. When the work was still new Fokine created two versions of the role of Zorbeide—the first for the dancer and actress Ida Rubinstein, who appeared in the premiere, and the other for Tamara Karsavina and for his own wife, Vera Fokina, both classically trained ballerinas. He later restaged and altered the work for various productions after he left Russia (he died in New York in 1942).

Questions of design were equally problematic, for Bakst created at least four versions of the *Schéhérazade* set. As for *Firebird*, Diaghilev was not entirely happy with Golovin's costumes for the Firebird and the Princess and had Bakst redo both. Furthermore, to save money, he made use of costumes from the production of *Boris Godunov* he had presented in Paris two years before. Eventually Diaghilev ran out of time and money, and Golovin's design for the final scene of *Firebird* was never constructed. This last, missing element Liepa was able to set right.

Fortunately, Liepa was helped by that fact that Fokine's son had made a gift of many of his father's papers, including original materials for *Petrushka*, *Firebird*, and *Schéhérazade*, to St. Petersburg's Performing Arts Library. He was also able to draw on some fifty hours of home movies owned by Isabel, which contain large portions of these three Diaghilev ballets as rehearsed and even danced by Fokine.

It is hardly an exaggeration to suggest that both ballets looked better at the

Mariinsky than they had in Paris. This was not just a matter of Liepa's realization of crucial missing elements, but one of lighting, which today is far more sophisticated, and the fact that the Kirov corps de ballet is superior to that of the Diaghilev company (we have the testimony of Balanchine, Diaghilev's last ballet master, as to the inadequacies of the Ballets Russes corps, as well as that of Anton Dolin).

True, there is no longer a Karsavina to dance the Firebird or a Nijinsky for the Golden Slave (he had initially pleaded for the role of the Firebird). But one would have to be hard-hearted not to be grateful for Makhalina's Zorbeide and Asylmuratova's Firebird on the same evening, or Ruzimatov as the Golden Slave and Liepa as the Prince. Classical dancing does not get better than this today, and these artists were the cream at the Kirov during my year there.

At later performances Zorbeide was danced exceptionally by Liepa's sister, Ilze, from the Bolshoi (she was far more sensuous than the Kirov ballerinas who danced the role and more in the mode of Ida Rubinstein), while the Firebird was alternately and superbly performed by the Georgian ballerina Irma Nioradze and the Mariinsky's shining young star, Anastasia Volochkova. In addition, there was a notable Golden Slave from another impressive newcomer, Nikita Shcheglov, and a fine Prince from the character dancer Dmitri Korneev.

More Fokine could be seen across town at the Maly (or Mussorgsky) Theater, the city's second home for opera and dance, which offered a revival of *Petrushka* in a replica of Benois's original set. Although it was a shoestring effort, it did give further credence to the idea that a full-scale Fokine revival might just be around the corner. Of course, the star turns he created for Pavlova (*The Dying Swan*) and Nijinsky (*Le spectre de la rose*) are always with us, and at the Mariinsky I saw the former danced by Uliana Lopatkina and the latter by Zhanna Ayupova and Ruzimatov. Neither Fokine's *Egyptian Nights* nor his *Papillons* was danced while I was in St. Petersburg, though both are in the company's repertory. But it was possible during the season to experience the fiery Polovtsian Dances he devised for Borodin's *Prince Igor* (and which Diaghilev also poached for Paris), as well as Fokine's last Mariinsky work, the dances for Glinka's *Ruslan and Ludmila*.

In October the Mariinsky offered its first performances of the season of two bedrock pieces of repertory—Petipa's irresistible *La bayadère* and that most exemplary of all his ballets, *The Sleeping Beauty*. The marvelous, ritualistic *Bayadère* has been aptly described by the critic Arlene Croce as "a poem about dancing and remembrance and time." It was virtually unknown in the West until the Kirov toured it to America on its first visit in 1961, and later its famous Kingdom of the Shades scene became part of the repertory of both the Royal Ballet and the American Ballet Theater. (I remember well the ABT production with first Rudolf Nureyev and later Mikhail Baryshnikov.)

Bayadère amounts to a journey into the past, for the company still uses sets from early in the last century. And while Petipa would easily recognize them, he would surely be taken aback to see today's costumes. Pavlova was demurely covered, but Lopatkina and those who followed her in the role of Nikiya—Makhalina and Asylmuratova—exposed a good deal of flesh, from their bare arms to their bare midriffs. Several choreographic elements might have surprised him even more, however—the role of Solor, as expanded and intensified by Vakhtung Chabukiani; the addition of a new character, the Golden Idol, and his virtuoso solo, created and first danced by Nikolai Zubkovsky; and the pas de deux between Gamzatti and Solor in which Gamzatti abandons her character shoes for a pair of slippers that allow her to go *en pointe*. It was Petipa's concept that Gamzatti should remain with both feet firmly on the ground while Nikiya reaches upward and symbolically toward more spiritual heights.

Petipa surely would have been dismayed to see that his final act and its apotheosis had been done away with (Makarova restored both in her London production, as have a few other theaters in Russia) and that the current Kirov production ends in the Kingdom of the Shades. This means, of course, that Nikiya's dance at the wedding festivities for Gamzatti and Solor is no longer a flashback—it is not a ghost that appears but a flesh-and-blood character who threatens the union of the prince and princess. Even so, this production as a whole exudes more of the atmosphere of the days when the Mariinsky was the home to the Imperial Ballet than do many others in the company's repertory.

The Sleeping Beauty was still being danced in 1995 in a revised version staged by Konstantin Sergeiev in 1952, which made extensive cuts and alterations in the choreography and included a new version of the prologue. Later, Vinogradov made further emendations in an attempt to make its choreography purer. This remained the official house version until a new production in 1999, which was based on a notation of the ballet by Vladimir Stepanov made at the turn of the century. The same source was used by Sergei Diaghilev for his 1921 *Sleeping Beauty* and later by England's Royal Ballet. Both these were staged by Nikolai Sergeiev, who had spirited Stepanov's notebooks out of Russia.

Taking this important source material (now housed in the Harvard Theater Collection) as the bible for the 1999 production, the dancer and choreographer Sergei Vikharev scrapped the Sergeiev-Vinogradov version in an attempt to regain a sense of the original—not just the dance pieces themselves, but also the ballet's extravagant mime scenes. This new production also attempted to recreate the spirit if not the letter of work's original decor and costumes. When *The Sleeping Beauty* was new in 1890, it was a source of profound inspiration to Benois, Diaghilev, and others of that clique, as it was to the young Stravinsky and his future artistic partner, Balanchine. A passion for this seminal piece remained with all of these men throughout their lives as a standard and a beacon. Today, its appearance on a poster outside the Mariinsky always ensures a sold-out house.

Balanchine, who was trained in St. Petersburg, remarked in his conversations with the Russian critic Solomon Volkov, "It is the best of the old ballets, second only to *Giselle*. Petipa was a wizard; he was the first ballet master to realize that . . . Tchaikovsky was a genius. That wasn't so easy: the composer was still around, the public didn't like him, the critics didn't like him. But Petipa surmised it, and he guessed that because the music of *Sleeping Beauty* was so lush and brilliant he should build his choreography on movement *en dehors*. . . . Petipa created 'the Tchaikovsky style' in ballet.

"No one knows anymore how to do *Sleeping Beauty* the right way. All over the world ballet companies do it horribly, because they don't understand it at all. In Russia at the Mariinsky Theater, *Sleeping Beauty* was done magnificently. The curtain went up, on stage there were lots of people, all dressed in opulent costumes by Konstantin Korovin; in our day dancers were dressed well, even we children were costumed beautifully. The waltz with garlands was begun by thirty-two couples, then, as Petipa conceived it, sixteen pairs of children would appear. The men lined up in corridors, and we children danced inside these moving corridors, while the dancers held the garlands over us. Then the men left the stage. They carried the garlands, the ladies followed, and after them came we children with baskets in our hands. The audience went wild.

"When they prepared the premiere of *Sleeping Beauty* at the Mariinsky, they spent fifty thousand rubles on the costumes alone—an enormous sum! And what stage effects and magical tricks! It was a grand *féerie*. *Sleeping Beauty* must be an extravagant spectacle. . . . In Russia, if I were in favor there, I could do it well; they wouldn't stint on this. But here, no one understands Tchaikovsky. It's music of such nobility! But they don't care. Because they don't know a thing about French or German fairy tales or about Russian music. Whatever you do is good enough for them. And if you do it better, they won't even understand that it's better."

One evening, after a performance of *The Sleeping Beauty*, Balanchine was part of a group of children who were presented to the imperial family. In later life he remembered the event clearly: "Everyone thinks the royal box at the Mariinsky is the one in the middle. Actually the czar's [personal] box was on the side. . . . It had a separate entrance, a special, large stairway, and a separate foyer. When you came in, it was like entering a colossal apartment: marvelous chandeliers and the walls covered with light blue cloth.

"The emperor sat there with his entire family. . . . The Czar was not tall. The Czarina was a very tall, beautiful woman. The grand princesses, Nicholas' daughters, were also beauties. The Czar had protruding, light-colored eyes, and he rolled his Rs. If he said, 'Well, how are you?' we were supposed to click our heels and reply, 'Highly pleased, Your Imperial Majesty!" We were given chocolate in silver boxes, wonderful ones! And the mugs were exquisite porcelain, with light blue lyres and the imperial monogram."

The designs for *Sleeping Beauty* prior to the 1999 overhauling were the work of Sergei Virsaladze, while Sergeiev's staging was kept fresh during my time in St. Petersburg in the main by the former Kirov prima ballerina Ninel Kurgapkina. The first performance during the 213th season was the 786th at the house since its premiere in 1890. On my last night at the Mariinsky, I witnessed the 790th performance. I saw all but one of the intervening ones, and each time the effect the work produced was nothing less than miraculous.

A particularly cherished memory was watching the exquisite Volochkova graduate from the role of the Lilac Fairy, which she danced early in the season at the age of nineteen, to the leading role of Aurora, which she danced at the last performance, just after she had turned twenty. The choreography, particularly in the first act, can vary depending on the availability of the youngsters from the Vaganova Academy. But with or without children, it remains the most evocative and poetic dance experience imaginable. Of all the classical ballets in the repertory, it is the richest, the most formal, and the warmest. It is a work that will rightly always be intimately associated with the Kirov, and one the company dances with special pride, luster, and purity.

There is one aspect of ballet at the Kirov, however, that bothers anyone with Western eyes and experience, and that is allowing—and blatantly encouraging—applause during the coda of a pas de deux, which breaks this climactic section into separate pieces. This happened time and again not only in *Sleeping Beauty* and *Bayadère*, but also in other standard pieces such as *Don Quixote* and *Swan Lake*. But Liepa reminded me that this was a convention dating from imperial times, and Fokine's attempt to do away with this practice in his ballets was one of the reasons Petipa was preferred to Fokine.

"You should be fascinated and grateful to have a chance to experience ballet as it was received in the great days of Mariinsky a century years ago," Liepa admonished me. "At that time the ballerina was queen, and the czar and the public wanted to see her bow after her thirty-two *fouettés*. No one really cared about the man and his variation. In fact, at that time there was not always a variation for the man. Ballet was more a social event than an artistic one a hundred years ago, and the response of the audience to *Sleeping Beauty* or *Swan Lake* at the Kirov today is much more what Tchaikovsky knew and expected than is the case when his ballets are performed in England or America."

Watching the Kirov at work night after night, I began mentally comparing its style with that of the Bolshoi, as well as with those of dance companies in the West. One evening I discussed these questions with Liepa. He was trained at the Bolshoi and spent half a decade with the Kirov, so he has an insider's view of both companies and their differing styles. He summed them up with an analogy: "There is a saying that the Kirov is the black caviar of dance, and the Bolshoi is the red. Personally, I would say the Kirov is cool, the Bolshoi hot. The Kirov is Russian, the Bolshoi is Soviet. Dancers at the Bolshoi are allowed more freedom of movement in order to make a dance step or gesture more exciting. If I made a gesture on stage in Moscow it would be a big one. At the Kirov it would be less. Yet, it would be fair to say that the Bolshoi dances an adaptation of the Kirov style. After all, [Leonid] Lavrovsky and Grigorovich were trained at the Kirov and spent their formative years there before coming to Moscow, where they developed a more heroic style.

"In my time in the Bolshoi there were about 300 dancers in the company, where here at the Kirov we have about 250. What these dancers share in common is the ability to feel the music they dance. Russian dancers never count. I was so surprised when I went to dance with the American Ballet Theater to find the dancers there counting all the time. They couldn't believe that I didn't count, that I simply felt the music—even in a Stravinsky-Balanchine ballet. This is one of the big differences between dancing in the East and in the West. When a Russian dancer hears music, he begins to fly with it. It is his soul that is dancing. In fact, he develops a sensory feeling for the music that lets him know instinctively when a peak is coming. Because of this, he is in the right position at the right time. A non-Russian who counts, ironically, is not always where he should be and does not give the same sort of illusion of flying. In the West, when you have an accent like 'ta-TA,' a dancer there tends to go down, where a Russian will go up. The big difference for me is that American dancers do not dance from the inside, like the dancers in the Kirov, but from the outside. To me, they are not feeling anything.

"I also think people born in Russia, and especially in St. Petersburg, are different from those born elsewhere, because they have a spiritual union with the earth. This is why so many of us who could stay in the West and make a nice life there come back here. There is something in this land of ours, for all its troubles, that we cannot get anywhere else and that is essential to our lives.

"When I decided to dance at the Kirov in the fall of 1990 as a guest—Vinogradov asked me to do *Spectre de la rose* as part of an evening in homage to Nijinsky —my agent told me I was crazy. 'Why are you going back to Russia,' he asked, 'when you could go to Chicago for ten performances of the *Nutcracker* at $10,000 a performance?' But for me the Kirov date was more important, and my instincts were right, for after *Spectre* Vinogradov asked me if I would like to be part of the company. This had never happened before. Kirov dancers had gone to the Bolshoi, but no Bolshoi-trained dancer had ever joined the Kirov.

"Vinogradov also told me that he would like to have me for the first performances of his new version of *Petrushka*, but I told him I had a contract for the next season with ABT. 'Well,' he said, 'it's up to you,' and we left it at that. From the Kirov I went to dance *Giselle* at La Scala at New Year's with Carla Fracci, and during those performances I had a few days off. With a friend I rented a car, and we drove to Venice, which I wanted to see in the snow. While we were there, my friend took me to the cemetery where Diaghilev is buried. We went early in the morning; there was no one there. I began dancing *Spectre de la rose* at his tomb. You probably think this is crazy. It was winter, I was in a heavy coat, but I danced. I didn't think about it, I just did it. It was at that moment that I decided, 'I am going back to the Kirov instead of to ABT.' But how? There was a contract to honor.

"I got to New York three days late, and the manager of ABT, Jane Hermann, was furious with me. 'You missed an important rehearsal for the gala that marks our fiftieth year,' she said. 'You cannot do this to us.'

" 'What is the problem?' I asked. 'It was *Sleeping Beauty*. I don't need to rehearse this.'

" 'Then we don't need you,' she said.

"That was it. In two weeks I was back in St. Petersburg, and this became my company, the place where I want most to be—to teach, to dance, to stage operas. My goal here is to make a standard that is higher, so that the person who follows me has an opportunity to then make the standard even higher. This way the theater remains alive and grows."

Although Liepa joined the Kirov at its top echelon and became one of the company's most cultivated dancers, the most popular remained Farukh Ruzimatov, and his first appearance of the 1995–96 season was at a Mariinsky gala, where he danced like a fevered apparition in a solo piece created by Maurice Béjart, *The Death of the Poet*, set to the Adagietto from Mahler's Fifth Symphony.

No question about it, Ruzimatov is the real thing when it comes to projecting star qualities. He is animalistic, lithe, and mesmerizing, with a face as mobile and expressive as his body. He danced this piece several more times during the season, and each time it was a wrenching experience, marking him as an artist to be reckoned with. He was less successful in purely romantic repertory like *Giselle*, although he could be a delight in an exotic piece like *Bayadère*. Other wonderful moments during the evening were the exceptional young baritone Vasili Gerello tossing off Figaro's "Largo al factotum" from *The Barber of Seville* and Julia Makhalina partnered by Alexander Kurkov in the pas de deux from the last act of *Don Quixote*.

It was at this gala that I realized the matter of our seats was far from permanently resolved. Box 14, it seems, had long been regarded as virtually the private property of one of Malkov's assistants, who used it for his friends and often sold it for his profit. He was hardly pleased to see Myron and me there night after night. About ten minutes before the curtain was due to go up for the gala, this officious official appeared with the head usher in tow and demanded that we move to other seats. I refused, knowing that if I gave in once it would be the first of many times. The man grew red in the face and louder in his demands, until Myron, in what was obviously less than cordial Russian vernacular, told him to stop bothering us. As the house lights dimmed, he had no choice but to comply, but the box that evening was crammed to overflowing.

This was the first of many such encounters that included people waving in our faces tickets that they had purchased and that bore our seat numbers. This increasingly unpleasant duel of wits would continue literally to our last week in St. Petersburg. After we lodged protest after protest with Gergiev and Katia, it was Myron who finally came up with a way to ease the situation. It is his contention that if you want something done in Russia you avoid the upper echelons; the women in this matriarchal society—the *babushkas*—control most things. Quietly he went to the box office and had a word with the woman in charge there. With a winning smile, he explained our problem and asked that she set aside the tickets for our two seats and sell them to no one. It seemed to work, or at least it did for weeks at a stretch.

Two nights later came the lowest point of my year at the Mariinsky—another *Salome*. What drew me to the performance were a soprano and a conductor new to me: Svetlana Volkova and Leonid Korchmar. Both were incompetent. The singing and the orchestra's playing were so rhythmically lax that the music had little shape or sense. The Salome barely knew the notes and faked many passages, as well as omitting phrases and certain high notes. It was grim. These two evenings were among the first I spent back at the Mariinsky after a quick trip to New York for the Met's new *Queen of Spades*, conducted by Gergiev. That night in New York in late October 1995 had been an alien evening for me, for I had grown so accustomed to the sort of sound Gergiev draws from the Kirov orchestra that something seemed amiss at the Met.

It wasn't, of course; it was just different. While the playing of the Met's orchestra was beautiful, precise, and professional, it lacked that hot-to-the-touch character of the Kirov's brass, timpani, and strings. Nor did the Met's musicians play with the sense of propulsion, the 100-percent-plus the Kirov Orchestra gives Gergiev night in and night out. The production was a grave disappointment and a far cry from the satisfying one at the Kirov, with its vivid evocation of scenes of familiar gardens and streets in St. Petersburg.

But there was no way the Mariinsky could match the overall impact of the Met's brilliant cast, which brought the Met debuts of the Kirov's Nikolai Putilin and Ludmila Filatova, as well as that of the baritone Dmitri Hvorostovsky (although he is not a Kirov artist, he has become identified with the company through his Philips-Kirov-Gergiev recordings). Where it could easily be argued that Vladimir Galuzin is the equal of Ben Heppner, who sang Herman at the Met, the Mariinsky has no soprano who is the equal of Karita Mattila, the Met's Lisa. The evening also drew an enormous amount of emotional impact from the farewell performance in America of the late Leonie Rysanek, an artist of Callas-like dimensions who was saying goodbye in the cameo part of the old Countess. No one knew at the time that she was fatally ill. She died three years later.

My longing for the unique sound of the Kirov Orchestra under Gergiev's direction was soon to be fulfilled as I left St. Petersburg to accompany the musicians and their maestro to Japan. The orchestra's first tour of that music-loving country would prove to be an experience to revel in, and it remains among the richest and longest-lasting memories of my year with the company.

CHAPTER FIVE

Nápravník and the Imperial Opera

A LEXANDER III ascended the throne in 1881 following the assassination of his father. Like his czarina, the Danish-born Maria Fedorovna, Alexander was fond of the arts, and the new czar committed a vast amount of funds to the Mariinsky and to other Imperial Theaters. He also provided an enormous boost to native opera in 1882 when he did away with the crown monopoly on theaters. This opened the doors for the formation of several remarkable private opera companies, like the one created by the music-loving millionaire Savva Mamontov in Moscow. Mamontov financed productions of adventurous new operatic works that did not find a welcome elsewhere.

Solomon Volkov, in his stirring cultural history of St. Petersburg, gives a clear idea of the extent of the czar's involvement in the running of his theaters, particularly the Mariinsky: "Every spring [he] personally approved the repertoire for the opera and ballet, often making significant changes; he did not miss a single dress rehearsal in his theaters. The emperor was involved in all the details of new productions—and not just from whim or pleasure; his motivations were also political. He knew that the imperial theaters . . . were the mirror of the monarchy; the brilliant and opulence of their productions reflected the majesty of his reign. . . . [His] Italo-Franco preferences [in repertory] reflected not only the sovereign's tastes but Russia's political orientation at the time. . . . Of the Russian composers, Tchaikovsky had long been a favorite of Alexander III. Knowing that, we can more easily understand why the emperor was rather hostile toward the music of the Mighty Five, a seemingly inconsistent position for a Russian nationalist."

The year after Alexander came to power, Igor Stravinsky was born in the nearby town of Oranienbaum, where his parents had a summer home. His father, Feodor, was a leading bass at the Mariinsky, and the composer grew up in an apartment building opposite the Mariinsky's stage door. He had his first operatic experiences in the Mariinsky, and it was his belief, expressed in his book *Exposi-*

tions and Developments, that "the operatic season was far more interesting than the symphonic."

While *Don Giovanni* and *The Marriage of Figaro* were the sum of Mozart at the time, Stravinsky recalled performances of bel canto operas such as *The Barber of Seville, Norma,* and *Don Pasquale.* Of Verdi, he heard *La traviata, Il trovatore, Rigoletto, Aida,* and *Otello.* He felt that "Verdi was always a controversial subject in St. Petersburg. Tchaikovsky admired him, but the Rimsky group did not. When I spoke admirably of Verdi to Rimsky, he would look at me as Boulez might if I suggested playing my *Scènes de ballet* at Darmstadt."

Stravinsky remembered the most popular non-Russian operas of the day to be *The Merry Wives of Windsor* (in which he often saw his father perform), *Manon, The Bartered Bride, Der Freischütz, Carmen, Cavalleria rusticana,* and *Pagliacci,* along with three scores by Giacomo Meyerbeer—*Les huguenots, L'africaine,* and *Le prophète.* Most of Wagner's mature operas (except *Parsifal,* which would not reach the Mariinsky until 1997) were given, and it seems that *Tristan* was a particular favorite of Nicholas II.

"The livelier and more exciting opera productions were of works of the Russian school, however," Stravinsky continued, "Glinka's operas above all, but also Dargomizhsky's, Rimsky's, Tchaikovsky's, Borodin's, and Mussorgsky's. I heard *Boris* many times, of course, not in the original version. Next to it in popularity was *Prince Igor.* (Borodin, incidentally, was a good friend of my father.) The Tchaikovsky operas I remember most clearly were *Eugene Onegin, The Golden Slippers,* and *The Queen of Spades.* . . .

"I must have seen all of Rimsky's operas. At any rate I remember seeing *Sadko, Mlada, The Snow Maiden, Mozart and Salieri, Christmas Night, Kitezh, Czar Saltan, Pan Voyevoda,* and *The Golden Cockerel.* . . . [The latter] had become a rallying point for students and liberals because of its having been banned several times by the czarist censor; the performance[,] when it actually did materialize, was not in the Mariinsky, but in a private theater in the Nevsky Prospect. . . .

"The star among the local St. Petersburg conductors was [Eduard] Nápravník. As the Nápravníks and the Stravinskys lived in adjoining apartment houses, I saw the eminent conductor almost every day, and I knew him well. My father had sung in his opera *Dubrovsky,* and we had been quite friendly with him at the time. As with most professional conductors, however, Nápravník's culture was primitive and his taste undeveloped. A small, hard man with a good ear and a good memory, he was absolute boss of the Mariinsky Theater.

"His entrance on the concert stage or in the opera pit was very grand indeed, but more exciting still was the act in which he removed his left glove. (Conductors still wore white gloves then, to improve the visibility of their beats—or so they said; Nápravník's left hand was employed chiefly in adjusting his pince-nez, however.) No ecdysiast at the moment of the final fall was ever regarded more attentively than Nápravník as he peeled this glove."

Stravinsky had been kinder to Nápravník earlier in his 1936 autobiography, writing that "in spite of his austere conservatism, he was the type of conductor which even today I prefer to all others. [There were] certainty and unbending rigor in the exercise of his art, complete contempt for all affectation, and showy effects alike in the presentation of the work; not the slightest concession to the public; and added to that, iron discipline, mastery of the first order, an infallible ear and memory, and, as a result, perfect clarity and objectivity in the rendering . . . what better can one imagine."

Born in what was then Bohemia in 1839, Nápravník was brought to St. Petersburg to conduct an orchestra of serfs at the Yusupov palace. It was by chance that he joined the music staff of the Mariinsky Theater: a pianist failed to show up for a performance of *Ruslan and Ludmila*, and Nápravník was spotted in the audience and drafted into the pit, where he sight-read the part. The theater's chief conductor at the time, Konstantin Liadov, later hired Nápravník as a répétiteur after Alexander II freed the serfs, and the Yusupov orchestra was disbanded. In 1867 Nápravník advanced to became Liadov's assistant.

During this same period the Mariinsky gave the first of its many performances of *Lohengrin*, the one Wagnerian opera that would persist well into the Soviet era. Liadov presided over *Lohengrin*, and Rimsky-Korsakov remembers attending it with Balakirev, Cui, Mussorgsky, and Dargomizhsky. "*Lohengrin* called forth our utter scorn," Rimsky writes in his autobiography, "and an inexhaustible torrent of humor, ridicule and venous caviling from Dargomizhsky." When Liadov retired in 1868, the year of the Mariinsky's first *Lohengrin* ("He was killing himself with drink," Rimsky observed), Nápravník replaced him. His reign would last nearly half a century. During his time at the theater Nápravník conducted some 4,000 performances of operas that ranged from Gluck's *Orphée et Euridice* to Wagner's *Ring*, and he was in charge of eighty premieres, half of which were of Russian operas. Among these were Mussorgsky's *Boris Godunov*; Rimsky-Korsakov's *The Maid of Pskov*, *May Night*, and *The Snow Maiden*; Tchaikovsky's *The Maid of Orleans* (which was dedicated to Nápravník), *The Queen of Spades*, and *Iolanthe*; Rubinstein's *The Demon*; and Nápravník's own *The People of Nizhni Novgorod* and *Dubrovsky*.

Nizhni Novgorod had its first performance in the winter of 1869, soon after Nápravník was appointed director of the Mariinsky. At the same time Nápravník was rehearsing Cui's *William Ratcliff* for its premiere (Cui would later be represented at the theater by the premieres of two further operas—*A Prisoner in the*

Caucasus, 1883, and *The Saracen*, 1899). As Cui was a leading critic in St. Petersburg, the side-by-side premieres of *Nizhni Novgorod* and *William Ratcliff* placed him, according to Rimsky, in "an awkward position." Afraid to write about the Nápravník opera, which he anticipated disliking, at a time when his own opera was being prepared by the conductor, he begged Rimsky to handle the assignment for him. Rimsky-Korsakov agreed and produced a review "smacking of Cui himself in style and method. Expressions like 'Mendelssohnian leaven' and 'bourgeois ideas' and the like were there aplenty. . . . Naturally it spoiled my relations with Nápravník for the rest of my life." Although he didn't like the conductor's music, Rimsky attended rehearsals for *William Ratcliff* and "marveled at [Nápravník's] ear, his executive ability, his familiarity with the score."

But it was the premiere of *Boris Godunov* that stands out as a watershed not only in the life of the Mariinsky but in the struggle to establish an authentic and meaningful school of Russian opera. It was also an event that has provoked heated debate ever since over Mussorgsky's ideas and ideals concerning the score. The original version of the opera was finished in 1869; it contained neither the Polish act nor the Kromy Forest scene and ended with the death of Boris.

Before the score was completed, Mussorgsky had spoken to Stepan Gedeonov, then the director of the Imperial Theaters, about a staging of the opera. He was told nothing was possible for the upcoming 1869–70 season, but Gedeonov said he would arrange for Mussorgsky to play the work for the selection committee; if they approved it, a place for it might be found in the following season. But when the committee auditioned it, the opera was literally blackballed. Queried about this decision, Nápravník answered, "What sort of opera is it without a female element? Undoubtedly, Mussorgsky has great talent; let him add another scene, then *Boris* would be acceptable."

But there was more to the matter than simply the lack of a heroine, according to Rimsky-Korsakov. He felt that "the freshness and originality of the music nonplused the honorable committee . . . much of [its] fault finding was simply ridiculous. Thus, the double basses *divisi* playing chromatic thirds in the accompaniment of Varlaam's second song were entirely too much for [Giovanni] Ferraro, the double bass player [and a committee member], who could not forgive the composer this device."

In preparing his second version, Mussorgsky not only added the character of Marina and the Polish act, but also substantially rewrote the music for the scene with Boris in his Kremlin apartment, adding the Nurse's song, a new version of Boris's monologue, and the concluding hallucination scene. Finally, he cut the scene before St. Basil and substituted the one in the Kromy Forest, which was eventually placed after Boris's death. (Nearly a half century later, when Mussorgsky was being trumpeted as a prophet of socialism, the official line in the Soviet Union among scholars was that the second version of the opera was feeble and had been forced on the composer by bureaucrats of the Imperial Theater system, an idea that persists in some quarters today.)

Following the reworking of the *Boris*, there were still two other hurdles to be surmounted. One was an edict by Nicholas I that forbade the portrayal of a czar on the stage. Only the current czar, Alexander II, could make an exception. This he did in April 1872. The other was the approval—again—of the theater committee. They were given the new score, which, interestingly enough, still contained those controversial contrabass thirds, and some believe it was rejected for a second time, though the point continues to be debated among scholars. Whatever the truth of the matter, it was finally approved (although provisionally, as the orchestration was not completed) in May 1872.

In 1873 the Mariinsky staged two excerpts from the opera—the inn scene and part of the new Polish act—and their success led to the opera's being scheduled for its premiere the next season on 8 February 1874. Nápravník held eighteen rehearsals; the cast was strong and the sets and costumes effective (they had been recycled from a 1870 production of the Pushkin play on which Mussorgsky's libretto was based). The evening was a benefit for the mezzo-soprano Julia Platonova, who created Marina, and all the tickets were sold. Mussorgsky's contract with the Mariinsky called for a royalty payment per performance of a tenth of two-thirds of the box office receipts. For the premiere, that amounted to about $99 (in contrast, Verdi had received nearly $12,000 for writing *La forza del destino*).

Cuts were made, including the scene in Pimen's cell and other pages throughout the score, and the Kromy Forest scene was played as a separate act, changes Nápravník got Mussorgsky to agree to on the basis that they detracted from the score's effectiveness. But as Caryl Emerson and Robert Oldani point out in their detailed study of the opera's history, "Simply put, the uncut *Boris* was too long for Nápravník's audience of the 1870s. In its final form . . . the opera lasts nearly three hours and fifteen minutes, without intermissions." The cuts reduced it by an hour.

Joining Platonova was Ivan Melnikov as Boris, Feodor Kommissarzhevsky as the false Dimitri, and Osip Petrov as Varlaam. Platonova was praised for "the refined musical taste of her phrasing, the tender nuances of her acting [and] her feminine grace." Melnikov, too, came in for his share of praise: "Melnikov obviously considered his role deeply and in his acting revealed both an extraordinarily subtle comprehension of the role and an enthusiasm that testifies to his great dramatic gifts, which he has never displayed before to such a high degree."

It was Melnikov who introduced into the part a sort of histrionic half-singing, half-speaking of certain lines that later became a norm. According to Ilya Tiumenev, a pupil of Rimsky-Korsakov's, Melnikov "sings scarcely half the time, but speaks and shouts without pitch. . . . One receives the impression not of opera but rather of melodrama, although not bad. What Modest Petrovich might have said of this, I do not know . . . but Boris' part itself, in several places, is delivered in pure, conversational speech."

Evidently the opera had a great popular success, and four performances were all sold out, but the press was disappointing. Hermann Laroache, writing in the newspaper *Golos*, felt that "the overabundance of dissonances and the incompetence in handling vocal parts in *Boris Godunov* reach the point where the listener cannot be sure of the composer's intentions and is unable to distinguish intentional wrong notes from the wrong notes of the performers." Alexander Famintzin in *Musikalnyi Listok* was even harsher: "His resources are represented by a pot of mixed colors, which he tosses indiscriminately into the score with no concern for harmony or elegance of design. This crudity is a perfect proof of the composer's ignorance of the art of music."

But what cut deepest was a long article by Cui that Mussorgsky described to a friend as "hateful." The crux of Cui's objections to the score were its "chopped recitative and looseness of musical discourse, resulting in the effect of a potpourri. . . . These defects are the consequence of immaturity, [of an] indiscriminating, self-complacent, hasty method of composition." Although Tchaikovsky did not go public with his opinion of the opera as Cui had, his reaction was even more devastating. In a letter to his brother Modest, he wrote, "I have made a thorough study of *Boris Godunov* [and] I consign it from the bottom of my heart to the devil; it is the most insipid and base parody on music."

Despite its unhappy critical reception, *Boris* returned to the Mariinsky's stage the next season for eight performances, and in the 1876–77 season it was revived, although minus the Kromy Forest scene. The theater gave *Boris* again after Mussorgsky's death on 16 March 1881, but the following season it had only a single performance, after which it was officially dropped from the Mariinsky's repertory. There was an attempt in 1888 to revive the opera, but Alexander III personally struck *Boris* from the theater's proposed repertory list.

It took a new century and a new version created by Rimsky-Korsakov for the opera to regain a foothold in the company's repertory. In 1908, Diaghilev presented *Boris* for the first time in the West—a production at the Paris Opéra with Feodor Chaliapin in the title role. Rimsky's score was used. Rimsky later prepared other versions of *Boris* in which he restored more of Mussorgsky's original material and ideas, but it was in his first version that the opera reentered the Mariinsky's repertory. This is not the place to delve deeply into the opera's complex performance history, but it should be noted that in 1928, the Mariinsky took another look at the work and came up with a hybrid version of the composer's 1869 and 1874 scores, and after 1960 the theater used almost exclusively a version prepared by Shostakovich until Gergiev introduced the critical edition prepared by David Lloyd-Jones. Finally in 1997, Gergiev conducted and recorded Mussorgsky's 1869, seven-scene original for the first time at the Mariinsky, although with the inclusion of some 1874 emendations, repaying an historic debt that was more than 125 years old.

The season before *Boris* was introduced, the Mariinsky offered the premiere of Rimsky-Korsakov's first opera, *The Maid of Pskov*, also known as *Ivan the Terrible*. (Rimsky had actually been represented at the Mariinsky the season before with the premiere of Dargomizhsky's *The Stone Guest*. The score, which had been left unfinished, was completed by Cui and orchestrated by Rimsky-Korsakov.) *Pskov* would be followed by fourteen other Rimsky operas, seven of which would be premiered by the Mariinsky. Not surprisingly, Nápravník was opposed to presenting *Pskov* but bowed to the wishes of the new manager of the Mariinsky, Nikolai Lukashevich, a man well disposed toward Rimsky and his circle.

During the rehearsals Rimsky found "Nápravník impassive . . . but his disapproval made itself felt." Still, Rimsky admitted that he "worked magnificently, pouncing upon all errors of the copyists as well as my own slips of the pen." The premiere took place on 13 January 1873, with some of the leading singers who would appear in *Boris*'s premiere—Osip Petrov, who sang Ivan the Terrible, and Julia Platonova, who sang Olga. It had ten performances that season.

Pskov was followed seven years later with the premiere of *May Night*. Again the conductor was Nápravník, and the scenery was recycled from sets created for Tchaikovsky's *Vakula the Smith*, which had been taken out of the Mariinsky's repertory after its world premiere in 1876. But, as Rimsky put it, "*The Maid of Pskov* received more praise, more censure, and more success than *May Night*." In 1882 Rimsky's next opera, *The Snow Maiden*, received its first performance. It too was conducted by Nápravník and featured Feodor Stravinsky as Grandfather Frost. Nápravník insisted on a number of cuts, which Rimsky accepted (he had vehemently opposed the cuts proposed for *Pskov*); but he was hardly happy about them and felt that many sections of the opera were "disfigured." Again he found Nápravník to be "exacting and cool" in the rehearsals and "magnificent" in the performances. In the press there were "reproaches for my lack of dramatic action, for the poverty of melodic inventiveness which manifested itself in my partiality for borrowing folk tunes, reproaches for insufficient originality."

The Snow Maiden was followed by three other Rimsky operas—*Mlada* (1892), *Christmas Eve* (1895), and *Servilia* (1902)—all little known today. The year after the premiere of *The Snow Maiden*, a committee at the Mariinsky was asked to consider for production Mussorgsky's last opera, *Khovanshchina*, which Rimsky-Korsakov had completed after the composer's death. It was rejected without debate, and the first performance fell to an amateur company in St. Petersburg the next year. The opera did not reach the Mariinsky until 1911, when Albert Coates conducted it with a brilliant cast that included Feodor Chaliapin as Dosifei, Ivan Ershov as Golitsin, and Evgenia Zbrujeva as Marfa.

The time of *Mlada*'s first performance was a period at the Mariinsky, according to Rimsky, when the theater "lacked a sufficient number of rehearsals. [When] the orchestra men are all on hand . . . the singers sing half-voice; now orchestra and singers function properly, but the scenery is lacking, because there is to be a performance in the evening, and there is no time to make the change; again, the scenery is in place but the lighting is out of order, or the rehearsal is held to the accompaniment of a piano, and so on. . . . Things at the Russian Opera . . . everlastingly shape themselves in such a manner that time was . . . lacking. Singers [were] constantly falling ill and [the] changes of repertory necessitated . . . innumerable extra rehearsals of old operas. Eternal haste, five performances a week, a stage that is not always free for rehearsals, being often occupied by the ballet—all these take time from quiet and serious rehearsals, such as are required for proper artistic execution. . . .

"Above all this there often reigns at the Mariinsky Theater a spirit of presumptuousness, routine, and weariness, in conjunction with fine technique and experience. Singers, chorus, and orchestra all consider themselves first *hors concours*, and, secondly, experienced artists . . . who are weary of everything [but] nevertheless feel they will manage quite well, even though it is not worth while to tire oneself too much for it. This spirit often crops out through all outward courtesy and even cordiality, when theatrical impresarios, warmly pressing the composer's hand, tell him how much pain they have taken on his behalf . . . nobody can so quickly grow tired, fall into routine and think he has fathomed all mysteries as do the native Russians and with them those foreigners who have grown up with us in Russia."

Rimsky-Korsakov's final Mariinsky premiere was a work many see as his finest achievement—*The Legend of the Invisible City of Kitezh and the Maiden Fevronia*. It was first given at the Mariinsky on 20 February 1907, conducted by Felix Blumenfeld, and featured Maria Kuznetsova as Fevronia, Ershov as Grishka, and Vladimir Kastorsky as the Bard. Wagner's *Parsifal* is sometimes mentioned when *Kitezh* is discussed, and at moments it does exude a similar mystique. But the radiance that emanates from *Kitezh* is as personal as it is moving, and the opera's roots are entirely Russian, with many of its pages recalling the folk elements in *Sadko* (a major Rimsky opera whose premiere was not at the Mariinsky but in Mamontov's private theater in Moscow).

The year after the premiere of *Pskov*, the Mariinsky presented for the first time Tchaikovsky's *The Oprichnik* (earlier the theater had rejected Tchaikovsky's first opera, *The Voyevoda*, because of "the ultramodern direction of its music, slipshod orchestration and unmelodiousness"). Neither *The Oprichnik* nor his next operas, *Vakula the Smith* and *The Enchantress*, lasted long at the Mariinsky or anywhere else (Tchaikovsky, incidentally, conducted the premiere of *The Enchantress* when Nápravník fell ill, and the chief ovations that evening were not for the composer but for Feodor Stravinsky). It was not until *The Maid of Orleans* in 1881 (a work that was long encountered under its French title *Jeanne d'Arc*) that Tchaikovsky truly came into his own as an operatic composer. The premiere of the *Maid* on 25 February 1881, with a cast that included the elder Stravinsky, seems to have been a popular success, but the press, and especially Cui, disliked it. He termed it "sheer banality" and later wrote that it was "a weak work of a fine and gifted musician, ordinary, monotonous, dull, and long, with rare flashes of brighter, vivid music and those are echoes from other operas."

The Moscow premiere of *Mazeppa* in Moscow a year later was followed three days later by the first Mariinsky production. Again Stravinsky was a member of the cast, singing the role of Orlik, along with Melnikov, who sang Kochubei. Moscow also had the professional premiere of *Eugene Onegin*, but when the Mariinsky first staged the opera in 1885, conducted by Nápravník, it was with a revised third act that included more dance—the *écossaires*—added at the request of Ivan Vsevolozhsky, the intendant of the Imperial Theaters.

Onegin and *The Queen of Spades*, both based on works by Pushkin, were Tchaikovsky's supreme operatic achievements. *The Queen of Spades* was a joint collaboration with his brother Modest, who adapted the original short story as a libretto. The idea of making an opera out of Pushkin's gripping tale had came from Vsevolozhsky, and curiously, a young composer named Nikolai Klenovsky was the one originally chosen to set the story to music. Modest had repeatedly urged his brother to write the music. But Tchaikovsky found little interest in the story initially: "It doesn't move me, and I shall only be able to write perfunctorily."

However, when Klenovsky pulled out of the project, Tchaikovsky had a radical change of heart. "A heroic decision," he termed it in a letter to his patron Madame von Meck. In late January 1890 Tchaikovsky arrived in Florence and began work on the score. The music poured out of him at a furious pace; within forty-four days the score was complete. Defending himself against later accusations that the opera was written in too great haste, Tchaikovsky said, "They do not realize that to rush through my work is an essential feature of my character.... The chief thing is to love the work. I have certainly written with love."

The opera was criticized for having "violated" the spirit of Pushkin's tale, in particular by resetting it in the late eighteenth century. In actuality, the brothers were trying to clear away extraneous subplots and strengthen the main story line —essential elements in recasting any book or drama as an opera. Herman, the center of the story's storm, was changed from a cold and calculating gambler to a man torn between his love of cards and his love of Lisa. The old Countess was made more human and vulnerable, and Tchaikovsky decided that Lisa should die in the icy waters of the Neva: "The audience must know what becomes of Lisa. She cannot drop out in the second act."

What seems to have disturbed Pushkinites most was Herman's suicide (in the original story, he spends the rest of his life in an insane asylum). Tchaikovsky's critics felt that if he had to die, at least his death should be ennobled by some grand melody. When Modest raised this point with his brother, Tchaikovsky was adamant about not changing a note. "No doubt it was Figner [Nikolai Figner, the tenor who created Herman] who thought of it; he probably wants something like the final aria in *Lucia di Lammermoor*, with dying gasps and pre-mortal hiccups. This is really impossible!!!"

Yet elsewhere he was kinder. In a letter to the theater's director he wrote, "I know already that Figner will be superb. What a rare artist is this Figner—and what a brilliant exception to the old saying that all tenors are stupid." Later, in another letter, he added, "I was impressed by his quick intelligence and grasp of my ideas. Everything he does matches exactly what I had in mind, answering my wishes to the fullest."

Even granting that the Tchaikovsky brothers sentimentalized Pushkin's gothic story, they were only acting in the name of opera, a form of theater with its own special dictates and needs. Opera, as practiced in the nineteenth century, was scarcely a congenial forum for subtlety. For so pessimistic a man, Tchaikovsky was inordinately pleased with what he had done in *The Queen of Spades*. Writing to his brother when the score was finished, he noted, "Either I am terribly or inexcusably mistaken, or *The Queen of Spades* is a masterpiece.'"

He was not mistaken, although the critics at the time were. Following the premiere on 19 December 1890, the press praised the orchestration but found the music uneven, and they attacked Modest's libretto. But time was on Tchaikovsky's side, and *The Queen of Spades* eventually became a world favorite. It remains indelibly associated with the Mariinsky.

Another Mariinsky premiere was Tchaikovsky's final stage work—the one-act *Iolanthe*, again with a libretto by Modest. To Tchaikovsky, this tale of medieval court life involving knights, dukes, and ladies "captured my imagination but not my heart." Rimsky felt it was "one of Tchaikovsky's feeblest compositions . . . everything in it is unsuccessful—beginning with impudent borrowings . . . and ending with [its] orchestration which in this particular case Tchaikovsky had somehow written topsy-turvy; music suitable for strings had been allotted to wind instruments and vice versa, and hence it occasionally sounds even fantastic in the most unsuitable passages."

Up to a point, Tchaikovsky agreed. "What's most sickening," he told his brother during the composition of *Iolanthe*, "is that I'm beginning to fall into repeating myself and a lot of [the love scene] has come out of *The Enchantress*." For *Iolanthe* Tchaikovsky again had Figner and his Italian-born wife, the soprano Medea Mei (the original Lisa), and they, according to Gennady Kondratyev, the chief stage director at the Mariinsky, "created a furore in the duet and, at the audience's insistence, repeated it." Although *Iolanthe*, which premiered 18 December 1892 on a double-bill with the first performance of the *Nutcracker*, fared much better initially than the ballet, the reverse has come to be the case in modern times.

Two weeks before Tchaikovsky's death the next year, the Mariinsky gave the fiftieth-anniversary performance of *Ruslan and Ludmila*. Igor Stravinsky had good reason never to forget the evening, and not simply because his father was in the cast or because "the Mariinsky was lavishly decorated that night, and pleasantly perfumed. . . . A ceremony and a parade had preceded the performance; poor Glinka, who was only a kind of Russian Rossini, had been Beethovenized and nationally monumented. I watched the performance through my mother's mother-of-pearl lorgnette binoculars. In the first intermission we stepped from our loge into the small foyer behind. . . . Suddenly my mother said to me, 'Igor, look, there is Tchaikovsky.' I looked and saw a man with white hair, large shoulders, and a corpulent back, and this image has remained on the retina of my memory all my life."

Three years before Tchaikovsky died, Borodin's only opera, *Prince Igor*, finally reached the stage. The composer had worked on the score on and off for eighteen years, and it was still unfinished at his death. The task of completing it fell to Rimsky-Korsakov and Alexander Glazunov, then only twenty-one. They not only retouched what existed of the orchestrations, but also scored the balance of the music. Glazunov actually composed much of the third act on the basis of existing sketches. In addition, he reconstructed the overture from memory, having heard Borodin improvise his ideas for it at the piano.

The debate has been long and heated as to where Borodin ends and the others take up. Yet so powerful is the music that emerged from this troika of composers that the validity of *Prince Igor* as a stage work has never been in doubt. Scenes and whole sections of the score have come and gone in various productions through the years (notably the controversial third act, which was omitted at the opera's first performance, given at the Mariinsky on 4 November 1890), but the opera in one form or another has steadfastly held its own in the operatic repertory.

This period, the era of the ascendancy of Russian opera, was also a time of extraordinary singers at the Mariinsky. Among the most prominent were its basses, headed by Feodor Stravinsky. He had joined the theater in 1876 and remained there until his death in 1902, singing 1,235 performances of sixty-four serious and comic roles. He took part in the premieres of Tchaikovsky's *Vakula the Smith*, *The Enchantress*, and *The Maid of Orleans*; Rimsky-Korsakov's *May Night*, *The Snow Maiden*, *Mlada*, and *Christmas Eve*; and Borodin's *Prince Igor*.

Although he was not part of the premiere of *Boris*, Stravinsky later sang Rangoni at the Mariinsky and was Varlaam in the premiere of Rimsky's first revision of the opera, a concert version presented in the conservatory. His non-Russian repertory included Mephistopheles in both Charles Gounod's and Arrigo Boïto's settings of Goethe's *Faust*, and other standard roles such as Marcel in *Les huguenots* and Gessler in *William Tell*. Tchaikovsky had given an inscribed photograph to Stravinsky's father after his portrayal of the Monk in *The Enchantress*, a photo that hangs today in Gergiev's office, and the composer paid a further compliment to the singer in a letter to von Meck: "The best of the singers were [Maria] Slavina and Stravinsky. A unique burst of applause and unanimous approval from the whole audience was evoked by Stravinsky in the second act monologue; his performance should be a pattern for all future productions."

The year Stravinsky made his debut at the Mariinsky was Petrov's final season, and Stravinsky was seen as his logical successor, and he remained the theater's preeminent bass until the arrival of Chaliapin. Where Petrov had been called an "idealist" of the Russian operatic stage, Stravinsky was dubbed the "realist." His voice was considered powerful but not especially beautiful. There is a telegram in Stravinsky's dossier in the Imperial Archives from Vsevolozhsky in 1882 that reads, "Inform the minister and pay attention yourself to the fact that Mr. Stravinsky doesn't have any voice." What prompted this comment is unknown—perhaps it was linked to the fact that a new contract was pending. Whatever the reason, it suggests that Stravinsky's voice was not to every taste. But there is plentiful testimony that he was a strong, convincing figure onstage, and his career at the theater continued up until the year of his death (his contract in 1896, for example, stipulated that he sing thirty performances a season). He celebrated his silver anniversary at the theater in 1901 with a benefit performance of a role for which he was thought to be ideal—Holofernes in Serov's *Judith*. He was only fifty-nine when he died in 1902, and he just missed making recordings (the Russian discs featuring Figner and his wife went on sale the year of Stravinsky's death). His dossier ends on a sad note with a telegram from the theater's director, Vladimir Teliakovsky, to Nicholas II in Livadia: "The outstanding, honored artist Stravinsky died. Due to his long illness when he was unable to sing and did not receive money, his family is now in poor straits. I ask permission to give them the money for the funeral . . . from the opera's budget." The request was granted, as was, later, a pension to his widow.

It has been said that after his first seasons at the Mariinsky (1894–96), Chaliapin chose to be active in Moscow because he did not wish to compete with Stravinsky. Whether this is true or not, he did not rejoin the Mariinsky until 1918, when for a time he also served as its artistic director. Igor Stravinsky remembers Chaliapin as "a man of large musical and theatrical talents [who] at his best was an astonishing performer. I was more impressed by him in *The Maid of Pskov* than in anything else, but Rimsky did not agree. ('What shall I do? I am the author, and he pays absolutely no attention to anything I say.') Chaliapin's bad characteristics began to appear only when he repeated a role too often, as in Boris, for instance, where he became more and more histrionic (there is no Russian equivalent for 'ham') with each performance. Chaliapin was also a gifted storyteller, and . . . I saw him frequently at Rimsky's and listened to his tales with much pleasure. Chaliapin succeeded my father as the leading basso of the Mariinsky Theater, and I remember the performance of *Prince Igor* in which my father explained this succession to the public by a gesture, as he and Chaliapin took their bows together, my father as the Drunkard and Chaliapin as the Prince."

It is difficult today to imagine the almost godlike status of Chaliapin in the world of opera. It has been said that had he been czar instead of Nicholas II, there would have been no Revolution. He dominated his age like a colossus and is considered by connoisseurs to be one of twentieth-century opera's three most influential figures, along with Caruso and Callas. His voice was actually more that of a bass-baritone than a true bass, for he lacked a girth of sound and those black, rolling low notes one heard later in such Russian basses as Mark Reizen. But he was a far greater personality and an actor of astounding variety and depth, one with a gift of willing himself into the skin of the character he was portraying.

Chaliapin was virtually responsible for public awareness of the greatness of *Boris Godunov* in Russia and in the West, from London's Covent Garden to New York's Metropolitan Opera. He was adored on all levels of Russian life, from the man in the street to Nijinsky (who was frequently seen standing in the wings in order to study Chaliapin's performances) and Rachmaninov, and became one of the highest-paid artists in the world. Whether playing a czar or a peasant, an inflamed lover or a sadistic devil, he breathed life into every role he undertook. Often the music was bent unduly by the force of his outsized instincts, but Chaliapin was one of those artists who wrote his own rules and created his own universe.

Unlike today, this was an era of outstanding basses at the Kirov, for in addition to Stravinsky and Chaliapin there were Vladimir Kastorsky and Lev Sibiriakov, to mention only two of the best. But great basses were not the sum total of the Mariinsky's roster. It had its share of outstanding tenors and sopranos as well. For Igor Stravinsky, "Three tenors of the Mariinsky come to my memory: [Leonid] Sobinov, who was light and lyric, an ideal Lensky; Ershov, a 'heroic' tenor, and an outstanding Siegfried (he later sang Fisherman in the Petrograd production of my *Nightingale*); and Nikolai Figner, the friend of Tchaikovsky, and the operatic king of St. Petersburg."

Sobinov, like Chaliapin, was a Russian who forged an international career. His performances at the Mariinsky were only a part of his activities, which took him as far afield as La Scala and Berlin. A wonderful and sensitive artist, he left numerous recordings that testify to his suave singing. It seems that after twenty years on the stage, however, he had put on weight, began having trouble with pitch, and refused to accept the fact that he had sung far beyond what had been his best.

The Mariinsky productions of Wagner's *Ring* cycle and *Tristan* would have been impossible without Ershov. After training in Italy, his career at the theater began in 1895 and lasted until 1929. He was dubbed the "Russian Tamagno," and his stentorian sound was matched by an equally impressive musical imagination and an admirable evenness of production. After his retirement, he founded the opera studio at the city's conservatory. To Levik, Ershov was "a complex of musical nerve, a fount of inspired rhythm, the immovability of marble and the dynamic of the storm, a lava flow of brilliant timbres, rapturous joy and unbearable melancholy . . . and above all, infinite Russian vocal breadth." With Ershov, "Siegmund and Siegfried's cries were of joyous victory and rapturous triumph, Kuterma's howls in *The Invisible City of Kitezh* were full of suffering [and] Hoffmann's [aria] 'Tale of Kleinzach' was full of cunning and ambiguity."

But as Stravinsky noted, the public's favorite was Figner. He had been trained in Italy and there married an Italian mezzo-soprano, Medea Mei, who soon switched to soprano roles. They returned together to St. Petersburg in 1887 and formed a legendary artistic partnership. (The year before, incidentally, both Figners had been part of an Italian opera company touring South America and were singing *Aida* in Rio de Janeiro the night the nineteen-year-old Arturo Toscanini stepped unheralded into the pit to make his debut as a conductor, supposedly at Figner's suggestion.)

Despite his immense popularity, Figner's voice was controversial. It has been described as "strident, with a weak middle register, and an uneven scale," although his recordings are certainly attractive if at times frayed. But what obviously turned the tide in his direction were his uncommon dramatic gifts, which were especially forceful in *The Queen of Spades*. After his retirement in 1907, he was appointed as director of the Narodny Dom Theater (the People's House, a large hall near the

Winter Palace, where opera was given from 1909 until 1923 at prices much lower than those at the Mariinsky).

Stravinsky's list of tenors omitted the name of another major artist, Dmitri Smirnov, no doubt because his career began at the Bolshoi, and it wasn't until 1910, after Stravinsky's departure from Russia, that he transferred to the Mariinsky for seven years. Like Sobinov, he was essentially a lyric tenor who excelled in bel canto operas, and many believed he was Sobinov's equal. The Mariinsky had its abundant share of outstanding baritones as well, among them Ioachim Tartakov (who from 1900 through the October Revolution was the director of the Mariinsky), Alexander Bragin, and George Baklanov.

As for sopranos, Igor Stravinsky recalled "Félia Litvinne, who sang a surprisingly brilliant Brünnhilde, surprising because she had such a tiny mouth; and Maria Kuznetsova, a dramatic soprano who was very appetizing to look at as well as to hear." But there were also Mei, Natalia Ermolenko-Juzhina, Maria Michailova, Evgenia Bronskaya, and Lydia Lipkovska, and to this starry list must be added the greatly admired mezzo-soprano Evgenia Zbrujeva. Levik felt the most illustrious of the women at the Mariinsky was Medea Mei. Of her debut in 1887 as Valentine in *Les huguenots* he wrote, "Her whole appearance was simply staggering—beauty of face, hair, singing, stage movement, and costume. It was an unconventional beauty, but its harmony was exactly right: finely chiseled features, black expressive eyes, . . . and all the languid movement of the south."

There were also occasional guest appearances in St. Petersburg by the Bolshoi's reigning prima donna, Antonina Nezhdanova. One of the most notable was her participation in a gala performance of Glinka's *A Life for the Czar* on 22 February 1913 celebrating 300 years of the Romanov dynasty. She was joined by Ershov, Kastorsky, and Zbrujeva. That evening there were appearances, too, by some of the Mariinsky's most renowned dancers (Pavlova, Kshessinskaya, Preobrazhenskaya, Legat, and Gerdt), and in the finale other outstanding singers took part, including Sobinov, Tartakov, Figner, and Mei.

By the turn of the century the Mariinsky at last had its own productions of *Tristan und Isolde.* A few years later the *Ring* was mounted as well, conducted by Nápravník and then by Emil Cooper, who remained at the Mariinsky until 1923. Later the theater would add *The Flying Dutchman* and *Die Meistersinger.* Other foreign works were being introduced about the same time, such as Giacomo Puccini's *La bohème* and Pietro Mascagni's *Cavalleria rusticana* (both mounted for the Figners); during the 1912–13 season, Richard Strauss's *Elektra* (staged by the influential stage director Vsevolod Meyerhold, with the composer in attendance) and Puccini's *Madame Butterfly* were added to the repertory.

As Nápravník neared the end of his lengthy career, the principal conductor at the Mariinsky came to be Albert Coates. Born in St. Petersburg the same year as Igor Stravinsky of a Yorkshire businessman and a Russian mother, he, too, was a pupil of Rimsky-Korsakov's. After his schooling in England, he became the assistant of Arthur Nikisch (who guest-conducted at the Mariinsky) in Leipzig. In 1910 Coates was engaged to conduct *Siegfried* at the Mariinsky, and in 1917 he was appointed its artistic director. But post-Revolution traumas and widespread famine led to his departure in 1919. He was later acknowledged as one of England's finest pre–World War II musicians and a preeminent conductor of Wagner's operas.

Fred Gaisberg, who, at the turn of the century, worked for what is now the EMI label in England, pioneered the recording of great Russian singers like Chaliapin, Sobinov, and the Figners during the imperial era. "I was recording Chaliapin in our studio in St. Petersburg," he recalls in his biography, "when the exuberant Albert Coates breezed in with, 'Oh, I heard that an English firm was running this show, so I thought I would look in. You don't mind, do you?' In those days he was first conductor at the Imperial Opera House under the eighty-year-old Czech Nápravník, and he stood every chance of becoming a dominating force in the Russian musical world.

"He was a tall magnificent fellow of undisputed genius, with the gift of making staunch and faithful friends. I can see him now conducting *Prince Igor* at the Mariinsky Theater with all-embracing gestures of those sweeping arms, and with his features glowing with pleasure and excitement. That was in 1912. He had Russia within his grasp then, and had the war not occurred I could imagine an Englishman becoming for the first time an international conductor of consequence. Anyone who dominated the musical world in the Russia of the Romanovs was, with their backing, a power indeed. That youthful, talented giant could have done it."

CHAPTER SIX

November: Survival on the Road

THERE WAS a palpable air of excitement at the theater in late October during my stay, for the word spread quickly that an on-again, off-again Kirov dancer, Igor Zelensky, was taking class with the company. Although this major artist had not formally broken ties with the theater, it was rumored he had had disputes with members of the ballet's staff that had led him to be more active in the West, where he joined the New York City Ballet for a while. But Zelensky frequently returned to St. Petersburg to visit his family and friends. On this trip home, speculation was running high as to whether or not he would dance. When the posters went up announcing him for a single performance of *Swan Lake* and one of *Le corsaire* in early November, you could feel the tension double inside the theater.

His appearances as Siegfried and Ali more than justified the advance word on this exceptional *danseur noble*. He is a beautifully proportioned man, somewhat reminiscent physically of the Bolshoi's Alexander Godunov, but more even and satisfying in the use of his body. Then, too, Zelensky is far of more a poet. Everything he did at the Mariinsky in November was elegant and suave and set within the context of an expressive, flexible, masculine line. There were no holes in his dancing, no lapses in his phrases, and for so big and tall a dancer, he became airborne in an amazingly easy manner, frequently descending to the stage to end a phrase in a riveting sort of tapered-off, winding-down way that was reminiscent of Yuri Soloviev.

In fact, his dancing on the whole appeared slower than that of others in the same roles, and the complete control he exercised over his body gave his slow-motion style a distinct and individual quality. It was as if he possessed the gift of suspending time and space, or better said, that he seemed to have the ability to reshape spatial elements at will. What he did and how he did it was, of course, more difficult than any facile, flashy, all-out virtuosity. Zelensky unerringly held an audience's attention—as if it depended for its life's breath on his perfect completion of a particular movement. Never did he let those of us down who were held rapt by his art.

He had two singular moments in *Swan Lake.* At the end of the first scene, he added the lovely solo from Nureyev's performances of the ballet. Liepa had also danced this solo in seasons past, but no one else did so during my time in St. Petersburg. Zelensky and his partner, the accomplished Georgian ballerina Irma Nioradze, gave no quarter to the audience during the Black Swan pas de deux, no wedge in which to insert the volleys of applause that were the norm at the Mariinsky. Despite Liepa's historical perspective on this practice, I found my excitement tripled by Zelensky's and Nioradze's dancing the coda at full tilt without a pause.

It was through a video performance of *Swan Lake* from the Kirov that many in the West first got to know Zelensky. Originally he was to have danced only the first-act pas de trois in this recording, but at the last moment Ruzimatov, scheduled as Prince Siegfried to the Odette-Odile of Julia Makhalina, was indisposed, and Zelensky took on the part of Siegfried as well. Although there was no precedent for a Siegfried to dance the pas de trois, this bit of serendipity made dramatic sense and helped to flesh out the slimness of the Prince's part in act 1.

Though Zelensky's performance in *Le corsaire* two nights later was equally exceptional, he had a less expressive platform on which to work his wizardry. Revived in 1987 by the Kirov, this Petipa ballet dates from 1863, although *Corsaire* had earlier been danced in St. Petersburg in a version by Perrot. Petipa based his staging on the work's original 1856 choreography for Paris by Joseph Mazilier. Today we are far removed from the work as conceived by Mazilier and Petipa, not only because of the span of time involved, but also because the ballet as a whole was long out of the Kirov's repertory, even though its well-known second-act pas de deux had maintained a foothold.

In the twentieth century, Petipa's choreography was reworked many times by many hands and always in accordance with the dance tastes and styles of each subsequent period (this latest *Corsaire* is largely rooted in a version created by Vakhtung Chabukiani; it was he, for example, who inserted the *rivoltade* with jetés and pirouettes into the coda of Ali's variation). What one sees at the Mariinsky these days is, in essence, a twentieth-century reinterpretation of a nineteenth-century staple seen through the sensibilities of its current choreographer, Peter Gusev, as well as those of the production's designer, Teimuras Murvanidze. Gusev, with additional touches by Vinogradov, has preserved more the spirit than the letter of Petipa, and what there is of that spirit is found in the structuring of the character dances, the mime, and the building up of the various dance pieces, which paid off in a series of crucial climaxes. There are also specific echoes of the Kingdom of the Shades scene from *Bayadère* and the garland dance in *Sleeping Beauty.* Although the score is a pastiche of music by Adolphe Adam, Cesare Pugni, Léo Delibes, and Riccardo Drigo, it is surprisingly homogenous. But the libretto, based on a poem by Lord Byron, is as preposterous as it ever was, with its repeated abductions and rescues and its once famous but now seemingly tacked-on finale "Le jardin animé."

Yet when danced to the hilt, *Le corsaire* can be a remarkably effective and affecting evening of ballet, especially in the Kirov production, which is filled with wonderful treats for the eye, from the opening storm-tossed shipwreck to the admitted but endearing kitsch of the finale. One striking throwback was the resurrection of the ballet's famous pas de deux as a pas de trois, with both Conrad and Ali acting as *cavaliere servente* to Medora and showing both men dedicated to serving and protecting her in their different ways.

November saw a return to repertory of Balanchine's *Scotch Symphony* and *Theme and Variations* and of Jerome Robbins's *In the Night*. The Russians have always had a love-hate relationship with Balanchine's American career as well as a burning curiosity about it. They have long known of his importance in West and the pathbreaking history of his New York City Ballet; after all, these were the undertows that had pulled Rudolf Nureyev and his fellow defectors westward in the 1970s.

But balancing this is a strong tendency among Russians to dismiss the accomplishments of their former artists and regard anything at home as better than whatever is done elsewhere. It is a deeply embedded Soviet inculcation. I remember, for example, returning from a trip to Paris and being quizzed by an employee in my hotel about the museums I had visited while there. She responded to each of my descriptions—defensively or gratuitously, I wasn't sure—with "Well, ours is not worse."

Balanchine was, of course, the strongest link in the chain that connected Kirov dance traditions with dance in the West, for he danced at the Mariinsky in both czarist and Soviet times. He began as a character dancer; Alexandra Danilova, another member of the post-imperial Mariinsky, remembered vividly how in the *Nutcracker* he always brought down the house in the Candy Cane variation, with his sensational jumps through a hoop. To her, "his distinguishing features … were speed, musicality, a big jump, and a sharp attack." Had he stayed in Petrograd he would probably have been assured of a long and successful career at the theater, but he chose instead to seek his fortune in the West in the 1920s as part of the Diaghilev company, first as a dancer and choreographer and then as its last ballet master. It was the demise of the company at Diaghilev's death that eventually brought Balanchine to America, where he altered forever the way Americans perceived ballet.

In 1962, Balanchine returned to Russia after an absence of nearly forty years, bringing his company to the East for the first time. It was a wrenching experience for him, and he left the troupe in the middle of the tour and fled back to New York. Still, he was persuaded to go back a decade later, with happier results. This second visit and a meeting with Vinogradov planted the seeds that eventually grew into the inclusion of several of his works in the Kirov repertory.

During a Kirov tour to the United States in 1986, following Balanchine's death, Vinogradov said in an interview he gave on the West Coast that he very much he wished to acquire certain Balanchine ballets for his company, but that the ballet master's heirs were difficult to deal with. Reading this, Barbara Horgan, Balanchine's longtime assistant, sent word to Vinogradov that they should meet and talk. When the company returned to the East Coast, Vinogradov invited Horgan to a performance. He told her that having Balanchine ballets as an active part of the Kirov's repertory was a " lifelong dream," adding that he particularly wanted to acquire *Scotch Symphony*, *Serenade*, and *Symphony in C*. Horgan in turn assured Vinogradov that the only requirement he needed to meet in order to fulfill this dream was to engage artists who had worked for Balanchine to mount the works. This he understood and agreed to, although it took several years before concrete plans could be laid.

It was decided that the Kirov should begin with two Balanchine works rather than attempt an all-Balanchine evening, as Vinogradov had originally envisioned. Part of this thinking was the result of the experiences of two guest artists from the Bolshoi, Liepa and Nina Ananiashvili, with the New York City Ballet. They were assigned the *Raymonda Variations* by the company's new head, Peter Martins, who reasoned that this would be a good piece for them, as it was a ballet Balanchine had derived from Petipa.

"That's when I saw what Balanchine had done with Petipa," Horgan recalled, "how different the two styles were. George had arranged Petipa and had made the choreography more interesting, more modern. The experience was a nightmare for the two Bolshoi dancers. So I thought that Vinogradov was making the same type of mistake, thinking that *Scotch Symphony* was in a Fokine style. With an interpreter, I delicately broached the problem, and Vinogradov turned to me and said in perfect English, 'You are absolutely right. There is an enormous difference between the school of Vaganova and the school of Balanchine. I know what you are saying because Mr. Balanchine told me this himself in 1972, which is when he recommended *Scotch Symphony* to me." Reassured, Horgan arranged for Francia Russell, the former ballet mistress of the New York City Ballet, to go to Leningrad and stage *Theme and Variations*, and for Suzanne Farrell to follow her and set *Scotch Symphony*.

Russell arrived in Russia in September 1988 and spent three weeks working with the company on *Theme and Variations*, a ballet to a movement from Tchaikovsky's Third Suite for Orchestra. It was difficult time for her, for even though Vinogradov had professed his admiration for Balanchine and his wish to have Balanchine repertory, he was—in true Russian fashion—less than supportive once Russell arrived. It was the love-hate scenario all over again, and one hardly unique to this particular situation. I discovered firsthand that while the Russians want help—even ask for it—once it is offered they become suspicious and begin questioning why it is being given.

During Russell's rehearsal period, according to Horgan, Vinogradov was away working with a Western company. Russell never saw the same group of dancers twice, and she never was given a complete run-through of the ballet. She is more sanguine in her memories of the experience than Horgan, however, describing it as "a real pioneering gesture." To her, "The Kirov Theater is not so large . . . they just think big. Out front it's kind of baroque and pretty, but the stage is for big effects. They think in terms of size and numbers of people. Mr. B. grew up on that stage. He loved making things like *Vienna Waltzes* and *Union Jack* because there were so many hordes of people. He was always talking about big sets and was fascinated by the size of the tree in the *Nutcracker* and always spoke about having more dancers. In Russia when he was a boy there were hundreds of people in the ballets, and he always wanted that."

Farrell went to Leningrad four months later. Evidently she had an easier time with *Scotch Symphony:* the ice had been broken, and, too, this ballet was more in a style the company was accustomed to. As Horgan put it, "It wasn't as fast, it wasn't as difficult technically. . . . We all talk about the Kirov dancers' wonderful upper bodies, but they can't bend those upper bodies. They are held there by an invisible iron ramrod, so Suzanne had to work very hard on getting the girls and boys to move from the waist."

In Elizabeth Kendall's *New Yorker* article, she takes the matter a step further. "Balanchine wasn't easy for the [Kirov] dancers. Their manners slowed them down; they didn't have time to become the grand folk they usually became on stage. Whereas Vaganova had stuffed as much as she could of the musical-aesthetic concept of Petipa's days into ballet steps, Balanchine had done the opposite: he had divested ballet steps of manners and period musicality, so they could be inflected in new ways, to different music. Sometimes Balanchine's steps happened on syncopated musical accents, which Kirov dancers weren't used to, or they asked for percussive action in the feet instead of the Kirov's gracious gestures with the arms. Most radical of all, they had to be danced to the tempo demanded by the music, and not to music slowed down by dancers in performance."

Alexandra Danilova, who was trained at the Vaganova school and began her career as a dancer at the Kirov, ended her days teaching in Balanchine's school in

New York. She takes the Vaganova-versus-Balanchine issue even further in her autobiography: "If Petipa would have you lift one leg slowly, Balanchine would in the same measure have you lift the leg twice or move the arms twice as fast. . . . *Pas de bourrée*, for instance, in Petipa would be: one, two, three. But in Balanchine's choreography, it would be slightly different: for example, one-and-two, hold three—the first two steps faster, so that you get where you're going more quickly. . . . The old way of doing *pas de chat* is to lift one leg, then the other—one at a time. But Balanchine sped up the timing so that the second leg immediately follows the first and you see a clear position—both legs up—in the air. Balanchine took classical ballet steps and sharpened the focus, so that you see a perfect fifth position or a jump at its height, and the time it takes the dancer to get from one position to the next is shorter."

Vinogradov was on hand when Horgan flew to Leningrad in February 1989 for the premieres, and this time he was more accommodating. As Horgan recalled, Vinogradov's "operation is like Balanchine's: it's a one-man show. Everything that goes on in that theater with regard to ballet is Vinogradov's policy. . . . I found him humorous, gentle, kind, and authoritative. He knows how to get what he wants. I admired him, and I enjoyed watching him at work. . . . I went to many performances and remarked how respectful the audiences were. He said, 'Yes, but you know, in Leningrad, our audience comes as though they are going to church.'" Horgan found that at the Kirov, "people wear the best clothes they can possibly put on. You can spot the tourists because they are the ones wearing T-shirts and sneakers. In Russia the arts are a solace."

Six years had elapsed between the premieres of *Scotch Symphony* and *Theme and Variations* and the revival I saw in 1995. For at least one person who had grown up on these works in New York, the St. Petersburg performances were a disappointment. The style still seemed not entirely comfortable for the Russians, and there was a marked heaviness to the dancing, particularly in *Theme and Variations*. For the first time I became aware that the Kirov Ballet could have clay feet.

Of the two, only *Scotch Symphony* had a degree of naturalness, but perhaps this was because *Theme and Variations* suffered from a seeming lack of interest on the part of Ruzimatov, who was far out of his element. With someone different and more sympathetic partnering Julia Makhalina, one feels she would have made a more positive impression, given her sharp style of dancing and its patently Balanchinesque qualities. The Robbins ballet was somewhat more plausible in its Kirov context, but it was sabotaged by the wooden playing of the pianist assigned to the ballet, who turned Chopin's nocturnes into nightmares.

At the same time, the opera season was hobbling along, awaiting Gergiev's return from the Met. He was scheduled for a single *Khovanshchina* at the Mariinsky before proceeding with the Kirov Orchestra on its first Japanese tour. Of cursory interest in the meantime was the first *Madame Butterfly* of the season, which turned up on the Kirov's stage in the old Met production dating from 1958. I had known it intimately in New York during the 1960s, and the effect of seeing it in Russia was disorienting, to say the least. It was not very well sung or played, and the Kirov staging was heavy handed and the lighting lurid. But then, the best of the company was away at the time in Portugal, where Gergiev joined it on his way home for performances of *Katerina Ismailova* and Berlioz's *Roméo et Juliette*.

For the tour to Japan, Gergiev programmed the Tchaikovsky Serenade for Strings, to which he added the composer's Sixth Symphony and the *Romeo and Juliet* Overture, Stravinsky's *Sacre du printemps* and the complete *Firebird*, the Prelude to *Parsifal*, and the Second Suite from Ravel's *Daphnis et Chloé*. The highlight of the tour, however, promised to be Gergiev's first collaboration with the pianist Sviatoslav Richter, who was already in Japan for a series of concerts. Gergiev had long ached to collaborate with this greatest of Russia's contemporary pianists, and he worked diligently to bring the union about. Earlier attempts had fallen through because of conflicts in dates and the pianist's often frail health.

Gergiev and Richter had agreed on Tchaikovsky's First Piano Concerto for the Japanese tour, but by November Richter had changed his mind, and the work now being rehearsed in St. Petersburg was Mozart's Piano Concerto No. 25. By the time the orchestra arrived in Japan, Richter was having second thoughts even about the Mozart, and although Gergiev did his best to save what would have been an extraordinary event, the pianist begged off, pleading fatigue and a wish to return home earlier than scheduled. In the end, the Richter-Gergiev appearances scheduled for Tokyo and Osaka were canceled. Richter died two years later, and so the longed-for collaboration never materialized.

The rehearsals for Japan were dominated by the Tchaikovsky Serenade, which Gergiev was conducting for the first time. He took great care with the work, preparing it in detail to set its accents and shape its lines. It was exciting to hear him lift the orchestra from a matter-of-fact beginning to a performance of great intensity and thrust. One day he spent nearly two hours on the first movement alone, which recalled his preparation of Beethoven's Ninth Symphony the summer before. But in this case the results were significantly different. Perhaps because it was Tchaikovsky's music and because the orchestra had played his ballets and symphonies so often, the lessons taught in the first movement were not lost when it came to the remaining movements. Whatever the reason, the search for the right colors and nuances paid off handsomely, and from the first performance of the work in Kagoshima, it sounded like a longtime staple with the orchestra and Gergiev.

After another memorable *Khovanshchina*—a performance that was bold and beautifully molded—we flew the short hop to Helsinki and then on to Tokyo, but without Gergiev. An acute sinus infection had caused his face to swell and kept him behind for an extra day. He finally arrived on his own just two hours before the first concert in Matsumoto, looking haggard but insisting on immediately beginning an hour and a half's rehearsal that kept the audience locked out until fifteen minutes before starting time. I was still very tired from the flight and the train trip to Matsumoto and could only imagine how Gergiev must have felt.

Yet with the first notes of *Le sacre* that evening it was obvious to anyone that something special was afoot. My fatigue melted away as the excitement of the performance built to the vivid proportions that had marked the playing of *Le sacre* during White Nights, which was the last time the orchestra and Gergiev had touched the score. Again they went deep inside the music to ferret out all its pagan forces. It hit with a particularly overwhelming impact at the Matsumoto concert hall, which was of a good quality and seated only 720.

But as powerful as *Le sacre* was, it was only a preamble to the searing performance of the Tchaikovsky Sixth that followed. This performance is beyond my power to describe for someone who was not there. In fact, it was more than a performance as such, it was an experience where every step of the way was dictated by the emotional content of the music. One could quibble over some obvious slips in the solo playing and overall ensemble, and even areas for interpretative disagreements surfaced; Gergiev, for example, saw the second movement in rather too dark and menacing a light. But the totality of the performance swept such concerns to one side.

Backstage afterward, Gergiev was obviously satisfied with the evening but termed it "a good dress rehearsal." When I protested, he waved my words aside saying, "A few more like this, and I'll really give you something in Tokyo." I was to discover that this was no idle boast.

The next day we moved on to the south of Japan and Kagoshima for an all-Tchaikovsky concert that included a repeat of the Sixth Symphony. It was good and even cleaner, but not the emotionally draining experience of two days earlier; this was especially true when it came to the final movement. When I asked about the difference in the finale of the Sixth in Kagoshima, Gergiev replied, "I basically have no tempo for this movement; it depends entirely on the hall we are playing in and how I feel at the time."

To be fair, the hall in Kagoshima was less fine and thinned out the orchestra's sound, especially that of the strings. Still, they managed to make their point in the Serenade. The *Romeo and Juliet* Overture that filled out the program was more mundane than not, and afterward, speaking of *Romeo*, Gergiev remarked in a matter-of-fact manner, "I didn't help the orchestra as much as I could have." I pressed him to elaborate on this, and he said his timing was off because key musicians who had rehearsed and performed in Matsumoto did not play in Kagoshima.

But this was his doing, he explained, the result of an apprentice program he has instigated in which young musicians—in this instance, the timpani and the four solo winds—alternate with and learn from a veteran member of the orchestra. There are even three alternating concertmasters. He established this program to ensure a continuity in the sound of the Kirov orchestra should he lose a principal player. With Richter's cancellation, the rehearsal time in Tokyo set aside for him was used by Gergiev to work out some of problems that cropped up in Kagoshima, and by the time of the first concert in the capital, an all-Stravinsky program, everyone was back in stride.

Both of the halls in Tokyo, as well as the one in Osaka, turned out to be superb. It struck me as amazing that three such halls of such exceptional quality existed in this small country and that two of them are in Tokyo alone, whereas London and Paris lack even a single good venue for making music. The first Tokyo concert was played in the fairly new Geijutsu Gekigo Hall in the city's Metropolitan Arts Center, and the second was in Suntory Hall, which is a bit smaller in size and brighter in sound, but was nonetheless complementary to the orchestra. In both the orchestra's sound was clean and solid, with a glowing post-reverberation.

For the tour, Gergiev used a body of strings made up of fourteen first and fourteen second violins, twelve violas, twelve cellos, and eight basses. There were four each of winds (with players doubling on alto flute, piccolo, and contrabassoon), eight horns, three trombones, three tubas (one a baritone tuba), six trumpets, two timpanists, six percussion, three harps, and two keyboard players. To these were added stage hands and administrative assistants. It was a large group to move from city to city by train, bus, and air, but each leg of the trip went off comfortably and securely.

There is no question that the peak of the tour was reached in Suntory Hall. I had heard Gergiev conduct the Prelude to *Parsifal* previously in New York and in St. Petersburg, and both times it was filled with warmth and mystery, as it was in Japan; but his conducting of *Daphnis* was new to me. It turned out to be highly personal and even willful in spots, just as Leonard Bernstein's had been, yet it was entirely convincing (despite a few obvious minor mishaps) and played as an all-out virtuoso showpiece. But the Tchaikovsky Sixth set a seal on the evening. Luckily, a recording of this performance has been issued so that I do not have to depend on notes or my memory to substantiate its impact (the concert was also taped in high-definition video).

As Gergiev had promised, it surpassed the Matsumoto performance. In Tokyo the expressive intensity was just as great, but this time it was wedded to finer, more finished playing. It was followed by forty-five minutes of cheering, emphasizing not only the quality of the evening, but the voracious appetite of the Japanese for music. They listened intently and applauded enthusiastically. The orchestra played three encores, and even after they left the stage, the applause continued without diminishing until Gergiev came out one last time to acknowledge it.

Early the next morning we left for the north and Morioka, but that evening's concert made it clear that the tour had begun to take a toll. The players were exhausted from traveling all day, and the concert was a letdown after the previous night's triumph. Yet it is remarkable how high a level it still managed to maintain under such trying circumstances. To my surprise, on the final night of the tour in Osaka, where Lexo (who was there for a solo recital) joined us, Gergiev and his players managed once more to scale the heights. There were four encores, and during the last—the Overture to *Ruslan and Ludmila*—Gergiev stopped conducting and simply leaned back against the railing of the podium to enjoy his orchestra along with the rest of us. He occasionally nodded his head or smiled, but that was all. A few times he turned to the audience with a trace of a grin on his face, as if to say, "Not bad, huh?" The effect was electrifying, with the orchestra playing as though possessed. It was a grand finale to a grand experience.

CHAPTER SEVEN

Petipa and the Imperial Ballet

AT THE TIME the Imperial Ballet moved to the Mariinsky Theater, Marius Petipa was at the height of his creative powers, and ballets continued to flow from his imagination and give pleasure to the theater's audiences: *The Tulip of Haarlem* with Lev Ivanov (1887), *La vestale* (1888), and *Le talisman* and *Les caprices du papillon* (1889). This crescendo of dance pieces climaxed on 3 January 1890 with the premiere of Tchaikovsky's *Sleeping Beauty*.

Mathilde Kshessinskaya, who became the czarina of dance at the Mariinsky, has written in her autobiography *Dancing in St. Petersburg* that "Petipa always spoke Russian, which he knew very poorly, despite a long stay in Russia. He called everybody 'tu.' He usually arrived at the theater . . . wrapped in a check plaid. He prepared his program beforehand, and never improvised during rehearsals. Without even looking at us, he merely showed us the movements and steps, accompanying his gestures with words spoken in indescribable Russian: 'You on me, me on you; you on mine, me on yours.' Which meant that we had to move from our corner ('you') to 'me,' where he was! To make his meaning clearer, he tapped his chest every time he said 'me.' But we understood his mime and vocabulary perfectly, and knew what he wanted us to do.

"I told him that I should like to dance Esmeralda. He listened carefully and asked me point-blank in his jargon, 'You love?'

"Confused, I answered that I was indeed in love, that I did love.

"Whereupon he continued, 'You suffer?'

"I thought it a strange question, and immediately replied, 'Certainly not!'

"Then he explained to me—a fact which I was to remember later—that only artists who had known the sufferings of love could understand and interpret the role of Esmeralda. . . . I was to recall his profound words later when I won the right to dance Esmeralda, a right which suffering alone could bring—when Esmeralda became my best role."

In the 1892–93 season Petipa created a work especially for Kshessinskaya's gifts: *Calcabrino*, a three-act ballet with a libretto by Modest Tchaikovsky and music by Léon Minkus. To prepare herself for this important step in her career, Kshessinskaya worked with Enrico Cecchetti, the famed Italian dancer and teacher who joined the Imperial Ballet in 1874 and later became Diaghilev's ballet master. He was her partner in *Calcabrino*, and she went to him to "attain the virtuosity which the Italian dancers were then demonstrating on the Russian stage. Italian technique called for abrupt, precise, clear-cut movements, while Russian and French techniques are more lyrical, softer, more expressive, even in steps most marked with brio and virtuosity. It was only later that I was to return to our own technique, realizing its grace and beauty."

The Bolshoi Kamenny was the home of the Imperial Ballet until 1886, although Petipa continued to supply ballets for opera productions in the Mariinsky and even an occasional full-length dance work such as *La vivandière* in 1881. But after the Bolshoi was condemned as unsafe and closed, his company had no choice but to take up full-time residency in the Mariinsky, which had just reopened after its first round of alterations. For the inaugural of the redecorated and expanded theater, Petipa created a ballet *féerie* in three acts with music by Minkus—*Les pillules magiques*.

Of the works Petipa fashioned while in the Bolshoi, only a handful that he either overhauled or created anew persist in some form or other in the company's current repertory—*Paquita* (1857), *Le corsaire* (1863), *Don Quixote* (1869), *La bayadère* (1877), and *La fille mal gardée* (1885). Petipa's versions of *Giselle* and *Coppélia* were later supplanted by productions that were based more on the choreography of others. A pivotal work such as *The Daughter of Pharaoh*, which sealed his importance to the theater in 1862, has vanished from the dance scene, although this and other of his dance works remained in repertory through the early decades of the twentieth century.

The great ballet master had come to St. Petersburg in May 1847 from France, where he was born in Marseilles on 11 March 1818 and trained by his father. He debuted as a dancer at the Bolshoi Kamenny on 26 September 1847, partnering Elena Andreyanova in *Paquita*, a production for which he helped revise Joseph Mazilier's original choreography. The next year he produced the ballet *Satanilla* in collaboration with his father, Jean, who had been engaged as a teacher at the Imperial Ballet School (following Jean's death, Marius would take up the post for a while). *Satanilla* was the first of a successful string of works fashioned for the czar's theaters in St. Petersburg and Moscow. The ballet that secured for Petipa the post of second ballet master under Saint-Léon (who had meanwhile replaced Jules Perrot), however, was the three-act extravaganza *The Daughter of Pharaoh*.

The work was fashioned for the benefit night and farewell appearance of the admired Italian ballerina Carolina Rosati. At first the theater's new director, Alexander Saburov, was against the project. His predecessor, Stepan Gedeonov, had left him with a deficit and no money for new productions. Saburov argued that so large-scale a work as *The Daughter of Pharaoh* could not be done in the six weeks that remained of the winter season. He finally gave way when Petipa promised to deliver the work on time, using existing scenery and costumes. He kept his word, and *The Daughter of Pharaoh*, with a score by Cesare Pugni, premiered on 18 January 1862. It was an immense success, for his choice of a libretto was an apt one: following the important archeological discoveries made in Memphis in 1851, interest in ancient Egypt had become rampant.

The ballet paralleled a similar appetite for grand opera, exemplified by the weighty, expansive stage works of Giacomo Meyerbeer, long a popular composer in Russia. Ballet under Petipa became a *grand spectacle* that lasted some four hours, made use of differing dance styles and techniques, and employed hundreds of dancers and supernumeraries. Petipa's ability to impose on classical ballet a structure and logic it had previously lacked was already in evidence. He introduced a strict division between mime and dance, carefully positioned the use of ensemble numbers to achieve visual harmony and balance, and established the strict ordering of the sections that made up the classic pas de deux (usually adagio, variations, and coda).

In 1869 Saint-Léon resigned his post as chief ballet master to return to France, and Petipa was named his successor. He would reign unchallenged for the next thirty-five years. So popular were his ballets and so great was the vogue for dance in St. Petersburg that the dance repertory for whole seasons consisted entirely of original or restaged works by him. The 1870s also brought Petipa's daughter Marie to the stage of the Mariinsky, where she captivated the public with her attractive physical appearance and her airy yet spirited style. She quickly established herself as one of the leading character dancers of the period.

Marie was one of the many vivid dance personalities who made the age of Petipa bright and appealing, but the dancer who would dominate the Mariinsky from the mid-1890s through the final years of Romanov rule was Kshessinskaya. She came from a family of dancers—her father, two sisters, and a brother were all members of the company. But it was Kshessinskaya who made the family name blaze. She was trained at the Imperial Ballet School and in her autobiography has left us a vivid picture of life in that institution:

"The part of the building where the girls lived was strictly separate from the boys' quarters. On the first floor were the girls' dormitories and classroom, and the rehearsal rooms, two large and one small. A wide corridor led from here to the School theater on the same floor. A small staircase led to the floor above, a copy of the one below, holding the boys' rooms and the inspector's office. Following the corridor which passed in front of this office and the classrooms, one arrived at a small but very lovely church, flooded in light, sparkling with the jewels encrusted in the icons which the artists had presented to the School. There were services on Saturday evening, Sunday morning, and holidays. When the girls went to church accompanied by their teachers wearing their long uniform dresses with little white hoods, their hair strictly smoothed down and plaited, they used the wide main staircase.

"Since all communication between boys and girls was strictly forbidden, many were the dodges which had to be used for an innocent exchange of looks, smiles or words. Naturally, the teachers did not let us out of their sight during rehearsals and dancing classes; however, despite our sentinels, we always managed to snatch a few seconds' flirtation, for these gatherings provided us with our only opportunities! These secret intrigues were part of the School's traditions, and each girl had her own particular boyfriend."

Kshessinskaya's first teacher at school was Ivanov, who, she recalled, "accompanied our dances himself on the violin. . . . His gifts never reached a full flowering, partly owing to his innate indolence. . . . In a lazy voice he would tell us: "*Pliez!*" or "*Genoux en dehors!*" but he never stopped us, made no corrections, did not interrupt the class to point out a pupil's wrong movement . . . instead of putting life into us he was content to teach us in a routine manner. . . . I stayed three years in his class, and, when I was eleven, moved into that taken by Catherine Vazem, ballerina of the Imperial Theaters, where less simple movements were already accomplished. Not only were the exercises taught with a care to their right execution, but gracefulness was also demanded.

"Vazem's class began with exercises at the barre, followed by adagios and allegros in the middle of the studio. The steps were not complicated: attitudes, arabesques, leaps, *pointes, pas de bourrée, sauts de Basque*, all the basic steps, in fact, which modern technique has preserved. Vazem saw that we adopted the correct position of the foot *sur les pointes*—a very important matter—and also that our *en dehors* was satisfactory. Her class was a kind of transition, preparing us for that of Johansson, a real school of virtuosity.

"Vazem carefully followed the pupils and did not hesitate to interrupt them if she thought the execution of steps incorrect or lacking grace. She was satisfied with me, and all she said, not unkindly, was 'Kshessinskaya! Don't frown or you'll grow old before your time!' But her lessons also seemed to be lacking in inspiration. I had learnt all these movements a long time ago, and my enthusiasm suffered accordingly.

"It was quite another matter in Johansson's class, which I entered when I was fifteen: so much so that later, as an artist, I was to go on working with him.... He was not only an excellent teacher, but a poet, an artist and inspired creator. He knew how to think, and he knew how to observe, and his pertinent remarks were highly valued by us. His art was noble because it was simple, and the man himself was as simple as he was sincere. Every movement he made had meaning, expressed a thought, reflected a state of soul, which he strove to pass on to us."

As a young girl, Kshessinskaya had a short-lived but intense liaison with the future czar, Nicholas II, when he was heir to the throne; later, after the Revolution, she married his cousin the Grand Duke Andrei. Her first meeting with Nicholas came following a dance concert given as a final exam by those graduating from the Imperial School, one attended by the royal family. Kshessinskaya danced a pas de deux from *La fille mal gardée*, and afterward, at a dinner in the girls' dining room, Czar Alexander III asked the young dancer, "Where are you sitting?"

"I have no special place," she answered.

"Sit next to me," said the czar. He then turned to the czarevitch and told him to sit on her other side, adding with a smile, "Careful now! Not too much flirting." Thus began one of the famous affairs of the time.

Although Kshessinskaya formally joined the Mariinsky Theater as a ballerina in 1890, her first appearance on its stage had come in 1881, while she was still a student at the Imperial Ballet School—a small part in *Don Quixote*. This was a period when Italian ballerinas still appeared as guests and dominated the dance scene. The most admired of these was Virginia Zucchi. Kshessinskaya was fourteen when Zucchi arrived in St. Petersburg. She remembers that at this time she "was seized with doubts: had I chosen the career which suited me? . . . Zucchi's arrival . . . immediately, and radically, altered my state of mind, revealing to me the true meaning of our art.... Zucchi was no longer young, but her exceptional gifts had lost none of their vigor. I felt an overwhelming, unforgettable sensation when I watched her. I felt that I was beginning to understand, for the first time, how one should dance in order to deserve the title of a great dancer....

"Zucchi had a wonderful gift for mime. She gave all the movements of classical ballet extraordinary charm and astonishing beauty of expression, filling the audience with enthusiasm whenever she danced. Her acting henceforth became true art for me, and I understood that the essence of such art does not lie exclusively in virtuosity and technique. I realized that technique, far from being an end, is only a means. Zucchi's movements, the line of the arms and back, were wonderfully expressive, and I wanted to seize them, to make a mental photograph of them, greedily following her acting with my childish eyes: later people were to say that I attained Zucchi's perfection in these movements. When, in my later career, I danced Esmeralda, I was inspired by memories of her interpretation which, in this ballet, had reached the most sublime dramatic expression. For me Zucchi was the genius of dancing." Interestingly, Ivan Vsevolozhsky, who became director of the Imperial Theaters in 1881 following Baron Karl Kister, and Petipa were opposed to the appearance of Zucchi and other foreign ballerinas because their styles, according to the ballet historian Roland John Wiley, "represented a concession to vulgarity incompatible with their standards." Still, a few others managed to arrive and leave a mark on Mariinsky history. The last to gain prominence was Pierina Legnani, Petipa's first Odette-Odile and Raymonda. It was in *Swan Lake* that she produced a prodigious thirty-two *fouettés*, which had never before been attempted in Russia. This feat left an indelible mark on dancing and became a measuring stick for ballerinas who followed her.

Kshessinskaya's dancing was not to everyone's taste, however; Bronislava Nijinska, Vaslav's sister, who was a member of the Mariinsky ensemble from 1908 to 1911 and later a Diaghilev dancer and choreographer, dismissed it as "vulgar acrobatics," while the critic Gennadi Smakov felt she "excelled mostly in lyrical, dramatic parts requiring good *terre-à-terre* technique." But Tamara Karsavina, who had good reason to be prejudiced against Kshessinskaya and who saw her both at the Mariinsky and later during 1911 and 1912 with the Diaghilev company, maintained that she was both a brilliant technician—she was the first Russian to attempt Pierina Legnani's thirty-two *fouettés*—and a superb actress. Whatever the truth of the matter, there is no denying her prominence and her place as the foremost and last of the prima ballerinas of the imperial era.

As a person, Kshessinskaya charmed some and repelled others. Among the latter was Teliakovsky. As Volkov puts it, Teliakovsky "hated her whims and intrigues and wrote in his diary that she was 'a morally impudent, cynical, and brazen dancer, living simultaneously with two grand dukes and not only not hiding it but on the contrary weaving this art as well into her stinking, cynical wreath of human offal and vice.'" Kshessinskaya danced little after the Revolution. She married the czar's nephew (the second of her grand dukes) and settled in Paris, where, as Princess Romanovsky-Krassinsky, she taught until her death in 1971 at the age of ninety-nine. Among her students were Tatiana Riaboushinska, André Eglevsky, Yvette Chauviré, and Margot Fonteyn.

Kshessinskaya's reign at the Mariinsky was also marked by a strong male contingent of dancers, headed by Gerdt and the Legat brothers, Nikolai and Sergei. Gerdt had begun dancing small roles with the Imperial Ballet as early as 1860, while still a student at the Imperial Ballet School. His life seemed to have been a charmed one. He was long admired, well paid, and given the title of "His Majesty's Soloist." It was Petipa who first recognized Gerdt's gifts as a dancer and actor and trained him in mime. Gerdt's unique abilities led Petipa to enlarge the prominence and virtuoso capabilities of the male dancer with such added virtuoso, aerial touches as the cabrioles and *assemblées* we now take for granted in a part such as Albrecht in *Giselle*.

Initially Gerdt appeared only in pas de deux, but he eventually moved from merely partnering a ballerina to full-length leading roles. His repertory embraced more than a hundred parts, crowned by his creation of Prince Désiré in *The Sleeping Beauty* in 1890, when he was forty-six, and Siegfried in the Mariinsky *Swan Lake* five years later. His career would continue until 1916. As a teacher, he numbered among his students Karsavina, Vaganova (who had worked with Johansson and would work later with Nikolai Legat), his daughter Elisaveta, the Legats, and Fokine.

Nikolai was the older of the two Legat brothers (he was born in 1869, Sergei in 1875) and had the longer and more influential career (Sergei, who married Marie Petipa and was one of Nijinsky's first teachers, committed suicide in 1905 at the age of thirty). Both men capitalized on Gerdt's example, and they offered the first formidable challenges for dance supremacy yet faced by the Mariinsky's ballerinas. The Legats' position of authority was consolidated in 1903 following the ouster of Petipa, when they became for a while joint ballet masters at the Mariinsky. After Sergei's death and with Gerdt's declining years, Nikolai became the premier danseur at the theater. He choreographed a dozen ballets for the Mariinsky, including the still popular *Fairy Doll*, which he fashioned with Sergei, and he reworked several Petipa works as well.

Although Nikolai was a noted teacher, he never managed to codify his dance theories into a formal system. But much that Vaganova did after he left Russia in 1922 was based on his ideas and his teaching. (Legat settled in London in 1930, where he opened a renowned studio whose students included Alexandra Danilova, Vera Zorina, Ninette de Valois, Alicia Markova, Anton Dolin, and André Eglevsky.) In a lighter vein, the legacy left by the brothers includes a wealth of caricatures that chronicle the heyday of the Imperial Ballet in a witty and at times caustic manner.

The years of Gerdt, the Legats, and Kshessinskaya coincided with a splendid and exciting dance era that began with Vsevolozhsky's appointment. A person of enormous culture and a designer of importance with twenty-five productions to his credit, Vsevolozhsky was willing to spare no expense where dance was concerned. Benois remembers him as a man whose conversation "was distinguished by simplicity, goodwill, evenness, . . . witticisms, and epigrams." Kshessinskaya believed that "under him the Imperial Theater progressed greatly in the artistic sphere. He brought Russian ballet and opera to a hitherto unknown height. The libretti of almost all the ballets and operas were either written by him or following his directions. He was also an excellent draughtsman with a profound knowledge of styles, and designed all the costumes most successfully."

One of the lasting reforms made by Vsevolozhsky was his elimination of the long-established post of ballet composer when Léon Minkus retired in 1886. This cleared the way for fresh ideas and new solutions to the challenge of writing for dance and opened the door to composers like Tchaikovsky, and Glazunov after him. It was with Tchaikovsky's music that the artistic collaboration of Vsevolozhsky and Petipa reached a pinnacle with the premiere of *The Sleeping Beauty* in 1890. It marked the birth of what has been termed "symphonic ballet." For the first time emphasis rested equally on music and dance.

The roots for *The Sleeping Beauty* actually reach back four years to 1886, when Tchaikovsky's opera *The Enchantress* was being rehearsed for its premiere at the Mariinsky. In the composer's diary, he notes, "I found a letter from Vsevolozhsky with an invitation . . . to talk over a ballet . . . Petipa and [Alexander] Frolov [supervisor of the ballet school] showed up and we immediately started discussions [with] my rejection of *Salammbô* and *Undine.*" Two years would pass before the proposed ballet began to take shape. In 1886 Vsevolozhsky writes to Tchaikovsky, "I conceived the idea of writing a libretto on *La belle au bois dormant* after Perrault's tale. I want to do the *mise-en-scène* in the style of Louis XIV. Here the musical imagination can be carried away, and melodies composed in the spirit of Lully, Bach, Rameau, etc. In the last act indispensably necessary is a quadrille of all of Perrault's tales."

Tchaikovsky was impressed and set about composing the score. His brother Modest tells us that Tchaikovsky asked of Petipa, who contributed to the libretto, "designations of the dances in the most exact way, the number of bars, the character of the music, the amount of time of each number," although the composer used these only as guidelines and went his way when his inspiration so dictated. The full score was completed in late summer of 1889, and Riccardo Drigo, the Mariinsky's principal ballet conductor, took it, made cuts, indicated tempos, and added expression marks. Emendations were being made right up to the premiere on 15 January 1890.

Alexander Shiriaev, a former St. Petersburg dancer and Pugni's grandson, has left us a fascinating portrait of how Petipa worked to create his choreography. The process began at home rather than in the rehearsal halls or on the stage. Petipa "usually summoned a pianist and a violinist. Ordering them to play fragments of the music repeatedly, he planned the production at his table making use of little *papier-mâché* figurines. . . . He moved them about in the most varied combinations, which he noted down in detail on paper. . . . At rehearsal [with Drigo at the piano] Petipa appeared with a whole pile of outlines and drawings made by him at home, and immediately began to rehearse on the basis of them. Ordinarily Petipa worked with groups and soloists separately, and then introduced the latter into the prepared ensemble."

As for the leading ballerina—in the case of *The Sleeping Beauty*, it was the Italian dancer Carlotta Brianza—Shiriaev notes that Petipa "carefully studied the particulars of her gifts, sought out interesting features, assiduously strove to develop them as far as possible and constructed the dance accordingly. If it happened that he showed the ballerina a new movement [and] she struggled and struggled with it to no avail, then he rearranged the *pas*." It appears, according to Shiriaev, that Tchaikovsky's music and his reluctance to change it presented Petipa with difficulties he had not faced before with composers like Pugni and Minkus, who were willing to alter their scores endlessly to suit Petipa's ideas. Although Tchaikovsky and later Glazunov were apparently ready to meet the ballet master at least half-way, Petipa was more reticent about demanding changes of them.

Among those present at the final dress rehearsal of *The Sleeping Beauty* was the designer and painter Léon Bakst, then a student. "For three hours," he later wrote, " I lived in a magic dream, intoxicated by fairies and princesses, by splendid palaces streaming with gold, by the enchantment of the fairy-tale. . . . All my being was in cadence with those rhythms, with the radiant and fresh waves of beautiful melodies, already my friends." Brianza tells us that Czar Alexander III was present at the dress rehearsal "with all his family," but the czar's reaction to Tchaikovsky—"Very nice"—crushed the sensitive composer, who recorded this lukewarm compliment in his diary, then added five exclamation points.

Others were more appreciative. Benois felt that "however brilliantly the young and pretty Brianza performed her role, however incredibly funny [Timofei] Stulkin was [as Catalabutte], however nightmarish Cecchetti in the role of Calabosse—and he was also enchanting in the dances of the Bluebird—however excellent were the dozens of other dancers who represented fairies, peasants, genies, courtiers, hunters, fairytale characters etc.—all their personal mastery and the charm of each one of them combined in the beauty of the ensemble. Thus the good fortune befell me in fact to see a genuine *Gesamtkunstwerk*."

It was left to Benois to beautifully sum up the significance of this extraordinary score: "There was something in it that I had somehow always been waiting for. And already at the second performance not the spectacle, not the dances, not the performance, not the executants captivated me, but the music conquered me, something infinitely close to me, something I could call *my* music." The success of *Sleeping Beauty* was solid enough for Vsevolozhsky to press Tchaikovsky for another ballet following the Mariinsky's premiere of *The Queen of Spades*, the same year as *Sleeping Beauty*. For the libretto, Vsevolozhsky proposed E. T. A. Hoffmann's tale of the *Nutcracker*. Tchaikovsky accepted, although he was not particularly delighted with the story. He was even less delighted when illness prevented Petipa from completing the new ballet; that assignment went to Ivanov.

Perhaps Tchaikovsky agreed to the commission because it included a companion piece, the one-act opera *Iolanthe*, for which he had higher hopes. At the premiere of this disparate pair of works on 18 December 1892, neither was the notable success *The Sleeping Beauty* or *The Queen of Spades* had been, although, surprisingly, the opera met with greater favor than the ballet. (*Nutcracker* did not reach the stage of Moscow's Bolshoi until 1919 or America until 1944, an odd fact for a work that is today the bread-and-butter of most ballet companies.) Modest Tchaikovsky, the composer's brother, felt that the children's scenes devised by Ivanov were "disastrous," and although Antonietta dell'Era, who created the Sugar Plum Fairy, was an able technician, she was unattractive and overweight.

As early as 1886, Vsevolozhsky and Petipa began to plan a revival of Tchaikovsky's *Swan Lake*, which had failed at its premiere in Moscow in 1877, and even as the *Nutcracker* was readied for its first performance, there is evidence that discussions concerning a new version of *Swan Lake* were underway. But Tchaikovsky remained uncertain that his music could be saved. It took the composer's death in 1893 for the idea to finally be realized. The full ballet was already planned for 1894, and the theater took the first step toward its resurrection with a remounting of act 2 by Ivanov as part of a Tchaikovsky memorial evening. Using suggestions by Vsevolozhsky, Tchaikovsky's brother Modest revised the plot lines, redefining Rotbart more sharply and making Siegfried the innocent victim of Rotbart's evil.

Modest would go on to revamp the entire story for the full-length version, for which Petipa joined forces with Ivanov to create the dances for acts 1 and 3 (he also contributed ideas to act 4). Despite Petipa's smooth exposition of the story in act 1 and the attractive national dances he created in act 3 (excepting the Hungarian and Venetian dances, which were the work of Ivanov), it is the affecting *ballet blanc* wrought by Ivanov for act 2 that remains the basis of *Swan Lake*'s prodigious success.

Modest's libretto plays down the original drama, which was conceived by his brother as a duel between good and evil. In its place, he came up with what amounts more to a fairy tale—a mixture of magic and deceit. The revamping of the score to fit the new story line was entrusted to Drigo, who deleted some pieces from the original, reorchestrated other passages, and added orchestrations of some of Tchaikovsky's piano works to fill in several dramatic gaps. Incidentally, Stravinsky has written that Leopold Auer, the famed teacher of violin at the St. Petersburg Conservatory, was required to play the solos in *Swan Lake* at the Imperial Ballet as "Soloist to His Majesty, The Czar." "I remember seeing him walk into the Mariinsky pit, play the violin solos (standing, as though for a concert), and then walk out again."

Whether he realized it or not, Tchaikovsky altered the course of ballet music in Russia. As Wiley has put it, in "a time and country where the success of a native composer was measured first of all in the opera house, in the concert room only after that, and not all in the ballet theater, Tchaikovsky made ballet composition a fit occupation. It is difficult to imagine anyone else who could have done this better—indeed, who could have done it at all." Without question it was Tchaikovsky who set the stage for the next significant, enduring symphonic ballet to be produced by Petipa—*Raymonda*, to a score by Alexander Glazunov.

Glazunov, who followed Rimsky-Korsakov as director of the St. Petersburg Conservatory, was just thirty when he was given the scenario for *Raymonda* in 1895 and commissioned by Vsevolozhsky to write the ballet. He took three years to complete the work, and it premiered in 1898 as a benefit evening for Legnani, who danced the title role with Sergei Legat as Jean de Brienne. Petipa was then eighty, but *Raymonda* showed no ebbing of inspiration on his part. It is rich in inventive ideas, and although a few more ballets would follow it, it remains Petipa's true valedictory. Indeed, it is a measure of both his gifts and those of Glazunov that the ballet has succeeded so well despite its limp scenario—a ridiculous plot laced with thwarted love and the supernatural. One critic went so far as to say it had "everything but meaning."

The new century brought a new director to the Imperial Theaters in St. Petersburg. Prince Sergei Mikhailovitch Volkonsky assumed the post in the last half of 1899, and Kshessinskaya, who had her difficulties with him, nevertheless later described him as "a highly cultured man and accomplished musician, [who] was an excellent pianist. He was also an admirable actor who often appeared on the amateur stage. His appointment was warmly greeted by all connoisseurs and promoters of art. . . . He always behaved like a man of the world, irreproachably educated, with delicate manners and without the slightest affectation."

Among Volkonsky's early appointees as an assistant was Sergei Diaghilev, then twenty-seven years old and the editor of an influential magazine, *The World of Art*. The hiring of Diaghilev and his firing six and a half months later must have seemed a minor matter at the time despite the controversy involved, but in retrospect it proved to be a pivotal moment in Volkonsky's short reign (he left his post in 1901). It is a matter that has dogged the heels of the Mariinsky ever since, for within a few years after leaving the theater, between 1908 and his death in 1929, Diaghilev established himself as a seminal figure in the performing arts of the twentieth century.

He secured his place by popularizing Russian art, dance, and music in the

West and by changing the face of ballet as few before or since have managed to do. In the beginning, however, the first dance company he brought to Paris in 1909 can and should be legitimately viewed as a touring version of the Russian Imperial Ballet. Its first repertory, in fact, was poached from the Mariinsky (although several of the works were modified by Fokine to suit Diaghilev's taste) and rehearsed in St. Petersburg. Originally, thanks to Kshessinskaya's intervention, patronage was obtained from Grand Duke Vladimir, and rehearsals began in the Hermitage Theater. But when Kshessinskaya, who was to be a part of the troupe, became dissatisfied with the roles assigned her, the grand duke withdrew his support and his funding, and the company was booted out of the Hermitage. After a few anxious days, during which other money was found, their rehearsals resumed in the German Club, a theater on the Ekaterinsky Canal.

Diaghilev's brief association with the Mariinsky is chronicled in a folder marked "secret" in the Imperial Archives. It contains a letter he sent to Nicholas II in the spring of 1901 following his dismissal from the theater. As this document has not been made public before, it seems only fair that after a century Diaghilev be allowed to air, in slightly condensed form, his side of the affair (the dates in are in the old style):

"Your Imperial Majesty . . .

"I have known Prince Volkonsky since before he became director of Imperial Theaters, as he wrote for *The World of Art* magazine, sponsored by Your Majesty, of which I am still editor-in-chief. Since I was admitted to civil service [3 September 1899], the Director has given me different errands, which I have done willingly. . . . Most of these errands involved my connections in the artistic world and were directly tied with my position as editor-in-chief of *The World of Art* magazine.

"Thus, with my help, the painter [Appolinary] Vasnetsov was commissioned to do the production of *Sadko* [at the Mariinsky], the painters [Léon] Bakst, [Eugène] Lancerey, and [Konstantin] Somov were commissioned to produce program books for the Hermitage Theater Performances, Bakst and Benois were commissioned for sketches for the opera *Cupid's Revenge* and for the pantomime *Le coeur de la Marquise* . . . for the Imperial Hermitage Theater.

"During the work on these commissions there arose many difficulties as very often the painters weren't able to supervise the exact execution of their artistic designs. When it was decided to include the ballet *Sylvia* in next year's repertoire, there was a suggestion to engage *The World of Art* painters [Valentin] Serov [for costumes], [Konstantin] Kolovin [for the second-act set], [Alexander] Golovin, Lancerey [for the third-act set], Benois [for the first-act set], and Bakst [for costumes]. I invited them on the part of the Director [and] they agreed to take part in the production, provided they would be guaranteed the exact execution of their designs. I informed the Director of their wishes, and as I was a close friend of the painters, he made me responsible for this production.

"Because I foresaw that problems would arise with other people engaged in this production, I asked Mr. Volkonsky to authorize me to be officially in charge of *Sylvia* and he agreed. The artists then set to work with great energy and enthusiasm, and I reported their progress to the Director. On 26 February of this year, at a meeting with Baron Kusov (the stage manager), Mr. Polenov (his assistant), Mr. Lopukhin (officer for special errands), and me, the Director announced his decision to place me in charge of this ballet. Then, after discussing several items—cost estimates, appointing a ballet master, and defining my relations with the stage managers—the Director said he would issue the following order to be written into the Register of Imperial Theaters: 'By the order of Director of Imperial Theaters, the officer for special errands Mr. Diaghilev is placed in charge of the production of *Sylvia*.' Those present at the meeting did not make any amendments or alterations to this order.

"On the evening of the same day, however, the Director, in a private letter, informed me that he could not place me officially in charge of *Sylvia*. As soon as the painters learned that he had changed his mind, they told me, and they notified Prince Volkonsky, that they wouldn't continue their work for Imperial Theaters for an indispensable condition for their success had been violated.

"Given these circumstances, I wrote a private letter to Prince Volkonsky telling him that I refused to participate in the production of *Sylvia*, and considering our crucial disagreement, I asked him to free me as well from the position of editor of the annual magazine of the Imperial Theaters. I told him that without the help of my painter friends I could not produce the annual on a proper artistic level. . . .

"On the same day, I was visited by Mr. Teliakovsky, the manager of [your] Moscow Theaters, who happened to be in St. Petersburg, along with Prince Volkonsky, and in the presence of painters, we discussed the problem. . . . The painters insisted that . . . Prince Volkonsky's change of mind had affected their position and that this was a matter crucial to them. This talk continued not less than two hours. . . . Prince Volkonsky promised to return later in the evening to finish the discussion, but, being delayed in the theater, he sent me a note inviting me to come to the theater after the performance. When I arrived, he declared once again that his original decision was no longer possible. . . . There was no suggestion or a hint of my dismissal.

"On 3 March I received a private letter from the Director in which he asked me to submit my resignation as officer for special errands. On 5 March . . . Prince Volkonsky notified me that not receiving any reply from me . . . he was forced to send another letter, this time an official one from the office of the Theater. The next morning in a letter to Prince Volkonsky I asked him to allow me to postpone my answer for a few days, but at 3 P.M. I received another letter from Volkonsky stating that his letter had already been sent and couldn't be retrieved.

"The same evening, I received his official . . . letter, and it stated that I was given a week to send in my resignation. On 13 March I informed the Director that I wasn't able to fulfill his wish, and on 15 March an order for my dismissal from service was issued. . . . In this order, the Director stated the reason for my dismissal was my refusal to continue in the position of editor of the annual magazine of the Imperial Theaters. . . . [Yet] I felt I had the right to resign [this position] because I receive an extra fee as a free-lance worker for it. And I had, after all, started working on the annual magazine before I entered the civil service. As to *Sylvia* [which was not mentioned in the Director's order of dismissal], I couldn't fulfill this task because the Director hadn't appointed me officially and because of the refusal of painters to cooperate.

"If my dismissal was caused [solely] by my refusal to send in my resignation, I dare to explain the following:

"After receiving the first letter from Prince Volkonsky asking me to resign, I realized that my future in the Civil Service would be endangered. This is why I asked the Director for a delay in order to investigate the possibility of transferring to another department. But although the Director received my request before his official letter was sent, he didn't stop the official one. . . . This meant I was given only two days for voluntary resignation from the service with the Imperial Theater. It's obvious that one can't find a new place in two days, this is why I refused to send in my resignation. . . . Then, on 15 March, I was dismissed under Article Three.

"Your Majesty knows the frightening meaning of such a dismissal. The Article provides the following reasons for dismissal: 'The inability to carry out professional duties, unreliability, and guilt known to the authorities but which can't be proved by facts.' None of these apply to me, and because of the gravity of such dismissal, the law demands that authorities be very cautious, objective, and unbiased in such cases.

"I dare claim to your Majesty that I am not guilty and can't think of any deed that could cause such a rare and severe punishment.

"Your Majesty's true subject,

Serge Diaghilev,

25 March 1901, St. Petersburg."

Volkonsky fills in some blanks in his memoirs. He writes that following the meeting between himself, Diaghilev, and other staff members, he was told privately by his staff that if Diaghilev were put in complete charge of the *Sylvia* production it "would cause such fermentations that they could not answer for the work being done." Diaghilev's biographer, Richard Buckle, attributes this to Diaghilev's "arrogance" and the enemies it was already making for him. Beyond this, it must have been a slap in the face to many at the theater that a minor official still in his twenties was given complete charge of a new production.

Although it doesn't come out in Diaghilev's letter to the czar, Benois tells us in his autobiography that Volkonsky was perfectly willing for Diaghilev to continue in charge of *Sylvia* (which was to star Olga Preobrazhenskaya, with choreography by the Legats), but without an official title. But even in his twenties, Diaghilev was not a man to allow others to take credit for his ideas. Buckle suggests that Diaghilev might have decided to be truculent on this matter because he felt he was in a strong position given his success in revamping the theater's annuals.

Benois writes that Diaghilev had hoped to "stagger the world with his annual. He thought that after that, it would become plain to everybody that he was capable of 'great deeds.' . . . It is just possible that our friend's ambitious plans—which he did not always hide from us—included the hope that he would, in time, replace Volkonsky himself and establish in the Imperial Theaters an era which would survive for posterity as 'The Diaghilev Era.' It is possible that Volkonsky was not quite blind to the dreams and ambitions of his brilliant subordinate. In any case in his relations with Seriozha [Diaghilev], a certain watchfulness not unmixed with suspicion began to appear."

In addition to his work on the annuals, Diaghilev no doubt believed he had a strong trump card in his close, carefully orchestrated friendship with Kshessinskaya, who was the same age as he. In her autobiography she notes that "I liked him from the first. . . . [He] had a rich head of hair with a greying lock in front, which earned him the nickname 'Chinchilla.' When he entered the Administration's box while I was dancing the waltz in *Esmeralda* my stage companions began to hum under their breath:

I've just heard that Chinchilla is in his box,
And I'm terribly afraid to make a mistake."

Benois has written that "there was always [a storm] when Diaghilev was anywhere near. . . . Dressed in his smart, faultlessly-fitting uniform [required of civil servants] he had a way of walking through the stalls, his head in the air, which made tongues wag and gossip about him." Obviously the strong personality that made enemies already had the power to attract attention and inspire awe and fear.

But it was Diaghilev who best summed himself up, no doubt in part with his tongue in his cheek. In 1895, in a famous letter to his stepmother, he wrote, "I am, first of all, a great charlatan, although brilliant, and secondly, a great charmer, and thirdly, very brazen, and fourthly, a man with a great amount of logic and [a] small amount of principles, and fifthly, I believe, without talent; however . . . I have found my true calling—patron of the arts. For that I have everything except money, but that will come."

As Kshessinskaya disliked Volkonsky, she might have hoped that Diaghilev would assume a more powerful role in the running of the Mariinsky and be in a better position to support her wishes. Whatever the truth, her lover at the time, Grand Duke Sergei, went to the czar's summer palace to talk the matter over with his nephew. After hearing the details from the grand duke, Nicholas is supposed to have said, "In Diaghilev's place I, too, would refuse to resign." At this point Diaghilev must have believed that victory was his.

But Volkonsky tells us otherwise. A minister of the court, making his usual report on household matters to the czar, showed him Volkonsky's letters to Diaghilev. After reading them, Nicholas agreed to sign the order for Diaghilev's dismissal. Benois writes that "the following day being [a] Sunday, there was no publication of the *Government Gazette*, but when Diaghilev unfolded the paper on Monday morning, secretly hoping to find in it Volkonsky's resignation, he found his own name accompanied by the disgraceful words: 'according to Article Three.'"

Article 3 was invoked only in serious cases involving misconduct. To Buckle "it was the equivalent of being cashiered from the army. Diaghilev may have feared that people would think he was being penalized for his homosexuality." As Benois puts it, "One can imagine Diaghilev's horror, shame and grief. All his hopes and plans had collapsed in one minute, and he, who dared to hold out against a very high dignitary, who had had the support of the Grand Duke, and even, [so] it seemed, that of the Monarch himself . . . was cast out."

Ironically, Volkonsky's own days at the theater were numbered after he crossed swords with the all-powerful Kshessinskaya. Unhappy with the hoops that were part of her costume for Petipa's *La camargo*—she felt that they hindered her movements—the ballerina refused to wear them. The following day a notice was posted that read, "The Director of the Imperial Theater fines the ballerina Kshessinskaya [so many rubles] for an unauthorized change in the costume prescribed by regulation for the ballet *La camargo*." The ballerina writes, "Bearing in mind my salary and position, the fine was so small that it was clearly meant to provoke and not to punish me. I could not submit to such an insult without taking steps to put it right. I had no other resource but to apply . . . to the Czar, begging him to have the fine remitted. . . .

"[Soon] a notice went up on the board: 'The Director of the Imperial Theaters hereby orders a remission of the fine imposed on the ballerina Kshessinskaya for an unauthorized change in the costume prescribed by regulation in the ballet *La camargo*.' Volkonsky felt that he should not remain at his post following this incident and handed in his resignation."

Kshessinskaya's concern for how she was costumed, however, would later have more positive results. When she danced Petipa's *Le talisman* in 1910, she had her costumer alter the traditional tutu, a decision that placed future ballerinas in her debt. As she writes, "Tutus generally began at the waist, and I [wanted] to lengthen the bodice. . . . I always seemed taller on the stage than I really was, and this illusion was strengthened by the new cut of the bodice. . . . My costume in the second act . . . so delighted Anna Pavlova that she asked me if she could have a similar one made for her foreign tour."

While Kshessinskaya reigned supreme on the stage of Mariinsky, it was Pavlova who came to epitomize the Russian ballerina for the rest of the world. In 1908, she became the first Russian dancer to undertake a foreign tour, which extended her name and fame throughout the Baltic region and later on to Berlin and Vienna. Born in St. Petersburg in 1881, the illegitimate daughter of a Jewish laundress and a soldier, she entered the Imperial Ballet School a decade later where she studied with Gerdt and Johansson, and upon graduation in 1899, she was accepted into the Mariinsky without an apprenticeship in the corps de ballet. She began as a *coryphée*, and her rise to the rank of prima ballerina was swift. From the start she attracted attention for her airy grace and easy technique. She quickly became a favorite of Petipa's during his final few years at the theater, creating leading parts in his ballets *The Seasons* and *Harlequinade*, and she also starred in the Legats' *Fairy Doll*.

Whereas Pavlova was initially admired for her vivacity and charm, it was Petipa who sensed in her an equal gift for pathos. He soon gave her the roles of Nikiya in *Bayadère* and Giselle, parts she made her own. There were noisy encounters at the Mariinsky between her emerging fans, the *Pavlovtzi*, and the followers of Kshessinskaya, setting off one of ballet's great rivalries. It was with Pavlova and Nijinsky in Fokine's *Chopiniana* that Diaghilev opened his first ballet season in Paris in 1909. She left Russia in 1914, and from then until her death in 1931 in the Netherlands, her life was one of incessant global tours. Her name, like Nijinsky's, came to be synonymous with dance.

The year of Pavlova's debut at the Mariinsky was the year Diaghilev joined the theater's staff. At that time he could not have known that in the ranks of the Imperial Ballet was a young soloist who would soon emerge as the next important figure in Russian choreography after Petipa and with whom his future fame would be closely aligned. Mikhail Fokine had joined the troupe in 1898 at the age of eighteen after graduating from the Imperial Academy of Ballet, where he had been a student of Gerdt, among others. As a dancer he was soon promoted to leading roles and was the frequent partner of Pavlova and Karsavina.

Of equal importance, he began his career as a teacher in 1902 and proceeded to institute major reforms both in the classroom and, as a choreographer, onstage. When his first group of students graduated, Fokine told them in an open letter, "I believe dance should express meaning, the spirit of the actors, their emotions, characters, and lives as they live them on stage. . . . In place of the dualism of mime and dance, ballet must become a harmonious blending of music, painting and plastic art." This was more than a manifesto. It was a battle cry that would bring Fokine into conflict with tradition. Balanchine once commented that with "Petipa everything was drafted along straight lines: the soloists in front, the corps in the back. But Fokine invented crooked lines. . . . For me he really invented the ensemble in ballet."

In her autobiography, Kshessinskaya writes that "Fokine rebelled against fixed poses [such as] the arms raised like a crown around the head. Without rejecting the framework of classical technique, he wanted a free expression of emotion. For his ballet, *Eunice*, . . . he went to the Hermitage Museum in order to study classical dances on vase paintings, and made a close inspection of everything which could reveal Greek and Roman art to him. . . .

"*Eunice* caused a great stir and provoked heated arguments and repercussions. There was a violent clash between the upholders of tradition and the supporters of what was new. Fokine had to wage a real war, both in the theater and out, against certain critics and balletomanes; but the conflict merely gave him more energy and strengthened his convictions. The old balletomanes reproached him with the taint of 'Duncanism' [as a young man Fokine had seen Isadora Duncan dance in St. Petersburg, and, although he later would attempt to repudiate it, her freedom and her barefoot, Greek-inspired movements had a profound effect on him and his dance aesthetics].

"Young people, on the other hand, gave an enthusiastic welcome to this breath of fresh air, which had come to give new life to the unalterable canons of classical ballet, which Fokine had certainly never intended to demolish. . . . The first night of *Eunice* was on December 10, 1906. I danced the main role. All the dancers were first class: Gerdt brought his admirable mime and style to the role of Petronius. Anna Pavlova gave a marvelous performance as Antonia. The part of Claudius the sculptor had been given to the excellent dramatic dancer, [Alexis] Bulgakov, who was so much at home in dramatic roles that he had once considered joining the Alexander Theater company . . . while the black slave was danced by [Leonide] Leontiev."

Along with *Eunice*, Fokine also created *Chopiniana, Le pavillon d'Armide,* and *Une nuit d'Égypte* for the Mariinsky (and all works that in altered forms would be the backbone of the Diaghilev's first Paris ballet season), but eventually conflicts at the theater would lead him to begin a separate, extraordinary, and more fruitful life in the West, where he created his most memorable works expressly for Diaghilev, including *Firebird, Petrushka, Le spectre de la rose,* and *Daphnis et Chloé.* Following a quarrel with Diaghilev over Nijinsky's emerging role as a company choreographer, the two men broke in 1912, although Fokine was persuaded to return to the Diaghilev fold in 1914 for a final season after Diaghilev abandoned Nijinsky. " To dance for Fokine," Karsavina said, "was to understand how to tell the world a story in which you believed."

His career at the Mariinsky was made easier when Vladimir Teliakovsky, the former director of Moscow's Bolshoi Theater, followed Volkonsky as director of the Imperial Theaters in 1901. Petipa's power base had begun to erode with Teliakovsky's appointment, for the director felt the venerable ballet master (then eighty-three) was too old for his post and new ideas in choreography were needed. The handwriting was on the wall when Teliakovsky had Alexander Gorsky—a former Mariinsky dancer who became ballet master at Moscow's Bolshoi Theater—create a new version of *Don Quixote,* which had long been danced in Petipa's choreography.

Teliakovsky also cut down the subscriber nights at the theater and the number of hereditary box holders, making room for a new and growing middle-class audience for dance and opera. This more open-minded public had begun to find fault with what to them were Petipa's dated productions. In addition, Teliakovsky started to modernize the look of productions on the Mariinsky's stage by bringing in the Moscow painters Alexander Golovin and Konstantin Kolovin. Many of their designs—*Don Quixote* and *Ruslan and Ludmila* among them—could still be seen at the theater during my year in St. Petersburg.

After the failure in 1903 of Petipa's last ballet, *The Magic Mirror,* which was scandalously received with whistles and shouts, he was unceremoniously eased out. From 1905 until his death in 1910, he was seen at the Mariinsky only in the audience, an embittered old man. He was buried in the cemetery of the Alexander Nevsky Monastery in the company of many of the artists who played major roles in the Mariinsky's history—Catterino Cavos, Tchaikovsky, Rimsky-Korsakov, Borodin, Mussorgsky, and Feodor Stravinsky.

The second year of Teliakovsky's reign in the new century brought the debut of a dancer who would create a major place for herself in the annals of dance alongside that of Kshessinskaya and Pavlova: Tamara Karsavina. The daughter of a Mariinsky dancer, Platon Karsavin, she arrived at the theater in 1902 when, she tells us in her absorbing memoirs *Theater Street,* the company "comprised about 180 persons, with a preponderance of women. The ranks were as follows—corps de ballet, *coryphées,* second and first solo dancers and ballerinas. Salaries went according to rank.

"Promotions were given every spring and announced by the *Journal of Orders*, an official weekly gazette. . . . Every morning, artists before entering the rehearsal room, tarried on the landing to scan the page of the journal. Remonstrances, fines, honorable mention and scanty words of gratitude appeared on that page. . . . I read the confirmation of my being received into the troupe as a *coryphée* on a raised salary of 720 roubles a year. It seemed a lot for the first year, as compared with the usual 600 of beginners."

Early on Karsavina had a run-in with Kshessinskaya that she never forgot. She had been paired for the first time with Nijinsky in a pas de deux from a now-forgotten Petipa ballet called *Roxana*. After a rehearsal, Karsavina writes, "an infuriated figure [Kshessinskaya] rushed up to me. 'Enough of your brazen impudence. Where do you think you are, to dance quite naked?' . . . It appeared that the strap on my bodice had slipped off and my shoulder had become uncovered, which I was unconscious of during my dance. I stood in the middle of the stage dumbfounded, helpless against volleys of coarse words hurled at me from the same cruel mouth. . . . By this time a dense crowd of sympathizers had surrounded me; my chronic want of handkerchiefs necessitated the use of my tartan skirt to wipe away the tears. Preobrazhenskaya stroked my head, repeating 'Sneeze on the viper, sweetheart. Forget her, and think only of those beautiful pirouettes of yours.' "

By the time Karsavina arrived on the scene, Teliakovsky had at last discontinued the policy of inviting foreign ballerinas, intent on building up the reputations of theater's leading dancers. This was a time, as Karsavina notes, when "none of our dancers had been abroad yet; Pavlova still belonged to our stage. There was a rare abundance of talent in the ballet at the time—adorable [Vera] Trefilova; frail, exquisite Pavlova . . . Preobrazhenskaya, witty and accomplished, the darling of the audience; brilliant to audacity, Mathilde Kshessinskaya; [Julie] Sedova, covering the stage in a few leaps; beautiful Marie Petipa; [Lubov] Egorova. . . . Round them grouped the spring garland of young dancers—the reserve. The corps de ballet was justly famous for accuracy and discipline. . . .

"The judgment of fellow-artists was more feared than the adverse criticisms of the newspapers, especially the judgment of the corps de ballet, where one met with the impartiality of professional knowledge unbiased by personal ambition. Seniority of age, respected from school days, made it possible for an obscure dancer of the corps de ballet about to retire to give advice to Preobrazhenskaya. 'Olinka,' the former would say, 'don't hunch your shoulders. I noticed you did so last night.' The advice was accepted gratefully."

The daughter of a civil servant, Preobrazhenskaya was not a beautiful woman, but she possessed excellent technique and a will of iron. For two years after joining the Imperial Ballet she danced in the corps de ballet, only occasionally being allowed to understudy a leading role. But gradually her abilities were recognized, and she was given excellent solo roles and built a loyal following. Beyond her vivid dancing, she, along with Karsavina and Fokine, played a dramatic part in the history of the company as one of the instigators of the 1905 strike at the theater.

The strike grew out of the unrest that resulted from an event in Russian history known as "Bloody Sunday"—22 January 1905. On that day the police in the capital fired into a large group of workers who had come to the Winter Palace to ask the czar for sufferance. Hundreds were killed, and the impact of these senseless murders led to an outburst of indignation throughout Russia. The massacre provided the impetus for a group of twenty-nine leading Russian musicians, among them Sergei Rachmaninov, Chaliapin, Sergei Taneyev, Alexander Gretchaninov, and Reinhold Glière, to publish a manifesto addressing their own grievances in a Moscow paper a few weeks later. It read in part: "Only free art is vital, only free creativity is joyful. . . . When in the land there is neither freedom of word and print . . . then the profession of 'free artist' becomes a bitter irony. We are not free artists, but, like all Russian citizens, the disfranchised victims of today's abnormal social conditions. In our opinion Russia must at last embark on a road of basic reforms."

Revolution was in the air on all sides, and by autumn it extended into the Mariinsky. Karsavina writes that the idea that "artists, so conservative at heart, usually so loyal to the Court, of which we were a modest part, should have succumbed to the epidemic of meetings and resolutions seemed to me like treason. Meetings were held everywhere; autonomy, freedom of speech, freedom of conscience, freedom of the printed word—even children at school were passing these resolutions. Whether in full conscience of the cause . . . or following a few leaders, our troupe also put forth claims and chose twelve delegates to negotiate them.

"Fokine, Pavlova and myself were amongst them. [We wanted] to choose our own committee to decide artistic questions and questions of salary [and] do away with the methods of bureaucratic organization." When the committee was rebuffed in its attempt to deliver the artists' grievances to Teliakovsky, who was away in Moscow, it was decided to try and prevent the performance the next day at the Mariinsky of *The Queen of Spades*, in which a number of dancers appeared.

"My duty," Karsavina recalled, "was to go round to the ladies' dressing rooms and call the dancers off. The task was distasteful to me, and my eloquence was not of the most persuasive. A few left the theater; the majority refused to strike. Within a few days the circular of the Minister of the Court [termed our action] a breach of discipline [and required] all who wished to remain loyal to sign a declaration. The great majority signed, leaving us, their chosen delegates, in the lurch. We represented nobody, yet continued to gather at Fokine's or Pavlova's flat. [At one meeting] the door bell rang. Fokine went to open [it]. A few moments later he staggered back into the room. 'Sergei has cut his throat,' and broke down sobbing. Sergei Legat, bitterly against his will, had been nagged into signing the declaration. The soul of loyalty, he felt himself a traitor. 'I am a Judas to my friends.' . . . He was found in the morning, his throat cut with a razor."

By mid-October the attempted revolution had been put down and amnesty was granted to those who had struck. Teliakovsky assembled his band of rebels, calling their action an act of flagrant insubordination, but adding that the act of amnesty had exonerated them. Karsavina ends this chapter in the theater's history by noting, "For a time an antagonism was felt between the two factions of the troupe, but that soon wore out. The funeral of Sergei brought us all together in a common grief. I felt thankfulness when resuming work; the theater became dearer than ever to me, the world in which I had almost despaired of living in again."

Fortunately, the career of Karsavina was not injured by this momentary lapse from grace, and she went on to forge an illustrious career at the Mariinsky that extended through the real Revolution of 1917. Fokine (who had been her lover and wanted desperately to marry her) was the paramount influence on her career both in St. Petersburg and abroad. With him and the Diaghilev company she had her most renowned triumphs, creating roles in such Fokine ballets as *Firebird, Petrushka, Le carnaval, Daphnis et Chloé,* and *Le spectre de la rose.* She remained in Russia until May 1918, when she escaped to Europe and rejoined the Diaghilev company.

Many of her chief roles were danced with Vaslav Nijinsky, with whom she formed a memorable partnership. His time at the theater was comparatively short, as was his career as a whole. In fact, his life has been summed up as ten years growing, ten years studying, ten years dancing, and thirty years mad. But he left an indelible mark on the dance, for, as Kshessinskaya reminds us, "Before his time, the male classical dancer, considered far inferior to the ballerina, was limited to supporting her and to dancing a few steps to give his partner a rest. Thanks to Nijinsky, he was raised to the highest level and became the ballerina's equal. [He] gave male dancing a new direction and style, which proved a veritable revolution in the art of ballet."

The son of Polish dancers who made their home and careers in Russia, Nijinsky came to the Mariinsky in 1907, although he had danced children's parts and small roles at the theater while still a student in the Imperial School, where his principal teacher was Mikhail Obukhov (he also worked with Sergei Legat). Karsavina, arriving early for class one day, noticed one of the boys who leapt higher than the others and seemed to linger in the air. "Who is that?" she asked Obukhov.

"It is Nijinsky; the little devil never comes down with the music," he replied.

Once, when asked if it was difficult to stay aloft, Nijinsky answered, "No! No! Not difficult. You just have to go up and then pause a little up there." He could toss off an *entrechat dix* with cool elegance, and the remarkable thing about Nijinsky's elevation was that there seemed to be no preparation. He simply shot upward. In time, however, he came to resent the attention paid to his seemingly miraculous technical abilities, and frequently he protested, "I am not a jumper; I am an artist." His sister, Bronislava Nijinska, had an explanation for his apparent defiance of space: "In the *allegro pas* he did not come down completely on the balls of his feet, but barely touched the floor with the tips of his toes to take the force for the next jump [thus] creating the impression that he remained at all times suspended in the air."

Kshessinskaya saw Nijinsky in his graduation performance in 1907 at the Mariinsky and asked to have him as her partner. Her interest in him meant that he was spared entering the company as a member of the corps de ballet. Later Fokine singled him out as well and gave him principal roles in his ballets *Le pavillon d'Armide* and *Une nuit d'Égypte* and in his revised *Chopiniana*, all ballets Nijinsky would dance in later versions for Diaghilev. At Fokine's invitation, Benois witnessed an early rehearsal for *Pavillon*, for which he designed the sets, and he too was impressed by Nijinsky's prowess.

"I would not have noticed him," Benois has written, "had not Fokine presented him to me as the artist for whom he had especially composed the part of Armide's slave, so as to give him a chance to display his remarkable talent. Fokine counted on amazing the public by the unusual heights of his *sauts* and *vols*, which the youth performed without any visible effort. I must confess that I was rather surprised when I saw this wonder face to face.

"He was a short [only five feet, four inches tall, weighing 130 pounds], rather thick-set fellow with the most ordinary, colorless face. He was more like a shop assistant than a fairytale hero." Karsavina, on the other hand, described him as "exotic, feline, elfin." Thanks to his role in *Pavillon* and other parts at the time, Nijinsky quickly became a local celebrity in St. Petersburg; it was in Europe and America that he became a god.

He was idolized not only for his prodigious technique, but for the enormous dramatic truth he brought to his roles and the wide range of emotions and moods they embodied, from ethereal to animalistic, from otherworldliness to sexual. His break with the Mariinsky occurred in 1911 after his first performance there of Albrecht in *Giselle* (he had danced the role first with Karsavina for Diaghilev in Paris the year before).

When Diaghilev decided to form his own company and no longer borrowed dancers and repertory from the Mariinsky, it was essential that he obtain the services of Nijinsky, with whom he was in love. But there were still two years left to run in Nijinsky's contract with the theater. The matter came to a head with Nijinsky's first *Giselle* in St. Petersburg. He decided to wear his costume from Paris, which did not include the usual trunks designed to be worn over a dancer's tights. Whether he was encouraged in this or not by Diaghilev remains uncertain, but by the Russian standards of the time the costume made him look provocative.

Some have said he failed to wear his dance belt, but like his biographer Richard Buckle, I feel that this tale is suspect. As Buckle puts it, this athletic support was "an article male dancers in classical ballet would feel very uncomfortable without." At any rate, an official protested Nijinsky's costume before the performance, but he refused to alter it. Although Teliakovsky was away at the time, the dowager empress was present at the performance and is said to have strongly objected to Nijinsky's appearance (though proof of this has never been established). The next day the *St. Petersburg Gazette* announced Nijinsky's dismissal, which freed him to join Diaghilev's upcoming season in Paris.

The impresario was quick to capitalize on the situation. He wired his partner in France, the impresario Gabriel Astruc, "After triumphant debut—present all St. Petersburg—Vestris was dismissed within twenty-four hours. Reason costume . . . Monstrous intrigue. Press indignant this morning. Interview director announcing willing take back Vestris who refuses. Appalling scandal. Use publicity . . . Serge." As a footnote, Karsavina, his Giselle on this controversial night, felt that Nijinsky "reached such heights of inspiration as never before."

Nijinsky and Diaghilev went on to create dance history in the West, while Nicholas ii and Russia set off on a disastrous course that resulted in a great casualty of World War i—the collapse of Russia's ruling house. During this time, Karsavina tells us, recruits could be seen drilling in the square in front of the Mariinsky. Yet life in the theater "followed an unhalting course. . . . The usual plan of giving a number of new productions in each season remained unaltered, although . . . for mere revivals, costumes and scenery would be brought out of the thrifty past.

"In those sorrowful years the stage remained strangely serene . . . [and] the same queues formed outside the box office; no empty seats disgraced the Mariinsky; but the physiognomy of the public was greatly altered—no more bright uniforms, no more lovely toilettes. Every night the audience demanded the national anthems. As new allies gradually joined the cause, our intervals became longer [for] now a full quarter of an hour would be required to go through the anthems."

The last important choreographic figure at the Mariinsky during its twilight as an Imperial Theater was Boris Romanov, who had graduated from the Imperial Ballet School in the same class as Fokine. He had made a name for himself first as a character dancer and appeared in the first seasons of Diaghilev's Ballets

Russes. But choreography gradually became more dominant in his life (for Diaghilev he created *La tragédie de Salomé* to music of Florent Schmitt in 1913 and staged Stravinsky's *Rossignol* the next year).

Although Romanov created new dance works for the Mariinsky as early as 1912, his most significant work would be done after the Revolution and Lenin's rise to power. By that time World War I had nearly run its course, the monarchy had fallen, peace had been made with Germany, Czar Nicholas II and his family had been assassinated, and life in the country and in the Mariinsky was shaken to its very core.

CHAPTER EIGHT

December: Spreading the Word—Audio

ERGIEV'S primary task on returning from Japan in early December of 1995 was to tape the first commercial recording of the original version of Verdi's *La forza del destino*, which he had returned to the company's repertory with a concert performance in 1994. Watching the proceedings over a week's time, I began to feel that either Gergiev was the most confident man in the world, with an unflinching belief in his forces and his own abilities, or one of the most foolish. He and the company had plunged into a major recording without rehearsal and without having performed *Forza* for more than a year. On top of this, he scheduled a performance of the Verdi Requiem for the evening of the first session, which was also being given on the fly.

The day before Verdi and *Forza* began to dominate life in the theater, however, the Mariinsky's singers, dancers, players, stagehands, and staff were assembled to meet Yuri Schwarzkopf, Malkov's replacement as the theater's new administrative head. He came to the Kirov from the directorship of the Komissarzhevskaya Musical Theater in St. Petersburg, and his appointment was made by Victor Chernomyrdin, the minister of culture in Moscow. It was said that Schwarzkopf was a close friend of Sobchok's, and certainly the mayor and Gergiev had been closely consulted before the decision to appoint him was made.

Addressing the assembled personnel, Gergiev registered his shock at how swiftly the ballet scandal had echoed around the world and the great shame he felt for what had happened and the way in which it had tarnished the Kirov's name. "The arrests and investigation have caused doubts everywhere, and there is the danger that people will lose faith in the theater," he continued. Even worse, he added, the ongoing investigations were draining needed energy from the theater. Instead of new performances and recordings, the company was having to deal with conflicts and arguments. "We have to prove we are the best with our fine, powerful work. We must keep all that is good here and make certain that it is not destroyed."

In introducing Schwarzkopf to the assembly, Gergiev stated, "I liked him from the first time we met when I saw how he showed his teeth at the mayor's office while struggling for funds for his theater." With his white hair and thick frame, Schwarzkopf bears more than a passing resemblance to Boris Yeltsin. He spoke softly as he told the company that his first concern was to bring the theater out from under the shadow of corruption. He added that the turmoil not only had hurt the ballet troupe, but also had damaged the aura of the Mariinsky. But, he quickly added, the theater was developing plans to combat the scandal and the fallout that went with it. "I do not like to speak a lot," he said in conclusion; "let's get to work, and I beg you not to come to me with rumors and gossip."

For *Forza*, Philips's engineers had set up their control room in Gergiev's office, and great lengths of cables stretched from it to a forest of microphones on the stage and in the pit. They were ready the next morning when those in the company involved with *Forza* reported to work at 11 A.M. But as Gergiev was two hours late, the session did not begin until early afternoon. In deference to the tenor Gegam Grigorian, the first item on the agenda was the treacherous third-act cabaletta Verdi composed for Don Alvaro, which he jettisoned later when he revised the score. Grigorian dispatched its high-lying and stentorian demands impressively. In fact, it is hard to imagine another current tenor who could deal so confidently with this frightening stretch of music.

With this hurdle out of the way, the session jumped back to act 1 to begin at the beginning. In the first scene Grigorian continued as strongly as he had started, although dark clouds soon gathered with the tenuous singing of the young bass Askak Abdrazakov, an inexperienced singer out of his depth in even so small a role as the Marchese, and the brittle vocalism of Galina Gorchakova, whose singing lacked variety of tone and was none too steady in pitch.

Nor was there much satisfaction to be had that evening from the performance of the Requiem. Abdrazakov was hopeless, and Olga Borodina was off form (she was ill during this period and persuaded Gergiev to postpone a new production of *Carmen* being created around her). Added to this was an unmusical, throaty tenor (Teimuraz Gugushvili) and a cipher of a soprano (Margarita Alaverdyan). As for Gergiev, he was not focused, and the chorus and orchestra were one-dimensional. The performance was among the weakest experiences of the season.

The next day's sessions started with *Forza*'s third act. Both Grigorian and Nikolai Putilin were in rousing form, although it took time for Putilin to work up a full head of steam. Gorchakova followed with a repeat of her first-act aria, which was more convincing and secure than her singing had been the day before. For the recording, Philips engaged an assistant conductor from La Scala, Gabrieli Pisani, to work with Gergiev and the company. It was clear from his recurrent interruptions and impatience that he was not sympathetic with many of Gergiev's tempos and phrasings.

Gergiev listened patiently to Pisani's suggestions, but he stuck to his guns, and his seeming willfulness made sense. Why record *Forza* in Russia with a Russian cast and chorus only to impose on them an Italian performance norm? A large part of the project's validity was a Russian perspective that would set it apart from Western *Forza*s. Still, a careful rehearsal period would have moved the sessions along more efficiently and wasted less time. Gergiev rehearsed as he went, which left the cast and chorus restless. Yet when he finally shaped a section as he felt it, the music was usually delivered with crushing power.

The third session was devoted to all of act 4 but Leonora's aria. It unfortunately unmasked a further glaring deficiency in the casting and, more significantly, in the company itself. Mikhail Kit lacked the sonority and imposing presence needed for Padre Guardiano (he would have better employed as the Marchese), and his performance emphasized the fact that the Kirov was for the moment woefully deficient when it came to exceptional bass voices. This is probably one reason *Boris Godunov* was, for the time being, absent from the repertory, and it was a drawback to the casting of Dosifei in the company's performances of *Khovanshchina*. Vladimir Ognovenko is easily the finest of the Kirov's present crop of basses, although he is actually a bass-baritone. Still, he would have made a more incisive, dramatic Guardiano than Kit.

The next day, the sessions moved backward to act 3, scene 3, where again Putilin and Grigorian generated tremendous energy and excitement. Borodina still did not feel well enough to record Preziosilla's parts, so Gergiev continued to work around her. The afternoon brought Gorchakova back for "Pace, pace, mio Dio," and it was soon apparent that whatever gains she had made with "Me pellegrina ed orfana," the last-act aria was a setback. There was not a hint of *pianissimo* singing. Every note was batted out *fortissimo*, and her top seemed sustained by her jaw more than by her breath.

I played hooky from the evening session to see Bronislava Nijinska's *Les noces* downtown at the Maly Theater, which was being paired with Fokine's *Petrushka* in a semblance of its original decor and choreography. *Les noces* was also a re-creation of the sets, costumes, and choreography created for Diaghilev's Ballets Russes, and, being new, it was one of the strongest productions I encountered at the Maly, which normally operates on a shoestring. More typical of the company was its threadbare *Petrushka*, in which the corps was uneven and the orchestral playing poor.

During intermission, I added another memorable malapropism to the collection I had begun while in Russia. A lady, noticing an empty seat by me, inquired in thickly accented English, "Is that chair busy?" I assured her it wasn't, and she quickly occupied it. Other of my favorite misappropriations of English included a sign in a hotel above the reception desk that read, "For room service, go to seventh floor," and one outside the locked door of a bar in the same hotel that informed a thirsty client, "This bar is broken."

Apart from some retakes and other patching needed to complete *Forza*, the sessions came to an end five days after they had begun. Borodina was at last on hand for Preziosilla's music and sailed through "Rataplan" and her other scenes with a bravura ease that was breathtaking. In contrast, Gorchakova inched her way through "Madre, pietosa Vergine," sounding cautious and precarious. The sessions were running a day overtime, and to complete his work, Gergiev was forced to postpone a scheduled departure for Amsterdam and a concert with the Concertgebouw.

On the final *Forza* day, Gergiev looked exhausted and perplexed, and he confessed he had lost any sense of the recording as a whole. He said he would have preferred to go through the opera from first note to last and then retrace his steps fixing problem spots. It would have been better still, he maintained, to record the work live, as he had done the fall before in San Francisco with Massenet's *Hérodiade*. That opera was taped over the course of several performances and then assembled for a commercial issue by Sony, one of the few times Gergiev has strayed from the Philips fold.

Recording *Forza* was more than just another Kirov-Philips venture. It was a calculated and important step (as was the Paris concert performance the following spring) toward easing the opera back into the company's stage repertory in a production that was to include a re-creation of the opera's original sets. During the next few years, this exciting plan was an on-again, off-again trial for all concerned. It did not become a reality until the White Nights festival in 1998.

But the project remained dear to Gergiev, and he hoped to interest Philips as well in a video recording of the opera. In 1995, though, the head of artists and repertory at Philips, Costa Pilavachi, was far from certain that a video *Forza* was possible at the time; it depended, he told me, on securing a coproduction (the opera was eventually taped in 1998). "We taped, for instance, a *Nutcracker* here, but only because a Japanese company wanted it. Still, Philips's video projects will continue at the Kirov every year or year and a half, or whenever we find others willing to go in with us financially on a specific work.

"Philips is considering taping, for example, *Love for Three Oranges* and *A Life for the Czar*, which Valery is planning to bring back to the theater. Personally, I would love to tape *Lady Macbeth*. The important thing is that our involvement in the Kirov is real, and I think our presence here stimulates the entire company to perform at a high level. As you know, the Kirov is practically the last true ensemble company left in the world, even though it is inevitable that there are going to be inordinate problems with a company that puts on a different opera or ballet each night under the conditions that exist in Russia at the moment.

"Let's face it, the Kirov was in the dark ages for so long, it is going to take another decade to bring it to a consistently high level. But for the next five or seven years our relationship with the Kirov will probably be as intense as it is now. If the company should develop into a more international theater, there is no reason why we can't do more than just Russian repertory here, for there are only so many Russian operas that can be recorded or videotaped. But eventually Philips's association with the theater may have to take a back seat to its association with Gergiev."

By 1996, according to Pilavachi, Gergiev's CDs were beginning to sell well, although, he reminded me, "they have all been in a very specialized area of repertory. But Russian music was, we felt, the best way to introduce him to a broad recording-buying public. Other music will come as well—Berlioz, Wagner, and even Beethoven and Bruckner. He excels in all of these, and we have important plans for him in the future. As far as Gergiev is concerned, Philips is in for the long haul." (Eventually, *Prince Igor* and *Betrothal in a Monastery* were also videotaped, but only *Forza* had been released commercially by late 2000.)

With *Forza* completed, Schwarzkopf in place, and Gergiev off to Holland for a round of concerts (he would be back in St. Petersburg in mid-December only for single performances of *Salome, The Maid of Pskov,* and *The Queen of Spades*), the theater began to settle into some semblance of its normal routine. In quick succession came another sublimely affecting *Giselle* by Asylmuratova that was lucid of step and fragile of gesture, and a peculiar first *Faust* of the season that was musically abysmal and used a corrupt version of the score. Apart from Vasili Gerello's handsomely sung Valentin, it was also vocally poor. But it had some curiosities worth noting. The production consisted entirely of old-fashioned painted drops that must have been at least fifty or sixty years old and gave it a time-capsule allure. The Soldiers Chorus was staged as a complete scene unto itself with a boisterous brass band on stage, the Walpurgis Night was presented with the complete ballet, and the prison scene eliminated the final chorus proclaiming "Christ is resurrected," no doubt a hangover from the anti-church Soviet days.

December brought the first *Nutcracker* performance of the season. During my year in St. Petersburg it was danced almost entirely as a showcase for the Vaganova Academy. In this *Nutcracker*, the adult dancers were in the minority and more along for the ride. One of the many contributions made each year by the school to the theater, it stressed the close ties, dating back to the imperial era, that still exist between the theater and the dance academy.

The 1995–96 season paralleled the 258th year of this renowned institution, whose ballet master during my year in St. Petersburg was the late Igor Belsky, a choreographer and former Kirov soloist. "The best of Russian ballet has passed through our doors," he told me with understandable pride, "and we are striving to carry on the tradition, to preserve those qualities which have always set the style of the St. Petersburg school apart from other ballet schools in Russia.

"Above all, this special St. Petersburg style is a combination of acting, academic discipline, a strict observing of the tenets of classical ballet, and, last but not least, a dancer's ability to control the hands and the body with absolute freedom. Of course, we are well aware of other ballet disciplines. In her own day, Vaganova did a great deal to unite the Italian, French, and Russian schools, and she put her ideas together in the world's first dance textbook, which set out her principles and methods of ballet teaching so that other generations could aspire to the same dizzy heights."

Belsky was quick to deny that the Kirov had been isolated from dance developments in the West, a defensive attitude left over from Soviet days. In his opinion, "Vaganova and her pupils [Marina] Semenova, [Galina] Ulanova, [Tatiana] Vecheslova, and [Natalia] Dudinskaya actively responded to every new development in world choreography, and today our graduates are capable of anything— choreography by Bournonville, Balanchine, Robbins, [Roland] Petit, [Maurice] Béjart, and other Western masters. According to John Taras, who staged Balanchine's *Symphony in C* for the Mariinsky, our dancers perform it better than most foreign troupes, so we have no reason to feel second best to Western companies. In fact, Western dancers don't enjoy the same range of possibilities that the Russian school offers. Not only have we reached the highest peak of professionalism and technique, but we have created an enormous repertory that has become a birthright.

"I was in New York not long ago for the graduation ceremonies of the School of American Ballet, and I can't honestly say that they've got an edge on the Russian system. I've seen plenty of other dance schools as well, and I've had long chats [about this issue] with many people, including Balanchine, who once partnered my aunt Nadezhda Bazarova. Although he's best known as a Western choreographer, Balanchine, after all, graduated from the St. Petersburg institute, and he learned the principles of Russian classical choreography there.

"I took over the Vaganova Academy after Konstantin Mikhailovich Sergeiev, who did much to enlarge and develop it, and I introduced a modern dance class and a jazz course to keep up with the times and give our young dancers an opportunity to find their feet in modern choreography. I also included modern works in the academy's repertory, especially Balanchine's."

The current workload is heavy for the children. Lessons begin at 9 A.M. and end at 5.30 P.M., and then there are rehearsals at night. This is especially hard on those who live a long distance away, although, like all the academy's students, they get a free lunch each day. The school is placing a great deal of emphasis on English today, and French is now taught only in terms of ballet terminology. It is also offering more fine-arts courses in the upper grades and staging many purely dramatic scenes and productions as well.

Belsky had hoped to reestablish the system used during the imperial era, when all the dance students lived in apartments attached to the school. He felt this would preserve their strength and improve discipline. And prior to his death, the academy was preparing a building in its courtyard for that purpose; in 1996 some members of the Kirov's junior company were already living there. There were plans as well to reopen the small chapel inside the school, left over from the czarist period.

"We're also trying to broaden the children's horizons and to introduce them to the cultural life of St. Petersburg," Belsky continued. "They go on regular trips to museums and conferences, and, of course, our students play an active role in productions at the Mariinsky. We even put on our own shows there, such as the *Nutcracker*, and our young dancers are an integral part of repertory pieces like *Sleeping Beauty*, *Don Quixote*, and *Cinderella*. These test their potential as performers even before they appear in our graduation productions each spring, held at the Mariinsky. Furthermore, we present each year a special program at the Hermitage Theater, and pupils from the first to the fifth grade regularly stage concerts in the Academy Theater.

"While there's been no drop in professional training at the school, we do face a real problem, unfortunately, in the deterioration of the quality of candidates we audition for admission, particularly the boys. It's also getting harder to find girls who make a strong impression, look good, and move well. While we conduct an extensive selection process each year, we take only about thirty girls from some twelve hundred candidates. We lose a lot of them along the way. This year we're dropping nine girls from the fifth grade.

"At present there's also a large contingent of foreigners studying with us from Korea, Japan, America, Canada, and even the United Arab Republics. We only accept foreigners from the age of seventeen and then for one or two years only. Some of them then stay on to work in Russia, as it's hard to find regular work abroad. But, as you see by our schedule this season alone, we keep very busy, and this activity has helped preserve our ballet in all its glory even through hard times.

"During World War II and the blockade of St. Petersburg, a lot of our young men died, and we lost several teachers from the old school as well. But one standard has remained, for we believe that technique should never be a substitute for artistry, otherwise the culture of dance will vanish forever. The most important thing for us and for dance is for the academy to continue to flourish. And we will, because we will always observe the same motto: Preserve the old but keep creating the new."

The *Nutcracker*, however, was one case where the old was not preserved and the new was unsatisfying, especially for anyone raised on Balanchine's production, with its greater sense of fantasy, its more beautiful proportions, and its finer dramatic logic. The Kirov's *Nutcracker*, apart from the opening scene, was poorly designed, weakly choreographed, and not the showcase it was meant to be for the young dancers. They were unequal to the divertissements in the last act, a fact underlined by pitting them against two leading Kirov dancers in the roles of the Sugar Plum Fairy and her Cavalier.

After a vivid *Sadko* the following evening, with Yuri Marusin in top form in the title role and the veteran tenor Konstantin Pluzhnikov sounding amazingly fresh and velvety as the Indian Guest, Asylmuratova undertook her only performance of the season in the role of Zarema in a favorite Soviet ballet, *The Fountain of Bakhchisarai*. This 1934 work, based on a Pushkin poem, was premiered at the Kirov and long served as a major vehicle for Galina Ulanova, who created Maria, the ballet's other leading female character.

Seeing this work without the affection the Russians have for it and minus any prior associations, it was difficult to be tolerant of the weak, derivative score by Boris Asafiev or the predictable choreography by Rotislav Zakharov (who in 1949 had another success when he restaged Glière's ballet *The Bronze Horseman* in Moscow; it had originally been choreographed for the Kirov by Sergeiev, who danced the premiere in 1948 with Dudinskaya). Not surprisingly, *The Fountain of Bakhchisarai* is rarely seen outside Russia except when the Kirov brings it on tour, and even so rare an artist as Asylmuratova could not infuse it with meaning or life.

During December, I had cause to recall an observation of the Marquis of Queensberry. In attacking his son's relationship with Oscar Wilde, Queensberry said that to look a thing was as bad as being it. His words came back to haunt me when Gergiev turned over his orchestra and chorus to the American businessman Gilbert Kaplan for a performance of Mahler's Second Symphony, the only piece in Kaplan's repertory. I would not venture to say that the Kirov can be bought, but this concert certainly gave the appearance that it was a possibility, and that in itself was bad.

This depressing evening, and the fact that the theater's exceptional musicians were subjected to such amateurism, was sad enough in itself. What others, such as the conductor Mariss Jansons, who was present in the royal box with Gergiev, thought, I can only imagine. Gergiev adamantly denied that the theater had received a cent from Kaplan, and the only reason behind the performance I could fathom was that Gergiev was planning to add the Mahler Second to his repertory (which he eventually did), and this was an occasion for the orchestra to try it out. He has used this ploy before with other guest conductors.

The Mahler performance especially rankled because it came on the heels of two other evenings where the line between art and commercialism was crossed, to the detriment of the theater. The first performance of the season of Liepa's Fokine evening had been sponsored by Christian Dior to promote a new perfume, and on a later occasion, a theater gala was backed by a local bank. It would have been one thing had the hard sell on either occasion been confined to the lobby, but in each instance it was allowed to invade the stage. The Kaplan evening was even more distressing, for it encroached on the music and was dispiriting for all concerned, especially the players, many of whom complained bitterly to me afterward.

Two nights later, Gergiev was back in the Kirov's pit for Rimsky-Korsakov's *Maid of Pskov*. I had seen it a month before, but this striking piece had not registered with quite the same impact it did under Gergiev's leadership, when it became gripping music theater. The orchestra was in peak form, the chorus equally sonorous and superb, and adding to the excitement was the stunning use made of the Mariinsky's peal of bells, which had been built into a back wall of the theater expressly for *A Life for the Czar*. Later they were used to spellbinding effect at the premiere of *Boris Godunov*, and they still ring out impressively today.

Beyond the sweep and pageantry of Rimsky's score, I loved the richness of the Mariinsky's old-fashioned production, with its canvas drops, lavish staging, and horses galloping at full tilt across the front of the stage in the last act. Like *La bayadère*, it made me feel I had been born too late and would have been more at home with the theater of a century earlier, when such trappings were the norm. The cast for *Pskov* was not extraordinary, but it did include one of the few performances of the season by the plaintive-voiced Tatiana Novikova, one of the theater's veteran sopranos and still an affecting artist.

A repeat two nights later of Bournonville's *La sylphide*, a dance work that exudes the very breath of romanticism, left me feeling that if *Giselle* is ballet's *La sonnambula*, this might well be its *Lucia di Lammermoor*. The title role was danced without great distinction by Veronika Ivanova, but I gained a deeper appreciation of Andrei Yakovlev, her partner, a Kirov workhorse who danced a wide variety of roles during the season, from Albrecht to Romeo. He may not be a poet, but he is a marvelously dependable dancer of consummate ease and an important asset to the company, with his well-defined technique and easy elevation.

The audience the next evening for *The Queen of Spades* was forced to play a waiting game when the 7:30 P.M. curtain time came and went. Gergiev had gone to Moscow for the day and bad weather delayed his return. The curtain was held twenty-five minutes, as no one backstage knew when, or whether, he would turn up. When his plane finally landed, he took a cab straight to the theater, pausing only long enough to don his tails before entering the pit. Not surprisingly, his energy level was low, and matters were made worse by the last-minute replacement of the scheduled Lisa with an indifferent soprano from the Maly Theater. What finally made sense of the evening, however, was Vladimir Galuzin's impassioned performance of Herman.

By Christmas morning, the temperature was down to twenty degrees below zero centigrade, and the Neva and the city's canals were frozen solid. I was reassured by a maid in my hotel, however, that this was really not such a bad winter. After all, she added laconically, the Baltic Sea had not yet frozen over. But the weather turned the walk to the theater the next evening for a lackluster *Don Carlo* into a wondrous moment. The leafless branches of the trees that lined the street were covered with ice and powdered with snow, and the streetlights shining through them gave them an inner glow that created a scene of indescribable wonderment. It was one of the compensations in a long Russian winter.

CHAPTER NINE

The Soviet Years: Opera

THE UNREST that led to Nicholas II's abdication peaked at the Mariinsky on 21 February 1917 during a performance conducted by Nikolai Malko. The chorus, demanding a salary increase, refused to sing, and the soloists onstage did little more than whisper. Malko stopped the performance and had the curtain lowered. Before long, however, it was raised again, the orchestra began to play and the dancers to dance, and the opera continued, undermining the strike. Malko also conducted the last performance in the Mariinsky as an Imperial Theater—*Eugene Onegin*. For a short while performances ceased.

When they resumed in March with Rimsky's *May Night*, the evening began with the chorus singing Alexander Tcherepnin's "Do not weep over corpses" and "The Song of the Volga Boatmen." Ivan Ershov read his poem "Freedom," and after the opera ended the "Marseillaise" was sung. "The only new thing in the theater," Malko has written, "was the talkativeness which was a characteristic of the entire company at the time. I personally was given many non-musical duties to perform. I was the chairman of five different committees, and, for a time, the chairman for the general meeting of the soloists."

The same month, Nicholas II bowed to the inevitable. The war with Germany was clearly a lost cause, and Russia was split in two by conflict, mounting casualties, and demands for change. With the czar's abdication in favor of his brother the Grand Duke Michael (who quickly abdicated the next day), a provisional government was formed. This was merely a prelude to a full-scale revolution, which was set in motion in November with a gunshot from the cruiser *Aurora* anchored in the Neva River. The gun could be heard across the Neva at the Narodny Dom, where Chaliapin had sung Philip II in Verdi's *Don Carlo* that evening. On his way home he had to dodge stray bullets. At the Mariinsky, the ballet was dancing a double bill of *Nutcracker* and Fokine's *Eros*, a ballet set to Tchaikovsky's *Serenade for Strings*. A few days afterward the theater was closed, and its doors did not reopen until December.

As part of his new government, Lenin appointed Anatoly Lunacharsky—who once described himself as an "intellectual among Bolsheviks, [and a] Bolshevik among intelligentsia"—as the people's commissar of public education, the man under whose authority fell the arts in the emerging Soviet state. His job, as outlined by Boris Schwarz in his absorbing book *Music and Musical Life in the Soviet Union*, was "to educate a vast, untutored mass audience; to win the confidence of the arts intelligentsia faced with new social responsibilities; and to convince political leaders that support of the arts was an integral part of mass education."

His hands were full, especially as Lenin had strong objections to what he termed the "pompous court style" of opera. This brand of theater smacked too much of what he was out to change. His priorities were clear: education first, the arts second. "While in Moscow perhaps 10,000 people will come to the theater," he said in 1920, "there are millions trying to learn how to write their name, how to count."

Soon after Lunacharsky's appointment, Malko remembers, the commissar came to "a meeting of singer-soloists at the Mariinsky Theater and made a one-hour speech, which dispelled the atmosphere of distrust and fright that nearly all the intellectuals felt toward the Bolsheviks." But, as Schwarz puts it, Malko's recollection of events of the time were "rose-colored," for "there was considerable friction and pressure before the artists yielded to party directives," and at the Mariinsky "there was open defiance of new government regulations, and some of the performances were disrupted.... So strong was the resentment of some members (including the chief conductor [Alexander] Siloti) that there were resignations in protest against any negotiations whatsoever with the Bolsheviks."

But Lunacharsky prevailed with his willingness to compromise and his determination to achieve his ends without undue pressure. Indeed, the man seemed to have not only a belief in the arts in the life of Russia's people but a personal love of them. When Malko gave Glinka's *Ruslan and Ludmila* at the Mariinsky as the theater's first new, post-Revolution production, Schwarz notes that Lunacharsky stepped before the curtain to address an audience that was largely new to opera: "To you, workers, will be shown one of the greatest creations, one of the most cherished diamonds in the wondrous crown of Russian art. On a valuable tray you are presented a goblet of beautiful, sparkling wine—drink it and enjoy it."

Schwarz also quotes Konstantin Stanislavsky, the fabled director of the Moscow Art Theater, as saying, "The doors of our theater opened exclusively for the poor people and closed for a time to the intelligentsia. Our performances were free to all who received their tickets from factories and institutions where we sent them. We met face to face ... with spectators altogether new to us, many of whom, perhaps the majority, knew nothing not only of our theater, but of any theater.... We were forced ... to teach this new spectator how to sit quietly ... how to come into the theater at the proper time, not to smoke . . . not to bring food into the theater and eat it there, to dress in his best so as to fit more into the atmosphere of beauty [and] at first this was very hard to do."

The former Mariinsky faced the same problems, but Schwarz reports a telling comparison made by Pavel Andreiev, a singer of the time, between the public during the imperial era and the new audiences: "We used to call the subscription public 'the guillotine.' There were times one wondered whether or not there was an audience in the hall. . . . Now, although the listeners sit in rags, the enthusiasm had no bounds."

In 1918 the Mariinsky became the State Academic Theater of Opera and Ballet, or GATOB, an acronym for the Russian name. At first, its repertory remained unchanged. The theater still mounted the standard Russian works, plus familiar operas by Verdi, Wagner, Gounod, Rossini, and Camille Saint-Saëns. But to many zealous party members these were too conservative; one of them even demanded that works of Tchaikovsky and Rimsky-Korsakov be removed because "they propagated ideas inimical to the proletariat." Declared the painter and writer Vladimir Mayakovsky, "We do not need a dead mausoleum where dead works are worshiped, but a living factory of the human spirit."

Once again Lunacharsky came to the defense of the theaters: "Only naive people can discuss seriously that our great opera houses must change their repertoire. No revolutionary repertoire exists, and we cannot afford new productions. It means that, at present, we can only preserve and replenish carefully and slowly the repertoire of the academic theaters." But although the repertory did not change fast enough to please zealots, the number of performances was increasing, and the old works were beginning to be rethought, restaged, and made to fit party ideals.

The controversial stage director Vsevolod Meyerhold was brought back to the GATOB in 1918 for a new production of Daniel Auber's *La muette de Portici*, now recast as a revolutionary drama and renamed *Fenella*. Singers were also allowed to take on the role of director as well: Chaliapin was given a production of Boïto's *Mefistofele* the same year, and a month later Ershov undertook Rimsky's *Kashchei the Immortal*, followed shortly by another Chaliapin production, Massenet's *Don Quixote*. The financing of Russia's major theaters, however, soon became touch-and-go, and in 1921 state subsidies were severely cut back. Both the GATOB and the Bolshoi were attacked again as being too bourgeois. By the next year the situation had become so desperate that there was talk of closing the GATOB. This potential catastrophe was sidestepped largely by a reduction in the costs of productions and the raising of ticket prices. But saving the theaters came at a high price: a renewed demand that the repertory be brought even more in line with socialistic aims and ideals.

Moscow, which was now the country's capital, led the way. An edict from Lunacharsky's office dictated that "the bourgeois opera of the capitalistic epoch must be transformed into the proletarian opera of the present day." The texts of operas were rewritten to conform to communist gospel. Glinka's *A Life for the Czar* became *Hammer and Sickle*, or *A Life for the Country*, in 1925. Instead of a peasant of 1663, Ivan Susanin (whose name eventually became the title of the Soviet-correct opera) is a peasant of the 1917 Revolution, and instead of saving the czar's life, he saves his fellow Bolsheviks by leading foreign invaders astray. The last act climaxed with the entrance of the Red regiments into the Kremlin and the interpolation of revolutionary songs.

There were transformations as well of *Carmen* (she became a Jewish communist in Poland), *Lohengrin* (who became an American socialist), and *Tosca*, which was recast as *The Battle for the Commune*. But perhaps the most bizarre of all was what happened to Gounod's *Faust*. Goethe's aging philosopher, who aches to be young again, is granted his wish in a way Gounod never dreamed of. He becomes "Harry," an American millionaire who, in his luxurious Berlin apartment, tells "Mr. Mephistopheles" that life is unbearable unless he has Margaret, a Hungarian movie star. Margaret, Siebel (her lover), and her brother Valentine are all communistically inclined and live in a Bavarian village. Mr. Mephistopheles places an enormous package of thousand-dollar bills on Margaret's windowsill, and when she finds it, she bursts into the "Money Waltz." This makes it easy for Harry to lead her from the straight and narrow Marxian path, while Mephistopheles, the evil genie of capitalism, laughs wildly at Harry's easy conquest. She is later deserted by Harry and condemned to prison for murdering their child. Filled with remorse, Harry comes to the prison to rescue her, but she kills him and is saved from Mephistopheles by the arrival of revolutionary troops. As if all this were not bad enough, Gounod's score was also pepped up with added bits of jazz.

The early 1920s were a difficult time at the GATOB. In his *Memoirs*, Levik notes that "an emigration of a number of important singers to the west . . . deprived the theater of a number of principal singers. There was a moment when the financial position of the theater and its existence as an enterprise that justified its expenses was called into question by the Finance Committee. A number of other circumstances had affected the company's discipline to a point where not even [Emil] Cooper's iron hand was able to deal with it."

Even with these problems, the GATOB was able to mount new productions of Wagner's *Rienzi* in 1923 (for which a new text was provided), Richard Strauss's *Salome* in 1924, Franz Schreker's *Der ferne Klang* in 1925, and the Russian premieres of Prokofiev's *The Love for Three Oranges* in 1926 and Alban Berg's *Wozzeck* the next year, with their composers in attendance. Of interest, too, were the nonoperatic visits to Leningrad during the 1920s by a number of other major Western composers, including Paul Hindemith, Darius Milhaud, Bela Bartók, and Alfredo Casella.

In 1925, the GATOB made its first attempt at a pure Soviet opera—Andrei Pashchenko's *Eagles in Revolt*. It was commissioned for the eighth anniversary of the Revolution, and its hero was an historic figure: the eighteenth-century Cossack Emelian Pugachev, who led a peasant uprising against Catherine the Great and was executed. In 1927, another effort, none too successful, was made at the theater to introduce new Soviet works with the premiere of *Storm of the Perekop* by Yuri Shaporin, who would later make his mark with his Tchaikovsky-like opera *The Decembrists*.

Through Lunacharsky's initiative, and as an alternate opera house to the GATOB, a second company was established in what had been the Mikhailovsky Theater, which had been the home of French drama in imperial times. It became known as the Maly (also called the Mussorgsky). Being a smaller house, it stressed more intimate opera, and it soon became the center for the experimental work of composers and stage directors alike. It was unhampered by the traditions ingrained at the GATOB, and it quickly attracted attention with works like Ernst Krenek's *Jonny spielt auf*, billed as a satire "on bourgeois decadence." In 1934, it premiered Shostakovich's *Lady Macbeth of Mtsensk*. About at this time a rivalry developed between the Maly and the more established GATOB that persisted until Temirkanov took up the reins of the Kirov and began to outdistance the other, weaker company.

An important parallel in the Sovietization of the city's institutions was the development of the opera studio in 1922 in what shortly became the Leningrad Conservatory of Music (the city's name was changed from Petrograd in 1924, the year of Lenin's death). In 1923, Ershov became its director, and within a decade it was supplying a third of the former Mariinsky's roster and half of the Maly's. It was here that the Kirov's future artistic directors, Temirkanov and Gergiev, cut their operatic teeth.

Despite its promising beginnings and the initial adventurousness of its repertory, the GATOB was soon overshadowed by Moscow's monolithic Bolshoi Theater, and by the 1930s it had become mired in routine, only occasionally making a gesture in the direction of a novelty. It remained a stronger house for dance than for opera, given the traditions of its ballet school and the presence on its conducting staff of a man such as Evgeny Mravinsky, who devoted a good deal of his effort to ballet. In 1935, with the death of the head of Leningrad's communist party, the GATOB was christened the Kirov Theater in his memory.

During World War II and the prolonged German siege of Leningrad, activity in the theater came to a virtual standstill, and the company was evacuated to Perm until the end of the hostilities. After the war ended and the damage from German shells was repaired, the theater took up virtually where it left off. In 1944, the music director of the Maly, Boris Khaikin, became the artistic director of the Kirov for a decade. After him, the theater's chief conductor from 1967 to 1974 was Konstantin Simeonov, who helped to fill the breach in the years before Temirkanov's arrival in 1977 to become the Kirov's artistic director.

Although new singers were discovered and developed during the postwar period, the best of them were taken away by the Bolshoi; but the routine was occasionally broken by the first visits of guest artists from abroad since the days before the Revolution. Among them were Sweden's Elisabeth Söderström and America's Dorothy Kirsten, George London, and Roberta Peters. There was also a 1964 visit to Leningrad by Benjamin Britten, Peter Pears, and the English Opera Group, performing *The Turn of the Screw, Albert Herring*, and *The Rape of Lucretia*.

By 1977, however, the Kirov had become so derelict that even the party politicos realized that something must be done about it. They turned to Temirkanov, then music director of the Leningrad Symphony, to reset the theater's course. At first, he refused their offer of the artistic directorship. "It was precisely the *laissez-faire* situation at the theater that had brought it to its knees artistically," he told me; "I wanted no part of it. Again they approached me, and again I refused. The pressure went on until it reached the highest authority—the party chief in charge of all of Leningrad. He was practically a dictator. He forced me to go. With those beneath him I could say 'No.' With him, this was impossible, although in theory I might have again refused. But I owed him.

"At the time I was in charge of Leningrad's second orchestra, and it had been with his help that I was able to increase the salaries of my orchestra 100 percent. He told me, 'When you asked for my help, I did as you asked, and it was very difficult. Now I am asking you for a favor on behalf of the city. So I am waiting to see if you are the kind of person who can be grateful or who pays his debts.' So you see, I had no choice. It wasn't quite blackmail because he was right. When I finally agreed to go, he asked me why I had refused the post, and I told him that the situation was absolutely out of hand. And he told me, 'Take a big stick with you. I give you carte blanche to do what must be done.'"

Fortunately, opera was not new to Temirkanov. He had conducted many performances of standard repertory at the Leningrad Conservatory, which produced a different opera every week. "After graduating," he told me, "I would have liked to have done more opera right away, but not under the conditions that existed in our theaters at the time. You see, the Bolshoi had already taken away Kirov artists like [Vladimir] Atlantov, [Evgeny] Nesterenko, and [Elena] Obratzsova because it was the national theater of Russia. The situation was a bit different with dance; the

Kirov Ballet still held a position that was strong in tradition and was considered more on a par with the Bolshoi. But even so, many dance stars of the Kirov who had been trained in Leningrad were later taken to Moscow.

"When I went to the Kirov, the situation at that time—not just in Leningrad but in all of Russia—was that of a 'court theater,' in that it belonged to the central government. Part of the entertainment for officials and their guests was always a *Swan Lake* or an opera. The government was, in effect, a patron of the theaters, and it was good to have its support, but it had its favorites among the singers and dancers. This created a difficult situation because these favored artists and even members of the staff didn't obey any sort of rules. One couldn't protest because they would immediately call a friend in the party and complain. The stars did as they wished. The day after a star sang, for example, she wouldn't turn up for rehearsals. This was considered normal behavior. A star could even ask a director she liked to come to the theater to build a production around her.

"I began at the very top, punishing artists for such behavior, knowing that the lesser ones would quickly realize I was strong and that I could do the same to them. And it had an effect. When the star came to complain, I was very rude and said, 'Leave me alone. You are disturbing my work.' But I had to show them that despite my age—I was then only thirty-nine—I was the person in charge and had the authority to do what must be done.

"They were amazed to learn that I was not a party member, for this meant that it would do no good to protest [against] me. You see, if I had applied for the post at the Kirov, the city officials would have demanded that I join the party. But as they came to me and forced me to take the post, nothing was said about my becoming a party member. Later they did ask me to join, but I refused, and there wasn't anything they could do about it. And by showing my teeth immediately, I had begun to establish the level of discipline I wanted within a year."

Temirkanov came to the theater with a very definite point of view, one that involved strong production values. "These didn't exist when I arrived. Things were being done in the same way they had been done for years. I started getting young singers who looked good and whom you could believe in as the characters they were portraying. Some of them came straight from the conservatory, like [Olga] Borodina. These were singers who could be trained, for they had enthusiasm and were eager to succeed.

"The repertory and life of a theater like the Bolshoi and the Kirov thirty years ago would probably have seemed strange to a Westerner, for the same productions had gone on for forty years, with the same staging and sometimes with the same singers. Can you imagine how these operas looked and sounded, and in what artistic state they were? My first job was to clean them up. I didn't want to change the repertory as such. You couldn't avoid certain operas like the great Russian classics; they had to be there, they are part of our heritage. My goal was to change how they were performed. Of course, it was necessary to add some new operas, and I am proud to have done the world premiere of Shchedrin's *Dead Souls*, which I believe is a work of genius; I conducted it first at the Bolshoi, and then I brought it to the Kirov.

"Premieres are important, but you should never do them just to do a premiere. The work must be important. I also wanted the theater to present more symphonic concerts, which was very difficult at the beginning, for there was no tradition for concerts, and it was difficult to find time to rehearse them within the regular schedule of the theater. I also wanted to take the opera and the orchestra abroad; they had never toured before, only the ballet."

During Temirkanov's time the theater was run by an administrator, but he was the artistic director for the whole theater—opera and ballet. "This was more or less in theory," Temirkanov commented, "because I never cared much for ballet and understood very little about it, so I left this all to Vinogradov. My only concern was that a part of the ballet be reserved for the operas that called for dance. The orchestra at the time was good—actually, we had what amounted to two full orchestras at the theater and they played both opera and ballet. But I felt they could be [made] even better by playing concerts as well.

"The chorus, however, was never very good after the Revolution—the Bolshoi's was better—and I found it difficult to improve it because I was not in daily contact with the chorus as I was with the orchestra. It had its own director, of course, and it was his job to see to the quality of the singing. Naturally, I complained to him, but my time was at a premium, and at first I could effect changes with the chorus only in the performances I conducted."

It was traditional at the time for the Kirov to mount two new productions of opera and three of ballet each season. Since culture in the Soviet period was well subsidized, money was always available for them. "This is not to say that everything was better then," Temirkanov interjected, "for I had to put up with trade unions whose main occupation was to protect those who couldn't sing, dance, or play. You couldn't touch such people. I had hoped to make records at the Kirov, for there had not been any for a long time. This situation has now changed because of the interest in the Kirov by Western companies. But this sort of arrangement didn't exist in my time. We had only Melodiya [the state record company], which paid artists very little. I thought this was humiliating—not for me, but for my players—so I refused to record with them. This was my way of protesting.

"In my time we employed about the same number of artists the theater has today, and there were six conductors on my staff, including the principal ballet conductor [Victor] Fedotov. The conductors I inherited could hardly be called fantastic, so I began looking for new young talent. This is how I heard of Gergiev, who had just won an international competition. I invited him to come to the Kirov as my assistant. He worked with me on the first Kirov production of *War and Peace*, and later he conducted some of the performances."

Gergiev's memories of the Kirov begin in 1972, five years before Temirkanov's arrival. "The first time I walked inside the Kirov," he recalled, "I went with a group of conservatory students and heard part of *Ruslan and Ludmila*, which did not make much of an impression on me. To be honest, in my first years in Leningrad I went more often to Philharmonic Hall than to the Kirov. Back then, it never occurred to me that I would have much to do with opera. This was true even after I won the All-Soviet Conductors' Competition in 1976, which for me was an important testing ground.

"For fifteen days, the three best orchestras in Moscow played under young conductors. It was in this competition that Russia used to find its generals and field marshals of music. Mravinsky was the first winner in 1938, so it meant a great deal. In 1946 something was held that was called a 'survey' or 'concours'—I don't know exactly how to translate the Russian word for it—but no prizes were given. Out of it came the great Simeonov. The actual competition was revived in 1966, and Temirkanov won. After that, in 1971, Alexander Lazarov, who became music director of the Bolshoi, was chosen."

For Gergiev, the turning point as far as opera was concerned came when he first encountered Simeonov, who was the Kirov's chief conductor. "He had been very ill and unable to conduct at the theater for more than a year," Gergiev recalled, "and when he returned there was a lot of excited talk about him among the conservatory students. I was curious and went to a matinee of *The Queen of Spades*. The performance was so magical and so unlike anything else I had ever heard, I began to think, 'Oh, the Kirov is an interesting place, after all.' We visited with him afterward for a few minutes, and he was kind to us. I remember his face well, especially his expressive blue eyes. He was a man from the very heart of the Russian musical tradition, and our finest opera conductor.

"Shostakovich called him 'the best interpreter of my music,' and his greatest years were in the 1960s before I came to Leningrad. People still remember with awe his *Lohengrin, Sadko,* and *Mazeppa,* and even some of the Soviet operas he performed. But Simeonov often came in conflict with the system. He was ordered, for example, to put the mezzo-soprano Irina Bogacheva, who had important friends in the party, in the opening night of the Kirov Opera's first tour to East Germany. He refused and told a party official, 'If you want Bogacheva, then you go conduct in Leipzig.'

"He was not fired, but eventually he stopped coming to the Kirov. That was the beginning of the end. To succeed in the Soviet Union you have to be an iron man. Simeonov was not. Mravinsky and Temirkanov were. Although Simeonov was not ideal as a functionary, he was the ideal conductor for Russian opera, and he should have been given the artistic directorship of the Kirov Opera. But one of the illnesses the Russians have always suffered is that they don't respect and love their own geniuses. The way Simeonov was treated was a perfect example of this."

There was a vacuum at the leadership of the theater in the years after Simeonov left until Temirkanov's arrival as artistic director. Actually, Temirkanov had already been at the Kirov as a guest in 1975 to stage and conduct a new opera, *Peter the First*, by Andrei Petrov—not a great composer, but he was a friend of Temirkanov's and a prominent man within the system, much like the composer Tikon Khrennikov in Moscow.

"I first met Temirkanov," Gergiev recalled, "when he came to my final examination at the conservatory, where I conducted a student orchestra. The reason he was at the examination was because of a letter he had received from a man in Ossetia who knew his father. The letter said: 'Dear Yuri, I write to you because I think I have a right to do so. Your father, who was killed by the Germans, was my friend. I want you to take a look at a young musician named Valery Gergiev, because I also knew his father, who died after the war.'

"I was twenty-two then. I think he was interested in me because I studied with his teacher, Musin, as had Simeonov [and Alexander Gauk, who had been a conductor at the Kirov in the 1920s and was music director of the Leningrad Philharmonic prior to Mravinsky]. Anyway, Temirkanov came to look me over. He must have been happy with what I did, for afterward he said, 'You,' in a very imperious manner, 'when you finish your studies, you will become my assistant.' Just like that.

"He was a strong man, proud, a beautiful artist and still young—only fifteen years older than me—but already brilliant and well known. He was only thirty-two when he got the Leningrad Symphony. It was not the highest post in the country, but it was a good one. I was thirty-five when I became chief conductor at the Kirov, also quite young. But even though I respected Temirkanov and finally had been excited by opera thanks to Simeonov, I still wasn't sure the Kirov was the right place for me, especially after I won a second important competition—the Herbert von Karajan contest in Berlin in 1977.

"When I returned to Russia, however, I was not allowed to go to the West for four years. You see, I was not married, I was not a communist party member, and I think the Ministry of Culture in Moscow still saw anyone connected with the Kirov as morally dangerous after the defection of Nureyev. Remember, too, Baryshnikov had defected just a short while before I went to Berlin. I was told later that

Karajan wrote several letters to the ministry in Moscow saying that I was a gifted young conductor whom he wanted to be his assistant in Berlin, but it did no good.

"There were other letters to Gosconcerts, the Russian state concert agency, from orchestras that wanted to engage me as the Karajan winner, but these letters were not even shown to me. Instead I was locked inside the Soviet Union. I'm not complaining, for this brought me to the Kirov. But a lot of artists in the Soviet Union did complain. What I hate about Russians is when they say they are not Horowitz because Gosconcerts was bad. What I would like to tell them is that you are not Horowitz because you are *not* Horowitz!"

With the West shut off to him, Gergiev decided to accept Temirkanov's offer. At the time the Kirov seemed to him like a good place to begin. "But when I came to the theater," he told me, "it was not easy for an Ossetian, a Georgian, an Armenian, or a Jew to be accepted there. There were fewer problems for a Ukrainian or a Belorussian, for they were not considered foreigners. But if you were an outsider, you had to prove yourself ten times more than others to show that you had something that could be good for the theater. This was what happened with me, and I think this challenge gave me a greater drive and focus than was the case with others."

Gergiev made his Kirov debut in January 1978, with the third performance of *War and Peace*; Temirkanov had conducted the premiere. Eventually he conducted four out of the eight performances that were given that season. He felt that "this was for me a very big thing, for *War and Peace* was the only new production that year. This was my first time in a pit as a professional opera conductor. I had only done a *Carmen* with students at the conservatory because Musin had said to me, 'Valery, if you want to have a diploma as a symphonic and orchestral conductor, you are going have to do at least one performance of an opera.' There were five or six choices. I picked *Carmen.*

"I have always felt that Temirkanov was a courageous man to give so important an opera as *War and Peace* to a young man like myself. I had only one or two rehearsals, and I don't think the orchestra even knew who this person was who was conducting—'somebody new,' they called me. But I established a very good relationship with the players, and three months later I was given Prokofiev's *Romeo and Juliet.* To me it was symbolic that my first assignments at the theater were Prokofiev. He is certainly my most beloved composer.

"The rehearsals for *Romeo* were very intense, and the orchestra gave me some wonderful moments. I approached the music in probably too symphonic a way. It was hard for the dancers. While I was holding a fermata, they were already moving on to the next piece. It was not that I was unable to feel the character of a dance piece; in fact, I tried to take the tempi exactly as we had agreed. But I became so caught up in shaping the music *as* music that a fermata was sometimes five or six seconds longer than what the dancers were used to with other conductors.

"After Prokofiev, I was given Tchaikovsky's *Mazeppa*, which had been out of the repertory for maybe five years, and the cast was completely new to the opera. This was difficult for me, because this opera was so associated with Simeonov. But it was important to work with singers and learn about them. I heard these wonderful voices, and at first I didn't know what to tell them. I knew, for example, that there were those who had interesting voices but not interesting interpretations. Sometimes the opposite was true. So I started to question these things and look for answers and learn how to work with singers. For me it was a very valuable time. I was only twenty-five.

"At that time the Kirov's orchestra was nothing like it is now. The strings were quite good when it came to making a beautiful sound. But you need more than that. You need a firm sound in a tutti and many different colors. The winds as a section were not great—they lacked an individual timbre, although there were some good soloists. The brass was impressive, but far less polished in intonation and *attacca* than it is now and had a less melting sound; it was typical Russian brass—loud and powerful. Now you hear everything, you hear the distinctive voice of each section, yet you hear an orchestral entity as well. We haven't lost the Russian character of the sound, but it became more polished and plastic.

"To me a real Russian sound—the good Russian sound—is energy, a feeling of gambling, of taking chances; you want to win. The Leningrad Philharmonic under Mravinsky was always aristocratic, but it was so intense. Besides the Philharmonic, the best Russian orchestras back then were the Bolshoi Orchestra, which was very athletic and powerful with great string players, and Svetlanov's orchestra, the State Orchestra of the USSR.

"Twenty years ago the Kirov could not be ranked with these. It was impossible at the time to compete with the Leningrad Philharmonic and Mravinsky. The Philharmonic had this extraordinary ability to switch from Beethoven to Mahler, from Berlioz to Mozart. They were better educated in matters of style. They knew how to play Ravel's *La valse* with the right sound and follow it with a Haydn symphony that also had the right sound. It was a real ensemble, the best in Russia, and one of the best orchestras in any country. This was the result of years of work on the part of Mravinsky.

"Temirkanov bravely started with some ambitious projects. Sometimes there were flops, sometimes there were successes. But under him the orchestra and the opera company started to grow. Instead of being content with a few big artists like Boris Shtokolov, Temirkanov began looking for important young talent for the theater. By the way, Temirkanov didn't like Shtokolov. He had an exceptional voice, but he went his own way onstage and did whatever he wanted to do. He was, however, the only real star in the company at the time.

"But there were other good singers as well, like the fantastic lyric soprano Galina Kovaleva, and Irina Bogacheva [who is still with the company], who had good successes outside of Russia. Bogacheva has a good, big voice, but she is not very musical, interesting, or high class. Unfortunately she cared more about being a good Soviet artist than being simply a good artist. She was happiest singing at galas for party celebrations and getting awards. It's a pity, for she could have grown. This was a talent wasted because of the political system. Boris Kiniaev, a baritone, was another singer with a very impressive voice, although he was quite dull as a musician. All of these were at the theater when Temirkanov took over, and then he brought new artists like Sergei Leiferkus and Alexei Steblianko.

"Life at the Kirov before Temirkanov had been slow. I can't speak firsthand about the 1950s or early 1960s, but I don't think that period was much better or worse apart from Simeonov's performances. The point is, the Kirov was not a world-class institution. There were too many weaknesses. With Temirkanov it continued much the same, but at least he brought to the theater new singers, put on important new productions, like his *Queen of Spades* and *Eugene Onegin* (both of which he staged as well as conducted), and offered new operas like [Rodion] Shchedrin's *Dead Souls*. As for myself, I went on to conduct *Lohengrin, Manon Lescaut*, and *Don Giovanni*. Certainly *Lohengrin* in 1982 was the most important for me. My stamp on that performance was very strong. I was becoming very serious about opera and demanded a lot of rehearsals for *Lohengrin* and got them."

For his part, Temirkanov believed that "Gergiev was the most talented conductor I had, and I believe I left the theater to him with a better atmosphere. I had managed to clear the air. Life at the Kirov was not always harmonious, but there was far less maliciousness than there had been. There were a lot of new young and eager singers and conductors. I also left him with some problems. One of the biggest of these that faced the Kirov and other major theaters around the world is the casting of the standard repertory. There are not enough adequate singers for many of the big roles.

"We have a saying that 'you shouldn't make beef stroganoff without good beef.' And if you don't have a good Herman, you shouldn't do *The Queen of Spades*. The same is true of *Aida*. It is a very nice idea to say, 'I am going to produce all the Rimsky-Korsakov operas.' It sounds good. But in reality it is a fantasy. There aren't the singers. When I wanted to do a new *Onegin* at the Kirov I didn't have an Onegin, a Lensky, or a Tatiana. So I went out looking for them, for I wouldn't do *Onegin* with just anyone. I found Leiferkus and Marusin at the Maly, and [Larissa] Shevchenko was a student at the conservatory in her final year. They became my Onegin, Lensky, and Tatiana. Everyone was against me taking Shev-chenko because she was so young, but the nice thing about being a dictator was that I got my way.

"Once I found the right singers I could begin work on the production, which took a year to realize. The system then in Russia allowed such careful preparation. I supervised the scenery, the costumes, the wigs, the chorus—everything. I have the idealistic view that the conductor is responsible for it all. *Onegin* was my first opera as a stage director, and then came *The Queen of Spades*. My *Onegin*, by the way, was televised in Russia, but very poorly, and I had no idea that later the tape had been sold to the West. This I learned by chance. If I had been asked, I would have refused to allow it to be issued.

"The *Queen of Spades* video was done after I left the theater and is even worse. Those pigs—I'm sorry, but I've no other word for them—changed much of the staging and filled it with the sort of routine elements I had fought to change. There are some things I can still recognize as mine, but the Herman, for example, is all wrong. I would never have allowed a Herman who looked like this and acted so poorly. In 1995 I was asked to return to the theater to conduct the production, and knowing how criminal the video was, I agreed to do one performance in or-der to set it right. This was the first time in six years I had been back in the theater, and it took me eight days of rehearsal to redo the staging.

"I am sometimes credited for the production of *Boris Godunov* at the Kirov during my time, but it is not really mine. In fact, during the rehearsals I decided not to conduct it because I didn't approve of what was happening onstage. But the stage director came to me and asked what I disliked, and we sat down together and worked to change many things. Finally I was able to accept what was happening and conduct the performances. I can't say I was happy to leave the Kirov. I had cre-ated a well-oiled machine with fresh young talent, and when I was appointed as music director of the Leningrad Philharmonic following Mravinsky's death, it was hard for me to just drop everything and leave. I gave so much during thirteen years there. Not just my time, but my soul."

Gergiev will tell you without hesitation that "Temirkanov's personality brought a fresh new philosophy to this old tradition-bound Soviet institution. When he came, the theater had no system, no level that was acceptable day in and day out. He was out to make the Kirov a competitor of the Bolshoi, and that was really ambitious because the Bolshoi had all the power and all the money. But this Temirkanov did. I have to say it was under him that the company began to grow and change, not under me.

"He was a dictator, but in the good sense of the word; he was not a Noriega. Democracy is not a good thing when it comes to music. When everybody is right, nobody is right. You cannot vote for the right dynamics or the right tempo. With Temirkanov, the Kirov was above politics or propaganda. Like everybody else, he had to adjust certain principles to the political system, but not the most important ones. He put music above everything else."

CHAPTER TEN

January: An Israeli Debut

WHILE THE OPERA was again on the road—this time for its first appearances in Israel in January 1996—it was decided in upper political echelons in the Russian government that the Mariinsky should be remodeled along the same lines as the Bolshoi, with a single, powerful head. In Moscow, the former ballet star Vladimir Vasiliev had been placed in charge of all artistic and administrative matters, with full powers to hire and fire (he was dismissed from the position in 2000 by Russia's new head of state, Vladimir Putin). Not surprisingly, the person advanced for the same role at the Mariinsky was Gergiev. This idea distressed some, particularly those connected with the ballet, for many among them believed Gergiev to be not only unsympathetic to the needs and repertory of the ballet but, like Temirkanov, unknowing.

Yuri Schwarzkopf, however, went on record as saying that should the appointment as absolute director of the theater not go to Gergiev, the Mariinsky would, without doubt, lose him. To Schwarzkopf, this would amount to "a disaster." Gergiev's comment was, "The next five or six months are crucial, for if the structure at the Kirov isn't different, I will not stay. And if I leave, it will automatically change for better or for worse. But it is difficult to imagine that the Kirov will immediately find a stronger, more experienced and well-connected artistic director than myself."

But there were those who felt that Gergiev's appointment might be precarious, given the on-and-off quality of his administration of the company, his reluctance to delegate authority, and his absentee record. At this time discontent was felt throughout the theater at various levels; some members of the orchestra in particular made no bones about being overworked and underpaid. The chorus and soloists were no happier, just a bit less vocal.

There were those, too, who felt that in the beginning of Gergiev's reign the atmosphere in the house was very different—he was more available to the company and shared its travel and work difficulties to a greater extent. Elena Prokina, formerly a major singer at the Kirov, believes that little by little Gergiev became more distant, less considerate of his artists, and more concerned with his own agenda than with the needs of the theater.

"When I first joined the Kirov," she told me, "all I had in my apartment was a couch to sleep on. I didn't even have a refrigerator. But I was happy to be part of the theater. And, I must say, during that first year Valery ran the house, he was really wonderful. He was like a god to all of us. It was a privilege to work with him. He even shared his fees with the players. But that soon changed, and he began to bring people into the theater who were not that good, but who were loyal to him because they knew they could not get work elsewhere. Those around him soon cut him off from us. We had to go through them to speak to him. They were protecting themselves by 'protecting' him.

"Still, I was very grateful for the parts he gave me, and I was proud of the premieres I took part in. After all, I was very young, and for me it was a big opportunity. But the problems started when he wanted me to do roles that I felt were not good for my voice and when I began to be invited to other theaters. One night I came to the theater to get ready for a performance and found someone else had been told to sing in my place. Nothing had been said to me about the change. After that I had few performances in the theater.

"Valery told me that if I didn't stop contradicting him and behave myself, he would take all my roles away from me. Before this I had always asked his permission to do auditions when my agent arranged them for me. But after the way I was treated I stopped doing that. Still, because of my respect for him, I felt guilty about this. I ran into him one day and tried to explain my feelings. I told him it was not enough to only sing once or twice a season and only Russian works. To grow, I needed to do some Mozart, some bel canto operas. At that time we had no such works in the repertory, not even any Puccini.

" 'If I sing Prokofiev,' I told him, 'then I must also sing something beautiful for my voice that will help me survive.' He seemed to understand and even told me he was planning a new *Magic Flute* in which he could use me. He asked me to speak to him later in the week after a rehearsal. I agreed, because I did not feel it would be right to refuse. So I went to this rehearsal, and when it was over he turned to me and said in front of everyone, "Oh it's you. Well, I can't take you on our American tour." I didn't know what to say. I had no idea what he was talking about. I already knew there were no parts for me in the repertory being taken to New York [for the full company's debut there in 1992].

" 'But this is not what we were going to talk about,' I answered.

" 'Oh, yes,' he said, 'you want back into the theater. Well, I can't take you back because it would not be understood after how you have behaved.'

"I was stunned. I didn't even realize that I was out. I saw I had made a mistake by going to see him. So I said, 'Well, thank you very much for everything. Bye-bye.'

"As I started to go, he shouted after me, 'What are going to do with your independence? You won't sing anywhere. I guarantee it." And there are those who are convinced that Gergiev has been responsible for keeping Prokina from joining the Metropolitan Opera's roster.

Prokina's husband, Kirill Chevtchenko, was later responsible for a book attacking Gergiev and the Mariinsky. Among the charges he levels are that "Temirkanov held up to one hundred rehearsals before the premiere of a new production, so that each performance sparkled like a diamond, each nuance [was] polished and prepared. Nowadays productions are cobbled together by a 'director' with neither talent nor training . . . the singers are [often] students who have studied their roles for a fortnight or so and do not know until the night before who will be smiled at by fortune from on high and told, 'You are taking lead in the premiere tomorrow. . . .' I recently met in the street an elderly lady with whom I had been discussing and arguing over performances for years . . . When we got to chatting she mentioned in passing that she had not been to the Mariinsky [recently]. . . . 'It's gotten expensive and boring, my friend. Expensive and boring.' "

Gergiev readily admits that he and Prokina parted company, but he gives a very different account of the break. "She was in our previous production of *The Gambler* and was the only good singer we had for the opera's main soprano role at that time. But she decided to go to Vienna for an audition when a performance of *The Gambler* was scheduled. I repeat, she didn't go to sing but only to audition. When her husband came to me to say his wife was sick in bed and had to cancel, I already knew she was in Vienna and told him to leave my office.

"A month later she herself came to me and said how sorry she was to have been sick, and that she was now well and anxious to do more with me. I told her, 'Not only do I know you were not sick, but I know that you went to Vienna for an audition and that nothing came of the audition. You let your colleagues down and they do not want you in this theater any more, and neither do I.' That was the end of the story. People have come to me since and said, 'Oh, Prokina is a nice human being.' Maybe, but I don't want to work with her." Whatever the truth of the matter, it is inevitable that anyone as strong as Gergiev is certain to have detractors, and he will tell you without hesitation, "Of course, I have enemies here and in other places, and there are complaints. But what I do is for the good of the theater."

Amid the grumbling, the Kirov arrived in Israel in January 1996 for nine performances of *Khovanshchina* (including a public dress rehearsal) in the new opera house in Tel Aviv as part of the Israeli Opera's season. Whatever the players and singers were feeling, on opening night they handled themselves with honor. These appearances, after all, were important to the Mariinsky, for they netted the company $20,000 a performance and each member $50 per diem, money that was carefully husbanded for the months back in St. Petersburg, when the pay scale for most of the troupe dropped to about $5 a day or less.

The opera house in Tel Aviv is the heart of Israel's new performing arts center. This handsome building, with its excellent sight lines and notable acoustics and costing about $45 million, had been dedicated only fourteen months earlier. On the first night, Gergiev amply demonstrated that the Kirov magic can travel and remain intact, for this was a memorable *Khovanshchina* with a superb cast: Olga Borodina as Marfa, Konstantin Pluzhnikov in the dual roles of the Scribe and Prince Golitsin, Nikolai Putilin as Shaklovity, Yuri Marusin as Prince Andrei Khovansky, Vladimir Ognovenko making his first appearance of the season as Prince Ivan Khovansky, and Mikhail Kit as Dosifei. It was an equally brilliant night for the orchestra and chorus, and even the Kirov's ancient production looked vivid and substantial.

This was a trying time for Gergiev, who during the same period was rehearsing *The Gambler* for his La Scala debut and commuting between Milan and Tel Aviv, sometimes with a morning rehearsal in Italy and an evening performance in Israel. Because of this he could manage only four of the Israeli performances; his assistant Alexander Polyanichko conducted the other four. These *Khovanshchina*s, however, were a welcome opportunity to witness in a concentrated span of time virtually the full range of artists who have this work in their repertory, as all the major roles were double cast and some triple cast.

With these cast changes, shifts in first-desk players in the orchestra, and the peregrine nature of Gergiev's schedule, it was unrealistic to expect the company to maintain the sort of standard it had set on opening night, and the second performance produced a decided drop in quality. The chorus was raw, Marusin had obvious pitch problems, and Bulat Minzhilkiev and Alexander Morozov were no match for Ognovenko and Kit, nor was Larissa Diadkova on the same inspired level as Borodina.

On the evening of Gergiev's last performance, we manage to grab a few minutes of interview time in his hotel room, although we were continually interrupted by phone calls, several dealing with editing problems in the *Forza* recording. The interview was cut short when one of his assistants reminded him that it was 7:15, and the performance of *Khovanshchina* started in fifteen minutes. We made a frantic dash for the theater, arriving at 7:30. As we walked into his dressing room the phone rang, and Gergiev asked me to answer it. It was the stage manager asking when they could begin. "Tell them two minutes," Gergiev said. To my amazement he had changed and was in the pit precisely two minutes later.

Valery Gergiev, pianist Alexander Toradze, and the Mariinsky Theater Orchestra in concert.
COURTESY JAPAN ARTS

Sergei Alexashkin and Irina Lostkutova as Boris and Katerina
in Shostakovich's *Katerina Ismailova.*
PHOTO: VALENTIN BARANOVSKY

Lubov Karzanovskaya and Konstantin Pluzhnikov as Salome and Herod in Strauss's *Salome*.
PHOTO: VALENTIN BARANOVSKY

Altynai Asylmuratova and Vladimir Ponomarev as Zobeide and Shakhriar in Fokine's *Schéhérazade.*
PHOTO: VALENTIN BARANOVSKY

Altynai Asylmuratova and Evgeny Ivanchenko as Giselle and Albrecht in Adam's *Giselle*.
PHOTO: VALENTIN BARANOVSKY

Galina Gorchakova.
PHOTO: VALENTIN BARANOVSKY

Olga Borodina in her dressing room.
PHOTO: VALENTIN BARANOVSKY

Andris Liepa and Julia Makhalina as the Prince and the Firebird in Fokine's *Firebird*.
PHOTO: VALENTIN BARANOVSKY

Farukh Ruzimatov as the Golden Slave in Fokine's *Schéhérazade*.
PHOTO: VALENTIN BARANOVSKY

Andrei Batalov as the Golden Idol in Petipa's *La bayadère*.
PHOTO: VALENTIN BARANOVSKY

Rimsky-Korsakov's *Maid of Pskov* at the Mariinsky Theater.
PHOTO: VALENTIN BARANOVSKY

Larissa Diadkova as Kashcheyevna in Rimsky-Korsakov's *Kashchei the Immortal*.
PHOTO: VALENTIN BARANOVSKY

Vladimir Ognovenko and Anna Netrebko as Glinka's Ruslan and Ludmila.
PHOTO: VALENTIN BARANOVSKY

The new production of Prokofiev's *The Gambler* at the Mariinsky Theater
for the White Nights Festival of 1996.
PHOTO: VALENTIN BARANOVSKY

Vladimir Galuzin and Nikolai Putilin as Otello and Iago in Verdi's *Otello*.

Alexandra Volochkova as the Lilac Fairy in the Petipa-Tchaikovsky *Sleeping Beauty*.
PHOTO: VALENTIN BARANOVSKY

Valery Gergiev.
PHOTO: PETER MOUNTAIN

The company returned to St. Petersburg in time for me to see one of the first *Raymonda*s of the season, which featured the leggy, regal ballerina Anastasia Volochkova's first performance of the title role. It happened to be the night of her twentieth birthday. Adding to the excitement was the presence in the house of her teacher Natalia Dudinskaya, a greatly honored dancer of an heroic style and the theater's most important Raymonda during the Soviet period. She is now in her eighties and still an active member of the teaching staff of the Vaganova Academy. It was touching to watch Volochkova pass on her many floral tributes to Dudinskaya, who was seated in an adjacent stage box.

Raymonda was the last great work created by Petipa and followed in the line of "symphonic" ballets that began with the Petipa-Tchaikovsky collaborations. It was first danced at the Mariinsky in 1898 and has remained in the repertory of the company ever since. A beautifully integrated, compelling piece of dance, it amply demonstrated Petipa's ability to change, adapt, and grow in old age. Although it has an impossible story and substitutes pageantry for spectacular dance moments, it has a finer, more even flow to its lines than some of the better-known pieces that he fashioned.

Volochkova was in every respect a compelling, attractive artist of marvelous height and a lyrical presence. In the echelon of leading dancers ranking just below Asylmuratova and Makhalina, she is, along with Uliana Lopatkina and Diana Vishneva, chief among the company's contenders for future international fame.

As for the Kirov's male contingency, the brightest newcomer is Andrei Batalov, who two nights later enlivened an otherwise sleepy performance of *Don Quixote*. A winner of several important dance prizes, he possesses an exquisite sense of timing and an almost perfect ability to maintain a firm perpendicular with his body whatever pyrotechnics are involved. In the last-act pas de deux he took breathtaking chances by daring to complicate his variation with additional virtuoso twists, all of which came off brilliantly. Unfortunately, he danced little at the theater during my year; there were murmurs of his somehow having incurred the displeasure of a ranking member of the ballet's administration. Still, Batalov also provided the theater with a dazzling Golden Idol in *Bayadère*.

Toward the end of January, the double-headed eagle, symbol of czarist supremacy, was restored to a place of prominence above the entrance to the former royal box at the Mariinsky. It was presented by the Duchess of Abercorn, a patroness of the British Friends of the Kirov, to Schwarzkopf, and the following May the regal setting was completed with the installation above the czar's box of a grand gilded crown. The eagle was in place in time for a gala evening at the theater given in tribute to former Kirov artists, which brought back to the theater its most acclaimed singer of the 1960s and 1970s, the bass Boris Shtokolov. Although he was in his mid-sixties, the size and darkness of his once thundering voice were intact, and he brought great sonority and dignity to his singing of Prince Gremin's aria from *Eugene Onegin.*

The highlight of the evening, however, was Ruzimatov's repeat performance of Béjart's *Death of a Poet.* If anything, it was even more compelling than his performance of this stark solo had been the October before. It became a wrenching dialogue between his body and the music. It was impossible to watch this performance and not applaud him as a great artist, whatever his shortcomings might be in other repertory, such as his weak Basilio in *Don Quixote* later in the month with the fascinating Diana Vishneva as Kitri. But even in the latter work, he sometimes would send a frisson through the audience, if only with his arrogant phrase endings and bows. The gala included as well a pure and evocative *Dying Swan* from Lopatkina, which probably came closer to Fokine's original concept than any other I have seen.

Dance continued to dominate the gala with Makhalina's demonic and rock-solid Black Swan and Vishneva and Kurkov in a sparkling version of the *Don Quixote* pas de deux. Among the singers, only Borodina's mesmerizing performance of "Mon coeur s'ouvre à ta voix" from *Samson et Dalila* was a match for the dancers. It was in vivid contrast to the singing of "O ma lyre immortelle" from Gounod's *Sapho* by Bogacheva, who is now but a tremulous shadow of her former self. The concert closed with the final chorus from Glinka's *A Life for the Czar,* which released once again the mighty ring of the theater's peal of bells.

January brought as well another evocative performance of *La sylphide* with the charming husband-and-wife team of Margarita Kulliak and Vladimir Kim, an appropriate match for the cool and calm choreography. This was followed the next evening with a performance of *Bayadère* given in memory of Anna Pavlova on the occasion of the sixty-fifth anniversary of her death. With Irma Nioradze as Nikiya, Irina Chistyakova as Gamzatti, and Victor Baranov as Solor, it was a comfortable rather than an illuminating tribute to one of the pillars of Mariinsky history.

As I had not managed to see the revival in October of Prokofiev's *Love for Three Oranges,* I attended a performance in January. It might better have been titled *The Love for Three Dozen Oranges,* for it was vastly overproduced, overdesigned, and filled with silly symbolism. The singing was poor, and Leonid Korchmar's conducting was heavy handed.

Of much greater operatic importance during the month was the return to the repertory of Borodin's *Prince Igor* in preparation for the Kirov's winter tour to Europe. What made this revival of special interest was Gergiev's decision to restore the second Polovtsian scene, which was being mounted for the first time at the Mariinsky, and to reorder the acts of the opera to conform more closely to Borodin's intentions (these ideas had been tested three years earlier when Gergiev recorded the opera for Philips). It made for an engrossing, if long, evening and provided the viewer a chance to savor Fokine's dazzling choreography for the first Polovtsian scene. Gergiev placed it after the prologue instead of in its more traditional spot following act 1, and he repositioned the overture between the prologue and the first Polovtsian scene to avoid a wait while the set was changed.

The Kirov edition amounted to a rethinking of this epic opera, for like *Boris Godunov*, many of the composer's original intentions had been overridden by Rimsky-Korsakov and Glazunov, who undertook what became the standard performing edition of this unfinished work. The eminent Russian critic Vladimir Stassov, who wrote the scenario for *Prince Igor*, was the first to challenge the Rimsky-Glazunov version; he was later seconded by the composer Boris Asafiev and the musicologist Paul Lamm. While acknowledging that Rimsky and Glazunov made Borodin's music available and plausible, Gergiev agreed with Asafiev and Lamm that the published edition confined the composer's ideas, and he pointed to the superior strength of the score in moments where Borodin's voice emerges unvarnished (the Polovtsian Dances were among the few sections Borodin left in finished form, and the composer was aided in his orchestration of them by Anatol Liadov).

In addition to orchestrating, completing the music, and reordering the scenes, Rimsky and Glazunov cut a large part of the autograph material. Their task in polishing the work was a nearly impossible one, for what existed of the score was at the time of Borodin's death in great disarray. Numerous changes were penciled in, with further changes added over them in ink; many of these alterations were undecipherable. In attempting to make sense of the manuscript and Borodin's sketches, Rimsky and Glazunov often hobbled the work dramatically, and important elements such as the tug-of-war between the Russians and the Polovtsians were left unresolved and largely unexplained.

With Gergiev's decision to separate the two Polovtsian scenes, the second took on a character of its own, while the first provided a needed contrast between the early Russian scenes and pointed up the difference in the Russian and Polovtsian societies. But of the greatest moment was the replacement of the opera's weak finale with a restatement of music from the prologue, which gave the opera greater cohesion, symmetry, and a vivid sense of healing and triumph.

Unfortunately, Gergiev was not on hand to lead what was in effect a dress rehearsal for the tour. *Prince Igor* was conducted instead by Polyanichko, who coped ably with the assignment, although I felt—and was later proved right—that when Gergiev finally took hold of the score it would rise to the heights. Putilin was masterful as Igor, but Evgenia Tselovalnik was uneven, sometimes woefully so, as

Jaroslavna. She made it painfully obvious again how deficient the Kirov was at this time when it came to casting lead soprano roles.

However, Ognovenko was a superb Galitsky, Marusin a fervent Vladimir, and Diadkova a respectable Konchakovna. The chorus and orchestra were thunderous and wonderful, but much more was needed when it came to the lead dancer in the first Polovtsian scene. This deficiency would be corrected, if only momentarily, during the company's upcoming tour appearances in Paris.

CHAPTER ELEVEN

The Soviet Years: Ballet

AFTER NICHOLAS II'S abdication in March 1917 and the "first days of furious excesses, cannonades, [and] blaze of fires, a calm settled over St. Petersburg," Tamara Karsavina recounts in her memoirs. "Proclamations of the new government enjoined the population to confidence. The militia paid domiciliary visits to reassure citizens. The Revolution [too] had its brief spell of optimism. In the theater, the artists went out of their way to bring 'Comrade' into the conversation. A new director had been nominated, a man of letters, an eminent professor. The artists having organized their own committees, I had been chosen a president of ours. . . . I tried hard to maintain my artistic work unimpaired, fitting my practice into early hours, leaving committee meetings for rehearsals, and rehearsals for a table piled with papers.

"The Mariinsky was shorn of eagles and imperial arms; greasy jackets replaced the former livery of the attendants. I remember one night of a charity performance. A small group, grey-haired and worn looking, sat in the imperial box. They were old political convicts, a couple of months earlier recalled from Siberia; and homage was being paid to their martyrdom. The second phase of the Revolution came, and they were swept off by the new wave and held in derision. That phase had done with optimism. The [Western] front was breaking; deserters [were] fleeing home; disorganized soldiers filled the trains, rode on the roof, clutched to the buffers. From the hungry towns crowds set forth daily in search of food.

"The Government made frantic efforts to carry on with the war. At every corner improvised meetings were held. Lenin arrived; he harangued the people from the balcony of Kshessinskaya's house, where he had established his headquarters. Every day rumors multiplied like microbes in a diseased body. Newspapers born overnight spread panicky information and coined libels." Karsavina herself was accused of being a German spy, a charge that was quickly retracted, but her time as a glittering figure of the czarist era was drawing to a close, even though "under

the new regime artists were treated with great consideration . . . shows were liber-
ally given to the people [and there was still] a genuine love for the theater."

That fateful Mariinsky season ended on 15 May 1917 with *La bayadère*, featuring Karsavina's Nikiya. She remembers "ovations to a degree high even for the
Mariinsky." It was her last performance in St. Petersburg. By then, she recalled that
the city had grown "visibly depopulated. It had a new tragic beauty of desolation.
Grass grew between the flagstones of its pavements, its long vistas lifeless, its arches
like mausoleums. A pathetic majesty of desecrated pomp." By February of the next
year, Karsavina and her British husband had received papers allowing them to
leave, and after a perilous few weeks, they arrived in London, where she faced, as
she put it, "the footlights of a new world."

For the moment the future of the ballet was uncertain. Its school was closed
and finally reopened only after the commissar of public education, Anatoly Lunacharsky, persuaded Lenin that dance and opera were not inherently decadent but
a heritage of the people that had been "stolen and perverted." More importantly,
he convinced Russia's leaders that dance, if properly used, was a powerful propaganda tool. The pragmatic Lenin was probably most impressed with Lunacharsky's argument that guarding an empty Mariinsky Theater to protect it against
vandals would cost almost as much as maintaining its artists.

Although the theater stayed open, there were no funds to heat the building,
even when the temperature dropped to below zero. But the audience still came,
bundled in furs and sheepskin coats, and the dancers—often in flimsy costumes
—all but froze to the stage as they held a pose. Offstage a struggle was underway
between those who wanted Fokine to head the company and his opponents,
among them Nikolai Legat, who remained in Russia until in 1922 he immigrated
to England, where he became a well-known teacher.

Fokine missed the opening of the 1917–18 season, and his foes used his absence
for a new attack. The *Petrograd Gazette* characterized him as a "deserter." Later
that fall, Leonide Leontiev, then chairman of the ballet theater's committee, stated
in an interview, "Our main problem is that with Fokine abroad we are left without a choreographer. We have concluded a contract with the composer [Alexan-
der] Tcherepnin to present his ballet *Narcisse et Echo* [a Diaghilev creation] . . . but
alas, there is no one to stage it! Our *Petrushka* is quite ready, but again, because of
Fokine's absence we cannot stage it."

Fokine managed to return in time to choreograph the dances for the new production of *Ruslan and Ludmila*, and the next year—1918—he left on a tour of
Scandinavia, never to return. For a while the void was filled by Boris Romanov,
but after a year Romanov moved on to Moscow, and Leontiev was appointed head
of the ballet company. A character dancer and, like Romanov, a graduate of the

Imperial Ballet School, Leontiev had also taken part in the Diaghilev seasons.

Leontiev's first major assignment at GATOB was to stage Fokine's *Petrushka* in the fall of 1920 (he also danced the title role). In this he was aided by Alexander Benois, who was then a member of the theater's administration. As Elizabeth Souritz writes, "The very fact that *Petrushka* appeared on the Russian stage was considered a great event bearing witness to the fact that the Petrograd Ballet was once again gathering strength."

Leontiev's reign was short, and he was replaced in 1922 by the theater's first Soviet choreographer of consequence, Feodor Lopukhov. Although he later switched his allegiance to the Maly Theater in 1930, he returned to the Kirov as artistic director from 1944 to 1946 and again from 1951 to 1956. Ironically, given the enormous influence he exerted in his time, no original works by him have survived in repertory, and his presence today can be felt only in the Lilac Fairy variation in *The Sleeping Beauty*, which he created for Lubov Egorova as part of an important revival of the ballet during his first year as head of the company.

As Joan Acocella points out in a *New Yorker* article written in July 1999 during a Kirov Ballet visit to Manhattan, "Imagine Lopukhov's position. The civil war was barely over. The company was painfully reduced. (Those who could flee to the West had done so.) There was no money, and little support for classical ballet. Indeed, many leaders of the new U.S.S.R. believed that ballet should simply be eliminated, as a bad influence.

"Under these conditions Lopukhov mounted not just a revival of *The Sleeping Beauty*, but a reconstruction of the 1890 text, which had been eroded over the years. . . . To him, Petipa-style classicism was compatible with revolution; both were utopian. According to George Balanchine, who was one of his young dancers, Lopukhov used to say to the company 'Forward, to Petipa!' "

Trained at the Imperial School along with his sister—Lydia Lopukhova, a Fokine pupil whose principal fame came with the Diaghilev company—Lopukhov's time at the theater was important, for with ballet per se under siege on all sides as "un-Soviet," he managed to rebuild the roster of dancers after many fled abroad, maintain the classic repertory and mount new productions of it, resist the sort of modernization that dance was subjected to by Alexander Gorsky at the Bolshoi, and introduce other momentous works by Stravinsky, including *Firebird* and *Pulcinella*.

Lopukhov responded to the call for dances with revolutionary dynamics by creating *The Red Whirlwind* (a ballet about the October Revolution and a surprising failure) in 1924, *The Ice Maiden* in 1927, *Bolt* in 1931 (to music of Shostakovich), and *Taras Bulba* in 1940. Despite their inability to gain a toehold in the company's repertory, these pieces reflect, in Souritz's words, "the classical lexicon, while at the same time making it the language of modern art . . . oriented toward the search for pure, abstract dance."

But perhaps the most provocative and influential of his works was his 1924 *Dance Symphony: The Magnificence of the Universe*, set to Beethoven's Fourth Symphony. Like *The Red Whirlwind*, it was performed only once; but its attempt at nondramatic dance continued to resonate long after a single viewing. Certainly it captured the imagination of Balanchine, who danced in the premiere. To him, *Dance Symphony* sounded a loud call for reform, and he went so far as to write an article in Lopukhov's defense after the ballet was greeted with a mixture of hissing and applause.

One of Lopukhov's more enduring contributions to the theater was his joint choreography with Vladimir Ponomarev and Leontiev for Glière's *The Red Poppy* in Leningrad (the ballet had premiered at the Bolshoi in 1927; Leningrad's version came two years later). The work set out to comply with a demand from the government "to make art serve the purpose of educating the people" and dance more accessible. Its libretto was topical, stemming from the murder of the Soviet consul in China (the setting for the ballet) and that of a consul in Poland. The ballet took these real-life events and romanticized them as an affair between a Chinese girl and a Soviet ship captain. She is ordered to murder him, but instead love makes her take the bullet intended for the captain. The ballet came complete with an opium dream sequence that included a Golden Buddha and a swarm of butterflies, birds, and dancing flowers. Its mixture of revolutionary and stock ballet clichés was put in perspective by the composer Alexander Tcherepnin: "You don't make a statue of a Red Army officer out of whipped cream."

In retrospect, it is obvious that Lopukhov went too far too fast for the times, and in 1931 he was replaced as ballet master by the more conservative Agrippina Vaganova, who headed the company for six years. Although not a choreographer in any original sense, she produced new versions of *Swan Lake*, *Esmeralda*, and *Chopiniana*, parts of which are still seen today. Her value to the theater, however, was not as a dancer, although she was evidently a strong and able one, nor as a director, but as a teacher. Elizabeth Kendall aptly summed up what Vaganova's presence and work had meant to the school named for her and its parent company: "In the Kirov system, manners are inseparable from ballet steps—a legacy of Agrippina Yakovlevna Vaganova. . . . Starting with a class of third-year girls she took over in the winter of 1920–21, Vaganova codified the various styles of dancing—the French, the Italian, and the newer Russian—that had already begun to fuse under Petipa. She also introduced a new bravura—bigger shapes, heroic gestures—into ballet technique, so that it would fit in with the program of the Revolution. As a cultural politician, Vaganova was an interesting blend of the conservative and the radical, but what is important to ballet history is her emphasis on the human manners inherent in the steps rather than on abstract properties. Her approach offered a rallying point for the whole ballet system after the Revolutionary culture began turning more conservative."

In codifying movements and giving precise corrections to her students instead of vague suggestions, and in being analytical when it came to the use of muscles, Vaganova, more than anyone else, created a truly unique Russian way of dancing. To Kendall, watching classes with Vaganova's heirs in St. Petersburg was "to see small children learning, and grown dancers reminding themselves, how to inhabit another theatrical time zone—a more leisurely, prideful, and sensual one than that of present-day Western ballet. The chin lifts on the up-breath at the beginning of a phrase and lifts again at the end, acknowledging a close. The hands and wrists round out the music, trailing after the movement as if trailing through water. . . . Over the years, the way that this aesthetic has excluded twentieth-century dynamics—anything jazzy or abrupt or violent—has obviously created a rare cohesion of style.

"When the little girls at the Vaganova school walk on and off center floor, they walk on the balls of their feet, and their hands mark the place of a phantom tutu. The angle of their heads forms part of the basic steps, and so do the positions of their backs, the bend of their torsos. . . . The teaching inculcates a physical memory in the dancers' bodies even before they know what they are remembering." This is Vaganova's legacy.

Danilova, who later became an American citizen and taught at Balanchine's school in New York, clarified the special qualities of the Vaganova-styled Russian dancers through a telling comparison with American dancers: "Soviet technique is . . . much more acrobatic than ours and often more thrilling to watch, but we are dancers not acrobats, and ballet is an art, not a sport. I think Soviet dancers sometimes overstep that line." To her mind, "[Russian] ballet has become the exhibition of dancing. Soviet dancers no longer want to show the story or the mood so much as they want to show their technique—this one can turn three times in the air, lifting both his legs, and that one can do something else. But it's no longer expression; it's exhibitionism." That, too, is part of the legacy.

Danilova also believed that "American girls are built differently from the way we were in Russia. The Russian woman is rather voluptuous; Americans are more sportive. Russian [dancers] don't do sports, they eat; but American girls are always aware of their figures, of how many calories they're taking in. . . . In Russia, dancers are not conscious of their looks. We didn't have the notion that a ballerina should be slender and good looking. At the Mariinsky there was no ideal. A pretty face was the main requirement. Karsavina was pretty and also slender. Vaganova was a big technician but never had a great career as a ballerina because she was rather ugly. Looking back now, I see that there were many girls at the Mariinsky who were not such good dancers but were kept on for their beauty."

In Danilova's mind, the concern with losing weight started with Olga Spessivtseva. "We had always considered her beautiful; but when she went away to dance with the Diaghilev company, she lost weight, and when she returned to Russia she looked ravishing. . . . When I came to Diaghilev . . . and was told that I had to lose weight, I was astonished—it had never occurred to me to think of the picture I was presenting. Our awareness changed. It was Balanchine, I think, who gave us the ideal image of a ballerina, who in his choreography made us realize how much more beautiful movement looks on a body that is streamlined."

Spessivtseva was the first great Soviet ballerina and one of Vaganova's favorite pupils. She had appeared during the czarist period in 1916, dancing what became her signature role, Giselle, but not until immediately after the Revolution did she emerge as the theater's reigning prima ballerina. Lopukhov has described her as having "a shapely body, a wonderful build, subtle movements of the arms, legs ideally formed, a cameo face with enormous eyes that were full of fire, a beautiful high and long leap . . . the public always saw her as an incarnation of beauty."

Diaghilev found her "a finer and purer being than Pavlova. . . . I heard our great maestro Enrico Cecchetti saying 'There was an apple in the world that was cut in two halves. One of the two became Pavlova, the other Spessivtseva.' I can only add that to me Spessivtseva has always been the side of the apple which is turned toward the sun." And although Balanchine made fun of some of the older Mariinsky dancers like Pavlova, he talked lovingly of Spessivtseva—"She was so exquisitely made"—and spoke of her feet being like hands. Bouts with mental illness brought on by severe depression ended her career in 1939, when she danced for the last time in Buenos Aires.

Another outstanding ballerina of this period was Marina Semenova, the first outstanding pupil produced by Vaganova. Although her name is less well known in the West than that of Spessivtseva, to the critic Vadim Gaevsky "she accomplished a virtual breakthrough into unknown spheres of classical ballet. Unusual, even superhuman energy of movement, and an equally unusual sweep of gesture gave classical dance in Semenova's performance a new dimension, and demonstrated the emotional possibilities of the human soul in a completely new way."

Gaevsky goes on to add other characteristics not associated with any of Semenova's colleagues. "Her dancing extended the limits of virtuoso technique and even annihilated the very idea of such limits. At the same time Semenova was very feminine in every involvement on stage, in every step, in every feature. In other words she was the ideal classical ballerina . . . capable of high tragedy, although from nature she had received a comic gift—the gift of joyous dancing, the gift of laughter through dance."

In 1929 Semenova transferred to the Bolshoi, but her career there was damaged when her second husband was arrested in one of Stalin's purges. Despite her great popularity and her status as Stalin's favorite ballerina, she was placed under house arrest, and when she was allowed to resume her career, she seemed almost indifferent to dancing, neglected classes and rehearsals, and grew heavier, losing her once unique aura of poetry. Upon her retirement in 1952, she became a noted teacher, counting among her students such major Bolshoi ballerinas as Maya Plisetskaya and Natalia Bessmertnova.

During Vaganova's time as head of GATOB's ballet there were premieres of two pieces destined to become Kirov staples, *The Flames of Paris* (choreographed by Vasili Vainonen) and *The Fountain of Bakhchisarai* (choreographed by Rostslav Zakharov). Their survival had to do more with their nature as spectacle than with their scores, both of which, by Boris Asafiev, are dreadful pastiches. As Boris Schwarz has sagely observed, "Asafiev's music is more compiled than composed." Although *Flames* has now disappeared from the Kirov's repertory, the *Fountain* continues to flow. This melodramatic, obvious work seems not to have lost its power to enthrall Russian audiences.

For *Flames*, Asafiev used French revolutionary songs, while the score for the *Fountain* was a weak assemblage of hackneyed nineteenth-century musical ideas. A Western critic, Kurt London, who saw *Flames* while visiting Russia in the 1930s, came away disappointed. "Russian ballet," he wrote, "makes an out-of-date and reactionary impression and is an anachronistic relic a good hundred years behind the times. . . . Soviet ballet . . . has become an art fit only for the museum." As for Asafiev, London felt he "cherished a misguided ambition to compose."

Russians have seen these two ballets in a different light, however. To historians of the time, *The Flames of Paris* was "the first of the Soviet heroic mass ballet representations," even if London found it no more than "pretty little dances with red flags." But no one could deny that this work, with its unusually large numbers of male dancers, was a brilliant showcase for two of the best of these at the Kirov. Vakhtang Chabukiani, a Georgian, joined the company in 1929, and Konstantin Sergeiev came to the theater a year later and established himself as virtually a Kirov legend. Both, of course, had studied at GATOB's ballet school.

Chabukiani's first major role at the theater was in Lopukhov's *Ice Maiden*, and he next starred in the choreography by Vainonen and Leonid Yakobson for Shostakovich's *Age of Gold* in 1930. He would also dance the classic parts of Albrecht in *Giselle* and Siegfried in *Swan Lake* (now renamed *The Count*, in Vaganova's reworking of the Tchaikovsky classic as a realistic, modern morality play).

Chabukiani was teamed in both *Swan Lake* and the premiere of *The Fountain of Bakhchisarai* with Ulanova, and in 1939 he also choreographed the once popular *Laurencia*, as well as creating its role of Frondoso. His last important parts at the Kirov were Andrei in Lopukhov's *Taras Bulba* in 1940 and Solor in a new version of *La bayadère* he helped fashion with Ponomarev in 1941. When the Kirov company was evacuated to Perm during World War II, Chabukiani returned to Georgia and became ballet master at the Paliashvili Theater in Tbilisi, where he remained until 1973. After the Petipa-Gerdt and Fokine-Nijinsky eras, it was Chabukiani who did the most to strengthen and extend the role of the male dancer in classic ballets. He could even be said to have altered the bodies of male dancers through the greater development of his legs and chest. In a piece like *Bayadère* he was able to give full range to his physical and technical prowess, and many today do not realize that Solor's variations are his work and not Petipa's. Chabukiani left behind several films, including a lengthy excerpt from *The Flames of Paris*, from which it is still possible to thrill to the spirit, energy, and brilliance of his dancing.

The much-admired ballerina Tatiana Vecheslova, who danced with Chabukiani in *The Flames of Paris* and created Pascuale in *Laurencia*, has said that "he was born and created for the dance. . . . At one moment, like a steel spring, he sped up his rotation, then gradually slowed it down, as if obeying some internal command. Nature had not given him a large jump, but his flight was compared to the flight of an eagle. From a leap, he never fell onto the stage, but came down simply to fly up again." The critic Igor Stupnikov completes the picture by terming Chabukiani "the archetype of the heroic male dancer on the Soviet stage. . . . When [Rudolf] Nureyev first burst on the world stage, for example, he was actually repeating many of the stylistic qualities that had first been seen in the earlier master: that savage attack on stage and that uninhibited male energy is something that began with Chabukiani."

Laurencia has been temporarily shelved by the Kirov, but it is a ballet ripe for revival. Based on an eighteenth-century story of a peasant uprising in Spain, it belongs, like the majority of Soviet ballets, to the genre of "choreodramas," which for a long time in Russia was the only accepted type of dance. But within its predictable plot lines, Chabukiani managed to achieve a remarkable and convincing blend of folk and classical dancing that was the ballet's strength. What a thrilling sight it must have been to see him and Natalia Dudinskaya, who created the title role, in full flight amid its dazzling and complex dance patterns.

Born in Ukraine, Dudinskaya joined GATOB a year after Sergeiev, her future husband. Together they became one of the most admired and acclaimed dance couples in Russia. A favorite pupil of Vaganova, she was still active, in her late eighties, as a teacher at the Vaganova Academy. Although she had appeared as

Princess Florina in *The Sleeping Beauty* at GATOB while still a student, her first major role after joining the company was the creation of Mireille de Poitiers in *The Flames of Paris*. Then came her creation of the title role in Aram Khachaturian's *Gayane*, which was danced for the first time in 1942 in Perm.

She repeated her success in *Gayane* when the Kirov returned home three years later, and she followed it with Odette-Odile in a new staging of *Swan Lake* by Lopukhov. In addition to all the standard parts, she created a dozen other ballets, the most important of which was the Kirov's 1946 version of Prokofiev's *Cinderella*, with choreography by Sergeiev, a year after the ballet's premiere in Moscow. Lopukhov said of her, "Dudinskaya reached the heights of virtuosity in classical dance. Here is a case where one can say that a great love of work forms a good half of the talent and guarantees its development." If Dudinskaya had a shortcoming, it was as an actress. But as a technician she had no rivals. The most complicated dance patterns presented no apparent difficulties. Not only did she dispatch them with unique élan, but she made them seem effortless. Her leap was prodigious and vivid, and it is not stretching the point to see her as the female counterpart to Chabukiani, who had a great influence on her career. From the 1940s through the 1950s she was the *prima ballerina assoluta* of the Kirov and powerful enough to reserve a role like Giselle for her exclusive use. Through the years she has remained a Kirov model for such parts as Kitri in *Don Quixote*, Nikiya in *La bayadère*, Odette-Odile, and Raymonda.

One of the finer Kirov dancers to languish in Dudinskaya's shadow was Alla Shelest. She joined the company in 1937, and Lopukhov has written that he did not "know any other ballerina whose career was as ill-fated as Shelest's. For sixteen years she was condemned to make-do with the second cast of every role. . . . What a tremendous amount of talent it takes not to lose confidence under such circumstances! [She] was a typically heroic ballerina: nervous, fiery, willful, and strongly magnetic." Her chief moments in the sun came when Yakobson, who was a staunch believer in her gifts, had her create Angina in the premiere of Khachaturian's *Spartacus*, and when Yuri Grigorovich cast her as Katerina in the first performance of Prokofiev's *Stone Flower*. To Ulanova, "Every ballet in which Shelest performed was remarkable not only for the ballerina's talent, but also for her mind and for the great inner level of culture that belongs to a genuine artist. The boldness and the innovation in her interpretation of each of her roles stunned me as an artist. . . . You can always recognize Shelest by the perfection of the sketch, by the emotion, and by the dancer's self-abandon."

After Vaganova left the company to devote herself exclusively to teaching, the next important artist to occupy the position of artistic director was Leonid Lavrovsky, who reigned from 1938 to 1944, when he moved on to become chief choreographer at the Bolshoi until 1956. He had been a principal dancer with GATOB since 1923, when he took part in Lopukhov's aborted *Dance Symphony*, and he created his first ballet at the Kirov in 1936. But his name will always be associated with the Russian premiere of Prokofiev's *Romeo and Juliet*, starring Ulanova and Sergeiev.

Lavrovsky's choreography for this contemporary masterpiece is rarely seen outside of Russia, but there it remains vibrantly alive and still involves one deeply. A good deal of its power stems from Lavrovsky's special response to the score. He felt Prokofiev "carried on where Tchaikovsky left off. . . . He was one of the first Soviet composers to bring to the ballet stage, genuine human emotions and full-blooded characters. The boldness of his musical treatment, the diversity and intricacies of his rhythms, serve to create dramatic development." The request for a ballet on this Shakespearean subject was tendered to Prokofiev by the Kirov in 1934, and the score was completed two years later. Oddly enough, it was considered "unsuitable" for dancing, an attitude that probably accounts for the delay of four years from its completion to its Kirov premiere. Prokofiev, impatient to have *Romeo* heard, extracted two orchestral suites from it as well as a set of piano pieces, and these were played and acclaimed before the ballet was first staged, not in Leningrad but in Czechoslovakia. But that premiere and the music's immediate popularity finally moved the Kirov to action. *Romeo* can rightly be seen as the supreme achievement of Soviet ballet.

From writings by Lavrovsky and Ulanova we know that a struggle ensued between the choreographer, who wanted more music, and the composer, who adamantly said, "I've written exactly as much music as is necessary. . . . You must manage with what you've got." On his own Lavrovsky decided to insert the scherzo from Prokofiev's Second Piano Sonata to meet his choreographic needs, and although furious at first, Prokofiev finally relented and agreed to orchestrate it.

As for the dancers, they found the score "too delicate" and complained that they could not always hear the orchestra. "I know what you want," Prokofiev shouted angrily at Ulanova and Sergeiev, "You want drums, not music." But ultimately he made further changes, albeit reluctantly. For his part, Prokofiev felt the dancers often moved "against the music," and certainly the score, with its intricate harmonies and the angularity of its rhythms, presented new and alien challenges to the performers. "At first," Ulanova said, "the music seemed to us incomprehensible and almost impossible to dance. . . . But the more we listened to it . . . the more clearly emerged the images the music created."

Eventually the problems were sorted out, and in time Prokofiev's music and Lavrovsky's choreography became second nature to subsequent generations of Kirov dancers. There would later be many other versions of the ballet in Russia and abroad (chiefly those of Sir Frederick Ashton, John Cranko, and Sir Kenneth MacMillan in the West), and, as Schwarz has put it, "Undoubtedly, many a western spectator will find the Soviet ballet version of *Romeo and Juliet* artificial and disturbing, as indeed did some Soviet critics. But to the Soviet dance world, the concept of this ballet opened new perspectives in terms of danced drama, of a psychological search in a basically extrovert medium. *Romeo and Juliet* was seen as the beginning of a new ballet era, revealing uncharted vistas."

Certainly, *Romeo and Juliet* will always be identified with Ulanova, who made her debut at GATOB in 1928 and remained a major figure at the theater through its years in Perm. Afterward she joined the Bolshoi company, where she had first appeared as a guest in 1935, to become Russia's official chief ballerina. Juliet, of course, was not her first significant creation. She had created Maria in *The Fountain of Bakhchisarai* and had been Odette-Odile in Vaganova's new version of *Swan Lake*, as well as Diana in Vaganova's version of *Esmeralda*.

After the premiere of *The Fountain*, the critic Natalia Roslavleva wrote that Ulanova's Maria was "imbued with an elegiac sorrow close to the spirit of Pushkin and gives a strong indication of her special quality as dancer." She had what we today would term "soul," which Roslavleva has described as "tapping the internal melody." Whatever words one uses, what is unmistakable is that Ulanova was as much an exponent of the emotions of her roles as she was a highly accomplished dancer. The poignant memories she left behind were not so much of the conquering of a difficult series of steps as of her gift for conveying the essence of a feeling.

Because of her questioning, seeking nature, she gradually began to drop more superficial parts such as the title roles in *Sleeping Beauty* and *Raymonda* in favor of parts in which she could get under the skin of a character. "To me," she has written, "the value of my work lies in the conviction that the language of the ballet can convey to people great and vital truths about life, about the beauty in life and in the human heart." While her glory years were spent at the Bolshoi, where she came to epitomize the Soviet ballerina and where she achieved a legendary status, her roots and her training were in Leningrad. The shadow of her art still today falls across the Kirov's aspiring ballerinas.

During the war years in Perm, Ponomarev took charge of the company as its acting artistic director, relinquishing the post to Lopukhov after the hostilities ended. When the Kirov returned to Leningrad, the post of chief choreographer went to Sergeiev. While dancing leading roles at the Kirov, he served as the artistic director of the Vaganova School from 1938 to 1940, a post to which he returned in 1961, remaining until 1970. His first achievement as a choreographer was a new version of Prokofiev's *Cinderella* that the company still performs today, in which he danced the Prince opposite Dudinskaya's Cinderella.

Called "the poet of dance" and "the king of the lyric phrase," Sergeiev was considered a prototype of the *danseur noble*. He graduated from the GATOB School in 1930 and was immediately absorbed into the parent company. Despite his commanding status as a lyrical artist, Sergeiev was able to bring strength to contemporary ballets as well, such as *The Flames of Paris*, in which he created the role of Mistral alongside Chabukiani's Jerome, and *The Fountain of Bakhchisarai*, where he was Vatslav opposite Ulanova's Maria. "What suited Sergeiev best," Stupnikov felt, were the themes of "grand, ardent and devoted love. . . . Sergeiev was a romantic Siegfried, a poetic Désiré, and an ironic and comic Prince in *Cinderella*. . . . One of his most interesting and compelling roles was Albrecht in *Giselle*, which he continued to perform with depth and incomparable lyricism for so many years on the Kirov stage."

The years between the two world wars were heady ones at the Kirov Ballet, and the peerless casts peaked with Sergeiev's Romeo paired with Ulanova's Juliet. Lopukhov felt that "the carefully considered finish to every gesture and every moment on stage, particularly in dance movements, was what made Sergeiev a worthy partner to Ulanova. They were created for one another . . . but alas, in the very flowering of their talents, circumstances broke up this partnership unprecedented in its formal and spiritual beauty." When Ulanova moved on to the Bolshoi, Sergeiev's principal partner became his wife, Dudinskaya, and they went on to forge indelible images of their own, which Stupnikov felt were notable for "the technical accuracy of their dancing and for their endless search for new shades of meaning and unexplored beauties in the roles they performed."

When Sergeiev's time as a dancer began to ebb, he was made the company's artistic director from 1951 to 1955 and again from 1961 to 1970, where he became an admirable curator of the company's repertory and reaffirmed its traditional values. He returned to the choreography of original works in 1957 with *Path of Thunder*.

During the 1950s, Sergeiev shared choreographic honors with Yuri Grigorovich and an iconoclastic figure at the Kirov, Leonid Yakobson. For the Kirov, Yakobson staged the first production of Khachaturian's *Spartacus* (1956), which would later be overshadowed by Grigorovich's better-known and more spectacularly lavish Bolshoi production. Yakobson created some 130 dance works during his career, most of them disliked by Soviet officialdom, as they were outside the boundaries of the socialist realist style. He preferred creating short ballets rather than full-length ones, which also went against the official grain (he termed them "choreographic miniatures"), and his eclectic choreography combined classical movements with turned-in positions, jazz, sculptured poses, and popular dance. But his work was greatly admired by many leading Russian dancers because it stretched their dramatic range. For Mikhail Baryshnikov he fashioned the amazing *Vestris*, and Natalia Markova danced the lead in Yakobson's 1974 Kirov ballet *The Bedbug*, which has been described as "a biting satire of Soviet life."

Grigorovich had joined the Kirov as a character dancer in 1946, and from 1961 to 1964 he shared the post of artistic director with Sergeiev before moving on to the same post with the Bolshoi Ballet. (According to Oleg Vinogradov, Grigorovich was fired from the Mariinsky and exiled to Novosibirsk for two years, where they met and became close friends; only later was he pardoned and given the Bolshoi position.)

Apart from being entrusted by Lopukhov in 1957 with the choreography for the Kirov's first production of *The Stone Flower*, his principal legacy to the theater was his 1961 *Legend of Love*, to a vivid score by Arif Melikov. Shostakovich later wrote that "his choreographic images are replete with genuine poetry. . . . Everything is expressed, everything stated in [an] original language of images that, I think, open a new stage in the development of Soviet theater."

With *Legend of Love*, Grigorovich did away with mime and exaggerated arm movements. Among the most striking elements of the work was the powerful use of the corps de ballet, which functioned almost as a Greek chorus, advancing the story while commenting on it. Everything was conveyed by classical dance alone and through only four leading characters. To the critic Igor Stupnikov, this ballet "was almost like a manifesto: 'Look back to Petipa, who understood how to create rich and beautiful ballets; let us follow his example in using the art of dance itself to the fullest. . . . In the middle of the twentieth century, we will explore and experiment and aim for something different, but we will do so by using the older tradition.' Grigorovich . . . dared to state yet again that it is *dance* which can express everything of importance in ballet."

These years at the Kirov might easily be termed the theater's third golden age of dancing. The first had come at the turn of the century during the imperial era, the second was in the 1930s, and in the 1950s the company boasted another extraordinary roster of dancers, with more to come in the 1960s. Nothing in the theater's provincial opera wing remotely approached the splendor of dance at this time. Just a listing of some of the names from the halcyon 1950s makes the point: Ninel Kurgapkina, Vladilen Semionov, Inna Zubkovskaya, Alla Osipenko, Irina Kolpakova, Rudolf Nureyev, Valery Panov, Nikita Dolgushin, Gabriela Komleva, Alla Sizova, and Yuri Soloviev. Any pair of them would have made the fortunes of another dance company, and the Kirov's renegade, Nureyev, later did just that by himself.

Of the ballerinas of this period, Kolpakova—Vaganova's last student—was without doubt supreme in her time. Her career was long; I saw her dance her most famous role, Aurora in *The Sleeping Beauty*, in New York during the Kirov's 1964 visit, with a cast that included Soloviev as the Bluebird and Makarova as Princess Florina. Twenty years later, when she was fifty-one, she was filmed in the same ballet; her poetic line and lyrical technique were still beautifully intact. Her acting did not have a great dramatic impact, but on a purely technical level her dancing was breathtaking in its ease and security. In comparison, Kurgapkina was more sympathetic, Sizova more individual, and Osipenko more decorative. But wonderful as they were, the three were overshadowed by Kolpakova's strong presence.

In 1961, the year *Legend of Love* was first seen, the company was shaken by scandal. While on a spring tour in Europe, Nureyev defected to the French police in Paris. He had long been the black sheep of the Kirov flock, a dancer who was always Nureyev first and the role second. He was headstrong and broke most of the rules imposed on artists during his time. But so incandescent were his gifts that his idiosyncratic behavior, while not forgiven, was largely overlooked. He was lucky to have become a pupil of Alexander Pushkin, one of the most celebrated teachers of the era, whose other students include Grigorovich, Dolgushin, Soloviev, Valery Panov, Makarova, and Baryshnikov. Pushkin was among the few people who could tame Nureyev and, at the same time, command his respect.

Baryshnikov remembers Pushkin as "a calm, serene man[;] he was not given to elaborate verbal instructions. His style was the simplest—quiet and direct, but never confining . . . early on in his students' careers he would steer them in one direction or another: this one toward the romantic-lyrical route, that one toward the virtuoso. He taught in such a way that the dancer began to know himself more completely, and that, I believe, is the first key to serious work—to know oneself, one's gifts, one's limitations, as fully as possible."

Pushkin was often a buffer between Nureyev and the theater, and like Nijinsky before him, Nureyev spent only four years as a member of the Kirov before decamping and attaining the sort of idol status that had been Nijinsky's. The critic Arlene Croce has written that Nureyev "is the kind of dancer who causes categories to have a nervous breakdown." Gennady Smakov agrees: "The paradoxical combination of his princely looks and his explosive, edgy style toppled all the classical criteria established by Russian academic training."

There was no one quite like him before or since, except perhaps Chabukiani. But Nureyev had greater bravura, a more animalistic quality to his dancing, and a more finely molded physique. Even so, he was not as ideal and neat a Kirov dancer as were Soloviev and Baryshnikov—his dancing was oversized, too tempestuous, too sensual, too emotional. But these characteristics were never so pronounced that they became a deficiency, and they were wedded to one of the most prodigious appetites for dancing the world has ever known.

He was exceptional in another way as well. He was admitted to the Vaganova Academy when he was seventeen; his training before that had been in his provincial hometown of Ufa, the capital of the Bashkir Republic and virtually another world compared to Leningrad. Although he was a raw dancer when he entered Pushkin's class, he never looked like a student, so immense was his personality and so fiery were his performances. As Kshessinskaya had championed the young Nijinsky, so Dudinskaya asked for Nureyev as her partner in *Laurencia*, which immediately set him apart at the Kirov and stamped him as an important comer; her support led to his swift promotion to major roles with the company.

Nureyev paralleled Nijinsky in another way as well. A performance of *Don Quixote* with Nureyev was held up for forty minutes while the management fought with him over his costume. He had shed Basilio's puffed breeches in favorite of white tights, which better displayed the lines of his legs. It caused a minor scandal at the time, but it soon because a standard practice. Nureyev had long been at odds with Sergeiev, and Sergeiev's jealousy and vindictiveness toward Nureyev surely played a part in his spur-of-the-moment decision to defect in 1961. It was a major upset in the life of the company.

Nureyev had gone his own way as usual on the tour, mingling with foreigners, shaking his KGB shadows, and staying out late. Sergeiev and the KGB tried to lure him back to Moscow in the middle of the tour for a fictitious concert, but he saw through the ruse and impetuously asked for asylum from the French police at a Paris airport just as the company was leaving for its next engagement in London. Inadvertently, as Smakov puts it, Nureyev "altered the landscape of western ballet over the [next] two decades."

After his defection, Sergeiev turned the Kirov into "a mini police state," Joan Acocella has written. "The repertory consisted either of nineteenth-century classics, restaged by Sergeiev, or of socialist flag-wavers. (Sergeiev himself, in 1963, made a ballet, *The Distant Planet*, inspired by Yuri Gagarin's spaceflight.) . . . The dancers were watched vigilantly for signs of insubordination. If they looked like defection risks—indeed, if they failed to attend company meetings or had the wrong friends—they were often barred from foreign tours."

Nureyev was the first of the Soviet defectors to make an uneasy peace with the government, and in 1989 he returned to the Soviet Union and danced for the last time on the Kirov's stage. He was fifty-one and undertook five performances of James in *La sylphide*. Of the prodigal's return, a Leningrad critic wrote that "not everyone waited for him with love. Many anticipated disappointment. . . . At the performance everything became strangely muddled; we tried to look through time to see the dance as it would have been thirty, or even twenty years ago. Our ovations were addressed to the past."

After Nureyev's brief time with the Kirov, its most prized male dancers were Soloviev and Baryshnikov. Had Soloviev, a troubled man who eventually took his own life at the age of thirty-seven, also defected to the West, there is little doubt that he, too, would have made a major international career. As it was, suicide was his sad means of defection. He possessed what has been described as "the greatest leap in the world" (because of it he was nicknamed "cosmic Yuri," after the Soviet Union's first space hero). Like Nijinsky, Soloviev had the gift of seeming to be suspended in the air after soaring upward, and he returned to the ground in a soft, deep plié, which gave his feat a further touch of unreality. He was the closest dancer to Nijinsky physically: short and with thick, well-developed thighs.

Soloviev joined the Kirov the same year as Nureyev, and they shared many of the same classical roles—Siegfried, Albrecht, and both the Bluebird and Prince Désiré in *Sleeping Beauty*. In fact, there were nights at the theater when both these giants could be seen in the same performance. Smakov feels that in effect Soloviev was "trapped by his physique—his pleasant, 'country boy' face, his solid body, and powerful, muscular legs. He could easily be cast as a sterling Soviet youth, one of the stereotypes that embodied the official image in so many ballets [of the times] . . . as for classical roles, he generally seemed to be at a loss with them, especially with Albrecht. . . . His flawless dancing, particularly in Act ii, was at odds with his diligent yet amateurish pantomime."

Makarova felt that "no one nurtured Soloviev's soul or fostered his mind; no one ever produced a ballet to tap his inner world. This was a Stradivarius which played beautifully but never sang. . . . And he was too weak to break through to self-realization." But in 1972 he was given a part that overwhelmed Leningrad's ballet public: God in the farcical *Creation of the World*, choreographed by Natalia Kasatkina and Vladimir Vasiliev. In this role, as Smakov recalls, "he gave the first indication of his extraordinary comic gifts: dressed in a long white shirt, with a beard, light brown hair, and a round trusting face, Soloviev's God resembled a hapless Russian peasant."

This ballet had actually been created for Baryshnikov, and in his way he was as charming and amusing as Adam as Soloviev was as God. With *The Creation of the World*, Baryshnikov, who had joined the Kirov in 1967, came fully into his own, and he began at last to be given such major roles as Siegfried and Albrecht, which had previously been considered beyond his expressive range. Nonetheless, so outstanding was his talent—he caused near pandemonium with his graduation performance of the *Corsaire* pas de deux—that he bypassed the corps de ballet and began his Kirov career with the peasant pas de deux in *Giselle*, Bluebird, and the Poet in *Chopiniana*. His second season brought one of his best roles—Basilio in *Don Quixote*—for it made the most of his lighthearted, boyish character.

But because he occupied a sort of neutral ground between lyric-romantic parts and *demi-caractère*, he was not an easy artist to cast. A turning point came when Yakobson, recognizing Baryshnikov's unique gifts, created *Vestris* for him, a showpiece that brought Baryshnikov first prize in an international competition held in Moscow in 1969. In *Vestris*, with amazing lightness, his face became a series of masks, as he shifted from the most complex classical sequences to others that were downright grotesque.

He was at the theater twice as long as Nureyev before defecting to the West in Canada during a 1974 tour (four months before, Pushkin had died of a heart attack at sixty-two on a Leningrad street, which might have contributed to Baryshnikov's decision). His art was cut from different cloth. He exuded none of Nureyev's sexuality, and although a highly individual dancer, he was a more disciplined one. Baryshnikov's appeal stemmed primarily from his incredibly pure technique, which was artfully blended with what Smakov has termed his "impish charm."

"I joined the company," Baryshnikov has said, "when it was falling apart." A period of repression had followed the political thaw instigated earlier by Nikita Khrushchev. Gergiev was a student in the Leningrad Conservatory when Baryshnikov defected, and he remembers that "it was a shock, but it was somehow expected—not particularly of him, but of someone. You see, the system was pressing, always pressing. When Baryshnikov, like Nureyev before him, felt too pressed, their solution was to defect. I don't think they wanted to leave. I just think the system gave them no choice. It pushed them out. This was stupid. They should have understood that talents like Nureyev and Baryshnikov happen once in fifty years, even in the Soviet Union, which is such a big and powerful culture. But there were always gray people who reported to their superiors in such a nasty way that the politicians turned their anger against such artists instead of against their informants.

"The Kirov, of course, was full of all sorts of KGB connections and party appointees. It was a combination of a great artistic society and a lot of functionaries. In the 1970s, the Soviet Union had fantastic people—scientists, musicians, actors, writers, poets—who were suffering but who did their work despite the horrors and hardness of the system. The functionaries are still there, although there are fewer of them to push buttons and do damage. I think Russia is forever destined to have great problems and great people who must survive within these problems."

Another defection of the cold-war era was that of Makarova, the one ballerina to leap westward. She had joined the Kirov in 1959, eight years before Baryshnikov, and had first attracted attention while still a student, dancing as Soloviev's partner in his graduation performance in 1958. She would remain with the Kirov for eleven years before becoming a symbol in the West of classical dancing at its most eloquent and feminine. "Like Pavlova," Smakov has written, "her fragile lines, thin, girlish neck, and long face with its finely chiseled features, as if drawn by some old Dutch painter, call forth an image of elusive femininity . . . [with] her seemingly effortless leap, her light step, the innate fluidity of her movements, and her flexible torso . . . she would have been Ulanova's legitimate successor. But Makarova, like her frequent partner Baryshnikov, was driven by enormous artistic curiosity that constantly challenged her to extend [her] limits."

Makarova came by some of this naturally, having grown up when controls in Russia began loosening compared to what they had been under Stalin. Then, too, she was always interested in what lay behind the face of the characters she was portraying, and she tried to bring to the familiar figures of classical dance a greater emotional truth and dramatic dimension. It was never enough for Makarova simply to dance. She wanted to live her roles, to get under a character's skin, to bring out of them their inner life, their soul.

She began slowly and at first was by no means the consummate ballerina into which she later developed. But the originality of her approach was often its own compensation, and, as Smakov notes, "To a certain degree, her shortcomings turned out to be her forte, an unmistakable stamp of individuality that distinguish her from her gifted Kirov colleagues." Not for her a meek, dreamy Giselle. Instead she gave the public a none too stable, flesh-and-blood creature whose madness was a result of having her world shattered by a lie, an approach Makhalina would later take. Although the theater attempted to reign in Makarova's rebellious spirit and vivid imagination, it could do only so much, and she continued to attract attention while striving to perfect her uneven technique so that it might better serve her inner visions and feelings. After her defection, Oleg Vinogradov, who had been her classmate at the Vaganova Academy, worked behind the scenes to engineer her return to the Kirov, just as Makarova worked on her end to bring the first Kirov artists to the West for guest appearances, beginning with Asylmuratova and Ruzimatov in 1988.

Vinogradov's patience paid off, and in 1989 Makarova danced with the Kirov during a company visit in London. The next year saw her return to Leningrad, where she performed a pas de deux from John Cranko's *Eugene Onegin*. Unlike Nureyev in his reappearance at the theater, Makarova triumphed. Baryshnikov has yet to return to St. Petersburg, although he did relent and in 1997 danced again on the stage in his native Riga. The late Russian poet Joseph Brodsky felt that had Baryshnikov remained in Russia, "He'd be a ruin by now both physically and mentally. Physically because of the bottle . . . mentally because of that mixture of impotence and cynicism that corrodes everyone there—the stronger you are, the worse it is."

Temirkanov feels that the defections from the Kirov Ballet eventually contributed to Sergeiev's downfall, and his reign ended in 1970, the year of Makarova's "leap to freedom." For a while there was a period of unrest during which various factions shared or vied for power. The company drifted into near chaos, standards dropped, and the Kirov Theater was officially decried as "incompetent." The decay did not come to a halt until 1977 and the appointment of Vinogradov.

Vinogradov ruled the Kirov Ballet virtually unchallenged for twenty years, although during the last two of these he held on tenaciously by his fingertips as his power base eroded beneath him. But he was in control longer than any artistic director since the Revolution. An egocentric man of decided tastes and little patience for disagreement, he shaped, for better and for worse, the Kirov Ballet as it stood in the 1990s.

CHAPTER TWELVE

February–March: Conquering Europe

THOSE who examined their programs carefully at a repeat of *The Sleeping Beauty* the first week in February 1996 discovered that beyond the pleasures of the eighteen-year-old Maya Dumchenko as Aurora, the aristocratic Prince Désiré of Stanislav Belyaevsky, and a vivid, airborne Bluebird danced by Nikita Shcheglov, the production was no longer being overseen by Ninel Kurgapkina, at one time a major ballerina at the theater and now a respected coach. Overall responsibility for maintaining *Sleeping Beauty* had passed to Olga Chenchikova, the wife of Makhar Vaziev and a dancer whose career had been ended by an injury.

This shift in authority was distressing to many concerned with the fortunes of the Kirov Ballet, for it seemed to them to be a lowering of standards; these two ballerinas—Kurgapkina and Chenchikova—reflected different eras, gifts, and backgrounds. To understand the distress, it must be remembered that a principal factor in keeping the company strong and operating at a peak level is its remarkable system of coaches. Of course, there are coaches wherever there is dance, for ballet is an art that is strongly dependent on live role models. Dance steps can be written down or learned from archival videos. But these means are second best to seeing and learning the step through another body.

Even so, the coaching setup at the Kirov is a special one. One of the company's trademarks is how it has managed to maintain its truth in spite of the upheavals of revolution, war, and an uncertain economy. This has been in large measure a result of the training offered at the Vaganova school and the coaching system at the Mariinsky. Changes in the style and manner of the company's dancing have been inevitable—a question of time and tide, as the Vaganova faculty and the theater's coaches have died or retired. But the basic setup of the coaching system has not altered.

All dancers entering the company are assigned a coach who prepares them in their roles and makes certain that company traditions are adhered to, while allowing a certain amount of stylistic leeway for a dancer's personality and individual strengths. The coach also frequently acts as a go-between for a dancer and the artistic director, lobbying for certain roles at home and on tour. Even star dancers continue to work and be inspired by their coaches throughout their careers, and on retiring, many in turn take up the mantle of coach and teacher themselves.

During my year at the Kirov, in rehearsal sessions conducted by Elena Evteeva and Andris Liepa, I saw the difference their example could make. I also felt the presence on ballet nights in the house of former ballerinas such as Gabriela Komleva, Inna Zubkovskaya, and Natalia Dudinskaya. They could be seen sitting, Norn-like, in stage boxes, following the work of dancers in their care, checking out the competition, and frequently being passed floral tributes given their protégées by fans.

Elizabeth Kendall has advanced the intriguing theory that many of the changes in the company have to do with the violent history of St. Petersburg itself and how past events shaped the lives of the older generation of dancers differently from those of today's dancers. The theater's senior coaches, she notes, "had all been children during the Second World War, when Leningrad underwent the horrific 900-day siege by the German military and lost approximately a third of its population, most to starvation. . . . This generation knew wartime hunger, cold and fear, the poverty that measured food in bread crumbs and bits of sugar, the separation of families, the agony of fathers dying on the Leningrad front. . . . They also knew the time of rebuilding after the war, when people returned to the exhausted city and began, in a life of bare subsistence, to reconstruct their heritage." This had to make a profound difference, she believes, in not only the lives but in the art of those who lived during these times. She asked Kolpakova if this idea was tenable.

"'Maybe,'" Kolpakova responded. "'All we had was the theater. . . . No clothes, no cars, no dachas. I lived in one room with my mother—one room in a communal apartment with seven other families.'" Her generation, Kendall wrote, "was the last to experience . . . collective traumas. . . . Life for the generation of dancers that followed seemed positively American by comparison. . . . Former dancers look back on a theater where reverence for elders, dedication to craft, and a Petersburgian concept of classical high culture all came together in what was an indissoluble ideal.

"Today they survey a theater where that ideal has come apart. To them, young dancers seem, as Kurgapkina puts it, 'lazy.' . . . Of course, older Kirovians have gilded their memories. They've left out the interventions of Party bureaucrats, and the sense of being shut away from the wider world which played such a part in the defections of Nureyev, Makarova, and Baryshnikov. But, even allowing for the warmth of memory, it was clear to me that what was now in place at the Kirov was the shell of a system that had functioned brilliantly in war and crisis and rebuilding but now, in 'normal' times, was breeding cynicism and melancholy—along with pockets of intense honorableness. It was a system riddled with factions."

Kendall discovered people in the theater who "had the feeling that Vinogradov's dancers didn't pay much attention to Vaganova standards—that they were more interested in showing themselves off as grand personages than in shaping dance steps." As for herself, Kendall found that "by the time I visited the Kirov, the liberties that the Vinogradov dancers took on stage and off had introduced a separate set of standards into the theater, which seemed to work against the Vaganova heritage, and the unacknowledged clash between these two ideas of dancing was demoralizing the older dancers and confusing the younger ones. One of the senior dancers sat by me watching Ruzimatov rehearse in a particularly roughshod mode. 'If he does it like that, why should we even bother to take ballet class?' the dancer said ruefully."

Kendall laid a good many of the changes that have taken place at the Kirov at Vinogradov's doorstep because of his "unprecedented concentration of power . . . Galina Mezentseva quarreled with Vinogradov in the fall of 1990, and left for the Scottish Ballet. Altynai Asylmuratova danced part time for a while with England's Royal Ballet. Irina Chistyakova went to the London City Ballet as a guest dancer, and on her return was denied roles. . . . Olga Moiseyeva, having been dismissed as a coach by her star protégée, Julia Makhalina, accepted a teaching position in Germany for a year, both Kurgapkina and Komleva spend chunks of the Kirov season out of the theater, teaching in Europe or America.

"If Vinogradov didn't actively cause these defections or absences, he created the climate in which they happened," Kendall wrote in 1992. "One St. Petersburg dance critic remarked to me, 'How strange that in Stalin's time, when you would have expected a single monolithic opinion to hold sway in the theater, there were many opinions. Many people watched over our ballet tradition. Now, in this time of so-called openness, there's just Vinogradov in charge, and he's a super-monopolist.' " When Vinogradov was dethroned in 1997, a host of people felt much the same could be said of the company's present director, Makhar Vaziev.

Ballet continued to be prominent in early February, with a dazzling Kitri in *Don Quixote* by Makhalina and the much-anticipated premiere of Balanchine's *Symphony in C*, coupled with a repeat of Robbins's *In the Night* and Fokine's *Spectre de la rose*, featuring Ruzimatov. *Symphony in C* was more solid and challenged the company in a less exacting way than had the *Scotch Symphony* a few months earlier. But then, it had been freshly set by John Taras, and beyond this, the Kirov had the experience of having lived for several years with two other Balanchine ballets. The chief problem with *Symphony in C*, however, was not the dancers, as it had been with *Scotch Symphony*, but Vinogradov's decision to smother the work with elaborate drops and a series of ornate candelabra that lined the periphery of the dance area and detracted from the sleek lines of Balanchine's choreography. He dismissed criticism of this decision with a wave of his hand, saying, "I like spectacle, I like things to be rich, as does our audience, and I wanted *Symphony in C* in the style of our theater. Besides, I think this richness is in the music. It is glamorous." But if *Symphony in C* had too much decoration, *Spectre* had too little, not even the proper windows for the entrance and exit of the Rose. Nor was Ruzimatov's dancing more than workmanlike. This skimpy decor was an odd inconsistency to encounter in a season that boasted designs based on the original decor for Fokine's *Schéhérazade* and *Firebird*.

February also brought an electrifying revival of the company's production of Prokofiev's *The Fiery Angel*. This landmark production, which was new in 1991, was the first time the opera had been given at the theater. Undertaken as a coproduction with London's Royal Opera, it helped put a seal on Gergiev's Kirov as a place of adventure and excitement. Although by 1996 the staging was becoming lax and the scenery, which was beginning to look dog-eared, was not assembled with the greatest of care (unfortunately a commonplace occurrence at home and on tour), the evening was courageous and stirring. This was the opera that launched the career of Galina Gorchakova in the West, and while Larissa Gogolevskaya was not the Gorchakova of four years before, she was impressive. Vladimir Ognovenko was again a powerhouse as the Inquisitor, Konstantin Pluzhnikov was a properly malevolent Mephistopheles, and Polyanichko did an admirable job filling in for Gergiev, who was away.

Gergiev returned to St. Petersburg in time to take over a performance of *Sadko*, which was substituted at the last moment for a revival of the Kirov's *Ruslan and Ludmila*. It seems that *Ruslan*'s costumes had not been returned after the San Francisco performances the fall before; they were being held hostage until the Kirov rectified the poor condition in which it had returned a *Tosca* production borrowed from the California company. The switch from *Ruslan* to *Sadko* was complicated by Gergiev's not having conducted the opera for a while and by his being faced with unfamiliar cuts in the score made by Sergei Kalagin, who was in charge of the recent *Sadko*s.

As the cuts could not be restored in time, Gergiev spent intermissions with the score sprawled out on his desk trying to get these cuts in his mind before the next act began. On top of this he was attempting to be charming to a couple of guests, answer the telephone, and field questions from those crowding his office. "Too often Valery concerns himself with little problems that someone else could solve for him," Alexander Tchaikovsky feels. "Why does he feel he has to deal with everything? This is a big mistake. It drains him unnecessarily. But no one around him takes any initiative. They stand around waiting to be told what to do. What they should be doing is screening those who want to see Valery. If their problem can be solved by someone else, Valery shouldn't be bothered with it." Yet even with these myriad distractions, which are part and parcel of Gergiev's daily life, he managed to bring to *Sadko* a luster and an excitement to the score that had been missing from earlier performances.

Three days later the company boarded a chartered Aeroflot jet to head for Paris, where it launched a winter European tour that would last five weeks. In the French capital, the Kirov appeared at the refurbished Théâtre des Champs Elysées, where the Diaghilev company had danced the world premiere of *Le sacre du printemps*. In fact, Gergiev and his company arrived ninety years after Diaghilev first laid siege to Paris with a still-famous exhibition of Russian portraiture. The repertory for the 1996 tour included staged performances of *Prince Igor* and *The Gambler*, concert performances of the original version of *La forza del destino* and *The Queen of Spades*, Berlioz's *Roméo et Juliette*, and the Verdi Requiem.

Paris was the only one of the seven cities to hear *Forza*, and the performance there on 15 February began the tour on a low note. The problems started with the illness of Gegam Grigorian, who was forced to cancel his appearance. He is one of the few tenors today equipped to deal with the murderous tessitura of Don Alvaro's original music. For a while Gergiev was afraid that the opera for the opening might have to be changed. Perhaps this would have been prudent, considering the eleventh-hour substitute found in the Puerto Rican tenor Antonio Barasorda. Gergiev (like Verdi in his later Italian version of *Forza*) cut Alvaro's cabaletta, but still Barasorda struggled to make his way to the end of the score. Galina Gorchakova was in poor shape as well, Nikolai Putilin's voice took time to warm up so that he started cold and husky sounding, and Gennadi Bezzubenkov was an inadequate, gruff Guardiano. Only the memorable splendor of Olga Borodina as Preziosilla gave off sparks. Nor was it much of an occasion for the orchestra, which had little resonance and sounded muffled in the theater's pit.

The first stage work presented in Paris was *Prince Igor*, and although there were trouble spots here as well—chiefly the watery singing of Valentina Tsidipova as Jaroslavna—the end result was decidedly superior. Putilin was commanding from his first notes, and Ognovenko was magnificent as Galitsky. Only Larissa Diadkova failed to project her appealing voice in Kontchakovna's music. One aspect of the evening that consistently rankled, and would continue to do so throughout the tour, was the sets—poorly lighted and looking as if they had been thrown together. Like many conductors, Gergiev has better ears than eyes. If the technical inadequacies of *Igor* had been musical shortcomings, he would have put them right immediately and probably dressed down the person responsible for the errors. But he said nothing, and the sets continued to look shoddy night after night.

Still, he infused extraordinary energy and life into *Igor* that made it—musically at least—unforgettable. Part of the evening's success was also due to the inclusion of a strong solo dancer for the first Polovtsian scene, Islom Baimuradov. After two performances, however, he returned to St. Petersburg, and it was back to business as usual as far as the balance of the *Igor*s on tour was concerned. For the first repeat of *Igor* a number of cast changes were made, but none for the better. Mikhail Kit was weak in the title role, Alexander Morozov a still weaker Galitsky, and Evgenia Tselovalnik an uneven, although at times imposing, Jaroslavna. Originally Gorchakova was scheduled to be the principal Jaroslavna for the tour, but she pulled out at the last moment, claiming she didn't know the staging.

The first performance was scheduled to begin at 7:30 P.M., but curtain time came and went and Gergiev was still not in the theater (he finally arrived at 7:40). The French manager, although obviously upset, was sanguine: "Oh, I see," he said with a sly smile, "tonight no conductor, eh?" The Russians backstage (who are accustomed to Gergiev's tardiness) were as unperturbed as the French were frantic, and these differing Gallic and Slavic attitudes struck me as an instantaneous distillation of two diametrically opposed cultures.

The third performance was the company premiere of Prokofiev's *Gambler*, using the sets Georgy Tsypin had created for La Scala the month before. Musically, it was triumphant. Gergiev's fierce love for and understanding of Prokofiev's music made the shape and interior landscape of the score crystal clear. His orchestra played like champions, and the cast, headed by Lubov Kazarnovskaya as Pauline, Vladimir Galuzin as Alexei, Sergei Alexashkin as the General, and a Bolshoi guest, Elena Obraztsova, as Babulenka, was evenly matched and brilliant.

The production was less convincing, for Tsypin employed a single and eventually tiresome apple-green set, broken only by the starkness of Alexei's bedroom, which was left onstage for the entire evening. Nor was Teimur Tchkheidze's direction appealing. It seemed more like a collection of stylized groupings and gimmicks than a truly intrinsic mirror of the music. But whatever its qualities and however debatable they might be, the performance had been honed to a fine point, and repeated performances during the tour were as well knit and free flowing as the Paris premiere.

In Lyons the company gave a concert performance of *The Queen of Spades*, and it was an unexpected and revelatory experience to hear this opera without staging and with no separation between pit and stage. There was a compelling concentration on purely musical values to an extent not possible in the theater and a greater awareness of the finely wrought quality of Tchaikovsky's score. Of special interest, too, was Larissa Diadkova's Countess, a role she made mesmerizing.

In a cavernous new theater in Montpellier, the company performed Berlioz's *Roméo et Juliette*, which, despite Marianna Tarasova's eloquent singing, was dealt a serious blow by Gergiev's decision (or one imposed on him) to take an intermission after the scherzo. When the performance resumed, he was unable to recapture its original thrust and atmosphere. A repeat of *Prince Igor* in the same town brought some unexpected and odd cuts by Gergiev, including the trio in the second Polovtsian scene and Jaroslavna's last-act aria.

The Spanish leg of the tour began in Valencia, in a fine new concert hall named for the pianist José Iturbi, a native son. Here *Igor* was presented in concert form, and like *The Queen of Spades*, it, too, offered new perspectives. Gergiev was able to put the overture back up front where it belonged, and tempos were generally crisper and quicker without the staging and dancing. Details emerged in an extraordinary way, and in the hall's lively acoustics, the Polovtsian Dances were overwhelming. Barcelona's remarkable art-nouveau edifice, the Palau de la Musica Catalana, was the venue for the first of three tour performances of the Verdi Requiem. Unfortunately, this amazing concert hall looks more inviting than it sounds.

It would be in Madrid's new concert hall that the Verdi would come completely to life—sweeping and detailed, with some demonic brass playing, superb winds, and blazing strings. The only problem was the soloists. Marina Shaguch seemed uninvolved and was unable to project the low notes of her part; Tarasova sounded tired; the guest tenor, Vladimir Grishko, was unstable; and Bulat Minzhilkiev was too rough-and-ready for this music.

Schwarzkopf joined the company in the Netherlands in March 1996 with word that Moscow's minister of culture had appointed Gergiev absolute head of the Mariinsky, a position that now placed him over Schwarzkopf (who would continue for a while as the theater's managing director) and Vinogradov. The appointment only needed Boris Yeltsin's stamp of approval. However elated Gergiev was over the news, he was also exhausted, stretched to the limits of even his robust constitution. He had before him performances of *Prince Igor* and *The Gambler* in the Hague, the recording of *The Gambler* for Philips in Haarlem in a new hall built for the Netherlands Radio Philharmonic, a concert *Queen of Spades* in Utrecht, and three concerts with the Rotterdam Philharmonic consisting of the Overture and Venusberg Music from Wagner's *Tannhäuser* and Bruckner's Ninth Symphony. Sometimes he fulfilled two of these tasks in a single day. He even dashed off to Brussels one evening for a concert there. All this fell between 12 and 18 March.

Gergiev finished recording *The Gambler*, after several all-day sessions in which the music seemed to leap off the page, and reached the Utrecht *Queen of Spades* with a hundred-degree-plus fever and a bad cold. Yet in many ways, this was among the most staggering moments of the entire tour. It was a conflagration of emotions that held one spellbound and exhilarated from the first note, especially with Galuzin on hand to sing a possessed, breathtaking Herman. But the evening took its toll. Gergiev had to withdraw from a final *Igor* in The Hague and was forced to cancel a second set of concerts in Rotterdam (Stravinsky's *Apollo* and the Berlioz *Te Deum*).

I arrived back in St. Petersburg to a mediocre evening by the visiting Argentinean Ballet, a meddling troupe headed by the top prizewinner in the 1985 Moscow International Ballet Competition, Julio Bocca. But the bad taste this evening left was eradicated by another lovely *Sleeping Beauty* featuring Irina Zhelonkina as Princess Aurora, partnered by Belyaevsky. As both were students of Natalia Dudinskaya, an uncommon unity and sense of stylistic common ground helped elevate the evening. This was followed two nights later by a magical performance of *Bayadère* featuring Altynai Asylmuratova as Nikiya with Bocca as her partner. It is a measure of the Kirov Ballet's supremacy that the company could provide such leading ballerinas as Zhelonkina, Diana Vishneva, and Elvira Tarasova for the smaller parts in the Kingdom of the Shades scene.

Even so, the major dance event of the month was a return to the repertory of Grigorovich's *Legend of Love*, first with Julia Makhalina as Mekhmene Banu and then, ten nights later, with Asylmuratova in the same role. This work, little known in the West, established Grigorovich's importance as a choreographer. *The Legend of Love* is a full-length work based on a play by the Turkish writer and revolutionary Nazim Hikmet. As the critic Igor Stupnikov has described it, "The story is rich in ideas and images, and was not simply a thin plot around which to arrange unrelated dances; it is a tale of blood, love, torment and sacrifice." In other words, it is a good deal more, both choreographically and musically, than that other popular Soviet ballet, *The Fountain of Bakhchisarai*.

With *Legend*, Grigorovich cleansed drama-ballet even further of its old-fashioned mime. Everything here is explained and the story advanced by dance alone. It is a riot of fascinating patterns, tense dramatic situations, and powerful movements. It was not easily accepted in the beginning; many officials found it too disturbing and stark. But the public and critics felt its power, and with them it was an instant success. It soon inspired a flood of words for Grigorovich's bold use of ensemble dancing and the way his dances were mirrored by the colors and moods of Simon Virsaladze's sets and costumes, which were still being used by the Kirov.

At the first night of *Legend*, Makhalina's stunning, sharply rhythmic performance was mirrored by Veronika Ivanova's more lyrical Shirien and complemented by Alexander Kurkov's Ferkhad and Konstantin Zaklinsky's commanding Vizir. When Asylmuratova took over as Mekhmene Banu, she brought softer tints to this Amazonian part and unfolded further aspects of the character. With her appeared Irina Zhelonkina as Shirien, Makhar Vaziev as Ferkhad, and Evgeny Neff as the Vizir.

Another *Don Quixote* two nights later finally gave me a chance to see Viacheslav Samodurov in a major role, and, as I had suspected from his earlier appearances as the Golden Idol in *La bayadère*, he turned out to be a dancer with marvelous agility who took enormous risks (triple turns instead of double ones) that sometimes worked and stopped your breath, but sometimes failed. Curiously, although the steps for *Don Quixote* are well regimented despite whatever personal touches a dancer might add, one never knew what would be worn by the evening's leading dancers. Kitri's costume in act 1, for example, would often be different from performance to performance and personalized in some way. Much the same variance was found in the principals' costumes in other Kirov ballets. Nor was Vinogradov's questionable penchant for tie-dyeing a welcome addition to the corps costumes for *Giselle* and other ballets.

March came to a close with a major discovery: my first visit to the theater's music library on Rossi Street. This is one of the most splendid and historic such libraries in the world, vying with those at La Scala and the Paris Opéra in the breadth and richness of its holdings. Full scores and parts are housed here for operas dating back to the eighteenth century, as well as the original manuscripts of operas and ballets inextricably associated with the Mariinsky—*The Sleeping Beauty, Boris Godunov,* and Glazunov's *Seasons*—not to mention important letters, books, and other primary documents. Here, too, parts are copied and readied for performances at home and on tour.

The library is in grave need of immediate first aid, however. There had been a recent leak during a heavy rainstorm, and water had saturated a cabinet full of scores. Gergiev asked Alexander Tchaikovsky to see how much damage had been done, and I went along with him. Sadly, there was a great deal, and the floor in the entrance room was littered with scores laid out to dry.

Beyond the preservation needed so desperately, the collection cries out to be computer indexed and stored in cleaner, climate-controlled quarters. But with the theater daily struggling to keep its head above water, the needs of the library have been submerged. Much the same was true of the archival material housed down the street in the Library of the Performing Arts and the Museum of Theater and Music. To spend time in any of these archives and see the riches and the needs was at once exhilarating and depressing.

CHAPTER THIRTEEN

Gergiev and the Opera

WHEN YURI TEMIRKANOV accepted the post of music director of the Leningrad Philharmonic in 1988, it was up to the minister of culture in Moscow to decide who would replace him as the artistic director of the Kirov Theater. When his choice was announced, the Kirov Orchestra, in a spontaneous reaction, protested the decision. As the political scene in Russia was changing under Mikhail Gorbachev, the minister backed down and allowed the musicians to vote for their new chief.

"I was not even in the city at the time," Gergiev told me. "I think I was in Prague conducting. Anyway, I got a call telling me that I had gotten 85 percent of the vote, which was quite a lot because there were others nominated for the post as well. I must say that I don't think I would have stayed on at the Kirov if someone else had been elected. I was perfectly happy to be number two to Temirkanov. He was, after all, a fine musician and the man who brought me to the Kirov. But with him gone, I felt ten years of service to the theater had given me the operatic experience I needed to go out into the world and make my own way. Even back then, I couldn't see the full extent or the possibilities of my future at the theater.

"At any rate, I returned to Leningrad as the newly appointed artistic head of the Kirov and was invited to meet with the party boss in the city. When he saw me, he was obviously shocked because I was so young. He was frightened that such an important institution was going to be given to someone who looked so inexperienced. This man knew only the important musicians in the city, like Mravinsky and Temirkanov, and I was unknown outside the theater. His first question to me was, 'If you are appointed, what would you do?' I answered that I would start with the Russian repertory and create a festival around an important composer. I already had in my mind that this would be Mussorgsky. I believed that concentrating or focusing on such a idea would help me to begin."

But Gergiev remembers that when he announced the Mussorgsky Festival, "everyone started laughing at me, especially in Moscow. And when I brought the

Tarkovsky production of *Boris* to the Kirov from Covent Garden, the music director of the Bolshoi, Alexander Lazarev, openly made fun of me on television. 'They have lost their way in the Kirov,' he said. 'They can no longer create a *Boris* of their own.' It became quite nasty. Russians, you see, have been taught to believe that we are the biggest country, we are the biggest nation, we have the biggest culture. They were told by Soviet propaganda that the Bolshoi was the best, the Russian opera stars were the best, Russian ballet was the best—period. If you live in the Soviet Union and are not Russian, you are made to feel that you are not the best and must do things better than others in order to prove yourself.

"For me this was not a disadvantage but a help. It made me work harder. I am very Russian if you talk about culture. But I have never subscribed to the idea that something is good just because it is Russian. I try to judge something with fresh eyes and ears, and then decide 'this is good' or 'this is no good.' And in this instance, I knew what I was doing. I had sat in Covent Garden watching [Luchino] Visconti's magnificent production of *Don Carlo* and listening to Carlos Kleiber conducting *Otello* and asked myself, 'What do they have that we don't have? What is needed to bring the Kirov up to an international standard?' Orchestra? I can make an orchestra as good as Covent Garden's. Chorus? There we have to work. We have no tradition of singing in Italian, German, or French, but we do have young people with good voices who are willing to learn. Singers? I knew we had interesting artists, like Gorchakova, Borodina, and Galuzin, but I knew we had to bring them along carefully to make them equal to the best in the world.

"And I realized that we lacked a strong scenic tradition. It might have happened when the great director Meyerhold came to the Kirov just after the Revolution, but his efforts were stillborn, and this important dramatic element never developed in our theaters. I felt we had to have productions that would be a discovery, a revelation. This why I brought Andrei Tarnovsky's *Boris,* why we did *The Fiery Angel* and *War and Peace* with English directors and designers. These productions were my immediate, forceful effort to change the Kirov in my first two years and turn it upside down."

The Mussorgsky Festival was only one part of the ambitious program Gergiev brought with him to the Kirov, and he was able swiftly to implement his plans because, in his words, "I had more freedom than Temirkanov did. Even before the fall of the Soviet Union, there was less control by the government. Also, I like to work more than Temirkanov did. This is no criticism of him. It is just my nature. If anything, I am probably the one who should be criticized, because I work too much and drive others too hard. I conduct more than sixty performances a year in Russia. It's ridiculous. But I don't see any other way; otherwise, there would be more bad performances at the Kirov.

"But conducting is only part of what I do. I am constantly after our ministers to help us. There are a lot of people who can do damage, but there are only one or two who can help. The prime minister can be a brave, strong man and say, 'We need a strong Mariinsky. Here is three or four million a year,' but he will be attacked by a shouting pack of dogs who say, 'No, we need to spend this money in other places.' They always find a reason to keep us from having what we must have. Our need is desperate, and if we don't have help now, there will be nothing to save.

"We brought in about $50,000 for the Kirov from the tour to Japan, for example. That means we cleared around $8,000 per concert after we bought some new brass instruments, covered unexpected expenses, and paid our people. We give the players the maximum we can: $50 a day. And this is not for him to buy a steak. We want him to be able to bring back some money to his family. In St. Petersburg, for example, our concertmaster makes only $150 a month.

"But compare us, for example, to the Leningrad Symphony, the city's second orchestra. The players there make only $100 a month. If they record, it is for some label you have never heard of, and they are paid something like $3 a CD. When we make a video, a performer earns about $600 or $700 after five days of hard work, and we put aside about $100,000, maybe $150,000, for the theater. This is divided among some five hundred Kirov employees who have nothing to do with this video. It is something extra so that they can eat. The ballet does much the same thing, but after seventy performances they bring back to the theater only about $50,000. This difference, of course, was part of the scandal at the theater last October. The orchestra, after all, brings the same amount back after just eight concerts.

"This means the orchestra must work very hard, although the Japanese tour was easier than most. After all, there were five days without concerts. The 'Crazy Tour' in October was longer, and we played every day. That brought in about $300,000 because there was a fund-raising gala in London, for which I didn't even take a fee. Still, we have a problem maintaining the standard I would like. It is going to take a great deal more money if the Kirov is ever to function as successfully as the Metropolitan Opera does, whose average level is higher than that of most opera houses."

Looking back at the institution he inherited in 1988, Gergiev maintains that it was "slow, lazy, and dusty, with only two productions worth looking at—Temirkanov's *Queen of Spades* and his *Onegin*. One of the first things I did was to cancel a new production of *La bohème*. The theater, of course, needed a *Bohème*—it still does—but I felt *Bohème* was not as important to the future of the Kirov as a new *Khovanshchina*. Mussorgsky is our bread and water; we cannot live without him. *Prince Igor* was another work I felt should be in the repertory and could be a showcase for the artistic potential of the company. And the Mussorgsky Festival did bring attention to artists like Borodina, Larissa Diadkova, Vladimir Ogno-venko, Sergei Alexashkin, and Bulat Minzhilkiev.

"It was a particularly important moment for Borodina, who was still a student at the conservatory when she auditioned for Temirkanov and was engaged for the Kirov. Her first role in theater was Siebel in *Faust,* which I conducted. But that did not make her a star. The star was born during the Mussorgsky Festival. I must say it was a controversial decision to give her the part of Marfa in *Khovanshchina,* because there were three other mezzos competing for the part. Olga was the youngest one and the least known. It was, I suppose, a daring move, but I think it helped to unite and focus the company.

"I made other unusual casting decisions at the time as well. Take Konstantin Pluzhnikov. He had been my Lohengrin and had sung all the romantic heroes, like Faust and Lensky. But I told him to study the part of the Scribe in *Khovanshchina,* for I felt he had enormous potential as a character tenor as well. And look at him today—he was a marvelous Herod in *Salome.* I must tell you, too, that no one wanted Alexashkin. Everybody was against him. They felt he was not up to the Kirov's level. But I saw that he had tremendous potential, and he has proven to be very valuable to the Kirov.

"These were all decisions I made in my first month at the theater. One year later, I was able to take the company on tour to Hamburg. There had been very little touring under Temirkanov—a few cities in East Germany, and once, I believe, to Greece. The most important date outside Russia had been a single visit to London and Covent Garden in 1987, where the Kirov performed *Eugene Onegin* and *Boris Godunov.* What I was out to create was a big, energetic atmosphere that would attract people. I felt that then everything else would follow—tours, records, video. In other words, people would come to you, and you would not have to go searching for them. And this is what happened.

"What helped me was that the mood had also begun to change in the country. The heavy accent was no longer on the Bolshoi. Before, even when Temirkanov was doing good things, the Bolshoi was more dominant. He didn't have singers like Vladimir Atlantov, Elena Obraztsova, Irina Arkhipova, Tamara Milashkina, Galina Vishnevskaya, or Evgeny Nesterenko. But Temirkanov made the first move, and it was an important one. Thanks to him, the way we perform *The Queen of Spades* today is perhaps comparable to, say, *Otello* at La Scala. It is part of us, and it has been good to have Temirkanov's production and take it to the West. There shouldn't be a season without it. When we finally do a new production of *The Queen of Spades,* I can assure you it will not be an experimental one, but again a classic one. The music and the story demand this. *The Fiery Angel* was a different matter. We took a more abstract approach, and our production is one I am exceptionally proud of. It was a first big step in a new direction, which we followed with *Salome* and *Katerina Ismailova.*"

Gergiev continued to find new singers and to promote others into leading roles, among them Elena Prokina, Galina Gorchakova, Gegam Grigorian, Vladimir Galuzin, Marianna Tarasova, and Nikolai Putilin. He feels that "our singers are continually learning and growing. Gradually we have been able to create something at the Kirov that did not exist after 1917—important names in opera, singers known everywhere through our tours and recordings. Before, such big names at the theater were only associated with the Kirov Ballet. Remember, too, only ten years ago there was no understanding and no support for singing in the original languages. Even five years ago it was a rarity in Russia."

Although the baritone Dmitri Hvorostovsky has never been an official member of the Kirov, he has become closely associated with the theater through his Kirov recordings. According to Gergiev, "He is one of the best friends the Kirov has. He went straight from opera in Siberia to the West, where he won the important Singer of the World competition in Great Britain. But he comes often to St. Petersburg as a guest and is beloved here. He never asks for big contracts or fees. He just wants to be happy artistically. He is planning long periods here—as much as forty days—to work with me. And I look forward to working with him. He is a much better ambassador for the Kirov Opera than our former principal baritones [Vladimir] Chernov or [Sergei] Leiferkus.

"I don't blame Chernov or Leiferkus for wanting greater financial stability, and their decision to leave us had to do not with me but with the difficult life here. The West is better organized and pays better money. We can't compete with that. But I believe Chernov, for example, could have had both worlds, say, 10 percent Kirov and 90 percent the Met. I don't think he handled this situation in the best way possible. Look at the career Borodina is making, and tell me—is she less successful than Chernov? Absolutely not. She was more clever. She took everything the Kirov could give her, which is a lot, and still performed in the best places outside of Russia.

"I don't want to make myself seem so important, but I built Olga's career and that of Gorchakova. They themselves have said this many times. But there is a big difference in their careers. Olga is not an artist who takes just one role, like Amneris, and sings it fifty times a year to earn as much money as possible. She welcomes new challenges. But Gorchakova is content to go around the world with the same few roles each season. How can I influence Gorchakova, for example, to be more than a great voice? We still haven't created in her an artist who can move convincingly or willingly from one repertoire to another and remain great. And this is important not only for her own reputation, but for the reputation of the company. After all, she represents us in the big world of opera.

"Leiferkus has made an effort to divorce himself from his past, but people still think of him as a Kirov artist. He sings a lot of Italian opera these days; some of it is good, some is less good. But nothing he has done has had quite the impact of his first, fresh appearances in the West with the Kirov. The same is true of Alexei Steblianko and Larissa Shevchenko. They were noticed when they were with the Kirov, but after they left they did not build important careers.

"But in Russia we have lost more than just singers. In the late 1980s, as the country began to open up, we started to lose many artists of importance—Gidon Kremer, Boris Spivakov, Evgeny Kissin, Vladim Repin, Maxim Vengarov—the list could go on and on. Dozens of fantastic names. It has been a great drain on our culture. Do you think anyone in the government—the minister of culture, the ex–party bosses, the new so-called democrats—was upset by this? The answer is No, with a capital N. It reminds me of the similar loss of artists when Hitler came to power in Germany.

"Yuri Bashmet was the only one who left and came back. He tried to take his whole chamber orchestra with him, but it just didn't work. His musicians immediately wanted lots of money and to have their families with them. When things didn't happen as quickly as they thought they should, they began to blame Bashmet, who had built the orchestra in Moscow and arranged its immigration to the West.

"I have been working to bring some of them back. Evgeny Svetlanov has conducted performances for us at the Kirov, but he now lives in Holland and is rarely heard here. And I have been lucky to have Mariss Jansons to do work with us as well. Temirkanov still has the Philharmonic, but most of his work is in the West. I hope he feels good about what is happening now in the Kirov, but a few years ago people began saying how much better the Kirov had become, and I think it was painful for him that his former assistant was doing so much more at the theater than he had done, especially as this came at a time when there was a crisis in his career.

"Still, I don't want to compare my career with his or anyone else's. Whatever others may say, I don't consider myself bigger than Svetlanov or Temirkanov. Svetlanov is as big an artist, to my mind, as Slava [Mstislav] Rostropovich, and much bigger as a conductor. To me, losing Svetlanov to the West was a great loss. Who of importance now conducts in Moscow? I'll tell you: nobody. As for Slava, I have invited him many times—too many times—to conduct at the Kirov. I wanted him to do our first *Lady Macbeth*, for example, because he knew Shostakovich so well. But now I am tired of trying."

Alexander Tchaikovsky feels that no conductor in Russia today can compare with Gergiev, and no orchestra in the land can compete with the prowess of the Kirov Orchestra. "In one rehearsal," he told me, "they can do what it takes a Moscow orchestra five rehearsals to achieve. They are absolutely phenomenal. And this is Valery's doing. For *Salome*, which had not been played in Russia for more than sixty years, he had a total of five rehearsals for the first performance, which was given in concert form. For *Katerina Ismailova*, there were only three rehearsals, and you heard how ideal it was.

"And look at the White Nights Festival. Every day the orchestra plays a different program. Remember, too, the Kirov Orchestra is really about three orchestras. There is a ballet orchestra, an opera orchestra, and a tour orchestra, and the personnel rotates. Valery has certain players he particularly likes, and they play his performances and go on tour with him. But those who remain behind are good, too. Of course, the standard of conducting is not as consistently good when Valery is away, and this affects the musical climate at the theater."

What makes a great deal of difference between a Gergiev and a non-Gergiev performance at the Kirov and elsewhere is his ability to create a sound that is his alone. "I am always trying to get my orchestra to play rounder, deeper, and warmer," he says, "to play with a feeling for texture. I think brass is one of my special concerns, whichever orchestra I am conducting or whichever piece is in front of me. Brass can destroy everything or make everything very interesting.

"Another important element is the percussion. I cannot enjoy working with other timpani players in the world after mine in the Kirov Orchestra. Not because the others cannot play, but because the level of personality and the variety of color and dynamics he gives me is so remarkable. This instrument we call the timpani is the foundation of the orchestra. It is not simply something that's beaten—it is a basic color in an orchestra's overall sound. A timpanist can give you a shock, a pleasure, can help you move from one section to another—from contrabassi to woodwinds—and it provides enormous support for a tuba or even a flute. This man—Sergei Antoshkin—played many years with Mravinsky. I feel very lucky to have him. He is my most interesting player."

To Gergiev, the sound of an orchestra must be tailored to the character of the music to create different feelings and moods. "If it is Berlioz's *Roméo*," he contends, "you must think of both Berlioz and Shakespeare, and how madly Berlioz was in love with this story. You have to recreate this feeling. You will never feel as strongly as Berlioz did, but you have to try to come as close as possible to the temperature and even the craziness of his music.

"You can't be exclusively intellectual about this. You have to feel it and make your orchestra feel it, and this of course is going to affect the sound. You have to analyze what is given to the strings, what is given to the percussion, what the role of tempo and color in the piece is. Often your ideas will change. For instance, I felt on the Japanese tour that we had not fully realized the second movement of the Tchaikovsky Sixth—it was too rushed, and there was not enough detail or intensity. So I rethought it and looked for another way to make it better. Sound must be a summary of your emotions, your intellect, your sense of fantasy, your artistic vision—and all of these elements must merge to form something that is yours alone."

As a conductor, Gergiev has compared himself to a thermostat in a sauna. "I turn up the heat when it is needed, and to secure the ensemble rhythmically sometimes I really have to punch—pow! I know when an orchestra needs help from me rhythmically, but I also know when it needs help emotionally. Sometimes the players have to be driven—like passengers in a car. You say to them, 'OK, we go.' But they do not know where. The conductor must know, and he must tell them. He supplies energy, logic, and explanations—for a phrase, a strange interval, or why a composer has written this or that. He has to give reasons for all these, and in performance he must give his reasons with his hands and his eyes."

Watching Gergiev at work with various orchestras over the course of dozens of performances, I found it curious that he sometimes used a baton and sometimes did not. Asked about this, he smiled and said, "It is something I still haven't figured out. I am not sure whether or not a baton really helps. But it is something you must experiment with. If I use a baton and feel an orchestra is watching only the movements of the stick, this is wrong. Players must look at the music they play, and when they occasionally glance in the direction of the conductor, what they must be aware of is his eyes. They give the players the key to unlock whatever problem has arisen. Those who think a baton makes all the difference do not understand conducting. It is the conductor that makes the difference, whether he uses a baton or just his little finger.

"When I led the Israeli Philharmonic for the first time in 1999, I did the initial concert with a baton and the next two concerts without one. A member of the orchestra told me he thought the first was good but the others were great, because there was more flexibility. Why were they different? I can't really say. The success of a concert depends on so many things—your mood, that of the orchestra, the hall."

Gergiev's way of preparing a score is as personal as his manner of conducting. "When I rehearse, I spend a lot of time with the orchestra looking at details, because the impact of the whole comes from paying attention to small things," he explains. "Many things during the concerts I can't control as much as I would like to, but in rehearsal I can tune the orchestra emotionally and give it the spirit of the piece, and this helps me build the music the way I want it to be during the performance. I don't try to prepare everything in a rehearsal, so that all the players have to do is repeat things exactly.

"Mravinsky did not like to improvise like this, but he had the enormous luxury of having a great orchestra and a great hall, and he always worked with the same players in the same acoustic. Remember, he led only one orchestra during the last fifty years of his life. Maybe there was an occasional concert with a Moscow orchestra, but it was rare—it didn't really count. What did count was his work with the [Leningrad] Philharmonic. He also had the luxury of seven or eight rehearsals for each program. This meant he could go deeply into details.

"I was lucky enough to witness what resulted from this unique partnership, and it was the strongest influence on my conducting. I believe very much in this sort of close relationship between a conductor and an orchestra. It is more difficult in my case to achieve the same sort of results, because my orchestra plays not only concerts, but a lot of opera and ballet, at home and on tour, and with many other conductors. Our situation is more difficult financially, however, because the Leningrad Philharmonic under Mravinsky existed in a very rich country, and I don't mean just money. The Soviet Union was a rich country musically. You might have five or six orchestras involved in a single festival of contemporary music. The minister of culture was required, as a part of the state's propaganda, to do such things. It was certainly not a democratic state, but it was one of the strongest structures ever for classical music. It has become very easy for people to see everything back then as black or white, but the Soviet Union was more light and shadows, pluses and minuses, water and fire. It was complex, a paradise or a hell. It was not that bad under the communists; neither is it that good under the new regime."

Always aware of who he is and the power he holds, Gergiev is not shy about admitting that "my name helps me in a country where highly placed politicians are not so easily reached. When I visited our prime minister to explain why we were a deserving case, he was very helpful. It is the smaller bureaucrats—the type who removed Gorbachev—who are the problem. These apparatchiks change their skins, but most of them learned their business twenty or thirty years ago. They hold on to power and don't want anybody to progress very far or become wealthy. That's why the working class remains the working class and why the Mariinsky Theater continues to have a small budget."

In August 1996, two months after the close of the 213th season, Russia's then president, Boris Yeltsin, formally vested the fortunes of the Mariinsky in Gergiev. With his new position as absolute head of the theater confirmed, Gergiev is said to have asked Vinogradov to go quietly so that the Mariinsky would no longer be tainted with the scandal surrounding his name. But Gergiev was not totally successful in cutting the former ballet master adrift from the theater. Vinogradov's influence had been too great in too many high places for too long.

There has been widespread talk that the ballet had strong mafia ties during Vinogradov's era, and it is rumored that they still exist. Such talk hangs like a black cloud over the theater. "This is a painful subject for me," Gergiev replies when such charges are raised. "This is not a place where the so-called mafia makes any decisions. My job is to keep this theater independent of any such pressures, and I'm going to do it. I did it with the Kirov Opera, despite all the problems we had, and I'll do it with the ballet. My appointment means that the payments that are addressed to the Kirov will go to the Kirov, not to other men."

Gergiev has learned to live with the realities of Russia's factions, current politics, and shaky economy—and with the government's dubious promises. For example, in 1997 he was to have received $10 million, but only $4.5 million materialized. Two years later, he told me, "I now get about 90 million rubles from the government, which is about $3 million, but much more is needed, of course. With the current tax system, the Kirov gives more to the country than the country gives to the Kirov. I find that scandalous and ridiculous. I think it should be the duty of the president—or the prime minister, or the mayor—to make sure the Hermitage and the Mariinsky are preserved when they hand over power to the next man. Otherwise, they will be in trouble with history."

CHAPTER FOURTEEN

April: Business as Usual

FROM MANY different angles the Mariinsky can be seen as a family theater, and this has proven literally and figuratively true of its ballet company, which through the years has included fathers and daughters, mothers and sons, and sisters and brothers. In several instances dance mini-dynasties have been created within the company. One of these, whose surviving members still play an active role in the theater's life, is the family of the much-admired character dancer Nikolai Zubkovsky. He joined the Kirov in 1931 and later married the ballerina Inna Zubkovskaya.

Their daughter Katei became a member of the Kirov's corps and wed the character dancer Vladimir Lepeev. During my year in St. Petersburg, their son, who had just graduated from the Vaganova Academy and who took his grandfather's name professionally, joined the company, dancing in the corps and beginning his career as a character dancer. He was then eighteen and had been a pupil of his mother, who, with her mother, continues to serve the company and the academy as a teacher and coach. From grandfather to grandson, the Zubkovsky family represents more than sixty years of Kirov history.

One evening over supper, in their handsome apartment crammed with souvenirs of a long life spent in the theater, they retraced their collective years at the Kirov. Zubkovskaya began:

"I graduated from the Moscow Choreographic School in 1941 and was accepted at the Bolshoi, but a few months later the war started and Germany invaded Russia. My parents and I were evacuated to Perm. At first I didn't want to go—I was anxious to begin my career. But because I was so young, my father wouldn't let me stay behind in Moscow and dance at the Bolshoi. It turned out to be lucky that I was forced to make the move, for the Kirov Ballet had also been evacuated to Perm for the duration of the war.

"I auditioned for the company there and was accepted as a member. After I met my first husband [she later divorced Zubkovsky and married the dancer

Sviatoslav Kuznetsov], I decided to stay with the Kirov. This was unheard of, for no one trained in Moscow had ever been taken into the Kirov, and I must say I was scared because even then the Kirov had a bigger reputation among dancers than the Bolshoi, and the performances in Perm were on the highest level."

Once back in Leningrad after the war ended, she danced in the corps de ballet and was given some small roles. Since she was an extraordinarily beautiful woman as well as an expressive dancer, more important parts gradually came her way. But Zubkovskaya felt she was not ready for the biggest roles and began working with Vaganova to gain courage and find an identity of her own. Her first major part at the theater was Odette-Odile, which she prepared in two days when the scheduled dancer fell ill. It went well and helped to build her confidence as a performer.

Zubkovskaya's repertory grew to include, among other parts, Maria in *The Fountain of Bakhchisarai*, Cleopatra in Fokine's *Egyptian Nights*, Kitri in *Don Quixote*, and Esmeralda. She appeared in Yakobson's *Spartacus* at its world premiere and later alternated with Olga Moiseyeva as Mekhmene-Banu in the first performances of Grigorovich's *Legend of Love*. She discovered that it wasn't as difficult as she had initially imagined to adapt her Bolshoi training to fit the Kirov's more reserved style, for this sort of restraint, she feels, came more naturally to her.

Zubkovskaya was part of the Kirov's European tour to Europe in 1961, and in Paris she danced with Nureyev in his last performance with the company—she was Nikiya to his Solor in *La bayadère*. In her opinion, "If Nureyev had stayed at the Kirov he would have danced 500 *Giselle*s, and that would have been it. He would not have been the legend he became. But he wanted new challenges; I think the money was secondary. His defection did not change our company at home, but some of our best dancers weren't allowed to go on future tours. When Nureyev finally returned here for *La sylphide* it was very sad. He was not the dancer I had known. I won't say it was a mistake, for we remembered how he *had* danced. But it was sad."

The fact that Zubkovskaya's first husband, her son-in-law, and her grandson were all character dancers is a reminder that in Russia dancers are cast according to type. Alexandra Danilova has written that "you are designated classical or soubrette or *demi-caractère* from the start, and for the length of your career you dance only the parts that are within your type—the roles that come naturally to you, that your temperament and physique are ideally suited for. When there are 250 dancers employed in a company, the directors can afford to be choosy: 'You are too short to dance the prince; you are too blond and so can't dance the Spanish variation.' I find [the] policy . . . in America better because it leaves room for surprises. Sometimes a dancer who is not by nature suited to a role triumphs in it and enlarges our thinking, giving us a new understanding of the ballet. After all, our notion of a role is mostly based on our memories of the people who have danced it in the past."

As we talked, Zubkovskaya and her family were very open about their discontent with Vinogradov's administration of the ballet. Lepeev felt that "Vinogradov was very lucky—he was in the right place at the right time. When he first arrived, he said he was going to save the Kirov, but actually he was saving his career. There was nothing wrong with the ballet."

Nodding her head, Zubkovskaya added, "The ballet was not better because of Vinogradov. It made him, he didn't make it. After the scandal last year any responsible artistic director would have left, but he stayed. He had no place to go."

"Vinogradov doesn't really understand dancers," her daughter continued. "You know he was refused admission to our ballet school. Look—he put a perfect dancer like Altynai Asylmuratova in the corps de ballet for five years after she graduated from the Vaganova School, and when my mother asked why he had put her best student in the corps, he said she still had much to learn. 'She can't even do the thirty-two *fouettés*.'

"'That's odd,' my mother replied, 'she can do them in my class.'

"'Well, if she can do them now,' Vinogradov answered, 'it's because I taught them to her!'"

"He's a dilettante," Zubkovskaya interrupted. "He didn't even graduate from the ballet school. What is he? He is not a teacher, and the Kirov didn't need his ballets. We lost a lot of important repertory when he came."

"I'll give him this," Lepeev chimed in, "he is a good manager. The company has good tours. Here in Russia I get only $10 a month. On tour I get $100. But there are always two pockets into which the Kirov's money goes; one is mine, the other is Vinogradov's. And his is much bigger." The family was equally concerned with a weakening of the coach system at the Kirov and the loss of many important artists to the West, and they blamed this on Vinogradov as well. Alla Osipenko became a teacher and coach in Connecticut with the former Hartford Ballet; Irina Kolpakova makes her home in New York and works with dancers at the American Ballet Theater; Vladilen Semionov heads a dance school in Indianapolis; and Eldar Aliev, his former student, directs Indianapolis's Ballet Internationale. How greatly this will influence American companies is still a question, for usually the Russian coaches do not come in contact with Americans until after they are well formed as dancers. But the departure of former stars from the Kirov's ranks, where coaches and dancers speak the same dance language, has had a debilitating effect on the company.

Zubkovskaya was equally worried that many gifted young Vaganova graduates (as well as those from other Russian schools) were leaving Russia en masse to seek their fortunes in America. I understood her concern better the year I returned home from St. Petersburg; three young men from the Kirov's junior company turned up in the Dallas area looking for work, a pattern that was being duplicated across the United States.

I asked her grandson if he was tempted to go west. He replied, "No. I have known this company from childhood; in fact, I have never known anything else."

"He was born in this theater," Zubkovskaya interjected. "It's his home."

"The odd thing," Nikolai continued, "was that I didn't want to go to dancing school and my grandmother didn't want me to go, but my father thought it would mean a better life for me. All of us but my father starting studying at around the age of ten; he was fourteen."

Yet when I saw Nikolai two years later in New York during the Kirov Opera's second visit to Lincoln Center, he seemed more enchanted with the idea of America. He had spent several weeks in San Francisco the previous year and was talking wistfully about America; he was thinking of giving up dancing and turning instead to acting.

A few days after my visit with the Zubkovsky family, I saw for the first time the breathtaking cache of costume sketches dating back to the nineteenth century that are housed in the Library of the Performing Arts, including those for the premieres of the *Nutcracker* and *Iolanthe* and for *The Sleeping Beauty, Prince Igor, The Maid of Pskov, La bayadère, Raymonda, The Queen of Spades,* and *Pavillon d'Armide.* Then, a few weeks later, I was allowed to view scenic designs for many of the same productions, which are housed next door in the Museum of the Performing Arts, along with many items drawn from a stunning collection of some twenty thousand photographs of Mariinsky productions and artists. Getting to them had taken time and patience, for like many other such treasures, they are jealously and suspiciously guarded where outsiders are concerned.

April was also brightened by the appearance in St. Petersburg of Eva Pasquier-Wagner, an old friend and the daughter of Bayreuth's Wolfgang Wagner. She now works in Paris at the Châtelet Theater (another daughter with close ties to the Mariinsky, Tamara Nijinska, turned up for an evening honoring her father). Eva was in town to hear the singers chosen for the finals of a vocal competition held in honor of Rimsky-Korsakov.

The concert with the Kirov Orchestra featuring the finalists provided no surprises, and while the winner—the Kirov's Olga Trifonova—was clearly worthy of the prize, the general level was not good. In retrospect, what made the occasion worthwhile was a guest appearance by Gorchakova, who was in exceptional voice. Her singing of the letter scene from *Eugene Onegin* was her one moment onstage during the 213th season.

In order to get his chorus and orchestra in shape for the upcoming new production of *Otello,* Gergiev conducted the opera in a concert performance honoring Gegam Grigorian, who was performing the title role for the first time. He was joined by Nikolai Putilin, singing his first Iago, and, as a guest artist, the Bolshoi soprano Asmik Papyan as Desdemona. It was a mixed bag. Grigorian was sorely pushed in Otello's music, Putilin was still feeling his way into the intricacies of his part, and Papyan was comfortable only in the quieter moments of her role. This left Gergiev and the orchestra to provide the principal pleasures of the evening.

More rewarding was the first *Ruslan and Ludmila* of the season. Glinka based his libretto for this, his second and last opera, on a Pushkin poem that tells a complicated story of love thwarted by evil and sorcery and regained by faith and valor. Musically the work as a whole might be described as Russian bel canto, for Glinka was greatly influenced by, among others, the operas of Donizetti, and of course, Italian opera was a dominant force in Russia when *Ruslan* was written. But although the vocal writing is often Italianate (including a bravura aria and cabaletta for Ludmila in act 1), the spirit of *Ruslan* is unmistakably Slavic, from its dazzling overture to its mighty choruses and the narrative storytelling of the Bard in act 1 and Finn in act 2.

With cuts, the performance ran nearly five hours, and not even Gergiev could will this uneven piece to work as a totality. But there were extraordinary compensations, notably the magical sets, based on designs by Alexander Golovin and Konstantin Korovin, which captured all the fantasy and color one associates with Russian folk art. One of the chief lures in *Ruslan* is Glinka's extensive use of dance; it includes two large ballet episodes as well as other, smaller dance moments.

The Mariinsky is currently using the choreography created by Fokine for *Ruslan* in 1917 (he had also staged the opera at the time), and it proved to be strikingly un-Fokinesque in its airy, Petipa-like patterns. Although neither Olga Kondina as Ludmila nor Valentina Tsidipova as Gorislava were more than workaday in their roles, Vladimir Ognovenko was a tower of strength as Ruslan, and Gennady Bezzubenkov was a rollicking Farlaf.

A further appreciation of Ognovenko's gifts came a few nights later when, as Basilio, he was the only artist who could be savored in the season's first and forgettable performance of *The Barber of Seville*. There was no sense of style to the performance, which had been staged by Pluzhnikov; the orchestra's playing was crude; and the sets and costumes looked as if they had been casually assembled from bits and pieces in the Kirov's warehouse. Providing the coup de grâce was the lurid lighting, which, to cite only one unfortunate example, flooded the stage in red during Basilio's "Calunnia" aria.

The next day was one of contrasts. Prokofiev's *Cinderella* was danced at the matinee, and in the evening the Vaganova Academy added to a mixed program of dance excerpts a complete performance of the disarming *Fairy Doll*. The latter was given in a version by Sergeiev of the Legat brothers' original and used a reproduction of the designs that marked Léon Bakst's debut at the Mariinsky. Since many of the Vaganova students were in *Cinderella* as well, this was a long, ambitious day for the school.

The Kirov dances a Sergeiev version of the Prokofiev work, and it turned out to be, like its *Nutcracker*, one of the Kirov's poorer efforts. The choreography never quite managed to peak, and the set, which was new in 1946, consisted of tatty painted gauze curtains.

One of the few things I salvaged from the performance was the memory of Viacheslav Samodurov's superb Prince and the suave conducting of Victor Fedotov. This veteran ballet conductor made his debut with the company leading *Cinderella* in 1965, but earlier he had been a member of the theater's orchestra while still a student at the Leningrad Conservatory. For a while during the years before Temirkanov's arrival, Fedotov was the theater's music director and principal conductor, doing both ballet and opera. Today, he is a familiar figure not only at the Kirov itself, but on the ballet's tours, and his trademark has been to conduct the large number of scores in his repertory from memory.

Fedotov was adamant from the beginning of his career as a conductor that he would use only the original versions of ballet scores wherever possible, and in this Sergeiev supported him. "I am always indignant," he said to me, "that many Russian and foreign choreographers tamper with a ballet like *Swan Lake* to suit their own convenience. After all, we do not draw beards on the paintings of Michelangelo and Raphael. It should be the same with *Swan Lake*. But restoring the true values of such scores was not easy. I was a young man when I began my career, and the Kirov musicians had long played the Prokofiev scores, for example, in a corrupt way. Not only were the orchestrations not correct, but there were many mistakes in the parts. When I attempted to correct them, the musicians said to me, 'I have been playing this music the same way for thirty years, why should I change now?' But I don't think they really loved Prokofiev then, certainly not as I did. The orchestra today is younger, far more receptive, and they work harder."

In the evening following the performance of *Cinderella*, the mixed program given by the Vaganova Academy opened with a dance version of Leopold Mozart's "Toy" Symphony and continued with pas de deux from *Giselle* and *The Little Humpbacked Horse*. There was a *Dying Swan* as well as a new work, titled *Coming Home* and set to Bach with a disco beat, that was an embarrassment. It came complete with flashing lights and a dancer in army fatigues who proceeded to throw a thinly clad partner about the stage.

What made the evening worthwhile was *Fairy Doll*. Originally danced as *Puppenfee* in 1888 in Vienna, where it still can be seen, the ballet was given a new twist by the Legats, who added more music by Tchaikovsky, Rubinstein, and Drigo to Josef Bayer's original score. The story takes a page from *Coppélia*, with an assortment of dolls coming to life in a shop after it closes. For the Legats' version in 1903, the Mariinsky pulled out its stellar stops with Mathilde Kshessinskaya as the Fairy Doll, Olga Preobrazhenskaya as the Baby Doll, Anna Pavlova as the Spanish Doll, Agrippina Vaganova as the Chinese Doll, Vera Trefilova as the Japanese Doll, Pavel Gerdt as the Shopkeeper, and Mikhail Fokine in a minor role.

Bronislava Nijinska and her brother took part in a performance of *Fairy Doll* at the Hermitage Theater, and in her memoirs she recalled that "it was our first contact with Bakst. Before this I had worn only stock costumes from the wardrobe, but for *Fairy Doll* each costume was individually designed, and we were all specially measured. . . . Bakst was not only meticulous about each costume, he also designed our makeup and applied it himself. . . . Vaslav was a wooden soldier and wore a blue jacket and black trousers, designed so that the soldiers really looked as though they were carved out of wood."

With Sergeiev's restaging, the ballet became a Vaganova Academy specialty. The young dancers were on the whole a delight, although none could be called amazing. But all were poised and generally solid—with the girls superior to the boys—and it was fascinating to watch these teenage (and younger) dancers go through their adult paces. Another *Raymonda* brought Lopatkina, with her limpid dancing of the title role, partnered by the strong and virile Andrei Yakovlev, and a repeat of the Fokine "Saisons Russes" had a lovely *Chopiniana*, in which Stanislav Belyaevsky partnered Zhanna Ayupova. However, Asylmuratova's soft Zorbeide and Makhar Vaziev's uneven Golden Slave were a mismatch in *Schéhérazade*. *Firebird* restored the balance with Anastasia Volochkova's predatory dancing of the title role to Liepa's ardent Prince (his wife, Ekaterina Katkovskaya, was the lithe, lovely Princess).

I had dinner after the performance with Liepa, who, without warning, unleashed a residue of anger aimed at Gergiev, no doubt left over from their ill-fated collaboration as stage director and conductor of *The Invisible City of Kitezh*. Liepa lashed out at what he felt to be Gergiev's use of the company "for his own sake," his "deals" with Philips at the "company's expense," the way he "surrounds himself with mediocre conductors at the Mariinsky," and his overworking of singers, dancers, and orchestra. While he added that Gergiev was doubtless a "genius," Liepa concluded that "he has no eyes and should only conduct."

I had to miss the season's first performance of the Prokofiev *Romeo and Juliet* to attend a program of Alexander Tchaikovsky's music at Glinka Hall downtown, but I caught up with it a few nights later in time to experience Altynai Asylmuratova's performance as Juliet, partnered by Andrei Yakovlev's Romeo (the dancers and the orchestra were well cared for by the conductor Alexander Titov, still a staunch and respected member of the Kirov's conducting staff). Of all Asylmuratova's expressive achievements during the season, this Juliet was the most perfect, poignant, and touching. Yakovlev was an animated, loving figure, and striking, too, were Dmitri Korneev's Tybalt and Ilya Kuznetsov's Paris. The joy of seeing this famous Lavrovsky staging danced in the original sets, which still had the power to impress one deeply, was in many ways the zenith of my time in St. Petersburg. There is more storytelling, swordplay, and pageantry, and less ardent dance, in the Lavrovsky than in better-known Western versions, but on the whole I found it more satisfying theater. One thing is certain—the month could not have ended on a more inspired note.

CHAPTER FIFTEEN

Vinogradov and the Ballet

WHEN GERGIEV was put in charge of opera at the Kirov in 1988 during the twilight of the Soviet era, he shared artistic responsibility for the theater with Oleg Mikhailovich Vinogradov, who had been the company's ballet master for eleven years. Like Gergiev, Vinogradov was a man who thrived on power and knew how to wield it, but he was also a talented and cunning product of the Soviet system.

During his twenty years at the theater, many saw him as a hero who kept the company together as Russia was falling apart, maintained standards, and created a new generation of major dancers. Others viewed him simply as a greedy villain who introduced scandal into the life of the Mariinsky. But however one chose to see him, there is no denying he has been an amazing survivor. "I fulfilled myself under communism," he told me in 1996. "Democracy may be the end of me."

He came to the Kirov in 1977 not out of choice, but having been drafted, like Yuri Temirkanov the same year, to help reverse a steady artistic decline that had become so pronounced that the theater's directorship was officially condemned by the government (Vinogradov has described this period in the Kirov's life as "a nightmare"). He was called before a committee formed to look into the problems at the theater, and when he was told he had been appointed artistic director and ballet master of the ballet, he stared in disbelief. "What for?" he demanded. "I have no wish to leave the Maly Theater [where he had reigned as ballet master for four years]. There I have been able to do everything I wanted to do at the Kirov but was prevented from doing" (Vinogradov had been the Kirov's second choreographer under Sergeiev from 1968 to 1972). He protested the appointment but soon reconciled himself to the task.

The mission Vinogradov was given was to maintain the Petipa heritage while acquiring new ballets and creating his own dance works. It was obvious, even to the politicos of the time, that things had to be loosened up and freshened up if the Kirov was to see better days and guard against future defections to the West. To challenge his dancers he gradually imported ballets by such important contemporary figures as Maurice Béjart, Kenneth MacMillan, and Roland Petit; created purer versions of *The Sleeping Beauty* and *La sylphide*; and introduced three Balanchine ballets as well as one by Jerome Robbins to complement the Kirov classics (like Temirkanov, Vinogradov was never a party member; this meant he had to walk a tightrope at first when introducing the work of foreigners).

Even so, Vinogradov was to have trouble keeping his stars at home in the new and freer Russia; but as this was less of a problem with major dancers than with singers, the ballet nights during my stay in 1995–96 tended to be stronger at the Mariinsky than the operatic nights. To Vinogradov this was a question of his dancers' discipline and their commitment to the Kirov and its traditions. He was quick to remind me that during his time at the theater dancers began younger, received greater encouragement, and were given leading roles quicker; this made them more fiercely loyal. He might have added that the parallel between the opera and the ballet is not entirely analogous, for a chorus member will always be a chorister, but a member of the corps de ballet can aspire to and attain stardom.

But certainly the broadening of the Kirov's repertory had an invigorating effect on the company, and in addition to importing new works by others, he produced a ballet nearly every year until 1991, including such stirring pieces as *The Inspector General* (1980) and *Battleship Potemkin* (1986). Alexander Tchaikovsky, the composer of both scores, had first approached Vinogradov, who was then at the Maly Theater, with the idea of a ballet on Gogol's satire. By chance, the choreographer not only had the same subject in mind, but had written a libretto.

"The day after I arrived in Leningrad to meet with Vinogradov," Tchaikovsky recalled, "the great dancer Yuri Soloviev committed suicide, and this was all that was being talked about in the city. His death was the last straw as far as the Kirov was concerned and one of the reasons it was decided something must be done about the theater. The atmosphere was bad, its reputation was low, and Vinogradov and Temirkanov were in charge to change things."

When Vinogradov went to the Kirov, he took the idea of *The Inspector General* with him. Being the successor to Sergeiev was especially difficult for him. Sergeiev had been very conservative; Vinogradov, on the other hand, was young and wanted to change things immediately. Thus, those who supported Sergeiev were against Vinogradov. The feeling then was that it was one thing for lesser dance companies to be experimental, but the Kirov Ballet should dedicate itself to the theater's traditions—like a museum.

"I think my *Inspector General* survived and reached the stage," Tchaikovsky said, "because, being a professional pianist, I played the score as if it were a concert piece—with intensity and emotion, not like someone who is only a composer. And this excited the committee that had to approve the score. But before *The Inspector General* was produced, Vinogradov asked me to orchestrate some of Edvard Grieg's *Lyric Pieces* for a ballet he called *The Fairy of the Rond Mountains*, and this actually became my first ballet for the Kirov.

"This was an important step for me. I studied carefully Prokofiev's *Romeo and Juliet*, with its delicate orchestral shadings, and I orchestrated these Grieg pieces in that style. This experience helped me when I came to score *The Inspector General*. It was premiered during the Olympic games held in Russia in 1980, which meant the ballet received a lot of attention. The dress rehearsal was attended by a committee of party members, and I sat in my seat frightened that they would cancel the work. After all, the ballet makes fun of government officials. But, surprisingly, there was no reaction from them, and the first performance was well received by the audience and the critics. But within the Kirov the reaction was very different. Many opposed it, not because of the story or the music, but just because it was new.

"I was very pleased with Vinogradov's choreography; it was witty and well made. And when the ballet was taken to Paris in 1982 it had a fantastic success. The Kirov planned to take it to Moscow the next year, but the party officials there demanded it be canceled. Vinogradov, however, told them, 'No *Inspector General*, no Kirov.' This took great courage. Finally Moscow gave in and permitted one performance—on a Sunday. This was important because no one works on Sunday, so the Bolshoi was filled. Again it had a great success, with twenty-five minutes of applause.

"This success meant as much to Vinogradov as it did to me, for after it, the attitude of those at Kirov who were against the ballet changed. The company later took *The Inspector General* to Berlin and Dresden, and again with success. This was the period during which I met Gergiev. He had conducted Vinogradov's first ballet at the Kirov—*The Hussar Ballad*, with music by Khrennikov—and he conducted 'my' Grieg ballet as well. He later conducted *The Inspector General* in Tokyo and the premiere of my next Kirov ballet, *Battleship Potemkin*, which was taken to America."

The two Alexander Tchaikovsky ballets and a reconceived version of *Petrushka* (1990) have contributed to Vinogradov's being considered a leading Russian choreographer of the latter half of the twentieth century and among the most progressive directors of the Kirov since Lopukhov. Not every move he made was a total success, however. While *Potemkin*, with its striking corps of thirty-two men, was widely applauded, his recasting of *Petrushka* was controversial, as were *La fille mal gardée* and *Coppélia* (the latter two originally created for the Maly). During one of the Kirov's visits to the United States, *Dance Magazine* commented that classic ballets had been ruined by Vinogradov's "streamlining" and the way in which he had "flattened the stories."

He was criticized for this at home as well, and for cleaning house so aggressively. He got rid of many older dancers (ninety-eight, by his count) that he felt were no longer an asset, and he made no secret of preferring malleable young dancers with trim bodies. Too, he liked their frequent arrogance and defiance, qualities he possessed in abundance. Early on, he supported and promoted such budding artists as Farukh Ruzimatov, Altynai Asylmuratova, Olga Chenchikova, and Julia Makhalina, easing them into leading roles and touting them to the press. While his bravura was admired, some saw it as the beginning of the end of what the Kirov had stood for so long and so staunchly.

Vinogradov's first memories of the Mariinsky Theater date back to the age of eight. He recalls that one day "I had twenty kopeks in my pocket. I was faced with the choice of buying a pie in the street or buying a ticket in the gallery to see an opera at the Kirov. But I chose the ticket. I don't remember what the performance was, and I didn't understand much of it, but for me it was an extraordinary experience. And when I had more kopeks, I went again to the theater—but this time there were no cheap tickets available. But opposite the Kirov was the conservatory. They were giving Rimsky-Korsakov's *The Czar's Bride*, and there was a ticket I could afford. And this experience I remember very well. When I returned home my grandfather asked me, 'Where have you been for such a long time?'

"I told him, 'I went to see an opera.'

" 'You are lying again,' my grandfather said. All my life I have indulged in fantasy, which to my grandfather was the same as lying. But to me my fantasies, my stories were real. I believed in them. I still do. So my grandfather asked me to tell him about the performance, and I began to sing words from the opera, for I was always musically very precocious. My family had come from a small village, and there life was unimaginable without songs. Everyone sang. And I had a very good ear for music, which grew and developed.

"Later at school I was in the chorus, and one day my aunt heard on the radio that there were to be auditions for the children's choir of the Kirov. Because I loved to sing, she decided I should go and try for this chorus. She took me to the theater, but we could see that the competition was very strong. I thought I didn't have any chance of getting in and decided to leave. But at the last moment something stopped my aunt; I went ahead with the audition and was accepted.

"My first assignment was in the *Nutcracker*, where we sang in the pit. I remember I kept one eye on the conductor and another on the stage. And I saw something incredible—ballerinas dancing as snowflakes. I was so mesmerized I came in late. Afterward I was reprimanded, but the impression of that dancing was overwhelming. Later, when I saw all of these fantastic creatures—the ballerinas—coming off the stage, I couldn't move. These impressions have stayed me all my life.

"As a child I hated school and was a very bad student. In fact, I have found that everything I disliked as a child—mathematics, chemistry—was of no use to me as an adult. But I was very bright when it came to history and, of course, music, and these were very valuable to me. Life, in fact, later confirmed that I had been right in the choices I made when I was young. . . .

"We lived in a communal apartment, which we shared with thirty other people—nine families. We had one toilet, one sink, one bath. Seven families were Jewish, and two were Russian. I felt very close to the Russian Jewish families but had little contact with the other Russians. When my father died, my mother was left a widow at twenty-nine with three children. We were very poor, and I hated our poverty. To me it was a nightmare, and I wanted to get away from it. My opportunity came when I was sent to join the Pioneers—a sort of Russian Boy Scouts. For me it was a paradise.

"We were housed then in the Anichkov Palace on Nevsky Prospect, and we lived among its beauties and treasures. It was like a fairy tale. We had our own theater there, and I took part in all the activities, trying to find myself. I sang in the chorus, built model airplanes and ships, learned puppeteering, and lost myself in their wonderful library. Nothing was wasted. I have used it all. Later I understood that I was special, a leader. I am a lion—literally a Leo, born on the first of August. I can't go slowly. I have little patience. I can never wait.

"I made a late start in ballet, like Nureyev, who was a classmate of mine in Alexander Pushkin's class at the Vaganova School. I had tried three times to be admitted to the Vaganova School but was refused because of my age. Finally they took me when I was fourteen. I studied just five years. What usually happens is that parents bring their children to the school when they are so small that the children do not understand what is happening—why they are being taught dance and what they will become. But I knew exactly what I was doing and what I wanted to do. Almost immediately I began creating dances [while still a student, Vinogradov started a dance jazz group with the dancer Nikita Dolgushin].

"Dancers who don't think, only leap; dancers who think, choreograph. My first choreographic experience was with Natalia Makarova. I made a dance for her to some music of Chopin, and within two years I made a full ballet. When I graduated at twenty-one, I left Leningrad thinking that I would never come back. I never dreamed of working at the Kirov. I knew if I stayed in Leningrad I couldn't be a leader, so I accepted a position in Novosibirsk [in southern Siberia], which, even though it was provincial, had a very good and respected dance company. Everything I achieved later was thanks to my years there.

"I went to Novosibirsk in 1958; the salary was low, food was not plentiful—my mother sent my wife and me bread from Leningrad—and we lived in an inexpensive hotel. That was normal for the time, but I wanted to live better than the others. So I started working outside the theater, staging shows for amateur groups, which brought in extra money [at the time he was also accused of illegally selling icons, foreign clothes, and furniture, although the charges were not proven]. The company numbered a hundred, and it danced all the standard repertory; I had to dance everything—corps de ballet, some leading parts, character parts. It was a wonderful experience.

"This way of learning became my credo. At the Mariinsky some of my finest soloists have come from the corps—Julia Makhalina, who was in our corps for three years, and Altynai Asylmuratova, for five years. They have stronger legs and have had fewer injuries than some of our younger stars, like Diana Vishneva and Uliana Lopatkina, who were never in the corps de ballet. In Novosibirsk I was also an assistant to the opera director and staged several productions, not just of opera but of operetta and drama as well. During these years I traveled a great deal to other theaters because I could make more money and learn more. I know theater as few know it, which is why no one can deceive me. By 1964, when I was twenty-six, I staged my first production, a version of *Cinderella*, and the next year I did my own version of *Romeo and Juliet*."

Both works provided vivid proof of Vinogradov's audacity and his belief in his gifts. These Prokofiev ballets were already renowned in Russia in their original stagings by Rotislav Zakharov and Leonid Lavrovsky. But Vinogradov felt that there was more to say about them than a simple retelling of two famous tales. He also returned to the original version of both scores, which had been corrupted by the orchestrations of others attempting to "enrich" the music and recast it in a more acceptable Soviet style.

Their success made his name in Russia's ballet world and led to an invitation to create a ballet for the Bolshoi Theater in Moscow, for they had a stark originality and immediacy combined with an undeniable theatrical wizardry. You see his sense of purpose and these principles returning in such later Kirov works such as *Battleship Potemkin*, *The Inspector General*, and the epic *Knight in Tiger Skin*. To him they were in part parables dealing with the struggle against prejudice and injustice—the determination of the individual to create a place in established society.

The idea had Soviet resonances, to be sure, and no doubt helped further Vinogradov's reputation within the political framework of the times, as did his *Petrushka*, which owes nothing to the original Diaghilev work beyond Stravinsky's score. It became a clash between an enslaved people and the hero who frees them. The dances for the people and their leaders are purposefully sterile, while those for the Petrushka figure were constructed on folk dances in combination with contemporary dance elements. What he was attempting to say with this strong juxtaposition of movement is that an oppressed people will be liberated by a return to their cultural roots, the factors that initially characterized their race.

Vinogradov's first experience at the Kirov as a choreographer during Sergeiev's reign (creating two original ballets—*Goryanka* and *Alexander Nevsky*—and new choreography for Britten's *Prince of the Pagodas*) increased the feeling of discontent that came from being number two and led him to accept the number one post at the Maly. Although that theater was undergoing a crisis—in his words, "collapsing"—he felt the Kirov was a dead end that offered him few possibilities.

When Vinogradov left the Kirov in 1973, he vowed never to return, and in four years he had made the Maly a true contender on the Soviet dance scene, giving it a new lease on life and taking it on its first Western tours; he was chosen for the job, interestingly enough, over the dancer Vladimir Vasiliev, who later headed Moscow's Bolshoi Theater. In particular, his ballet *Jaroslavna* at the Maly was a notable success and was taken abroad.

But return he did, and upon assuming the directorship of the Kirov Ballet, Vinogradov brought to it a background more diverse than that of any previous company head. It was soon obvious that the job was challenging him as much as he was challenging the company. Gradually he began generating not only choreography, but also librettos. He worked closely with the composers he chose for his new ballets and even designed productions, another skill he had learned in Novosibirsk.

But it was the choreographer that dominated. "In my choreography," Vinogradov told me, "I am trying to enhance the expressiveness of pure dance by employing the enormous potential of the elasticity of the human body. I love the abundance of complex coordination, leaps, and complicated, risky situations. My choreography is a synthesis of free elasticity and the possibilities of the Russian school of male dance." He was in the vanguard of those who sought to forge links between the Russian classical and traditional folk dances.

As the company's ballet master, he took an understandable pride not only in the soloists he created, but in the company's remarkable corps de ballet, which he feels is the company's glory and superior to that of the Bolshoi. In fact, he maintains that the biggest difference between the two companies is their respective corps. "Dancers at the Vaganova Academy are given from the beginning the dance elements they will need on our stage, so that when they come to the Mariinsky they already know what is expected of them—the stylistic movements, the ensemble coordination. Our strength is that we take our dancers from one source. Our former dancers teach there, and here in the theater they work as coaches.

"The foundation dancers receive in our school gives them a very clear understanding of the dance positions and the use of the feet and hands. Our arms are the best in the world, and this is yet another major difference between the Mariinsky and the Bolshoi dancers. Their style is thicker, with less refined use of their hands. Here, never. All our movements are carefully coordinated to create a harmonious whole. Our legs may betray us at times, but our arms never do. My formula for ballet is that the legs work, and the head, the hands, and the arms dance. Our ballerinas are incapable of moving their arms without their eyes and their body following naturally. This is ingrained in them as little girls. We start with this idea, and we finish with it.

"We at the Mariinsky do not like simply visual or acrobatic effects. We like long lines. Ballerinas should be tall with long legs; Balanchine thought so too, but after all his taste was molded here. Our mission, his and mine, has been not simply to serve tradition—we are not just a museum—but to use it creatively. And we started from the same point, Petipa, specifically the Kingdom of the Shades scene in *Bayadère*.

"But Balanchine could never get arms such as he knew and saw in St. Petersburg. So he created his own American style of ballet. I remember so well that once after we danced in New York, Lincoln Kirstein came to me with tears in his eyes, saying, 'You have created what Balanchine only dreamed of. You created his legs with your arms.' I have worked for six years in my school in Washington, D.C. [a school funded by the Reverend Sung Myung Moon that Vinogradov runs with his ex-wife, Elena], and every year I audition hundreds of dancers who come to me from dozens of cities across America. They don't have arms, only legs, because no one knows how to teach this."

By the late 1980s Vinogradov had virtually stopped producing new works, the company had retreated into a predictable repertory, and its life was largely dominated by its tours, which were stringently criticized at home. In a letter from the Kirov Theater Veterans to the city's main art newspaper, *Literaturnaya Gazeta*, in 1987, twenty disgruntled former dancers claimed the tours abroad led to a "decrease in the quality of ballet" and fostered a "bourgeois mentality" in the dancers. This prompted another letter from several dancers still active in the company, who complained about "the poor moral and psychological atmosphere in the theater" and an administration that was filled with "people who are far from talented and who think of everything but creative work."

This was not the first time Vinogradov had been attacked publicly. The year before had brought echoes of the charges leveled against him in Novosibirsk when the Leningrad Public Prosecutor's Office investigated complaints that he had "stolen costumes and furniture from the theater, had given away [an] expensive china service belonging to the theater to furnish a bribe, and had even smuggled into the country pornographic videos." Again, the charges were not substantiated, and Vinogradov insisted that these were simply ploys to discredit him.

The charge that wouldn't go away, however, was the gradual loss of adventurousness in the company's repertory. To Gergiev's thinking, the ballet under Vinogradov took "a very commercial turn. . . . Twenty years ago there was no doubt that the Kirov was the best ballet company in the world. But now I believe we should think very hard before we insist that we are [still] the best. In modern choreography, in whatever has happened over the past twenty years, we are not."

Although Gergiev and Vinogradov were, on the surface, civil to one another, it was no secret that they were men of differing ideologies when it came to running the ballet, and were usually at loggerheads. "I'm very much against the sort of touring that took place under Vinogradov," Gergiev says. "This is one of the reasons I was appointed head of the theater and why I accepted. Some people think that artists should work hard in order to make them rich. Vinogradov was one of these people. The ballet worked very hard to make him and his associates some of the wealthiest people in the business. I do not want someone here who will take the Kirov Ballet away for a hundred days a year to do two productions. You can't just dance twenty-eight *Nutcracker*s in twenty-eight days. That why the company's reputation has diminished.

"When the opera goes to a festival like Edinburgh's, we do five operas in one week, not just one *Boris* twenty times. I think the way the ballet tours is not artistic or good." As to the question of the ballet's future, Gergiev says, "There will be a lot of disagreements, fights, struggles, and maneuvers before the question is answered. These are all bad and destructive things, and the dance company is too important to let them drag on."

But despite what he said publicly, Gergiev seemed unable or unwilling to make a decision about a new ballet master and allowed the status quo—in other words, Vaziev—to prevail. In 1996 he approached Dmitri Briantsev, of Moscow's Stanislav Ballet, about taking over the company, but nothing came of it, and rumors were flying that he had even offered the post to Mikhail Baryshnikov. More recently Gergiev has shown an interest in the work of the choreographer Boris Eifman, who supplied two ballets for the Kirov in the 1970s and whose company debuted at the theater in 1998. But the feeling persists that the ballet's interests are not as paramount for Gergiev or as pressing a priority as many would like them to be.

In the winter of 1996, as if to answer his critics, Vinogradov created his first new dance work in five years: *Resurrection*, which he set to the Prelude and "Liebestod" from Wagner's *Tristan und Isolde*. It was built around his second wife, the Kirov dancer Alexandra Gronskaya, and he based it on his own resurrection after what he termed "a nightmare year, which I barely survived." If you can accept Vinogradov's account of the year, he is not exaggerating. Thugs were hired to beat him up, his apartment was burglarized, and there were blackmail attempts. Afterward, half of his salary supposedly went for bodyguards.

Some saw these attacks as mafia attempts to remove Vinogradov. When a British reporter asked if this was true, Vinogradov replied, "If they are paid enough the Russian mafia will give its services to anyone."

"Paid by people in the ballet world?"

"Absolutely."

"In the Kirov Ballet world?"

"Why not?"

Yet little of this offstage drama and tension translated itself into an effective stage work. The critic Dmitri Tsylikin called *Resurrection* "a ballet about creative impotence."

By the summer of 1997, Vinogradov's days of domination and influence had been eroded by routine, intrigue, and scandal, and Vaziev, his once-subordinate assistant, was firmly lodged in the driver's seat. "Vinogradov is just a name," observed the ballerina Altynai Asylmuratova. "Vaziev decides everything." The British critic Nadine Meisner described Vaziev as exuding "macho charm on the surface and the menace of a razor underneath. His wife, Olga Chenchikova, who . . . retired as a ballerina [in 1996] and is now a company coach, reputedly has the toughness of a Siberian permafrost. They make a formidable combination."

Although Vinogradov spent a good deal of his time after his ouster overseeing entrepreneurial interests elsewhere, principally in America—his Kirov Academy in Washington, D.C.—and South Korea, he could still be glimpsed backstage once or twice a year at the Mariinsky, a still trim, natty figure in his sixties dressed at times in a leather jacket, cowboy boots, and baseball cap, a phantom of the opera moving silently behind the scenes, and a man unwilling to give up the few last vestiges of power he had managed to hold on to for so very long as a part of the city's artistic and political establishment—one who knew too much about too many others.

Even back in 1996 he seemed to have resigned himself to a parting of ways with the theater, for one day he reminded me that Petipa had been turned out of the Mariinsky without so much as a thank-you after sixty years. In fact, he was barred from entering the building. With a shrug of his shoulders, Vinogradov added laconically, "I will probably one day come to this theater and be told by the guard, 'I cannot allow you in, Mr. Vinogradov.'" But that day has not yet arrived.

CHAPTER SIXTEEN

May–June: Spreading the Word—Video

ANYONE WALKING by the Mariinsky in early May 1996 must have been puzzled by several large vans parked at one side of the theater with lengths of heavy, black, umbilical-like cords that stretched from them into the theater. The trucks were from England, and Philips had brought them in by sea through the Gulf of Finland to videotape the Kirov's new production of Tchaikovsky's *Mazeppa*. Inside the theater, the first two rows of seats had been removed to make room for eight high-definition cameras manned by six American and two German cameramen, all under the command of Brian Large. He is the director for telecasts from the Metropolitan Opera and other major theaters and has been in charge of all of the Kirov's opera videos but one.

"Everything we have done here has been in high-definition except *The Fiery Angel*," Large remembers, "which was very low-def because at that time England was still resisting the new technology, as it had earlier resisted stereo. But today the best high-def equipment is in England and Germany. I first came here to tape *Khovanshchina* and *The Queen of Spades*, which were a Japanese venture, but I, of course, had an American crew. Back then the equipment had to be shipped from Japan to Hamburg and driven to St. Petersburg. This was necessary because the Russians are on a different television system than the West, and if we used Russian cameras we would have to convert everything, and there would have been a loss of quality.

"We started with *Khovanshchina* because the production was very old and we wanted to capture it while it still looked good. But it is a classic, and it conveys what the company is all about it. At the same time, Valery told me, 'We mustn't always be seen as a museum. We are a modern company and must do productions that reflect contemporary thought.' By this he meant the stage works of Prokofiev and Shostakovich. When he decided to tape *Mazeppa* I must confess I had my doubts, but then I really didn't know it. But he convinced me of its importance. 'I assure you,' he told me, 'this piece is at the heart of Russian music. It is one of the

239

greatest operas ever written.' I managed to find a score and started playing through it and found out he was right. It is extremely rich. It is the most Wagnerian of all the Tchaikovsky operas. He wrote it after he had been to Bayreuth, and the brass parts in particular, I think, reflect this.

"When I told Valery this, he said, 'You see, I told you *Mazeppa* was great. Now we have to next follow it with a work that shows the company in a different light. I have in mind Prokofiev's *Betrothal in a Monastery.*' Luckily this time I could agree with him, for I had seen it often when I lived in Prague. It is a comedy, a wonderful piece. It is *Love for Three Oranges* in a more brilliant, charming way. 'Then,' he said, 'we must do *Lady Macbeth* and *The Gambler,*' and I am certain both will eventually happen, for Philips believes in this man. He has become virtually their flagship. Despite the uncertain market for operatic videos these days, they are willing to go along with him [as of the publication of this book, the videos of *Mazeppa*, *Prince Igor*, and *Betrothal in a Monastery* remain commercially unissued].

"I love working here. I have the same feeling that I had in Bayreuth when I taped the *Ring*. It is like touching a nerve. To learn these touchstones of Russian literature and hear them performed here is brushing shoulders with history. It inspires you. This past week I had only two performances in five days to tape an opera I had never seen before, with a cast that was changing daily. The odds were stacked against us, but, as immodest as it will sound, I think what we got last night—which will easily be 95 percent of the finished video—is as good as anything I've ever done.

"Valery makes me realize that I am in this industry because of people like him. I am overwhelmed by his consuming passion to make music, to communicate it, and to bring it across the footlights to the public and through the camera to the world. He believes in video, [in] how it represents the company, and sees it as a platform that will carry the message of what he is attempting to accomplish at the Kirov—a documentation of the great classics of the Russian repertory. Simply put, he is an ambassador for the company and for music, and he sees videos and CDs as part of his ambassadorial mission.

"As far as theaters go, the Mariinsky is ideal for video. It is the right size, and the management is responsive and helpful; they want television and will adjust their schedule whatever way works best for you. For example, I needed some extra time with the orchestra, and it was immediately arranged—there are no unions, after all, and you can go on rehearsing and working as much as you want. This was a great advantage. Another was that we were able to light the entire orchestra for the prelude—and this during a public performance. That's something I couldn't do at the Met.

"But there is a downside as well. You often don't know who is going to sing because the casting is sometimes left to the last minute. But this is all part of Valery's nature. He pushes himself, his players, and his singers to the cliff's edge. But no matter how hard he pushes others, he pushes himself further. He believes in working to the last nerve, getting the last bit of energy and effort out of everybody. This means that in rehearsal you get things that are not there in performance, or vice versa. This also means you can't count on anything because it's going to change.

"In the control room, I have a camera that is always on Valery so I can see what is going on as we tape *Mazeppa*, and I can tell you he gives his life for this piece. And he does this not just in a recording session or at the Met, but wherever he is conducting. The place doesn't matter. The performance does. He is a performing animal, and this animalistic instinct in him demands he give the best he can. It is as if he is saying at every performance, 'I believe in the Kirov, I believe in this music, I want to create a standard, I want to make an indelible impression.' Gergiev doesn't know what it is to mark, or to hold back. For him, his life is on the line every time he steps on the podium. We all fear for his health, because no one can give a thousand percent every day.

"I remember in New York while he was conducting with the Philharmonic, we had a meeting about *Mazeppa*, and we didn't quite finish. I asked what time he could meet again the next day. 'Oh, I can't tomorrow,' he answered, ' because after today's concert I have to fly to Hamburg. I am conducting *Lady Macbeth* in Karlsruhe tomorrow night.'

" 'But Valery,' I said, stunned, 'You're crazy. You have another Philharmonic concert the next night.'

" 'Don't worry,' he said, 'I'll be back in time.' My God, we were talking about Karlsruhe, not Berlin. But for him it didn't matter. If it were in the Hebrides with an audience of twenty seagulls, he'd go there and give them a hell of a performance.

"This is what I love about him, even with all the frustrations involved—you can't always get decisions, you can't rely on him being on time. In the West, with its unions, you would be paying thousands of dollars in overtime for these delays, but these are not significant matters in Russia. Here what is significant is the quality of the performances, and the talent of this man is amazing. There are really only a few top conductors today. Carlos Kleiber is one, Valery is another. Both are crazy, both are geniuses. But to me Kleiber's craziness is pure craziness. Valery's craziness is with a purpose."

Although the old production of *Mazeppa* was still in use earlier in the season and radiated a sturdy, old-fashioned look similar to that of the Kirov's *Khovanshchina* and *Prince Igor*, the new one that was videotaped was in stark contrast, and a drab compromise between realism and the abstract. Its unit set provided little variety for the eye beyond a series of banners that came and went during the course of the opera, though the rich costumes did convey something of the flavor of this historical music drama. But the good thing about video, as Large reminded me, is that "the camera can be selective. I shot *Mazeppa* like a play with music; the set just disappeared into the background. There is nothing operatic about the video; it is intimate but, I think, strong."

Despite its visual shortcomings, *Mazeppa* was a gripping musical experience, even though Gergiev was left high and dry by the last-minute withdrawal of Galina Gorchakova; her replacement as Maria, Irina Lostkutova, was only adequate. Gergiev hoped to offset the crisis by making a separate audio recording with Lubov Kazarnovskaya, who had not sung the role for five years and could not restudy it in time to take part in the video production. But she was willing to do the CD version, for which she could use a score. However, the CD eventually marketed was taken from one of the videotaped performances.

For *Mazeppa*, Gergiev turned up a promising new tenor, Viktor Lutsiuk, for the part of Andrei, and Nikolai Putilin in the title role was a hero in every sense of the word. Excellent, too, were Sergei Alexashkin as Kochubei and the ever-dependable Larissa Diadkova as Lubov. As for Gergiev, his belief in this work, which some consider to be lesser Tchaikovsky, was palpable, and the orchestra responded to his dynamic conducting with its very best. "I don't remember the exact budget for making this video of *Mazeppa*," Large said, "but I know if it were at the Met it would cost $1.2 million. Here the money is divided up three ways. Philips provides the technical personnel, the equipment, and the post-production costs; Japan has made a heavy investment of money only; and the theater provides the production and pays the artists. Philips gets the video for cassette and laser disc, and Japan gets the television rights. The profits, if there are any, are shared, but no one will probably see a return on their investment for five or six years."

Later, Gergiev became disenchanted with the new sets for *Mazeppa* and commissioned another production that was more experimental. He then discarded it as well. Ironically, when the Kirov returned to New York in the spring of 1998, it wound up presenting the old *Mazeppa*. This was another instance in which Gergiev's ambivalence, lack of design savvy, and inability to make up his mind cost the theater dearly. There were two productions of Rimsky-Korsakov's *The Invisible City of Kitezh*, neither of them satisfactory, and an ugly *Prince Igor* was created for the 1998 New York visit to replace the superb old production (which, fortunately, was the one employed for the company's video of the opera). A year later, the company offered a new and equally distressing *Queen of Spades*, a reminder that for every new production during Gergiev's directorship that worked and made dramatic sense, there was a production that did no credit to any one.

While *Mazeppa* was being videotaped, aftershocks from the previous October's scandal were reverberating in the theater, and rumors were flying. The latest one was that Vinogradov's American patron, the Reverend Sung Myung Moon, leader of the Unification Church, had put up a half million dollars to settle the case pending against the ballet master. There was also talk that Vinogradov had demanded that Yuri Schwarzkopf remove Makhar Vaziev from the ballet. It looked like Vinogradov was still in the saddle; but the question was, for how long? Meanwhile, the ballet went confidently forward with two more strong, vibrant *Bayadères*, the first with Lopatkina as a fluid, melting Nikiya, and the second with Ruzimatov, displaying all the trappings of a champion, from the snap of his head to the stretch of his neck, the fire in his eyes, and the high arch of his back.

Added to this was a *Corsaire* with everyone—Volochkova, Ruzimatov, and Yakovlev—in red-hot top form, and another *Romeo and Juliet*, highlighted by the first Romeo of the season by Andris Liepa. He and the ballerina Maya Dumchenko had to perform the work before the daunting presence in a stage box of Ulanova. But the primary dance focus of the month was the premiere of Vinogradov's *Resurrection*. It was not dance so much as a knotting and unknotting of bodies featuring the ballerina Alexandra Gronskaya and a dozen men—a struggle and twisting that finally breaks out in its final moments into unencumbered dance. It was not a major work, but it did have a few undeniably effective moments.

Gergiev left his rehearsals for a new *Otello*, a production from the Bonn Opera staged by Giancarlo del Monaco, to make a rare appearance in the pit as a ballet conductor. In his hands, *Firebird* had a shimmer and power that had been missing throughout the season, and Irma Nioradze, razor-sharp in the title role, was the very essence of fantasy. Would that Gergiev could have worked as much magic with Stravinsky's *Rossignol*, with which it was paired; but *Rossignol* was sluggish and earthbound.

Otello reached the stage toward the end of May, and it was something to hear —even though it was not much to see. Its single set was dominated by a massive metal cross attached to a chain that had the look of having crashed and shattered huge blocks of stone. The cast spent the evening weaving their ways through the rubble and around the cross, and del Monaco had Nikolai Putilin, as Iago, climb up and down the cross, as if he didn't have enough to preoccupy him musically. The set and the direction were hardly an evocative or practical solution for the needs of the drama.

The title role was sung by Galuzin, the theater's finest tenor, and one who has the muscle and staying power to make this mighty role his own. His performance ranged far beyond the labored one of Grigorian in the Kirov's concert *Otello* the previous month. While Galuzin did seem at times in a rush to put some of the high-lying phrases behind him as quickly as possible, the role was a new one for him, and he was obviously still making adjustments in his pacing of the part. But already there was an authentic ring to his singing of Otello's music, and he cut a powerful, absorbing figure on stage. Putilin tended to snarl more than sing, and there was nothing of particular beauty to the singing of Larissa Shevchenko as Desdemona, who accompanied the production from Bonn along with her husband Alexei Steblianko, Galuzin's cover. Gergiev and the orchestra gave an impressive account of themselves, often stretching phrases to create huge spans of sound that threw the music into an entirely new and absorbing light.

But underlying this new *Otello* was a current of criticism that was best summed up by Alexander Tchaikovsky: "Why *Otello*, when Grigorian and Galuzin will not be easily available for future performances, and the theater has no one else to sing the title role?" The pressing question of finding new singers led Tchaikovsky to set up a system of bimonthly auditions in the house to replenish the theater's roster. This was motivated in part by his belief that "we don't have enough repertory that can be successfully done when the main company goes on tour, taking with it the full chorus and our best soloists. During these tours we are forced to put on more ballet than opera because we lack works that don't require large choruses.

"Then, too, the theater does not have a contract system with its artists. I think at the moment only Marusin and Borodina have contracts with the theater. Olga is required to sing six performances each season, while Marusin is engaged for the entire season. But without contracts for everyone, we cannot count on having Galuzin, Gerello, Gorchakova, and other important singers when we need them. It's a big problem."

As far as other repertory goes, Tchaikovsky feels that "the Kirov has got to do more contemporary works, like those of [Leos] Janáček. I would even like to see the theater hold a competition to find new operas. And there are other works in the West which we do not hear—[Strauss's] *Ariadne auf Naxos* or [Puccini's] *Turandot*, both of which we should be doing. Of course, Valery has done an amazing job when it comes to new productions—sometimes he has made five or six a year when before him there were only two—but I can't always agree with the repertory choices."

Otello was followed by the final performances of the season of *Don Quixote*, *Swan Lake*, and *Romeo and Juliet*, each illuminated by their respective lyrical ballerinas. In *Don Quixote* it was Anastasia Volochkova, a lovely, agile Kitri; in *Swan Lake*, Uliana Lopatkina's limpid, imperiled Odette-Odile; and in *Romeo*, Zhanna Ayupova's willowy Juliet. Only Ayupova had a consummate partner. The passion and ardor of Andris Liepa's second Romeo of the season was an ideal foil for his Juliet's vulnerability.

Don Quixote, incidentally, was a special evening for Vladimir Lepeev and his son Nikolai Zubkovsky. Lepeev was dancing his last Gamache, and Zubkovsky was appearing for the first time in the second-act gypsy pas de deux. His flashing, smoldering performance with Galina Rakhmanova brought his first bow before the Kirov's curtain, as his mother and grandmother applauded in a nearby box.

The 213th season came to an unpromising halt with three evenings featuring the graduating students of the Vaganova Academy. These annual spring evenings are held as a sort of combination showcase and public final exam. Each program began with the Kingdom of the Shades scene from *Bayadère*, still the ultimate test piece for a ballerina, budding or not, star or corps member. It was followed by a string of pas de deux from such standards as *Le corsaire, Nutcracker, Sleeping Beauty, Raymonda, Harlequinade,* and *Fairy Doll.* Each was a disappointment; there were no auspicious upcoming talents to be seen, although four of the girls held out varying degrees of promise—Ekaterina Zhithukhina, Veronica Part, Svetlana Ivanova, and especially Svetlana Zakharova, who had a small role in *Don Quixote* during the regular season.

So unpromising were the graduating males, however, that several regular Kirov dancers had to be recruited for the various pas de deux. This necessity produced one of the more spectacular dance moments of the year, as Andrei Batalov soared through *Corsaire* with a finish and an exuberance that left one gasping for breath. Here was an unprecedented and prodigious feat of balance, line, and speed, capped by dazzling pirouettes and bravura leaps. In a brief flash of brilliance, his dancing summed up what is both good and bad about the Kirov Ballet these days. That it boasts a dancer of Batalov's staggering prowess makes it special; that it fails to capitalize more on his gifts demonstrates the lamentable degree to which politics can still override art at the Mariinsky.

The first two weeks in June marked the end of the regular season of performances and were darkened by local elections in St. Petersburg that saw the ouster of Anatoly Sobchok (who died in 2000), the city's progressive mayor and a friend to Gergiev and the Mariinsky. Many feared that his loss to a more conservative candidate might work to the detriment of the arts in the city. But, according to Gergiev, the role of the mayor "is not that big in the life of Mariinsky. More important is the government in Moscow, as we are a federal theater, and the budget is made there by the minister of finance and the prime minister. Sobchok came often to the theater, but he didn't make enough of an effort to turn Petersburg into one of the cultural capitals of the world. You have the Hermitage, the Mariinsky, other important theaters, the libraries, the museums, the palaces, an enormous tradition. But you just can't continually point at these and say, 'We're great.' You must develop these great resources and make them more, and neither he nor the city was successful in doing this."

At the moment Russia is a restless and unhappy land, one at a perilous cross-roads. It is too far down the highway of change to revert to its former communist days, despite a groundswell in that direction, yet not far enough along the democratic road to right the economic and social wrongs that make life unbearable for so many. The country's future remains a perilous question mark.

A great part of the difficulty in making adjustments to a new system of government and living was that the average Russian had, from czarist times, never been encouraged to think or act on his or her own initiative. With the Revolution, the people simply exchanged one autocratic style of leadership for another. Granted, many old inequities were offset by the Soviets, and there was more widespread abundance in daily life than there had been previously. But counter-balancing this were the gulags and the purges. Monumental injustices were still the rule rather than the exception, and Russians were still told what to think and how to act. Independence of thought was no more a part of Soviet Russia than it had been of imperial Russia. Even the new Russia is rife with a self-absorbed elite. This makes the idea of democracy more theoretical than practical—in fact, at the outset of the twenty-first century, it is little more than an abstract concept. It has become imperative, according to Gergiev, to solve the interior strife in the land, upgrade the economy, and give people confidence in the government.

Gergiev believes the arts are all tied to these questions. "I want a strong man to head the government, someone who understands that peace, education, and culture are as necessary to cultivate as are our natural resources. I don't care if the prime minister is red, green, or yellow. I don't pay attention to his political colors. I can't say, 'I don't want to deal with this man because he is not so nice.' If he is a mayor or a prime minister I must deal with him. Our future depends on it."

EPILOGUE

Beyond White Nights

URI SCHWARZKOPF had been administrative head of the Mariinsky for a little more than five months as the theater geared up for the 1996 Stars of the White Nights Festival. This short period of time, however, had been enough for him to decide that his new duties were basically not a great deal different from those he had performed at St. Petersburg's Komissarzhevskaya Theater. Both jobs, as he described them to me, involved "coordinating the work, making things run smoothly, and allowing the creative staff to do its work with a minimum of problems." The challenge, for him, was coping with the higher aims and greater volume of work at the Mariinsky.

When I queried him about the extent of his involvement in artistic matters at the theater, he replied matter-of-factly, "I have practically no say in this side of the Mariinsky's life," but then added that "the director of any theater, of course, becomes involved to a degree in artistic decisions if he is responsible for the theater's finances, as I am at the moment. But ideally these are questions that should be discussed between the administrative head and the artistic director and a careful balance found. However, if something happens on our stage that I don't approve of, there is little I can do about it beyond giving the artistic director my point of view and hoping that he will respect it and think about it. Even if the administrative director here were still number one, which was the setup before I arrived, I would not interfere. I feel the leader of any artistic community such as the Mariinsky should always be a dictator with the final say. I don't think you will find an instance in an important theater in Russia or elsewhere where this is not the case."

When asked about Gergiev's critics, Schwarzkopf was sanguine. "Any director is going to have those who are for him and those who are against him. This is normal. I agree that Mr. Gergiev is not here enough; it is one of our problems. I know, too, that there is a big difference between the casts abroad and those here at home. But part of this problem is that Mr. Gergiev does too much, and he hasn't always time to correct such matters. We must try to find a way to protect him from himself."

Schwarzkopf had reason to be concerned for Gergiev's well-being, for during the thirteen days of the 1996 White Nights Festival, he conducted nine times—five performances of four operas and four different concert programs. His schedule had intensified when he decided to take over the new *Carmen* production after Mariss Jansons withdrew following a heart attack. Nor was he helped by the defection of Borodina and Galuzin from the cast (they were replaced by Marianna Tarasova and a new tenor, Viktor Lutsiuk), or by the fact that the production was put together virtually at the last moment.

During the season Gergiev had gone through several sets of designs as well as several stage directors, considered and discarded several editions of the score, and finally settled for something that was in essence a muddle. *Carmen*'s unit set consisted chiefly of several angled gray walls that conveyed no sense of Spain or the sun and looked flimsy and cheap, while the staging was largely from stock and did little more than perpetuate some of the opera's more familiar dramatic clichés. But the biggest disappointment was Gergiev himself. He used the standard edition of the score with the standard cuts and the Guiraud recitatives, and he had female choristers replace the children's chorus in act 1, corruptions he would never have allowed in a Russian opera. As for the orchestra, it did little more than skim loudly and quickly across the surface of the music.

Adding to the production's debits, Tarasova was thin-voiced and had little allure, Lutsiuk was raw and his French poor, and Nikolai Logvinor and Liya Shevtsova as Escamillo and Micaela were routine. A good many of the problems could have been avoided had Gergiev been willing to give the production to another conductor who would have had sufficient time to prepare a plausible edition, or had Gergiev chosen to recreate the brilliant designs made in the 1920s by Alexander Golovin. These were once a glory of the theater; bringing them back would have added immeasurably to a further awareness of the Mariinsky's history.

The second night of the festival was little better—a dance gala with England's Princess Margaret in attendance. It was to have centered on the premiere of a new ballet, *Paganini*, choreographed by Andris Liepa and starring Ruzimatov. But Ruzimatov suddenly became "ill" the day of the dress rehearsal (which went ahead, nonetheless, with Liepa himself dancing the main role), and the work was canceled. There were murmurs that Liepa's enterprise in creating the piece and raising the funds to pay for its production was resented. Losing *Paganini* cost the theater not only an intriguing new work, but Liepa as well. Soon afterward he left St. Petersburg and the theater for good, taking his ballet with him.

In place of *Paganini*, the best the company could muster were repeats of Vinogradov's *Resurrection* (which seemed much thinner on a second viewing), Robbins's *In the Night*, and Balanchine's *Symphony in C*. While the latter had grown stronger and more cohesive with repetition, it was marred on this occasion by noisy fans of Uliana Lopatkina, who did their utmost to manufacture an ovation for her at the expense of the music and the dance.

White Nights got back on track with Gergiev's first concerts, which were split equally between the Mariinsky and Philharmonic Hall. He began with Shostakovich's masterful *From Jewish Folk Poetry*, an orchestral song cycle that featured soloists Marina Shaguch, Larissa Diadkova, and Konstantin Pluzhnikov, and Mahler's Sixth Symphony. (There was an ironic subtext to the evening: here was a program of two "Jewish" works written by an atheist and a Christian convert, respectively.) Oddly, the Mariinsky has acoustical problems when Gergiev takes the orchestra out of the pit and places it onstage. He has tried to find several solutions for this dilemma, even removing all the parterre seats and seating his players on the main floor of the theater. While these problems were not a deterrent with the transparent Shostakovich, the Mahler came off sounding thin, and the orchestra lacked resonance.

These shortcomings doubled the pleasure of hearing the orchestra back in the warmth of Philharmonic Hall two nights later. Although Gidon Kremer was on hand for a deep, mesmerizing performance of the Tchaikovsky Violin Concerto, the centerpiece was a strange, uneven, overly long, yet powerful oratorio by Nikolai Karetnikov, a composer who died in 1994 and is little known outside of Russia. His *Mystery of Apostle Paul* was being given its Russian premiere; the score had first been conducted by Gergiev the previous fall during a guest appearance by the Kirov in Hannover. This difficult ninety-minute work exudes a mighty aura, and bringing it to such a gripping fulfillment was an awesome feat of concentration and dedication.

Gergiev and the orchestra returned to Philharmonic Hall for an incandescent performance of Berlioz's *Roméo et Juliette*, with Olga Borodina, Sergei Alexashkin, and Nikolai Gassiev as soloists. Here was Gergiev at his best—involved, confident, commanding, and persuasive. The performance seemed over much too quickly, and although Borodina had only a small section of the whole to sing, she did it in so shaded and atmospheric a way that her singing haunted one's memory for months to come.

For the final White Nights concert, the orchestra was back in the Mariinsky for a program of Russian rarities—Shostakovich's Symphony No. 11 and Prokofiev's Fourth Piano Concerto (with Toradze) and *Cantata for the Twentieth Anniversary of the October Revolution*, based on writings by Marx, Lenin, and Stalin. The Shostakovich and the Prokofiev concerto were arresting; not so the jingoistic cantata. It seemed in questionable taste to play this blatantly communistic score at a time when Russia was on the brink of a decisive national election and with all sides calling for abandoning the country's democratic course. Gergiev even introduced an actor dressed and made up to look like Lenin as part of the performance. Later in the summer, when Gergiev repeated the work in New York, he told interviewers that Prokofiev had secretly implanted an anti-Stalin message in the cantata. That may be true, but this knife cuts two ways. Although the propagandistic aspects of the score were distressing, what rankled most were the paucity and raucousness of Prokofiev's bottom-of-the-barrel score.

With the 213th season consigned to history, Gergiev next plunged into his festival in Mikkeli, where he and Lexo completed their recorded survey of the five Prokofiev piano concertos, later issued by Philips; reinforced his ties with Finland's Savonlinna Opera Festival; and returned to America for the Lincoln Center Festival in New York and the company's first appearances at the Tanglewood Festival. Gergiev continued to pile his plate higher and higher as he moved on to make his debut at the Salzburg Festival with *Boris Godunov*, which brought him together with the Vienna Philharmonic for the first time. The next summer they would be rematched for *Parsifal*, a work that dominated the 214th season of Kirov.

St. Petersburg was to have been the first city to stage *Parsifal* the day its copyright ran out—13 December 1913—but the scheduled performance had to be delayed three days because of the illness of the Kundry, Félia Litvinne. It was finally given privately in the Hermitage Theater before the imperial family, the diplomatic corps, and government officials. Two further performances followed for students of the Imperial Military Academy, and then the production moved to the Theater for Musical Drama, a new operatic enterprise inaugurated in 1912 (it performed in the Conservatory Theater, where it renovated the stage and increased the seating capacity; among the novelties the company presented was the first Russian performance of Debussy's *Pelléas et Mélisande*). With the coming of World War I, all German operas were removed from the repertories of Russia's theaters, but *Parsifal* returned to the Theater for Musical Drama in its 1917–18, and next to last, season.

Gergiev had long dreamed, with an almost messianic passion, of performing Wagner's last opera, and in a statement after the Kirov premiere, he said, "I regard the staging of *Parsifal*, an opera that brings together all of Wagner's main lines of thought, as a prelude to the revival of the Wagnerian cycles that were part of the Mariinsky repertory at the start of the century. And the enthusiasm with which the premiere was acclaimed both here and abroad shows that we made the right choice."

The press agreed. Typical of its enthusiasm was John Allison's coverage for *Opera* magazine. He felt Gergiev "caught the score's ecstatic beauty and all the pain too. Each act was carefully paced, and the performance swept along compellingly.

The Kirov Orchestra's rich strings and blazing brass sounded thrilling. This was an idiomatic, world-class account in a theater without a living Wagner tradition." His words were echoed by Richard Fairman in London's *Financial Times*: "Close your eyes and this was a Wagner Orchestra to equal any in the world." The English filmmaker Tony Palmer, who staged *Parsifal* for the Kirov, said in an interview with the *St. Petersburg Times*, "By no stretch of the imagination do I want to describe [the production] as a Russian *Parsifal*," but as the critic George Loomis pointed out, it had a decidedly Russian flavor. Palmer began the evening with 150 people walking down the aisles of the theater to the stage, "as though," he commented, "a Russian village was awakening and arriving to perform this great morality play . . . wearing ordinary Russian, sort of medieval costumes." A year after the Mariinsky premiere of *Parsifal*, the opera was the subject of a film made by Palmer in St. Petersburg and Rapallo, with Gergiev conducting and Placido Domingo in the title role.

The *Parsifal* season also brought a new *Boris Godunov* in the composer's original 1869 version, which Gergiev and the Kirov recorded, adding to it the 1872 version as well. Prokofiev's little-known and brilliant comedy *Betrothal in a Monastery* (soon followed by another neglected Prokofiev opera, *Semyon Kotko*) returned to the theater's repertory, as did a revised version of Sergei Banevich's opera *The Story of Kay and Gerda*, an opera the Kirov had premiered in 1981. There were also concert performances of Rimsky-Korsakov's *The Czar's Bride* (recorded by Philips) and Verdi's *Rigoletto*, and Gergiev established a new festival in Rotterdam in his name and made return visits to Japan and Israel while maintaining a strong presence in major cities in Europe.

For its part, the ballet offered José Antonio's *Goya Divertissement*, to music of Glinka, as a vehicle for Ruzimatov, and the first Kirov productions of two Stravinsky perennials, both of which were conducted by Gergiev: *Le sacre du printemps* (choreographed by Evgeny Panfilov) and *Les noces* (choreographed by Alexei Miroshnichenko). It also presented Fokine's *Polovtsian Dances* as a ballet work separate from Borodin's opera, as had Diaghilev, and later added a production of Stravinsky's *Le baiser de la fée* to its repertory as well.

Among the needed new blood added to the opera company's roster were the bass Vladimir Vaneev, who had also joined Gergiev for the Salzburg *Boris*; the baritone Evgeny Nitikin; the Moscow soprano Olga Guriakova; and the tenor Evgeny Akimov. The 1996–97 season saw the rise to prominence of two young sopranos already with the company, Anna Netrebko and Olga Trifonova, and there were also losses—the deaths of the bass Bulat Minzhilkiev, whose final role with the Kirov was Titurel in *Parsifal*, and of the soprano Evgenia Tselovalnik; these were followed by the death, in 1999, of Igor Belsky, the director of the Vaganova Academy.

When Lexo returned in the summer of 1997 for the fifth Stars of the White Nights Festival, he found the theater calmer and in less of a ferment, and he had a reason for it: "It has to do with the Russian character. When no one knows who is in charge, there are complaints and unrest. But once a Russian knows without question who the boss is, everyone settles down and does their job. And at the Kirov there is no question that Valery is the boss." With this awareness seems to have come a fuller acceptance of the demanding working conditions at the Kirov and of the fact that its tours are the core of the company's life and continue to make its seasons at home possible.

With the 215th season there was more Wagner (*The Flying Dutchman*) and a new production of *The Marriage of Figaro*. In the spring of 1998 the Kirov journeyed to Moscow, bringing four pieces of repertory—its two recent Wagnerian ventures, along with *Katerina Ismailova* and *The Fiery Angel*—to the Bolshoi, and the Moscow company reciprocated with a series of performances at the Mariinsky. This historic exchange gave St. Petersburg audiences a chance to hear for the first time in a long while operas that had once been standard fare at the Mariinsky, Tchaikovsky's *Maid of Orleans* and Glinka's *A Life for the Czar*. It also included Rachmaninov's *Francesca da Rimini*; two Verdi operas, *La traviata* and *Aida*; and Sir Peter Ustinov's new Bolshoi production of Prokofiev's *Love for Three Oranges*.

Almost immediately following its Moscow performances, the Kirov journeyed to New York, where it presented two weeks of repertory at the Metropolitan Opera during April. This engagement had a special significance, for the previous September Gergiev had been named the Met's first principal guest conductor and had committed himself to conducting eight operas for the New York company over five years, further tightening the bonds between New York and St. Petersburg.

News of this appointment was not received happily in Russia's higher circles, however, and the government publicly chastised Gergiev for accepting the position without official approval. "Gergiev must not take unilateral steps and sign foreign contracts without informing the Russian government of this and coordinating the matter with it," Igor Shabdrasulov, a government spokesman, told the TASS news agency. Yet the matter of his acting independently had hardly been raised before, and the entire episode smacked of a tempest in a teapot. Perhaps Russia was becoming nervous that it might lose so valuable a member of its cultural establishment.

The Met, however, was delighted to have a man of Gergiev's reputation and stature make a firm a commitment to the company. "Over the years," the Met's general manager, Joseph Volpe, told me in 1999, "there was always a criticism of the Met that Jimmy Levine [the company's artistic director and chief conductor] takes all the good productions and performances, and they don't really hire any other conductors. The truth was, of course, that we hired the best we could, but it was very difficult because of the amount of time a conductor has to spend at the Met for a new production. In Europe, they are all over the place; in two hours, they can fly to another opera house. Well, you can't do that in the States.

"Probably the most alarming thing in opera today is that you bring in conductors—and we had one, but I won't mention any names—doing a standard piece, and they were approaching it as though it were a symphonic piece and not an opera with singers and staging. How can you conduct opera and not be tuned in to the singers? If you don't support them, breathe with them, then the whole thing goes badly. That's why I have so much respect for Seiji Ozawa. I could only get him to do *Eugene Onegin* at the Met because he realized that he wasn't first of all an opera conductor and wanted to be very careful about what he chose to do. My goal has been to find conductors who knew their business and were willing to spend the amount of time with us we required. We turned to Valery when Jim was unable to do our new production of *Otello* in 1994—Domingo was actually the one who recommended him to me—and we all hit it off right away. I thought, well, maybe here is the person that might agree to do more with us, particularly if we offered him a position like principal guest. So we created the post for him. He was *the* candidate—there was no one else. He accepted, and I hope this arrangement will continue for a long time."

Gergiev began his Met contract conducting two operas there a season, but the way the scheduling worked out, he was able to do only one—*Katerina Ismailova*—during the 1999–2000 season. "That schedule of his!" Volpe said, throwing up his hands. "He's a crazy man. I'm prepared to say that both he and Jimmy are crazy men. Jimmy does sixty performances here, concerts with the Met Orchestra, chamber music, voice recitals, and, of course, he is music director of the Munich Philharmonic. As for Valery's schedule . . ." Up went the hands again.

Part of the ongoing relationship with Gergiev and the Met is a coproduction of Prokofiev's *War and Peace*, which will come to New York during the 2001–2 season, and the Met has already given the Kirov its former production of *Madame Butterfly*. "I think there are many ways the Met can help the Kirov," Volpe continued, "and we're prepared to do as much as we can, because it has to be a horrendous job keeping that theater going, given the current circumstances in Russia."

Ernest Fleischman, the charismatic former manager of the Los Angeles Philharmonic and himself a former conducting student of Albert Coates, has said that there are often problems for orchestras working with Gergiev for the first time because of his personal rehearsal and conducting technique. But it is worth any effort involved, Fleischman believes, because of the results Gergiev achieves. "Has the Met's orchestra experienced any such problems?" I asked Volpe.

"Yes, there are members of our orchestra who don't care for Valery's style of working, but there are also those who take exception to James Levine. Musicians are musicians. You are not going to please them all. To me it is the end product that counts, and while there are easy ways and hard ways to get to where you are going, in the case of both Valery and Jimmy the end result is at such a high level and so exciting nothing else really matters."

I asked Volpe to contrast Gergiev and Levine. "Jimmy is extremely intelligent, as is Valery," he said. "When discussing a problem or situation, Jimmy is thoughtful, considerate, and comes to a conclusion in a very precise way. Valery, on the other hand, has the computer running in his brain all the time, doesn't share every aspect of the information he has, but comes to a decision more quickly than Jimmy. Recently the secretary-general of the United Nations was here at a performance Valery was conducting, and I said to Valery, 'If you have a minute, come up and join us for a cup of coffee at intermission.' He left the pit, came running up, had his coffee and a conversation, and rushed back for the next act. Jimmy would never do that. He prefers to sit down quietly, contemplate what is ahead, and rest between acts. I don't think Valery ever rests. He's never been late for a performance at our house, but sometimes he is there at 7:59 for an 8:00 P.M. curtain. He can't bear to waste time or sit still. He always wants to plunge right into the music the moment he arrives anywhere.

"There is a difference as well in their conducting. Valery has a tendency to vary from night to night, and that can be very exciting. Jimmy does not do that. He knows exactly how he wants a piece to be, and that's how he does it. Now, he will vary if a singer has problems, but not otherwise, and that of course appeals to an orchestra because there are no surprises. Valery is definitely more mercurial, and there are always a lot of surprises with him, but that's the beauty of his music making. Thank heavens we have both."

There have been rumors that Gergiev might be in line for Levine's job, if and when Levine ever leaves the Met, but Volpe says this will never happen: "Valery is so committed to the Mariinsky that if the revenue they have now—which is not very much—were cut by 50 percent, he'd still be there. He goes around the world raising money and doing incredible things to keep that company going, and I must believe that, given this struggle, things have to get a lot easier. But whatever its future, my guess is that Valery would never give up the Kirov. Besides, Jimmy has an equal commitment to the Met, and I've always said that when I'm long gone, Jimmy will still be here."

According to Volpe, Gergiev has signed two contracts with the Met—one as principal guest and another purely as conductor. His commitment under them includes such diverse repertory as *The Flying Dutchman, Don Carlo, Otello, Parsi-*

fal, Salome, The Gambler, and *War and Peace.* In addition, the Met is making plans to bring the entire Kirov company for a post-season appearance in the summer of 2002 or 2003 (the schedule still has to be finalized). Volpe could not speculate about repertory, but he did say one of the works the Met is anxious for the Kirov to include is the original version of *La forza del destino.*

This will be the second time the Met has sponsored the full Kirov company; the first was in 1998 (according to Volpe, both the Met and the Kirov came out with a surplus at the end of the two-week run, for the ticket sales were better than what the Met had budgeted for). That visit provided an opportunity for me to be again in close proximity to the company, and the first thing that was abundantly clear was that its orchestra had lost none of its edge and excitement. I also savored a number of singers of whom I had heard little or nothing during my year in St. Petersburg: Netrebko, a delight in Prokofiev's *Betrothal,* and Trifonova, whose silvery voice was ideal for Ludmila in Glinka's *Ruslan and Ludmila.*

Among the newer singers, Akimov was a delight, but Vaneev's performances were a reminder that the Kirov still lacks a major bass voice apart from Ognovenko, who was sorely missed in *Ruslan's* opening-night cast; Nikitin was not half as good. As for Vaneev, he proved to have a dark, burly sound, but his voice seemed short in his lower register, and his singing had more bluster than character and finish.

But several Kirov veterans gave superb accounts of themselves. In poise and elegance there was little during the visit to match Larissa Diadkova's exceptional Ratmir in *Ruslan,* and my admiration for her singing doubled when she dispatched with equal ease the witty part of the Duenna in *Betrothal.* Yet, oddly enough, she was less effective as Konchakovna in *Prince Igor,* especially to one with memories of Borodina in the part (Borodina, who had just become a mother, had been unable to be a part of this second New York season). Matching Diadkova's unexpected comic flair in *Betrothal* were Nikolai Gassiev as Don Jerome and Sergei Alexashkin's Mendoza.

The biggest trial that beset those sympathetic to the Kirov came on opening night with the company's new production of *Prince Igor.* For some inexplicable reason Gergiev had left the company's rich traditional sets at home and substituted new ones that were a betrayal of the music and the Kirov's traditions. They were a glitzy, crass, uneven set of stage pictures, which looked as though each had been created by a different designer. Compounding the problem, Gergiev turned away from the edition of the score he had helped pioneer and employed a different finale.

In true Gergiev workaholic fashion, he conducted all but five of the seventeen performances, and from what I heard, he did so with what could only be described as his customary superhuman concentration and intensity. Watching his performances with special interest was Sarah Billinghurst, Volpe's assistant at the Met. She worked at the San Francisco Opera when Gergiev made his American debut there in 1991 and has followed his career closely and devotedly. She was a staunch supporter of the Met's sponsorship of the Kirov visit.

"I don't think the Kirov would have toured here under our auspices if Valery hadn't been our principal guest conductor," Billinghurst commented, "and Valery had very good reasons for accepting this post: he has a strong relationship with Joe Volpe, Jimmy Levine, and me—we first met in 1989. He loves the orchestra here, and his association with the Met can do positive things for the Mariinsky. In other words, we can bring the Kirov here every four or five years on tour, we can bring the ballet here, we can give or lend them a production, and we have engaged many of the Kirov's fine singers for our company. There's a lot of back-and-forth between our two theaters.

"In the years since I first saw Valery conduct, I think he has established his own style—I mean the actual, physical way he has of conducting. Some people tend to think that he is always a very driven conductor. Not at all! He can be as spacious and warm in his approach to an opera as Jimmy, and his conducting of works like *Parsifal* and *Lohengrin* is just as relaxed and lyrical. Jimmy admires him enormously. In fact, he has invited him to be the first guest conductor ever of the Met Orchestra at its concert series in Carnegie Hall, and we hope our orchestra in turn can appear in St. Petersburg."

The souvenir program for the New York visit provided a clear picture of the hierarchy at the Mariinsky at the time. With Gergiev in place as director of the theater and Schwarzkopf as its administrative head, it listed Leonid Korchmar as director of the opera company and Makhar Vaziev as director of the ballet. A year later, however, there was a shakeup at the theater when Gergiev replaced Korchmar with the veteran tenor Konstantin Pluzhnikov and restructured the rest of the theater's administrative staff.

"I was forced to tell Schwarzkopf," Gergiev informed me, "that the Kirov was advancing every day, and that we cannot go backward; we must always go forward. And if you can't go forward with us, you will have to find another theater to work for. You see, he just doesn't understand the workings of international theaters. I couldn't send him to talk to Joe Volpe at the Met or Gérard Mortier at Salzburg. He has no idea what to say to them. So I decided to put him in charge of ticket sales and the maintenance of the theater and its staff.

"My position remains as general and artistic head of the theater, and I delegated several important areas of our activities to three of my assistants. One is in charge of long-term planning. If we commit to performances at the Châtelet Theater in Paris or Covent Garden in London, this assistant works out details after I decide what operas we will do and what singers we want to use. Then the contract is signed. Another assistant is involved with handling customs, visas, insurance, and transportation, and the third takes care of marketing and development. All three report to me directly, not Schwarzkopf, and I think the running of the company is more disciplined now."

Other important changes included the formation in June 1999 of a junior Kirov orchestra of 65 players. This was a necessity, Gergiev felt, for many reasons. "The Kirov orchestra has changed about 80 percent in personnel since I became its director back in 1988. Some players retired, and some left Russia to make their life elsewhere. Today there are now 180 players in the regular orchestra, and with the 65 in the junior orchestra we have a total of 245 musicians. These young players will gradually take over as older players leave or become less active. You can't expect, for example, a player in his sixties to spend a lot of time on tour or learning difficult repertory for the first time, like the Wagner operas. This is easier with new, eager musicians. I also want to find young conductors whom I can bring into this program and help develop. For the concert the Kirov gave in memory of Musin I had eight young conductors participate, something I think would have pleased him, for when he was still alive he was always encouraging me to seek out promising conductors and give them all the help I could.

"The junior orchestra is in the hands of Gian Andrea Noseda, an extremely gifted conductor from Milan whom I met when I taught a master class in Siena in 1993, which he attended. I liked him immediately, and our meeting resulted in Gian Andrea coming to watch my rehearsals and hear my concerts in the Netherlands, in England, and in America. I then asked him to make his debut with the Kirov, which came at a concert in Italy that included the Tchaikovsky Sixth Symphony. This was the ultimate test. I told him, 'Gian Andrea, you will grow very quickly with us. I will give you *Boris*, *Queen of Spades*, and *War and Peace* to conduct, but you will give us correct readings of *Rigoletto*, *La traviata*, *Don Carlo*, and *The Marriage of Figaro*.'

"The junior orchestra is a unique chance for him to have his own orchestra, which, although young, is already quite virtuosic in many respects. We will try to give these beginning players a feeling of confidence that I hope will keep them happy in Russia and at the Kirov, where they are already playing side by side with our more experienced players and are being treated as part of the family. This means the apprentice program I started earlier has now been transferred to the junior orchestra, which has its own management and has already proven itself with a tour in Italy and performances of *Don Giovanni* at our festival in Finland. It returned to Italy to play a coproduction we created with the Ravenna Festival of

Bellini's *I Capuletti ed I Montecchi*, and I plan to have it accompany our ballet on tour."

The important next move came in January 1999 with the formation of a Mariinsky Academy for Young Singers. Gergiev placed his sister Larissa and Pluzhnikov at its head. As with the youth orchestra, members of the academy work side by side with the company's veterans and have taken part in master classes of such renowned Western artists as Renata Scotto and Fedora Barbieri, as well the Bolshoi's former leading contralto, Elena Obraztsova. The school has already presented its own productions: Rimsky-Korsakov's *Snow Maiden* at White Nights, Prokofiev's *Maddalena* at the Kirov's Mikkeli Festival in Finland, and Giovanni Pergolesi's *La serva padrona*.

On the stage of Mariinsky itself, members of the academy were featured in a much-praised production of Bellini's *La sonnambula*, conducted by Noseda, which used the exquisite sets created by Mauro Pagano for La Scala, while others appeared in the theater's revival of *The Marriage of Figaro*. And one academy soprano, Tatiana Pavlovskaya, was given a number of leading roles such as Tatiana in *Eugene Onegin* and Paulina in *The Gambler* in regular Kirov performances, and she is featured in the new Kirov recording of Prokofiev's *Semyon Kotko*.

"When they are ready, our singers immediately go to the stage," Larissa Gergieva told the critic George Loomis in an interview for *Opera* magazine. "Of the initial twenty [singers] in the first season, fifteen were used often, at different levels." She went on to point out that while "we are in contact with other programs, including at the Met . . . Russia is unusual, and we couldn't repeat their systems even if we wanted to." One crucial difference she cited was the fact that Western companies attract young singers from around the world, while the Kirov Academy has only one primary source for its talent—Russia. While the academy does not bar Western singers, most of the participants thus far have come from the Moscow and St. Petersburg conservatories, but there have been some as well from Georgia, Kazakhstan, Ukraine, and even Korea.

"Eventually," Gergiev hopes, "at least 80 percent of the theater's new artists will come from the training programs of our junior orchestra, the academy, and the ballet school. This way we will keep our sound and our tradition. I often tell the young players that what is important is not just playing the violin or timpani well, but playing them in the Kirov Orchestra. I work all the time with them and the young singers, and I don't have a problem telling the singers, for example, 'You sound good, but it's uninteresting. Your Italian is still not perfect, so you can't sing, for example, *The Marriage of Figaro*. I am sorry if you have wasted five months learning a role, but if you don't polish your languages seriously until they are at an international level, we can't use you.'

"My responsibility is to give them the best possible training and help, and part of this is putting them on the stage with a Borodina. Imagine appearing even in a small role with an artist like this. But they have to learn to be competitive. It was what she herself had to learn a dozen years ago. So I demand the highest standards from our young singers; this is why they hear 'no' from me more often than 'yes.' Sometimes it not so pleasant, but it is the only way for them to grow."

A lot of the support for the junior orchestra and academy comes from outside of Russia and from Gergiev's own pocket. "I have already donated $50,000, and occasionally I am given prizes that carry money with them—like $100,000 recently in America. I divided this money between the Kirov's young artists and my music school in the Caucasus." That school was part of a festival Gergiev began in Ossetia, "Peace for the Caucasus," which was held in 1997, in 1998, and again in 2000. One immediate and unexpected dividend from the school was Gergiev's introduction at the first Peace Festival to a young student named Natalia Dzebisova. The school was renamed for Gergiev in 1994, the year she enrolled; it is the same school where he first studied piano and conducting, and which, ironically, had at first rejected him as a student. Natalia graduated in 1999 and that summer became Gergiev's wife. On 2 October 2000, a son, Abissal Valerianovich, was born to them.

"She's nineteen, and I'm forty-six," Gergiev said with a broad smile. "It's a scandal. She's too old for me!" While in school Natalia concentrated on Ossetian folk music, and she performs on a native instrument akin to the accordion. "She really plays magnificently and makes real music," Gergiev added, "but now I want to redirect her interests and her knowledge of repertory. It is important that she understand the operas of Prokofiev and Wagner as well.

"For me, our marriage is a very important link to my people in Ossetia, whose problems are always uppermost in my mind. I am convinced that music can serve not only the Caucasus, but other trouble spots in the world. I must believe that anyone who loves Mozart and Tchaikovsky and comes to our concerts, where Russians, Chechens, Armenians, Azerbaijanis, and Georgians make music together, will be influenced by this fact. After the concerts people began asking themselves, 'How did a conflict between Georgia and Ossetia ever start?' It was something the politicians wanted, not the people. It was a question of ambition and bad leadership. It was practically *mafiosi*. These things start with political slogans that attempt to turn one people against another. Great Georgia. Great Serbia. Great Albania. And people, when they are hungry, listen to these slogans, and they say, 'Yes, we don't need minorities that take our jobs.'"

The conflict between Ossetia and Georgia was very painful for Lexo and Gergiev, and to do something about it they organized the first Peace Festival. "The people who came to our concerts were amazed to see not only the two of us—

a Georgian and an Ossetian—making music together," Gergiev says with pride, "but his friends and my friends came together in an incredible demonstration of friendship. And I asked myself after seeing this, how can they ever take up a rifle again? The possibilities in the Caucasus are tremendous if people can be convinced to live in peace. Business could flourish—and tourism. This is a place with fantastic air, clear water, breathtaking mountains, unbelievable landscapes. But instead people choose to kill each other."

Gergiev's interest in peace through music has extended to Israel and a festival he help begin in Elat, on the Dead Sea. To him this was more than an Israeli event. It was an Elat-Aquba, an Israel-Jordan, event. Then in 1999 he, Lexo, and the Kirov Orchestra went to the People's Republic of China for the first time. They were the first Russian ensemble to appear there in thirty years and the first foreign artists to play in Shanghai's new opera house. After a concert in Beijing for eight thousand, Gergiev and Lexo were invited to a private meeting with China's President Jiang Zemin. Before it was over the president had secured a promise from Gergiev that he would inaugurate the city's new concert hall in 2002.

At a press conference later, Gergiev talked of China's vast potential for absorbing classical music, its need to develop its own talent, and the power of music to bring people closer and make them better. Within twenty-four hours of arriving in China, he was already discussing plans for a second visit—on the condition that the Chinese help to underwrite it; the first tour had been something of a gamble, financed at the last moment by Philips and a group of private donors. The Chinese agreed to help, and Gergiev returned to conduct the first performance there of Mahler's Third Symphony and to give staged performances of *Eugene Onegin* and *The Marriage of Figaro*. He also speaks wistfully of bringing Wagner's *Ring* to the Chinese.

As far as the future of the Kirov is concerned, Gergiev says that the theater must continue to do its *Borises*, *Khovanshchinas*, and *Lady Macbeths* extremely well, but "if we announce a production of a Berlioz opera or Debussy's *Pelléas et Mélisande*, we put ourselves in danger, for now we risk comparisons with the world's leading opera houses, which also do these works. It's not enough if Russian audiences are happy with a soprano who sings *The Fiery Angel*, Senta, or Elsa. I knew when we brought our *Lohengrin* to Germany to open the festival at Baden-Baden, we would be compared to the best at Bayreuth or Berlin. We were, and we came off very well.

"Audiences today are international. They go to London, to the Met, to Bayreuth. Back in 1996, it was important for us to do *Otello*. Now it's important for us to do an excellent *Otello* that can stand beside *Otellos* at the Metropolitan Opera or La Scala. When people come to the White Nights Festival they compare, and we must be worthy of being put alongside the best. This is my goal.

"Verdi, by the way, is a composer we will concentrate on a great deal more in the future, probably beginning with productions of *Un ballo in maschera*, *Falstaff*, *Simon Boccanegra*, and *Macbeth*. I think we have more and better voices for his music than many other opera houses. There are Putilin, Borodina, Diadkova, Tarasova, Galuzin, and Gorchakova, who may be sometimes up and sometimes down, but hers is still one of the major voices of our time.

"None of this is easy, and I know I am asking a lot. Look, we are in the process of returning Wagner's *Ring* to the Mariinsky in a new staging by Johannes Schaaf —a difficult but brilliant man—and this means our chorus must memorize thousands of German words. This is very hard for them, but I tell them that it is no easier for the Metropolitan's chorus to learn *Khovanshchina*, *Boris*, and *Onegin* in Russian, and they must be on the same level."

The Kirov *Ring* began with *Das Rheingold* in June 2000. *Die Walküre* and *Siegfried* were scheduled to follow in March and June 2001, respectively, and the cycle will conclude with *Götterdämmerung* in the spring of 2002. The entire work will premiere at the White Nights Festival in June 2002. Afterward the cycle will go to the Teatro Colón in Buenos Aires and to Venice (depending on the restoration of the burnt-out Fenice Theater). "I want to make a sort of pilgrimage with the production," Gergiev said, "take it to all the places associated with Wagner. This means, of course, Germany, too. Whatever people may say about this cycle, they will see that the Kirov now has the strength to produce a *Ring*, and this will be an accomplishment that can't be ignored."

As for other new repertory, Gergiev wants to add Debussy's *Pelléas* "in a few years." I thought at first he had said "in a few days." Laughing at my mistake, he said, "Well, give me a couple of hours, and I'll arrange it!" He also speaks avidly of mounting Berlioz's *Les troyens* and bringing Alban Berg's *Wozzeck* back into the company's repertory. In fact, Gérard Mortier has offered him the Peter Stein production of the Berg opera. He is interested too in Britten's *Peter Grimes* and *Billy Budd*.

Beyond his operatic plans, Gergiev says he is trying to spend more time with the ballet than before. "I conducted several of the Balanchine nights, as well as *Romeo* and *Sacre*. And now I am planning a new *Nutcracker*, and I told the company, 'Sorry, the tempos are going to be Tchaikovsky's.' I want a *Nutcracker* that is dynamic, powerful, elegant, energetic, brilliant. It is a production we hope to film as well—perhaps something different, like an animated film.

"I am having to interfere more with the ballet than ever before, for although Vaziev is all right as its manager, he is not accepted as a great artistic leader. So I have gone to our finest dancers like Lopatkina or Asylmuratova and said, 'I am not a choreographer or a ballet master, but I have been at this theater for more than twenty years and I know its history and traditions. Tell me what you need for this company and your talent to grow and develop.' And they are open with me. Some of them have said I need to take more control, for there are some things that Vaziev should not decide by himself—for example, who should be invited as choreographers to the theater. So I have taken the initiative and invited several new choreographers myself.

"We now have Roland Petit's *Carmen* and his *Le jeune homme et la mort*, and the Balanchine Trust has licensed us to do *Jewels*. Of course, with the ballet we have the great responsibility of maintaining our traditional works—the Petipa repertory—and we recently did a new *Sleeping Beauty* that attempted to go back as closely as was possible to how this classic was danced at its premiere. In general, I think people were impressed with it, though the scenery was perhaps a bit over the top. But I think we gave the public a feeling for this ballet as it looked a hundred years ago at the Mariinsky.

"I also want to bring back Fokine's *Petrushka* in the original Benois production, and I am seriously considering the restored staging of Nijinsky's *Sacre*. We have a *Sacre* now—a modern one—which I want to repeat for a couple years, but after that I want to do the Nijinsky version. And I am concerned, too, about the future of the ballet school. I have asked Asylmuratova to become its director, and I told the minister of culture in Moscow, to whom the school now reports, that if Asylmuratova is given the job we will continue to open the doors of the Mariinsky to the school on a level with our new vocal academy or junior orchestra. If not, then we will create our own ballet school." (The post went to her shortly afterward.)

But these elements are just part of the biggest goal in Gergiev's life. He dreams of the theater and its schools becoming the heart of a cultural center. "Imagine creating a Lincoln Center or a Kennedy Center in St. Petersburg—a place where there is more than music. I want there to be restaurants and a modern art center, and we must make use of all the tremendous technological advances that are taking place every day, including the resources of the Internet. I hope, too, we can help integrate the conservatory into the plan, for the building badly needs restoring.

"Actually, there is nothing new to construct in order to accomplish this. Peter the Great did it for us nearly three centuries ago. I have my eye on a small island very near the theater, known as 'New Holland.' It contains a series of wonderful brick buildings constructed by Peter to store the wood and others materials he needed for shipbuilding. Today it belongs to the military, and there have been plans to convert it into a tourist district, with shops and hotels. But I want to convince the government to let the Kirov use it, so that we can remodel the buildings to create more rehearsal and performance space and storage facilities for the theater's sets and costumes. But this must be done in a way that will not spoil the atmosphere of the island and the historic role it has played.

"For these dreams to materialize it is extremely important that we continue touring, creating coproductions with other companies, and maintaining the festivals we have started around the world in London, Finland, Israel, and Holland. The Kirov has become a formidable force in the opera world, and there can be no turning back. Each year we must be better than we were before."

To devote even more time to the task of making the Mariinsky all he wants to be, Gergiev has cut back on his guest conducting. "I find time, of course, for the Berlin and the Vienna Philharmonics," he says, "but the only American orchestras I conduct now are the New York Philharmonic and the Met's, which is a pity because I always enjoyed the Chicago Symphony, for example. And my debut with the Philadelphia Orchestra was a good experience, too.

"In particular, I see my future with the Vienna Philharmonic as very important as well as gratifying to me, because, you know, conductors are invited by the orchestra itself; it is self-governing. I made my formal debut with the Philharmonic at the Musikverein in 1999 conducting its Herbert von Karajan memorial concert after we had performed and recorded together in Salzburg. Naturally, this was a special moment for me, for here was someone who had won the Karajan competition as a young man and had now returned to conduct an important concert in his memory. You can imagine the emotion and the responsibility I felt.

"One half of the concert was Debussy and the other half was Tchaikovsky. My preparation for this concert, however, was not just the five days of rehearsal I had. It was the last thirty years of my life. It started with my discovery of and affection for Debussy and Tchaikovsky. And by the way—this may be a surprise—Debussy probably came first. As a pianist I played through *La mer* more often than I did Tchaikovsky's Sixth, I was so fascinated by the harmonies and the colors.

"Working with Vienna is a totally different experience than working with the Kirov Orchestra. There I often have to be a teacher as well as a conductor, but not in Vienna. These players are masters. You can do things with this orchestra—with its brass, its strings—you never dreamed of before. I don't even know how or why it happens. But something remarkable, something truly creative takes place. Now they've asked me, 'Why not *Tristan* with us? The *Ring*? What about the New Year's concert?' I tell them, 'Let's wait and see.'"

On a purely personal level, Gergiev says that "80 percent of my life is related to music, but I do look forward to getting away from it when I can and having a few days or weeks in the forests of Finland or the mountains of the Caucasus and Switzerland. There I walk for hours on end. This is my way of unwinding. When you spend time with something you love—music or fresh air—it gives you energy.

I also watch television sometimes for two or three hours, especially after a performance, when it is difficult to get to sleep. I am very attracted to nature programs, especially the National Geographic programs or those on the Discovery Channel. But when I see shows on snakes, crocodiles, hyenas, lions, wolves, birds—how they protect themselves, attack others, vie for leadership, mark their territory— I smile to myself and can't help but be reminded of opera! An animal with its tail up, for instance, means 'I am the one.' That's Pavarotti-Domingo or Callas-Tebaldi, isn't it?"

In 2003, when the city of St. Petersburg marks the three hundredth anniversary of its founding, Gergiev will celebrate his fiftieth birthday, his twenty-fifth year at the Mariinsky, and his fifteenth as its director. As this confluence of anniversaries approaches, it should be clear to anyone not emotionally involved in the victories and defeats of the theater that it has reached a point where it needs Gergiev far more than he needs it. His career outside of Russia is enormous and high profile, and as vacancies open up with major orchestras around the globe, Gergiev will surely be prominent among those being wooed.

But whatever the future holds, there can be no doubt that the focal point of his life and work is, for the present, the Mariinsky. Because of his presence there, the theater is a hot spot in the world of opera. The big question is whether it could continue to command a leading position at home and abroad without a one-man show and stellar attraction like Gergiev.

Bibliography

Acocella, Joan. "The Soloist." *New Yorker*, 12 January 1988, 45–46.

————. "Lost and Found." *New Yorker*, 26 July 1999, 88–91.

Alovert, Nina. *Baryshnikov in Russia*. New York: Holt, Rinehart, and Winston, 1984.

Art du ballet en Russe. Paris: Editions du Mécène, 1991.

Bakst, James. *A History of Russian-Soviet Music*. New York: Dodd, Mead, 1966.

Ballet [Russian magazine]. Special Petipa issue, 1993.

Bartlett, Rosamund. *Wagner and Russia*. London: Cambridge University Press, 1995.

Beaumont, Cyril. *A History of Ballet in Russia*. London: C. W. Beaumont, 1930.

————. *Michel Fokine and His Ballets*. London: C. W. Beaumont, 1945.

Benois, Alexander. *Reminiscences of the Russian Ballet*. London: Putnam, 1941.

Berlioz, Hector. *Memoirs*. Translated and edited by David Cairns. New York: Alfred A. Knopf, 1969.

Bogdanov-Berezovsky, V. *Kirov Opera and Ballet Theater*. Moscow, 1959.

Bogolenova, Y., and I. Golubovsky, eds. *Kirov Opera and Ballet Theater*. Leningrad, 1972.

Bohlen, Celestine. "Long Nights, Longer Days, All Filled with Music." *New York Times*, 16 July 2000.

Borovsky, Victor. *Chaliapin*. New York: Alfred A. Knopf, 1988.

Bowers, Faubion. *Scriabin*. Mineola, New York: Dover, 1996.

Bremser, Martha, ed. *International Dictionary of Ballet*. Detroit: St. James Press, 1993.

Brown, David. *Tchaikovsky*. 4 vols. New York: W. W. Norton, 1978, 1983, 1991 (vols. 1–2, 4); London: Victor Gollancz, 1986 (vol. 3).

————. *Tchaikovsky Remembered*. London: Faber and Faber, 1993.

Buckle, Richard. *Diaghilev*. New York: Atheneum, 1979.

————. *Nijinsky*. New York: Simon and Schuster, 1971.

Buckle, Richard, and John Taras. *George Balanchine: Ballet Master*. New York: Random House, 1988.

Caruso, Enrico, Jr., and Andrew Farkas. *Enrico Caruso: My Father and My Family*. Portland, Oregon: Amadeus Press, 1990.

Chaliapin, Feodor. *Pages from My Life*. Translated by H. M. Buck. New York: Harper, 1927.

————. *An Autobiography, as Told to Maxim Gorky.* Translated by N. Froud and J. Hanley. New York: Stein and Day, 1969.

Chevtchenko, Kirill [Kirill Veselago, pseud.]. *The Phantom of the Opera in the City of N'.* St. Petersburg, 1996.

Chujoy, Anatole, and P. Manchester, eds. *The Dance Encyclopedia.* New York: Simon and Schuster, 1967.

Clark, Katerina. *St. Petersburg: Crucible of Cultural Revolution.* Cambridge, Massachusetts: Harvard University Press, 1995.

Clark, Mary, and Clement Crisp. *Ballerina: The Art of Women in Classical Ballet.* Pennington, New Jersey: Dance Horizons, 1988.

Cohen, Selma Jeanne, ed. *International Encyclopedia of Dance.* 6 vols. New York: Oxford University Press, 1998.

Cone, John Frederick. *Adelina Patti: Queen of Hearts.* Portland, Oregon: Amadeus Press, 1993.

Craine, Debra. "Shining White Knight of the Podium." *Times* (London), 2 July 1997.

Danilova, Alexandra. *Choura.* London: Dance Books, 1987.

Deten, A., and Igor Stupnikov. *Leningrad Ballet, 1917–1987.* Leningrad, 1988.

Dianin, Serge. *Borodin.* Translated by Robert Lord. London: Oxford University Press, 1963.

Doeser, Linda. *Ballet and Dance.* New York: Excalibur Books, 1977.

Dolin, Anton. *Olga Spessivtseva: The Sleeping Ballerina.* London: Dance Books, 1966.

Dunning, Jennifer. "Life's a Global Roller-Coaster Ride for the Kirov's Director." *New York Times,* 12 June 1995.

————. "Russians Are Springing Up All Over." *New York Times,* 5 November 1997.

Emerson, Caryl, and Robert Oldani. *Modest Mussorgsky and Boris Godunov.* New York: Cambridge University Press, 1994.

Fitzlyon, April. *The Price of Genius.* New York: Appleton-Century, 1964.

Fokine, Mikhail. *Memoirs of a Ballet Master.* Boston: Little, Brown, 1961.

Frangopulo, Marietta. *Leningrader Ballett.* Berlin: Henschelverlag, 1967.

Gaisberg, F. W. *The Music Goes Round.* New York: Macmillan, 1942.

Gattey, Charles. *Tetrazzini: The Florentine Nightingale.* Portland, Oregon: Amadeus Press, 1995.

Golubovsky, I., ed. *Kirov Opera and Ballet Theater.* Leningrad, 1967.

Gregory, John. *The Legat Saga.* London: Javog, 1992.

Gregory, John, and Alexander Ukladnikov. *Leningrad's Ballet.* London: Zena, 1981.

Gurewitsch, Matthew. "Valery Gergiev's Esthetic Brinkmanship." *New York Times Magazine,* 19 April 1998, 32–35.

Hetherington, John. *Melba.* New York: Farrar, Strauss, and Giroux, 1967.

Holmes, John. *Conductors on Record.* London: Victor Gollancz, 1982.

Jennings, Luke. "The Czar's Last Dance." *New Yorker,* 27 March 1995, 71–86.

Karsavina, Tamara. *Theatre Street.* London: Dance Books, 1981.

Kendall, Elizabeth. "Reflections: The Kirov." *New Yorker,* 8 June 1992, 77–89.

Kennett, Audrey. *The Palaces of Leningrad.* New York: Thames and Hudson, 1973.

Keynes, Milo. *Lydia Lopukhova.* New York: St. Martin's Press, 1982.

Khrushchevy, Iraida. *Kirov State Opera and Ballet Theater.* Leningrad, 1957.

Krasovskaya, Vera. *Nijinsky.* Translated by John Bowlt. New York: Schirmer, 1979.

Kruntyaeva, T., ed. *Kirov Opera and Ballet Theater.* Leningrad, 1982.

Kshessinskaya, Mathilde. *Dancing in St. Petersburg.* Translated by Arnold Haskell. Garden City, New York: Doubleday, 1961.

Kutsch, K. J., and Leo Riemens. *Grosses Sängerlexikon.* Munich: K. G. Saur, 1997.

Larue, C. Steven, ed. *International Dictionary of Opera.* Detroit: St. James Press, 1993.

Lazzarini, John, and Roberta Lazzarini. *Pavlova.* New York: Schirmer, 1980.

Leiser, Clara. *Jean de Reszke and the Great Days of Opera.* London: Gerald Howe, 1933.

Leningrad Ballet of Today. Leningrad, 1967.

Leshkov, D. *Marius Petipa.* London: C. W. Beaumont, 1971.

Levik, Sergei. *An Opera Singer's Notes.* Translated by Edward Moran. London: Symposium Records, 1995.

Lieven, Prince Peter. *The Birth of the Ballets-Russes.* New York: Dover, 1973.

Mahler, Alma. *Gustav Mahler: Memories and Letters.* New York: Viking, 1969.

Makarova, Natalia. *A Dance Autobiography.* New York: Alfred A. Knopf, 1979.

Maksitovskogo, C., ed. *Kirov Opera and Ballet Theater.* Leningrad, 1975.

Malko, Nikolai. *A Certain Art.* New York, 1966.

Mason, Francis, ed. *I Remember Balanchine.* New York: Anchor Books, 1991.

Massie, Suzanne. *Land of the Firebird.* New York: Simon and Schuster, 1980.

—————. *Pavlovsk: The Life of a Russian Palace.* Boston: Little, Brown, 1990.

Meisner, Nadine. "A Dying Swan?" *Times* (London), 15 December 1996.

Money, Keith. *Anna Pavlova: Her Life and Art.* New York: Alfred A. Knopf, 1982.

Mooser, R. *L'opéra-comique français en Russe au XVIIIe siècle.* Geneva: Éditions René Kister, 1954.

Nekhidzu, A., ed. *Marius Petipa.* Leningrad, 1971.

Newman, Ernest. *The Life of Richard Wagner.* New York: Alfred A. Knopf, 1933.

Nijinska, Bronislava. *Early Memoirs.* Translated and edited by Irina Nijinska and Jean Rawlinson. New York: Holt, Rinehart, and Winston, 1981.

Noble, Jeremy. *Kirov Ballet.* St. Petersburg: La Fondation Ballets Russes, 1995.

O'Mahony, John. "Demon King of the Pit." *Guardian* (London), 18 September 1999.

Osborne, Charles. *The Complete Operas of Verdi.* New York: Alfred A. Knopf, 1970.

Ostwald, Peter. *Vaslav Nijinsky: A Leap into Madness.* New York: Carol, 1991.

Parry, Jann. "Mugging, Money, and the Moonies," *Observer Review* (London), 2 February 1995.

Poznansky, Alexander. *Tchaikovsky: The Quest for the Inner Man.* New York: Schirmer, 1991.

Rimsky-Korsakov, Nikolai. *Chronicle of My Life.* London: Eulenberg, 1974.

Roné, Elvira. *Olga Preobrazhenskaya: A Portrait.* Translated by Fernau Hall. New York: Marcel Dekker, 1978.

Roslavleva, Natalia. *Era of the Russian Ballet.* New York: E. P. Dutton, 1966.

Ross, Alex. "The Maestro of Midnight." *New Yorker,* 20 April 1998, 86–93.

Sadie, Stanley, ed. *The New Grove Dictionary of Music and Musicians.* 20 vols. London: Macmillan, 1980.

—————. *The New Grove Dictionary of Opera.* London: Macmillan, 1991.

Schwarz, Boris. *Music in Soviet Russia, 1917–1970.* New York: W. W. Norton, 1972.

Scott, Michael. *The Great Caruso.* New York. Alfred A. Knopf, 1988.

—————. *The Record of Singing.* 2 vols. New York: Charles Scribner's Sons, 1977.

Shtokolov, Boris. *Shine, Shine, My Star.* St. Petersburg, 1995.

Slonimsky, Nicolas. *Lexicon of Musical Invective.* 2d ed. New York: Coleman-Ross, 1965.

Smakov, Gennady. *The Great Russian Dancers.* New York: Alfred A. Knopf, 1984.

Sobinov, Leonid. *Letters.* Moscow, 1970.

Souritz, Elizabeth. *Soviet Choreographers in the 1920s.* Translated by Lynn Visson. London: Dance Books, 1990.

Stravinsky, Igor. *Stravinsky: An Autobiography.* New York: Simon and Schuster, 1936.

Stravinsky, Igor, and Robert Craft. *Expositions and Developments.* Garden City, New York: Doubleday, 1962.

Stuart, Otis. *Perpetual Motion: The Public and Private Lives of Rudolf Nureyev.* New York: Simon and Schuster, 1995.

Svetloff, V. *Anna Pavlova.* Translated by A. Grey. New York: Dover, 1974.

Taper, Bernard. *Balanchine: A Biography.* New York: Harper and Row, 1963.

Taruskin, Richard. *Stravinsky and the Russian Traditions.* Los Angeles: University of California Press, 1996.

Teliakovsky, Vladimir. *Theatrical Memories.* Moscow, 1965.

Tommasini, Anthony. "Met's New Maestro: A Dashing Career, a Beat All His Own." *New York Times,* 20 December 1997.

Vaganova, Agrippina. *Basic Principles of Classical Ballet.* Translated by Anatole Chujoy. New York: Dover, 1969.

Volkov, Solomon. *Balanchine's Tchaikovsky.* New York: Simon and Schuster, 1985.

—————. *St. Petersburg: A Cultural History.* Translated by Antonina W. Bouis. New York: Free Press, 1995.

Watson, Peter. *Nureyev.* London: Hodder and Stoughton, 1994.

Williams, Neville. *Chronology of the Modern World.* New York: David McKay, 1966.

Wiley, Roland John. *A Century of Russian Ballet.* Oxford: Clarendon Press, 1990.

—————. *Tchaikovsky's Ballets.* Oxford: Clarendon Press, 1985.

—————. *The Life and Ballets of Lev Ivanov.* Oxford: Clarendon Press, 1997.

Yastrebtsev, Vasily. *Reminiscences of Rimsky-Korsakov.* Translated by Florence Jonas. New York: Columbia University Press, 1985.

Yearbook of the Imperial Theaters: Mariinsky Theater, 1895–1915. St. Petersburg.

Zakrzhevskaya, T., L. Miasnikova, and A. Storozhuk. *Rudolf Nureyev: Three Years in the Kirov Theatre.* Translated by Kenneth MacInnes. St. Petersburg: Pushkinsky Fond, 1995.

Mariinsky/Kirov
Discography and Videography

I. The Imperial Recordings

The 78-rpm recordings made in turn-of-the-century St. Petersburg are too numerous to list, and many are no longer available as reissues. Currently, the most comprehensive collection, with recording dates ranging from 1901 to 1924, is to be found on a series of five two-CD sets from Pearl Records. The series also includes a number of artists associated with other Russian houses as well as the theater in Warsaw, but only those artists principally active at the Mariinsky are listed below.

Volume 1 (9997). Ivan Ershov, Medea Mei-Figner, Nikolai Figner, Ioachim Tartakov, Leonid Sobinov.

Volume 2 (9001). Vladimir Kastorsky, Andrei Labinsky, Dmitri Bukhtoiarov, Vasili Sharonov, Gavril Morskoi, Oskar Kamionsky, Polikarp Orlov, David Juzhin, Natalia Ermolenko-Juzhina, Antonina Panina, Lev Sibiriakov.

Volume 3 (9004). Nadezhda Zabela-Vrubel, Maria Kuznetsova, Lydia Lipkovska, Dmitri Smirnov, Evgenia Zbrujeva.

Volume 4 (9007). Alexander Davidov, Alexander Bogdanovich, Lev Sibiriakov, Nikolai Shevelev.

Volume 5 (9111). Lev Sibirakov, Maria Michailova, Maksimilian Maksakov, Alexander Bogdanovich, Nikolai Seversky, Daria Zakharova, Mikhail Karakash, Elena Katulskaya, Evgeny Vitting, Maria Davidova.

The Pearl sets omitted recordings by Feodor Chaliapin, as there are many separate discs of him available. Among the most representative are *Chaliapin: Russian Operatic Arias* (EMI 7610092; with excerpts from *Boris Godunov*, *A Life for the Czar*, *Ruslan and Ludmila*, *Rusalka*, *The Demon*, *Prince Igor*, *Sadko*, and *Aleko*) and the *Chaliapin Song Book* (Preiser 89207), which includes a broad selection of songs in Russian, German, and English. Of special interest, too, are the records of Olimpia Boronat, whose main career was centered in St. Petersburg. Her complete recordings are available on Marston CD 51001.

II. The Soviet Recordings

Irina Bogacheva

Recital of songs and arias by Martini, Purcell, Bach, Pergolesi, and Handel. Melodiya LP 06263-64.

Dargomizhsky

Rusalka: Miller's aria. Shtokolov. Kirov Orchestra, Eltsin conducting. Columbia LP 34569.

Dzerzhinsky

Man's Destiny: Andrei's arias. Shtokolov. Kirov Orchestra, Eltsin conducting. EMI LP 40038.

Quiet Flows the Don: "Villain fled." Zhuravlenko. Kirov Orchestra, Samosud conducting. Lys CD 235.

Glinka

A Life for the Czar: "They guess the truth." Shtokolov. Kirov Orchestra, Eltsin conducting. Columbia LP 34569.

Ruslan and Ludmila: Farlaf's rondo. Zhuravlenko. Kirov Orchestra, Khaikin conducting. Lys CD 235.

Handel

Alcina and *Julius Caesar*: arias. Petrova. Kirov Orchestra, Dalgat conducting. Melodiya 78-rpm 03097-8.

Kabalevsky

The Taras Family: excerpts. Yashugin, Preobrazhenskaya, Kolyada, Alexeiev, Kashevarova, Ivanovsky, Nechaiev. Kirov Orchestra and Chorus, Khaikin conducting. Melodiya LP 38607.

Kazhlayev

Goryanka: ballet suite. Kirov Orchestra, Dalgat conducting. Melodiya 78-rpm 03237.

Khachaturian

Gayane: excerpts. Kirov Orchestra, Khaikin conducting. Melodiya 78-rpm 2410-1, 2372.

Mozart

Concert arias K. 272, 383, 486a. Petrova. Kirov Orchestra, Braudo conducting. Melodiya 78-rpm 03097-8.

Mussorgsky

Boris Godunov: act 2 (Shostakovich version). Shtokolov, Slovtsova, Kuzentsova, Grudina, Ulianov. Kirov Orchestra, Eltsin conducting.Columbia LP 34569.

Boris Godunov: Inn Scene. Zhuravlenko, Kommissarova, Gontariov, Krutiakov. Kirov Orchestra, Grykurov conducting. Lys CD 235.

Khovanshchina. Preobrazhenskaya, Freidkov, Nechayev, Reizen, Ulianov, Shashkov. Kirov Orchestra and Chorus, Khaikin conducting. Arlecchino CD 103.

Khovanshchina: "All is quiet." Andreiev. Kirov Orchestra, Pokhitonov conducting. Arlecchino CD 103.

Rachmaninov

Aleko: "Moon is high." Shtokolov. Kirov Orchestra, Eltsin conducting. Columbia LP 34569.

Rimsky-Korsakov

Sadko: "I'd sail for the sea." Petrov. Kirov Orchestra, Lazarev conducting. Arlecchino CD 23.

Sadko: Lullaby. Stepanova. Kirov Orchestra, Steinberg conducting. Arlecchino CD 23.

Sadko: Song of Viking Guest. Shtokolov. Kirov Orchestra, Eltsin conducting. Columbia LP 34569.

Czar's Bride: Duet, act 1. Preobrazhenskaya, Cesnokov. Kirov Orchestra, Pokhitonov conducting. Myto 992.028.

Tchaikovsky

Eugene Onegin: Gremin's aria. Shtokolov. Kirov Orchestra, Eltsin conducting. Columbia LP 34569.

The Maid of Orleans. Preobrazhenskaya, Ulianov, Shaskov, Runovsky, Solomiak. Kirov Orchestra and Chorus, Khaikin conducting. Myto 992.028.

The Queen of Spades: "It is evening." Bolotina, Preobrazhenskaya. Kirov Orchestra, Pokhitonov conducting. Arlecchino 142.

The Queen of Spades: "Forgive me." Pechkavsky. Kirov Orchestra, Wolf-Izrael conducting. Arlecchino 142.

The Queen of Spades: "Mon gentil petit ami." Khalileeva, Vebitskaya. Kirov Orchestra, Pokhitonov conducting. Arlecchino 142.

The Queen of Spades: "Je crains de lui." Preobrazhenskaya. Kirov Orchestra, Eltsin conducting. Arlecchino 142, Myto 992.028.

The Queen of Spades: Tomsky's aria. Andreev. Kirov Orchestra, Pokhitonov conducting. Arlecchino 142.

The Queen of Spades: "What is our life." Pechkavsky. Kirov Orchestra, Wolf-Izrael conducting. Arlecchino 142.

Tishchenko

Symphony No. 3. Kirov Orchestra, Blazhkov conducting. Melodiya 78-rpm 01974.

III. The Soviet Videos

Adam

Le corsaire (with additional music by Pugni, Delibes and Drigo). Asylmuratova, Neff, Zaklinsky, Ruzimatov, Pankova. Kirov Orchestra, Fedotov conducting. Nonesuch Laserdisc 40165.

Giselle. Mezentseva, Zaklinsky, Selyutsky, Terekhova. Kirov Orchestra, conductor unknown. Pioneer VHS 24332.

Arensky

> *Egyptian Nights* (Fokine choreography). Asylmuratova, Kullik, Ruzimatov, Kim. Kirov Orchestra, conductor unknown. JPN Laserdisc 1182.

Backstage at the Kirov Ballet

> Documentary focusing on the rise of Asylmuratova. Excerpts from *Swan Lake* with Mezentseva, Zaklinsky, Asylmuratova; interviews with Vinogradov, Gusiev, Moiseyev; Dudinskaya and Kurgapkina teaching. Kultur VHS 1382.

Ballet Legends: Ninel Kurgapkina

> Excerpts from *Don Quixote, Harlequinade, Le corsaire,* and *The Sleeping Beauty,* and waltzes by Richard Strauss and Shostakovich. View VHS 1220.

Children of Theater Street

> Documentary on Vaganova Academy, narrated by Princess Grace of Monaco. Excerpts from *Swan Lake,* act 2 pas de deux with Mezentseva, Zaklinsky; *Raymonda* with Dudinskaya, Sergeiev; *Satanilla*; *Paquita*; interviews with Dudinskaya, Sergeiev; Kultur VHS 1111.

Classic Kirov Performances

> Excerpts from *The Sleeping Beauty* with Vecheslova; *La bayadère,* pas de deux with Dudinskaya, Chabukiani; *Don Quixote,* act 1 excerpt with Kurgapkina; *Gayane* with Vecheslova, Zubkovsky; *Chopinana* with Ulanova; *Ruslan and Ludmila,* first ballet sequence with Komleva; *Nutcracker,* pas de deux with Kolpakova, Semenov; *Don Quixote,* act 1 excerpt with Terekhova; *Cinderella* with Efremova, Vikulov; *Prince Igor,* Polovtsian Dances with Kashsrina, Gumba; *Dying Swan* with Pavlova; *Chopiniana* with Likhovskaya, Vikharev; *Raymonda* with Dudinskaya, Sergeiev; *The Sleeping Beauty* with Komleva; *Fountain of Bakhchisarai* with Sizova, Bosov, Ostaltsov; *Romeo and Juliet* with Ulanova, Sergeiev; *Taras Bulba* with Chabukiani, Dudko; *Esmeralda* with Asylmuratova, Melnikov. Kultur VHS 1341.

Delibes

> *Coppélia* (Vinogradov version). Shapchits, Zavialov, Rusanov, Tarasova. Kirov Orchestra, Viliumanis conducting. Nonesuch VHS 40182.

Farukh Ruzimatov

> *Don Quixote,* pas de deux with Pally; *Bolero* with Trofimova, Stashkava, Polosulchina; *La bayadère,* pas de deux with Kunakar; *Tango.* TDK VHS BAL-01.

Farukh Ruzimatov: Profile

> Excerpts from *1830* (choreography: Béjart); *The Knight in Tiger Skin*; *Giselle* with Asylmuratova; *Le corsaire* with Asylmuratova; *Albinoni Adagio*; *Don Quixote,* pas de deux with Terekhova; *Gayane*; *Theme and Variations* (music: Tchaikovsky, choreography: Balanchine); interviews with Vinogradov, Makarova. JPN Laserdisc 1182.

Glory of the Kirov

Swan Lake, act 3 pas de deux with Dudinskaya, Sergeiev; barre exercises with Karsavina; *Raymonda*, pas de deux with Kolpakova, Semenov; *Viennese Waltz* with Kurgapkina, Bregvadze; *Reflection* (music: Tchaikovsky, choreography: Yakobson) with Osipenko, Nisnevich; *Le corsaire*, pas de deux with Sizova, Nureyev; *Laurencia*, pas de six with Kurgapkina, Nureyev, Soloviev; *The Tale of Serf Nikish* (music: Kamilov, choreography: Laskari) with Evteeva, Baryshnikov; *The Dying Swan* with Makarova; *Pas de quatre* (music: Pugni, choreography: Dolin) with Evteeva, Komleva, Galinskaya, Kovaleva; *Syrinx* (music: Debussy, choreography: Alexidze) with Osipenko; *Spartacus*, excerpt with Moiseyeva, pas de deux with Zubkovskaya, Makarov; *Romeo and Juliet* (choreography: Rizhenko, Smirnov-Golovanov), excerpt with Dolgushin; *The Ice Maiden* (music: Grieg, choreography: Lopukhov) with Osipenko, Markovski; *Chopinana*, excerpt with Komleva, Vikulov; *Le corsaire*, pas de deux with Kurgapkina, Budarin; *Swan Lake*, act 2 pas de deux with Ulanova, Sergeiev; *The Dying Swan* with Moiseyeva. NVC Arts VHS 4509-99619.

Kirov Ballet: Classical Night

Carnival in Venice, pas de deux with Efremova, Emets; *Diana and Acteon*, pas de deux with Terekhova, Berezhnoi; *Esmeralda*, pas de deux with Komleva, Afanaskov; *Flower Festival at Genzano*, pas de deux with Bolshakova, Guliaev; *Vivandière*, pas de deux with Sizova, Blankov; *Pas de quatre* (music: Pugni, choreography: Dolin) with Kolpakova, Komleva, Evteeva, Mezentseva. View VHS 1203.

Kirov Ballet in London

La bayadère, Kingdom of the Shades with Chenchikova, Zaklinsky, Kullik, Sitnikova, Likhovskaya; *Esmeralda*, pas de deux with Evteeva and Aliyev; *Vivandière*, pas de deux with Pankova, Vikharev; *Le papillon* (music: Offenbach), pas de deux with Kolpakova, Berezhnoi; *Swan Lake*, act 3 pas de deux with Makarova, Zaklinsky; *Don Quixote*, pas de deux with Terekhova, Vaziev; *Le corsaire*, "Le jardin animé" with Ruzimatov, Asylmuratova, Makhalina. Kultur VHS 1259.

Kirov Soloists: Invitation to the Dance

Narrated by Kolpakova. *Diane and Acteon*, pas de deux with Terekhova, Kovmir; *Notre dame de Paris* (choreography: Petit), excerpt with Chenchikova, Berezhnoi; *Pas de deux* (music: Burgmüller, choreography: Timofeev) with Kunakova, Daukayev; *Carnival de Venise* with Efremova, Emits; *Bachianas* (music: Villa-Lobos, choreography: Lebedev) with Bolshakova, Gulayev; *Le papillon* (music: Offenbach) with Kolpakova, Berezhnoi. Chenchikova coaching with Kurgapkina; Kunakova coaching with Kolpakova. View VHS 1208.

Leningrad Legend

Documentary narrated by Makarova. Excerpts from *Raymonda* with Dudinskaya, Sergeiev; *Giselle*, act 1 pas de deux with Asylmuratova, Ruzimatov; *Cinderella*;

1830 (choreography: Béjart) with Ruzimatov; *Albinoni Adagio* with *Ruzimatov;* *The Knight in Tiger Skin*, excerpt; *Battleship Potemkin*, excerpt; *Chopiniana*, excerpt; *La bayadère*, Kingdom of the Shades; *Paquita*, excerpt with Asylmuratova; *Gayane*, excerpt with Gensler; *Paquita*, mazurka with Vaganova students; *Swan Lake*, polonaise; *The Stone Flower*, Gypsy Dance; *Swan Lake*, act 3 pas de deux with Zelensky, Ayupova; Vaganova students in class; Ruzimatov in rehearsal and interview; Kolpakova teaching; Mezentseva coaching; Vinogradov interview; Dudinskaya interview and teaching; Sergeiev interview and teaching; Zaklinsky interview; Makarova teaching. Kultur VHS 1298.

Magic of the Kirov Ballet

La bayadère, Kingdom of the Shades and act 2 Indian Dances with Strogaya, Ostaltsov; *Le corsaire*, pas de deux with Terekhova, Ruzimatov; *The Sleeping Beauty*, pas de deux with Soloviev; *Raymonda*, Spanish Dance with Gensler, Ostaltsov; *Swan Lake*, act 2 pas de deux with Mezentseva, Zaklinsky; *Paquita*, pas de deux with Chenchikova, Daukayev. Kultur VHS 1216.

Makarova Returns

Documentary on Makarova's 1989 return to the Kirov. Excerpts from *Chopiniana*; *Swan Lake*, act 2 pas de deux; *Onegin* (choreography: Cranko), pas de deux; interviews with Makarova, Osipenko, Vikulov, Vinogradov; Kurgapkina, Dudinskaya, Sergeiev teaching. Kultur VHS 1209.

Mariinsky Ballet

Chopiniana with Asylmuratova, Zaklinsky; *Petrushka* (Vinogradov version) with Vikharev; *Barber Adagio* with Evteeva, Aliev; *Le corsaire*, pas de deux with Kunakova, Ruzimatov; *The Fairy Doll*, excerpts with Lezhina, Gruzdev, Fadeyev; *Markitenka* with Pankova, Vikharev, Sitnikova, Koltun, Zhelonkina, Melnikov; *Paquita*, act 3 excerpt with Makhalina, Zelensky, Panova, Sitnikova, Chicherin; *Don Quixote*, pas de deux with Terekhova, Ruzimatov. Home VHS 090.

Minkus

La bayadère. Abdyev, Terekhova, Komleva, Selyutsky, Potemkin. Kirov Orchestra, Shirokov conducting. Kultur VHS 1113.

Don Quixote. Terekhova, Ruzimatov, Ponomariov, Bruskin, Luniov, Lepeev, Korniev, Asylmuratova, Pankova, Gumba, Makhalina. Kirov Orchestra, Fedotov conducting. Kultur VHS 1217.

Prokofiev

The Stone Flower. Polikarpova, Guliaev, Terekhova, Babnin, Christyakova. Kirov Orchestra, Viliumanis conducting. Nonesuch Laserdisc 40153.

Purcell

The Moor's Pavane (choreography: Limon). Dolgushin, Semenova, Komleva. View VHS 1221.

Russian Ballet: Glorious Tradition

Excerpts from *Classical variation* (choreography: Gorsky, music: Drigo) with Semenova; *Swan Lake*, act 2 variation with Semenova; *Don Quixote*, pas de deux with Semenyaka and Baryshnikov; *Nutcracker*, pas de deux with Lezhina, Zelensky; *La bayadère*, pas de deux with Dudinskaya, Chabukiani; *Harlequinade*, pas de deux with Kurgapkina, Kovmir; *The Dying Swan* with Ulanova; *Chopiniana*, pas de deux with Makarova, Onoshko; *Don Quixote*, variation with Baryshnikov; *Raymonda*, pas de dix and variations with Kolpakova, Semenov; *Grand pas classique* with Komleva, Soloviev. Video Arts International VHS 69201-69203.

Story of the Kirov

Excerpts from *Swan Lake*, act 2 pas de deux with Ulanova, Sergeiev; *Le papillon* (music: Offenbach) with Kolpakova, Berezhnoi; *Giselle*, act 1 pas de deux with Asylmuratova, Ruzimatov; *Esmeralda*, pas de deux; *The Little Humpbacked Horse*; *The Sleeping Beauty*; Vaganova teaching; *The Dying Swan* with Pavlova; unidentified dance with Pavlova; *Giselle*, act 1 excerpt with Spessivtseva; *The Flames of Paris*, excerpt; *Romeo and Juliet*, excerpt with Ulanova, Sergeiev; *Laurencia*, excerpt with Dudinskaya, Chabukiani; *Swan Lake*, pas de deux excerpt with Dudinskaya; *La bayadère*, pas de deux with Dudinskaya, Chabukiani; *Taras Bulba*, excerpt with Chabukiani, Dunko; unidentified ballet with Dudinskaya, Sergeiev; *Gayane*, Sabre Dance; *Spartacus*; *The Stone Flower*; *Hamlet*; *Swan Lake*, act 2; *Don Quixote*, pas de deux with Semenyaka and Baryshnikov; *Nutcracker*, pas de deux with Kolpakova, Semenov; *The Knight in Tiger Skin*; *La bayadère*, Kingdom of the Shades. Laserlight VHS 80545.

Tchaikovsky

Eugene Onegin. Novikova, Diadkova, Marusin, Leiferkus, Okhotnikov, Gorokovskaya, Filatova. Kirov Orchestra and Chorus, Temirkanov conducting. Kultur VHS 1165.

Hamlet (choreography: Rizhenko). Garallis, Komleva, Dolgushin. Kirov Orchestra. View VHS 1221.

Romeo and Juliet (choreography: Rizhenko, Smirnov-Golovanov). Semenova, Semenchukov, Dolgushin. View VHS 1221.

The Sleeping Beauty. Sizova, Soloviev, Panov, Makarova, Dudinskaya, Bazhenova. Kultur VHS 1280.

The Sleeping Beauty. Kolpakova, Berezhnoi, Kunakova, Lopukhov, Evteeva. Kirov Orchestra, Fedotov conducting. Pioneer Laserdisc 83055.

The Sleeping Beauty. Asylmuratova, Zaklinsky. Kultur VHS 1477.

The Sleeping Beauty. Lezhina, Ruzimatov, Makhalina, Guliayev, Ayupova, Christyakova. Kirov Orchestra, Fedotov conducting. Polygram VHS 440070296.

Swan Lake. Mezentseva, Zaklinsky. Kultur 1475.

Swan Lake. Makhalina, Zelensky, Aliyev, Fateyev, Kashirina. Kirov Orchestra, Fedotov conducting. Nonesuch Laserdisc 40158.

White Nights of Dance in Leningrad

Excerpts from *Chopiniana*; *Notre Faust* (choreography: Béjart) with Chenchikova; 1830 (choreography: Béjart) with Ruzimatov; *Swan Lake*, act 2 pas de deux with Mezentseva, Zaklinsky; *Potemkin*; *Le corsaire*, "Le jardin animé" with Asylmuratova; *Heliogabale* (choreography: Béjart) with Asylmuratova, Ruzimatov; *La bayadère*, Kingdom of the Shades; *Le soldat amoureux* (choreography: Béjart). Kultur VHS 1305.

World's Young Ballet

Documentary on the 1969 International Ballet Competition in Moscow. Excerpts from *Vestris* (choreography: Yakobson) and *La bayadère* with Baryshnikov; unidentified film of Pavlova; Baryshnikov receiving Gold Medal; jury members Ulanova and Sergeiev; Baryshnikov rehearsing with Yakobson; Dudinskaya teaching. Kultur VHS 1275.

IV. The Kirov Today on CD

Borodin

Prince Igor. Gorchakova, Kit, Grigorian, Ognovenko, Borodina, Minzhilkiev, Gassiev. Kirov Orchestra and Chorus, Gergiev conducting. Philips 442537.

Prince Igor: Igor's aria. Hvorostovsky Kirov Orchestra, Gergiev conducting. Philips 438872.

Prince Igor: Polovtsian Dances. Kirov Orchestra and Chorus, Gergiev conducting. Philips 442011.

Prince Igor: Polovtsian March. Kirov Orchestra, Gergiev conducting. Philips 442011.

Glinka

Ruslan and Ludmila. Netrebko, Ognovenko, Kit, Diadkova, Bezzubenkov, Gorchakova, Pluzhnikov, Marusin. Kirov Orchestra and Chorus, Gergiev conducting. Philips 456248.

Ruslan and Ludmila: Overture. Kirov Orchestra, Gergiev conducting.Philips 442011.

Khachaturian

Gayane: Sabre Dance. Kirov Orchestra, Gergiev conducting. Philips 442011.

Spartacus: Adagio. Kirov Orchestra, Gergiev conducting. Philips 442011.

Liadov

Baba Yaga. Kirov Orchestra, Gergiev conducting. Philips 442011.

The Enchanted Lake. Kirov Orchestra, Gergiev conducting. Philips 442775.

Kikimora. Kirov Orchestra, Gergiev conducting. Philips 442011.

Mussorgsky

Boris Godunov (1869 and 1872 versions). Vaneev, Putilin, Lutsuk, Galuzin, Okhotnikov, Pluzhnikov, Gerello, Kuznetsov, Borodina, Nikitin. Kirov Orchestra and Chorus, Gergiev conducting. Philips 462230.

Boris Godunov: Coronation Scene. Kirov Orchestra and Chorus, Gergiev conducting. Philips 442775.

Khovanshchina. Borodina, Galuzin, Steblianko, Okhotnikov, Alexeev, Minzhilkiev. Kirov Orchestra and Chorus, Gergiev conducting. Philips 432147.

Songs and Dances of Death. Hvorostovsky, Kirov Orchestra, Gergiev conducting. Philips 438872.

Prokofiev

Betrothal in a Monastery. Netrebko, Gergalov, Gassiev, Diadkova, Akimov, Tarasova, Alexashkin. Kirov Orchestra and Chorus, Gergiev conducting. Philips 289462.

Concertos for Piano nos. 1–5. Toradze, Kirov Orchestra, Gergiev conducting. Philips 462048.

The Fiery Angel. Gorchakova, Leiferkus, Kit, Diadkova, Galuzin, Pluzhnikov. Kirov Orchestra and Chorus, Gergiev conducting. Philips 446078.

The Gambler. Kazarnovskaya, Galuzin, Obratzsova, Alexashkin. Kirov Orchestra and Chorus, Gergiev conducting. Philips 454559.

Love for Three Oranges. Akimov, Netrebko, Kit, Diadkova, Morozov, Pluzhnikov, Gerello, Vaneev, Bulycheva, Shevtsova. Kirov Orchestra and Chorus, Gergiev conducting. Philips 462913.

Romeo and Juliet. Kirov Orchestra, Gergiev conducting. Philips 432166.

Semyon Kotko. Pavlovskaya, Lutsiuk, Solovieva, Filatova, Akimov, Gassiev, Chernomortsev, Zhivopistev. Kirov Orchestra, Gergiev conducting. Philips 464605.

War and Peace. Prokina, Grigorian, Borodina, Marusin, Okhotnikov, Bogacheva, Morozov. Kirov Orchestra and Chorus, Gergiev conducting. Philips 434097.

Rachmaninov

Aleko: Moon is high. Hvorostovsky. Kirov Orchestra, Gergiev conducting. Philips 438872.

Symphony No. 2. Kirov Orchestra, Gergiev conducting. Philips CD 34569.

Rimsky-Korsakov

The Czar's Bride. Shaguch, Hvorostovsky, Bezzubenkov, Alexashkin, Akimov, Borodina, Gassiev, Loskutova. Kirov Orchestra and Chorus, Gergiev conducting. Philips 462618.

The Czar's Bride: Gryaznoy's aria. Hvorostovsky. Kirov Orchestra, Gergiev conducting. Philips 438872.

The Invisible City of Kitezh. Ohotnikov, Marusin, Gorchakova, Galuzin, Putilin, Kit, Gassiev, Minzhilkiev, Ognovenko, Diadkova. Kirov Orchestra and Chorus, Gergiev conducting. Philips 464225.

Kaschei the Immortal. Pluzhnikov, Shaguch, Gergalov, Morozov. Kirov Orchestra and Chorus, Gergiev conducting. Philips 464704.

Kashchei the Immortal: Prince Ivan's aria. Hvorostovsky. Kirov Orchestra, Gergiev conducting. Philips 438872.

The Maid of Pskov. Gorchakova, Ognovenko, Galuzin, Filatova, Bezzubenkov, Gassiev, Zastavny, Laptev. Kirov Orchestra and Chorus, Gergiev conducting. Philips 446678.

Sadko. Tsidipova, Galuzin, Tarassova, Minzhilkiev, Gergalov, Grigorian, Alexashkin, Diadkova. Kirov Orchestra and Chorus, Gergiev conducting. Philips 442138.

Sadko: Song of Venetian Guest. Hvorostovsky. Kirov Orchestra, Gergiev conducting. Philips 438872.

The Snow Maiden: Mizghir's aria. Hvorostovsky. Kirov Orchestra, Gergiev conducting. Philips 438872.

Rubinstein

The Demon: "Do not weep." Hvorostovsky. Kirov Orchestra, Gergiev conducting. Philips 438872.

The Demon: "I am he you called." Hvorostovsky. Kirov Orchestra, Gergiev conducting. Philips 438872.

The Demon: "On the airy ocean." Hvorostovsky. Kirov Orchestra, Gergiev conducting. Philips 438872.

Nero: Epithalamium. Hvorostovsky. Kirov Orchestra, Gergiev conducting. Philips 438872.

Scriabin

Prometheus. Toradze. Kirov Orchestra, Gergiev conducting. Philips 4467715.

Poem of Ecstasy. Kirov Orchestra. Philips (to be released).

Shostakovich

Symphony No. 8. Kirov Orchestra, Gergiev conducting. Philips 446062.

Stravinsky

Firebird. Kirov Orchestra, Gergiev conducting. Philips 446715.

Le sacre du printemps. Kirov Orchestra, Gergiev conducting. Philips (to be released).

Tchaikovsky

Capriccio italien. Kirov Orchestra, Gergiev conducting. Philips 442775.

Eugene Onegin: Letter Scene. Gorchakova. Kirov Orchestra, Gergiev conducting. Philips 446405.

Eugene Onegin: Polonaise and Waltz. Kirov Orchestra, Gergiev conducting. Philips 442775.

Iolanthe. Gorchakova, Grigorian, Alexashkin, Hvorostovsky, Putilin, Gassiev, Bezzubenkov, Diadkova. Kirov Orchestra and Chorus, Gergiev conducting. Philips 442796.

Marche slave. Kirov Orchestra, Gergiev conducting. Philips 442775.

Mazeppa. Putilin, Alexashkin, Diadkova, Lostkutova, Lutsiuk, Luhanin, Zhivopistev, Gassiev. Kirov Orchestra and Chorus, Gergiev conducting. Philips 462206.

Nutcracker. Kirov Orchestra, Gergiev conducting. Philips 462114.

Overture "1812." Kirov Orchestra, Gergiev conducting. Philips 442011.

Oprichnik: Natasha's aria. Gorchakova. Kirov Orchestra, Gergiev conducting. Philips 446405.

The Queen of Spades. Guleghina, Grigorian, Leiferkus, Chernov, Borodina, Arkhipova. Kirov Orchestra and Chorus, Gergiev conducting. Philips 438141

The Queen of Spades: Lisa's aria. Gorchakova. Kirov Orchestra, Gergiev conducting. Philips 446405.

Romeo and Juliet Overture. Kirov Orchestra, Gergiev conducting. Philips 454580.

The Sleeping Beauty. Kirov Orchestra, Gergiev conducting. Philips 434922.

The Sorceress: Where are you? Gorchakova. Kirov Orchestra, Gergiev conducting. Philips 446405.

Swan Lake. Kirov Orchestra, Fedotov conducting. JVC 6500.

Symphony No. 6. Kirov Orchestra, Gergiev conducting. Philips 454580.

Verdi

Aida: "O patria mia." Gorchakova. Kirov Orchestra, Gergiev conducting, Philips 446405.

La forza del destino. Gorchakova, Grigorian, Putilin, Borodina, Kit, Zastavny. Kirov Orchestra and Chorus, Gergiev conducting. Philips 446951.

La forza del destino: "Madre pietosa Vergine." Gorchakova. Kirov Orchestra, Gergiev conducting. Philips 446405.

La forza del destino: "Pace, pace mio Dio." Gorchakova. Kirov Orchestra, Gergiev conducting. Philips 446405.

Messa da Requiem: Fleming, Borodina, Bocelli, D'Arcangelo. Kirov Orchestra, Gergiev conducting. Philips (to be issued).

Otello: "Salce, salce . . . Ave Maria." Gorchakova. Kirov Orchestra, Gergiev conducting. Philips 446405.

Il trovatore: "Tacea la notte placida." Gorchakova. Kirov Orchestra, Gergiev conducting. Philips 446405.

V. The Kirov Today on Video

Adam

Le corsaire, pas de deux. Tarasova, Zelensky. Kirov Orchestra, Fedotov conducting. Philips Laserdisc 440070259.

Le corsaire, pas de deux. Kullik, Ruzimatov. Philips Laserdisc 440070266.

Bizet

Carmen: Final duet. Borodina, Domingo. Kirov Orchestra, Rostropovich conducting. Lumivision Laserdisc 9220.

Carmen: Prelude, act 1. Kirov Orchestra, Rostropovich conducting. Lumivision Laserdisc 9220.

Borodin

Prince Igor. Putilin, Borodina, Gorchakova, Vaneev, Akimov, Alexashkin, Gassiev, Karasev. Kirov Orchestra, Ballet, and Chorus, Gergiev conducting. Unissued.

Prince Igor: Finale, act 2. Tselovalnik. Kirov Orchestra and Chorus, Gergiev conducting. Philips Laserdisc 440070259.

Bull

God Save the Queen (British national anthem). Kirov Orchestra, Gergiev conducting. Philips Laserdisc 440070259.

Dvořák

The Cypresses (music: Dvořák, choreographed as *The Leaves Are Fading*). Asylmuratova, Zaklinsky. Kirov Orchestra, Fedotov conducting. Philips Laserdisc 440070266.

Gergiev: Catching Up with Music

Documentary with interviews with Gergiev, Musin, Toradze; recording sessions; excerpts from concerts, *Ruslan and Ludmila*, *Eugene Onegin*, *Khovanshchina*, *Prince Igor*, *Salome*, *Aida*. Unissued.

Glière

The Bronze Horseman: Anthem to a Great City. Kirov Orchestra, Gergiev conducting. Philips Laserdisc 440070259.

Glinka

Ruslan and Ludmila. Kit, Netrebko, Ognovenko, Diadkova, Bezzubenkov, Gorchakova, Pluzhnikov, Bogacheva, Marusin. Kirov Orchestra, Chorus and Ballet, Gergiev conducting. Philips VHS 075 102.

Haydn

Concerto for Cello in C (first movement). Rostropovich, Kirov Orchestra, Domingo conducting. Lumivision Laserdisc 9220.

Meyerbeer

L'africaine: "O paradis." Domingo. Kirov Orchestra, Kohn conducting. Lumivision Laserdisc 9220.

Minkus

Paquita, pas de deux. Chenchikova, Vaziev. Kirov Orchestra, Fedotov conducting. Philips Laserdisc 440070259.

Paquita, Polonaise and Mazurka. Vaganova Academy. Kirov Orchestra, Fedotov conducting. Philips Laserdisc 440070259 VD.

Mussorgsky

Boris Godunov (Lloyd-Jones version). Lloyd, Borodina, Steblianko, Leiferkus, Morosov, Boitsov, Ognovenko, Filatova. Kirov Orchestra and Chorus, Gergiev conducting. London Laserdisc 440071.

Boris Godunov: Kromy Forest scene. Gassiev, Ognovenko. Kirov Orchestra and Chorus, Gergiev conducting. Philips Laserdisc 440070259.

Khovanshchina. Borodina, Marusin, Minzhilkiev, Pluzhnikov, Trofimov, Tselovalnik, Okhotnikov. Kirov Orchestra and Chorus, Gergiev conducting. Philips Laserdisc 10053.

Salammbô: Salammbô's scene. Borodina. Kirov Orchestra, Gergiev conducting. Philips Laserdisc 440070259.

Penella

Gato montes: "Me llamabas." Verdera, Domingo. Kirov Orchestra, Kohn conducting. Lumivision Laserdisc 9220.

Prokofiev

Betrothal in a Monastery. Netrebko, Diadkova, Tarasova, Gassiev, Alexashkin, Gergalov, Vaneev, Akimov. Kirov Orchestra, Ballet and Chorus, Gergiev conducting. Unissued.

The Fiery Angel. Gorchakova, Leiferkus, Kit, Diadkova, Galuzin, Pluzhnikov. Kirov Orchestra and Chorus, Gergiev conducting. Philips Laserdisc 440070298.

War and Peace. Prokina, Grigorian, Borodina, Marusin, Okhotnikov, Bogacheva, Morozov. Kirov Orchestra and Chorus, Gergiev conducting. Philips Laserdisc 440070527.

War and Peace: Natasha's aria and Epilogue. Prokina. Kirov Orchestra and Chorus, Gergiev conducting. Philips Laserdisc 440070259.

Pugni

Diana and Actaeon, pas de deux. Lezhina, Ruzimatov. Kirov Orchestra, Fedotov conducting. Philips Laserdisc 440070259.

Rimsky-Korsakov

Sadko. Tsidipova, Galuzin, Tarassova, Minzhilkiev, Gergalov, Grigorian, Alexashkin, Diadkova. Kirov Orchestra and Chorus, Gergiev conducting. Philips Laserdisc 440070539.

Sadko: Song of India. Grigorian. Kirov Orchestra, Gergiev conducting. Philips Laserdisc 440070259.

Sorozabal

Tabernera: "No puede ser." Domingo. Kirov Orchestra, Kohn conducting. Lumivision Laserdisc 9220.

Tchaikovsky

Eugene Onegin: Lensky's aria. Domingo. Kirov Orchestra, Rostropovich conducting. Lumivision Laserdisc 9220.

Eugene Onegin: Polonaise. Kirov Orchestra, Gergiev conducting. Philips Laserdisc 440070266.

Mazeppa. Lostkutova, Diadkova, Putilin, Alexashkin, Lutsiuk, Luhanin, Gassiev. Kirov Orchestra and Chorus, Gergiev conducting. Unissued.

Mazeppa: Maria-Lubov duet. Diadkova, Tselovalnik. Kirov Orchestra, Gergiev conducting. Philips Laserdisc 440070259.

Nutcracker. Lezhnina, Baranov, Vaganova Academy. Kirov Orchestra, Fedotov conducting. Philips Laserdisc 440070273.

Nutcracker, pas de trois. Vaganova Academy. Kirov Orchestra, Fedotov conducting. Philip Laserdisc 440070259.

Overture "1812." Kirov Orchestra, Rostropovich conducting. Lumivision Laserdisc 9220.

The Queen of Spades. Guleghina, Grigorian, Putilin, Gergalov, Borodina, Filatova. Kirov Orchestra and Chorus, Gergiev conducting. Philips Laserdisc 440070534.

The Queen of Spades: Lisa's aria and duet from act 3. Guleghina, Grigorian. Kirov Orchestra, Gergiev conducting. Philips Laserdisc 440070259.

Sérénade mélancolique. Chenchikova. Kirov Orchestra, Fedotov conducting. Philips Laserdisc 440070266.

The Sorceress: "Where are you?" Gorchakova. Kirov Orchestra, Gergiev conducting. Philips Laserdisc 440070259.

Swan Lake, act 2 pas de deux. Makhalina, Liepa. Kirov Orchestra, Fedotov conducting. Philips Laserdisc 440070259.

Torroba

Luisa Fernanda: "De este." Domingo. Kirov Orchestra, Kohn conducting. Lumivision Laserdisc 9220.

Verdi

La forza del destino. Gorchakova, Grigorian, Putilin, Tarasova, Kit. Kirov Orchestra and Chorus, Gergiev conducting. Kultur VHS 2079.

Luisa Miller: "Quando le sere al placido." Domingo. Kirov Orchestra, Kohn conducting. Lumivision Laserdisc 9220.

Wagner

Parsifal, excerpts. Urmana, Domingo, Putilin. Kulture VHS 1850.

VI. Gergiev's Non-Kirov CDs and Videos

Anonymous

Hymn of the German Democratic Republic. German-Soviet Youth Philharmonic. National Anthem of the Soviet Union. German-Soviet Youth Philharmonic. Eurodisc C 8409/10.

Beethoven

Concerto for Piano No. 5, Op. 58. Frantz, German-Soviet Youth Philharmonic. Eurodisc C 8409.

Beriot

Scènes de ballet. Bashmet. Moscow Philharmonic. Melodiya 1000540.

Borodin

Symphonies Nos. 1, 2. Rotterdam Philharmonic. Philips 42296.

Massenet

Hérodiade. Fleming, Zajik, Domingo, Pons. San Francisco Opera. Sony 66847.

Mussorgsky-Ravel

Pictures at an Exhibition. London Philharmonic. Philips 426437.

Prokofiev

> *Ivan the Terrible.* Sokolina, Putilin. Rotterdam Philharmonic. Philips 456645.
>
> *Scythian Suite.* Rotterdam Philharmonic. Rehearsal with analysis. Unissued video.

Rachmaninov

> Concerto for Piano No. 2, Op. 18. Kissin. London Symphony. RCA 7982.

Stravinsky

> *Le sacre du printemps.* Rehearsal with analysis. Unissued video.

Tchaikovsky, Alexander

> Concerto for Viola No. 1. Bashmet. Moscow Philharmonic. Melodiya 1000540.

Tchaikovsky, Peter Ilyich

> *Eugene Onegin*: "You have written to me," "Can this be the same Tatyana?" Hvorostovsky. Rotterdam Philharmonic. Philips 426740.
>
> *Francesca da Rimini.* London Philharmonic. Philips 426437.
>
> *Iolanthe*: Robert's aria. Hvorostovsky. Rotterdam Philharmonic. Philips 426740.
>
> *Mazeppa*: "O Maria." Hvorostovsky. Rotterdam Philharmonic. Philips 426740.
>
> *The Queen of Spades*: Yeletsky's aria. Hvorostovsky. Rotterdam Philharmonic. Philips 426740.
>
> *The Sorceress*: Kurtyatev's aria. Hvorostovsky. Rotterdam Philharmonic. Philips 426740.
>
> Symphony No. 5, Op. 64. Geman-Soviet Youth Philharmonic. Eurodisc C 8409.
>
> Symphony No. 5, Op. 64. Vienna Philharmonic. Philips 462905.

Verdi

> *Don Carlo*: "Per me giunto . . . O Carlo ascolta." Hvorostovsky. Rotterdam Philharmonic. Philips 4226740.
>
> *Luisa Miller*: "Sacra la scelta." Hvorostovsky. Rotterdam Philharmonic. Philips 426740.
>
> *Macbeth*: "Pietà rispetto." Hvorostovsky. Rotterdam Philharmonic. Philips 426740.
>
> *La traviata*: "Di provenza." Hvorostovsky. Rotterdam Philharmonic. Philips 426740.
>
> *Il trovatore*: "Il balen." Hvorostovsky. Rotterdam Philharmonic. Philips 426740.

Index of Names and Works